SLEIGHT OF HAND
A Practical Manual of Legerdemain
for Amateurs & Others

EDWIN SACHS

Dover Publications, Inc.
New York

Published in Canada by General Publishing Company, Ltd., 30 Lesmill Road, Don Mills, Toronto, Ontario.

This Dover edition, first published in 1980, is an unabridged republication of the second, greatly enlarged, edition of the work as published by L. Upcott Gill, London, 1885.

International Standard Book Number: 0-486-23911-X
Library of Congress Catalog Card Number: 79-54184

Manufactured in the United States of America
Dover Publications, Inc.
180 Varick Street
New York, N.Y. 10014

CONTENTS.

PREFACE TO SECOND EDITION.

———

It is always a matter for self-congratulation on the part of an author to be called upon to furnish a Preface to a second or subsequent edition of some "bantling of his brain." In the present instance the task is more satisfactory than usual, the author not coming before the reader empty-handed. Since the publication of the first edition, conjurors have not been idle, and numerous new methods for producing magical surprises have been invented. Such of these as are suitable or worthy — for, in their haste to be novel, many have failed to be satisfactory—the author has incorporated; and, by a thorough revision of the work, he has placed before the aspiring conjuror, written up to date, all that it is possible for him to know in the region of Sleight of Hand.

E. S.

London,
   April, 1885.

SLEIGHT OF HAND

INTRODUCTION.

"It is as pleasant to be cheated as to cheat," is a maxim
that must have been framed expressly for conjuring, for the
more completely one is deceived by its medium (and, be it
said, by its medium alone) the better one is pleased.

The date of the origin of conjuring, as we now understand
the art, is not known, but there must have been proficients
in the practice of it as early as the time of Chaucer; for that
ancient writer speaks of one Coll Tregetour (Tregetour signi-
fying a juggler) producing a windmill from beneath a walnut
shell. There is doubtless some slight exaggeration in this
statement, or else modern wizards are far behind those of
early days—an hypothesis I cannot accept. In the superstitious lands of the East, jugglery was doubtless at the
bottom of the many manifestations that were mixed up with
religion, and the wily priests made the best (or worst) uses
of its influence on the uncultivated mind. When we consider
the effect that is even now produced on the minds of an enlightened audience by a skilful manipulator, the wonderment
of people who were but half civilised, and who were taught
to believe in spirits, is scarcely a matter for surprise.

Although superstition has not died out—if, indeed, it ever *will* die out—there are now very few people who attribute the successes of a conjuror to any other agency than that of his own skill; always excepting that of the everlasting "confederate," who, as the reader of the following pages will discover, exists, in ninety-nine cases out of a hundred, only in the imagination of the spectator.

Formerly, conjurors appeared clothed in long robes and tall, pointed hats, both covered with mystic signs and symbols; Robert Houdin, whom we may consider the father of modern conjuring, being the first to perform in the now conventional evening dress. This innovation had the effect of increasing the genuineness of the performance, as it was an easy matter to conceal large articles beneath a flowing robe, such as had been previously worn; but the close-fitting dress suit affords no means of concealment—to the minds of an audience, at any rate. Houdin was the means of elevating the art in the eyes of the public, besides investing it with nearly all that it possesses of the graceful; and, as it has undergone still more improvement since his time, it has now become a pursuit well worthy the attention of anyone inclined to follow it up, as much for the amusement of himself as of others. Besides its power of amusing, conjuring affords an immense amount of instruction to its student, and is useful in inculcating coolness, precision, and an endless amount of resource, which will always stand one in good stead on the world's wide and ever-changing stage.

It is my intention to give, in the following pages, such instruction as shall enable the merest tyro to become an adept in the art of Legerdemain, providing that a due degree of attention is given and a reasonable amount of practice undertaken. Practice, indeed, is what is required in order to achieve success in any pursuit or amusement, whatever its nature may be, and without it the best of instruction is given in vain. For this reason, I must exhort such of my readers as may seek to amuse their friends through the medium of what

I shall impart to them to devote as much time as they can spare to practice at the outset, in order that they may acquire a neat method of manipulation, which is the keystone of success in a conjuror, and which, once attained, will never leave them. If to this delicacy of manipulation is added a suavity of manner, accompanied by a never-failing cool daring, then the perfection of a conjuror is attained.

Magic may safely be divided into two parts, Drawing-room Magic and Grand Magic. As it is in the family circle that every amateur conjuror mostly exhibits his attainments, I shall first treat of drawing-room magic; indeed, it is absolutely necessary to be a master of that branch, in order to undertake grand magic successfully. The success of the conjuror who can perform only on the stage, far removed from all inquisitorial interference, will be but of short duration. I find it has been the case with most amateurs, who rarely find opportunities for performing on a stage, that their greatest successes have been achieved in the drawing-room.

The very first thing a conjuror must procure is a conjuring-wand—an implement that is always supposed by the audience to be for show only; and for such they must always be made to think it is. It is, however, an absolutely indispensable article, both to beginner and proficient, as it serves as an auxiliary to the concealment of any article in the hand, as will be explained hereafter. For the present, all the learner has to do is to procure a round stick of ebony, about 18in. long, fitted with ivory, silver, or brass ferrules (not caps) countersunk at each end, and to trust to me to its being necessary. It is best to have the wand made to suit the taste, as those sold at conjuring-shops are invariably too short. Any walking-stick manufacturer will make it.

PART I.
DRAWING-ROOM MAGIC.

———

THIS derives its chief beauty from the fact that it is almost entirely dependent on pure sleight of hand, a fact which audiences are never slow to appreciate. The most familiar objects are dealt with, and are made to vanish and re-appear in unexpected places, as though they really were disembodied and reinstated. The amateur will find, after a few years' experience, that the impromptu performances he may, from time to time, be called upon to give in the drawing-rooms of his acquaintances, will be much more satisfactory to both himself and his audiences than the more pretentious affairs given upon stages, which call for a great deal of management, apart from ability, to render them successes. When once the performer has attained the credit of being better than the ordinary ruck, it will become incumbent upon him to keep up the level of skill by means of practice, as wonder must follow wonder in ever-increasing proportion.

Coins, from being so readily procurable, and from their adaptability, are deservedly favourite media, and with them I shall first deal. For all general purposes, a well-conditioned florin will be found the best coin for the beginner; although, of course, he must, in time, be able to manipulate slippery half-crowns and pennies with equal ease. Florins, as a rule, are more readily procurable in these days, but few half-crowns being coined in comparison with them. But as the conjuror must be provided against all emergencies, I shall give directions for the best method of treatment for each coin. The means adopted for the temporary concealment of a coin in the hand is known as Palming, and I shall commence Drawing-room Magic with a description of the various methods.

CHAPTER I.

PALMING.

Method 1. *The Palm Proper.*—Hold the coin firmly between
the thumb on the one side and the middle and third fingers
on the other, the first and little fingers taking up graceful
positions, as it were, to cover the movement about to be
made (Fig. 1). Remove the thumb to its ordinary position

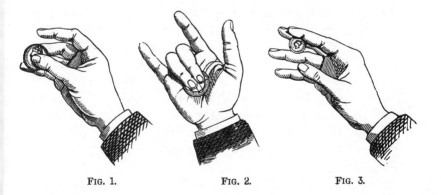

FIG. 1.   FIG. 2.   FIG. 3.

of repose, and, at the same instant, let the two fingers (second
and third) press the coin into the palm of the hand, half
way down the root of the thumb, the muscles of which
must be brought to bear against the edge of the coin, so

that it is held firmly and forms a bridge over the hollow of the hand (Fig. 2). A backward and forward swing should be given to the hand whilst the coin is being palmed, as it not only covers the movement, but also facilitates the operation in a marked degree. In pressing the coin home, it will be found that the third finger will be more used than the middle one. The instant the palm is effected, the hand must be made to assume the most natural position possible under the circumstances, the little finger being well thrown out, after the dainty manner ladies affect when holding a cup, so as to give the hand breadth. Some beginners think that in holding the hand perfectly flat they are effecting a very beautiful palm; but this is not the case, as can be seen at once by looking at the hand without any coin in its palm. That is the model the conjuror must copy: any unnatural position at once betrays the fact that something unusual is going on. For this method, the florin will be found the best coin, its edge affording a better hold than that of any other piece.

Method 2. *The Finger Palm.*—The coin is held between the thumb and forefinger, and the latter then slid aside, so that the coin rests upon the side of the middle finger. The forefinger then takes the place of the thumb, and the coin is held as in Fig. 3. The action is simplified if the coin is held in the first instance between the thumb and middle finger, but it looks awkward and suspicious. This method will be found particularly adapted for concealing coins of the size of a shilling and less. Larger coins should not be treated thus, except in emergencies, when anything is allowable.

Method 3. *The Thumb Palm.*—This palm is not generally known, which is to be wondered at, for it is a very safe and easy one. The coin is simply held between the thumb and forefinger, and then slid to the root of the latter, where it is held, as in Fig. 4. The only objection to this palm is that it keeps the thumb a close prisoner, to the manifest loss of grace, but it is exceedingly useful for large and slippery coins, such as half-crowns, pennies, and crowns.

Method 4.—Two, three, and four coins may be palmed by the first method, but the method shown at Fig. 5 is the

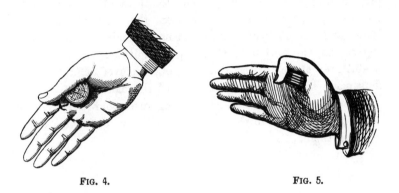

FIG. 4.   FIG. 5.

safer. There is a rather unnatural disposition of the thumb about it, but the fingers are left free play.

Method 5. *Reverse Palm.*—It is sometimes required of the

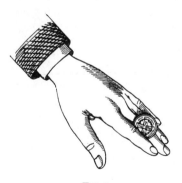

FIG. 6.

performer to show that his hands do not contain any coin. If a coin is palmed in one of them, he must first exhibit the other open in a very ostentatious manner, and, whilst the audience is momentarily engaged in looking at it, press the coin, by means of the thumb, through the fingers of the hand in which it is held, so that it protrudes at the back, and cannot be seen from the front (Fig. 6). Some performers have brought this palm to a great state of perfection. One very telling effect is to pretend to throw the coin away. For this purpose, it is held between the tips of the first finger and thumb, whilst lying upon the side of the middle finger. As the action of throwing is imitated, the forefinger is slid over the coin, the thumb being removed, and the coin thus made to protrude at the back of the hand.

Other fanciful methods of palming exist, but they will be of no practical use to the conjuror, so I have omitted descriptions of them.

CHAPTER II.

TRICKS WITH COINS.

THE uses of the palm will make themselves manifest in every
trick in which money is used as a medium, but the beginner
can astonish his friends, and, at the same time, make himself
perfect, by any of the following minor tricks :

(a) Throw the coin backwards and forwards, from hand to
hand, three or four times, in a careless manner, always taking
care that the left hand is shut well over each time the coin
is contained in it; and then make a feint of throwing, but, in
reality, palm the coin after the method that best suits its

size. The hand (in most cases it would be the left, as the majority of conjurers palm with the right; with left-handed people it would be, of course, reversed) which is supposed to receive the coin must be closed smartly, so as to make a noise similar to that caused by a coin thrown into the palm. This is effected by the ends of the two middle fingers striking the fleshy part of the thumb (Fig. 7). If this is properly executed, the illusion is perfect, and all eyes will be directed to the left hand, when the coin can be quietly placed in a side or tail pocket, to which receptacle it may afterwards be made to pass from the left hand, where it is supposed to be, in a

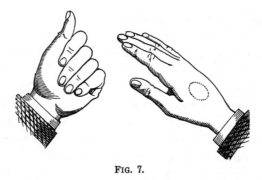

Fig. 7.

(The dotted line represents the coin palmed in the right hand.)

magical manner. I would recommend the beginner to practice this movement sedulously in private, as it teaches quick and neat palming, and will prove a most useful auxiliary to many important tricks. By "passing" a coin from place to place "in a magical manner" is implied the act of *pretending* to do so; it being an accepted axiom amongst conjurers never to "pass" anything invisibly to any given spot until the article is already safely located there. This practice will, of course, commend itself to all as avoiding untoward mistakes. To "pass" a coin from the hand, wave the wand over it, and say whatever you think will go down best with the particular audience you have before you. A sharp rap on the knuckles will complete the operation, but always take care to show the hand empty, otherwise the trick is spoilt. If the wand is not handy, pretend to rub the coin away between the fingers, or affect to give it to one of the audience. (See Figs. 8 and 9 for an effective method.)

FIG. 8.

(*b*) Have a coin palmed in the left hand, and borrow a similar one from the audience, and have it well marked (always have coins marked where possible, " to prevent changing "). Make a movement as though you placed the marked coin in

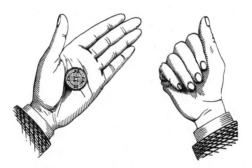

FIG. 9.

the left hand, but in reality palm it. At the same time, open the left hand, and the coin that has been snugly concealed there will look as if it had just left the right hand. By this means a change is effected which you can utilise according to circumstances. By fidgeting about among the audience, you may be able to place the marked coin under one of them; the other coin being held by someone who is directed to hold it "very high, sir, very high, so that everyone can see it"—the real object being to keep him from examining it too closely. By standing the holder of the coin on a chair, an opportunity for slipping the palmed coin into his pocket presents itself, and should be taken advantage of. The marked coin being once safely hidden, it is an easy matter to palm the unmarked one (which, of course, the audience has been led to believe is the marked one) and make it "pass" invisibly to wherever the other may be. The conjuror's own coin should always be provided with a very distinct mark—a cross is invariably a safe one to employ—as it is rarely that one meets with people who can refrain from instituting an illicit investigation so soon as the conjuror's back is turned. When the holder of the coin is seen to be surreptitiously examining it for the mark, the conjuror should not prevent him, but call the attention of the audience to the fact, and ask if the mark be visible. The holder, seeing the cross, will answer in the affirmative; he not being aware, of course, that the borrowed coin was possibly marked with a very different sign. This incident will add to the effectiveness of the trick.

In tricks *a* and *b* the wand will be found very useful. It should always be carried under the arm, after the manner in which soldiers carry their canes; and when any palm has been effected, and the coin has to remain concealed in the hand, the wand should be taken in the hand containing the coin. Beginners, especially, will find this of great assistance, as in the case of a somewhat defective palm the coin can be pressed well home by clenching the wand hard. Besides this, the fact of carrying a wand in the hand keeps the idea of the coin being there from the minds of the audience; and the mind is what the conjuror has to deceive.

(*c*) Have a coin palmed in the right hand (Palm No. 2), and procure a similar one, marked, which hold up to the audience by the left hand. Pretend to take it in the right, but let it fall into the hollow of the left hand (Figs. 8 and 9); the unmarked coin in the right hand being exhibited. In order to effect this daring change naturally and without detection, the thumb of the right hand must be passed through the ring formed by the thumb and forefinger of the left and the coin held between them, and the fingers closed well over the coin, which will appear to be grasped by them. Now place the left hand under the table, the right hand remaining above. Covered by the action of bringing it on the table, execute Palm No. 1 with the right hand, but keep the fingers formed as though they still held the coin, which you then pretend to lay on the table with a sharp "click." This "click" is made by the coin in the left hand, under the table, in order that the illusion may be perfect. The right hand will then affect to rub the coin through the table, and eventually the one in the left hand, which has in reality never been out of it, will be produced. The noise of rubbing is also made by the coin under the table, only it must not be continued too long; and care must be taken that the two hands act in perfect unison, as it will not do for the noise to continue when the action of rubbing with the right hand has ceased. This trick is not so difficult as it looks on paper, and is very effective. The whole trick consists in pretending to take the marked coin from the fingers of the left hand without doing so.

(d) Conceal a number of coins in the left hand. As a quantity cannot be easily palmed, they must be held in the hand with the wand. If that is not handy, hold the flap of the coat; but care should be taken that the wand is at hand for this trick. Borrow a hat, taking it in the right hand (in which a solitary coin is palmed), and transfer it rapidly to the left in such a manner that the crown is always towards the audience, and the fingers holding the coins are inside. The coins must not be jingled, or the trick will be exposed. Tell one of the audience that he must be very rich if he can afford to carry money about in such strange places as you perceive he does. Surprise will, of course, be expressed on his part, when you will fumble about in his hair, and eventually find the coin which you have had palmed. This is a much better method of commencing than merely saying, "I have here a shilling." It is sure to amuse the audience, and put you on a good footing with them; besides which, it is always well to mingle as much with them as possible, as then people go home and say, "Oh! he came right down among us, and found money in people's heads," &c. Also take care to find the money in an elegant and inoffensive manner. Having spun the coin in the air, in order to show that it is a real one, retire to the end of the room, as far away as you can, if the room is small, and hold the hat, still in the left hand, before you, with the crown towards the audience. With the coin in the right hand, make a pass at the hat, palming the coin (Palm No. 2), and letting one from the left hand fall. You will then appear to have passed the coin from the right hand into the hat, by way of the crown. Should the coin by accident fall on a soft place in the hat, and make no noise in so doing, shake the hat about to show that the coin really is inside, or no one will know what is supposed to have taken place. Now advance a step or two, looking cautiously forward as if you saw something in the air, and suddenly make a dart out with the right hand, at the same time bringing the coin to the extreme ends of the fingers. The idea conveyed is that the coin has been caught in the air (Fig. 10). Pass it through the hat, letting another fall from the left hand, and shaking the hat so as to ensure the two that have been dropped jingling together, and find another in the air a little farther on. Proceed in this way till all the coins in the left hand are exhausted (varying the proceedings by occasionally finding one at your elbow or foot), and then show the hat with coins to the audience, a member of which will doubtless have "just one more" seated on the tip of the nose, which coin is put into the hat in the ordinary way. The beginner should use shillings, seven or eight only in number, for this trick, although larger coins are certainly more effective at a distance. It is best to use two palms, viz., the finger palm when the coin is to be caught in the air or in the flame of a candle (a very pretty effect), as it is more readily brought to the ends of the fingers from that position; and either of the others (No. 1 for choice), when the coin is to be found on the body or elsewhere. It is as well to occasionally pretend to put the coin into the hat in the ordinary way, instead of through the crown. Some conjurors object altogether to passing through the crown; but this is merely a matter of fancy. It sometimes happens that the person in whose hair

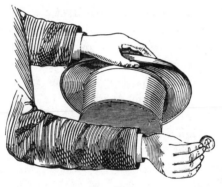

FIG. 10.

you find the first piece will, from his being a "funny man," or otherwise privileged person, ask you to give him back his property. Acquiesce at once with his request, of course after your own manner, which will be to palm the coin, and pretend to give it to him, much to his discomfiture. In borrowing the hat, be sure that it hides the left hand in the act of being taken, so that any accidental exposure of the coins held there, which might occur through inexperience, will be covered. Also observe the greatest caution in dropping only one coin into the hat at the first pass. After the first coin has fallen, it does not matter if two or more are accidentally let fall at once, as the error could not be detected;

but at the commencement it would be simply fatal to do so. Under cover of the hat it is easy to separate one coin from the rest for the first drop. If the number of coins is very limited, you must give the hat a short, sharp shake, which will serve in lieu of letting one fall; but only do this now and then. This trick will be treated in an enlarged form, under the head of "Grand Magic." When any number of coins are required for any other trick, they should always be collected in this manner, it being a most effective method. Always take a step in advance each time a coin is found. For this reason the performer should stand well to the right on the stage on commencing.

(e) The following makes an excellent "follow" to the preceding trick: Suppose that you have sixteen coins in all in the hat; conceal four of them in one hand. If the hat is then held by the same hand, it will not be noticed that it contains any coins. Now ask someone to count the coins in the hat, and, of course, there will be twelve. Take four of these away, and give them to be held by another person. Hold the hat high in the air, and tell the person who has the remaining eight coins to drop them into it when you have counted "three." Watch the action of his hand narrowly, and, as the eight coins fall, release the four concealed in the hand which holds the hat so that they all fall exactly together. The great thing to avoid is the sound of two distinct drops, which would be fatal. Leaving the hat, covered with a handkerchief if you please, in the hands of your temporary assistant, who will, of course, be enjoined to "hold it very high," you take the four coins just previously given to be held, and "pass" them invisibly into the hat, where, of course, twelve coins will be found. The method for passing used is the same as that depicted at Fig. 7, with the difference that the coins are not palmed. They must be held in the fingers loosely (Fig. 11) so that when the false movement of placing them in the out-stretched palm is made they will come together with a clash, which is highly necessary for the

success of the pass. The hand actually containing the coins
must instantly seize the wand, which article will then cause
the magic journey from left hand to hat to be made. Be
careful that the counting of the coins is done in a very
deliberate manner, and in a loud voice, so that everyone in
the room knows how many coins are supposed to be in the
hat before you pass the rest into it. If this is not done, the
effect of the trick is lost.

Here let me advise my readers to assiduously practise
quick palming, for which purpose I would recommend trick
a as a most effective exercise. So much depends upon a
quick and secure palm, that too great a stress cannot be laid

FIG. 11.

upon it. Indeed, I cannot too strongly impress the learner
with the necessity of practising everything, to the minutest
detail, in private, before venturing to perform before others.
By so doing, much chagrin and disappointment will be
averted.

(*f*) The trick I am now about to describe will, I have no
doubt, be known to many of my readers; but I ask no
excuse for giving it here, as those who can claim a previous
acquaintanceship with the trick will, perhaps, here learn a
wrinkle or two worth knowing: Borrow a handkerchief.
When I say "borrow a handkerchief," I do not mean simply
borrow one without any comment. On the contrary, make
a great fuss about never using your own handkerchief, &c.;

and be particular to hand round all borrowed articles for inspection, to show that you "have no confederates." By making your audience thoroughly sick of looking at borrowed articles, they are more likely to pass over anything of your own that will not bear minute examination. This should be borne well in mind. Spread the handkerchief out upon the table, and place a coin, not heavier or larger than a shilling (borrowed and marked), in the centre of it. Beneath the nail of the middle finger of the right hand (which hand is immaterial, but for the purpose of illustration it is necessary to use the terms "right" and "left") you have a small piece of bees' wax (on no account cobblers' wax) which you have previously made tolerably adhesive by working it about. Place this finger on the coin, saying, "Now, in order that all may see that I do not for one instant move the coin from its position, I place this finger upon it," and, taking up one of the corners of the handkerchief in the other hand, fold it over the coin so as to well cover it, and press it down hard, allowing the wax to come off on the coin, and to cause a mutual adherence between it and the handkerchief. Fold the remaining three corners over one another with great deliberation, exhibiting a portion of the coin each time, to show that there is "no cheating." When all four corners are folded over, the handkerchief will still be in the shape of a square, but of course much smaller than it was at the commencement, and it will have an aperture running from the centre to each corner. Note the portion of the handkerchief to which the coin is stuck, and place the two hands, side by side, in the aperture formed by this portion and the one next to it (Fig. 12). If the hands are now separated briskly, and the sides of the handkerchief allowed to slide through the fingers, it stands to reason that, the coin being fast to the corner of the handkerchief, it will, when the corner is reached, find its way into the hand. The handkerchief must be shaken hard, as soon as the coin is safe in the hand, for effect. The operations of opening the handkerchief and shaking it must be practised until they can be compassed both smoothly and quickly in one movement. The trick is easy, but requires some little practice. Common soap is an excellent substitute for wax, but it has the disadvantage of being less portable. The beauty of the wax is that it can be so easily concealed beneath the nail, and comes off the coin cleanly. The coin successfully vanished from the handkerchief, it rests with the performer to reproduce it in what manner he pleases. If he has already found coins in the

FIG. 12.

heads of the audience, the reproduction can be varied. For instance, if a tiny piece of wax be affixed to the flat end of the wand, and that end brought into contact with the coin whilst in the palm, and a little pressure used, the coin will adhere. Then, if the wand be passed rapidly behind a curtain, or inside the coat of one of the audience, a great effect can be caused by slowly producing the vanished article from its supposed place of concealment at the end of the wand. The trick can be further prolonged by having about 15in. of human hair, with a tiny bead of wax at the end, affixed to a waistcoat button. Affix the coin to the waxed end, and place it in a wineglass, in which it can be easily made to dance by slightly moving the glass or depressing the hair with the wand, which is supposed to be beating time. Such a combination of tricks, each one easy in itself, affords invaluable practice to the beginner. The conjuror, like the chess-player, must always see, in his mind's eye, two or three moves ahead, so that no hitch or hesitation occurs. For example, the instant the coin reaches the hand from the handkerchief, it must be palmed, the wand taken up, and the handkerchief ostentatiously given round for inspection to show that there is no hole in it, or for any other plausible reason. Perhaps you will only gain five seconds by this, but that is time enough to enable you to press the wand against the coin. You must not, after this, allow the least pause to occur, but at once seize someone, and have your wand inside his coat before he knows what you are about; for it must be remembered that, if the action is noticed, the coin will be noticed too, as it is in a tolerably conspicuous position at the end of the wand. Then, whilst you are rating the individual soundly for having endeavoured to spoil your trick by concealing the coin, and drawing universal attention to him, one hand will be busily employed in pressing the waxed end of the hair against the coin. The trick of dancing a coin in a glass is so well known that no one with any desire for a reputation as a prestidigitateur would introduce it by itself; but, in the illustration I have just given, the coin has been in such a variety of places and situations, that the idea of its being fixed to anything does not enter the minds of the audience. Half-a-minute's dancing is quite sufficient, and at the end of it the attention of the audience must be at once drawn into another groove by your showing the coin to be the veritable one marked some time since, the wax being removed by a finger nail.

(g) Another very pretty trick is the following, although also well known. Procure (a "magical repository" will be found

the best place to go to in the long run) a "nest" of round
boxes, one fitting inside the other. If the outside one is of
the size of a crown piece, and the inner one large enough to
contain a shilling, the "nest" should consist of nine or ten
boxes. Have the lids arranged in order, one within the other,
and the bodies in the same manner, beside the lids. If you
are performing with a retiring screen, the boxes can be
arranged behind it. Lacking this, the next best plan is to
have them at the bottom of a bag, which will stifle the noise
made by shutting them. Borrow a marked coin, which you
will exchange for a similar one in your palm (Palm No. 1).
Give this to be held. Say, "Now, here I have a small box."
But as you have purposely left the "small box" behind your
screen or in your bag, as the case may be, you will have to
go and fetch it. As soon as your hands are out of sight,
pop the coin (which will be the marked one) into the smallest
box, and shut all the lids down together. If you have to do
this inside the bag, and consequently in full view of the
audience, your face must bear an anxious and slightly annoyed
expression, as if the box could not be found. As soon as the
manœuvre is executed, exclaim, as if much relieved, "Ah, here
it is. Now, ladies and gentlemen," &c., &c. The operation
of shutting all the boxes down at once is a very simple one
if the lids are taken in one hand and the bodies in the other,
the two halves meeting, as it were, half way. A little practice
will soon show the futility of attempting to *turn* the lids
over on the bodies. Place the box in a prominent place (do
not give it to be held, as a slight shake will reveal the fact
that there is a coin already inside), and, taking the coin out
of the handkerchief, "pass" it into the box, which now ask
someone to open. Of course, box No. 2 will be found
inside, at which you will say, "Dear me!" or make any other
expression of surprise. Boxes Nos. 3, 4, and so on will in
turn be revealed, amidst great amusement, and in the innermost one, which the performer must, on no account, open
himself, the coin will be discovered. You cannot very well

avoid allowing an examination of the boxes, but always take care that the lids are in one place and the boxes in another, and all in great confusion as to gradation of size, and at the earliest opportunity sweep them away. It is the fashion to perform this trick with a coin previously sewn in a handkerchief, which handkerchief is whisked in the air. The effect is decidedly good, if not spoilt (as it certainly will be, ever and anon) by a demand to examine the handkerchief, which demand, I need hardly say, it is impossible to accede to. This sort of thing the conjuror must never indulge in. Let him borrow and return his handkerchief like a man, and trust to his sleight of hand.

(*h*) Palm a penny (Palm No. 1); borrow another, and a florin. Ask one of the audience to extend his or her hands (palms open and upwards) towards you; give the borrowed penny to be held by someone else, hold the florin at the ends of the fingers of the left hand, and execute the pass described in trick *c*, which will leave the florin in the palm of the left hand. The penny in the right hand must not, however, be actually exhibited, as is the coin in trick *c*, but be immediately placed in one of the outstretched hands before you. If the owner of them is at all restive, and anxious to see what is in his or her hand, or is a person you know or think you cannot trust, ask the nearest person to assist in the operation by holding the hand in one of his or her own. This, you will explain, is to show that you have no confederates. If the two parties are of opposite sexes, you can improve the occasion by some gentle sally about the gentleman being honoured by holding a lady's hand, &c. This operation concluded, the audience, including the holder of the coin, is, you may have no fear, under the impression that the florin is in the holder's hand. You have now to make believe to place the penny into the other outstretched hand. To do this, you must execute the same pass as before, only reversed; *i.e.*, the right hand will hold the penny, and the left the palmed florin. This trick affords an instance where palming with both hands is a requisite accomplishment. If the performer is not able to palm with both hands, an opportunity must be made for getting the coin in the left hand back into the right. By repeating the change as before, you will be supposed to place the penny in the other hand of the holder, and, drawing particular attention to the exact position of the coins, command them to change places. This trick, so simple to look at, is one of the most difficult to perform of those yet described; for not only must the sleight of hand be well executed, but the whole demeanour of the performer must be impressive of the fact that he really is doing what he says he is, instead of exactly the reverse. Yet the impressiveness must not be too pointed, or the natural suspicion in human nature will be aroused The "happy medium" is well hit if the performer, in giving the florin (in reality the penny), says, " Now, sir " (or " madam," as the case may be), "I will ask you to take great care of this coin for me. Conjurors are but poor people, and cannot well afford to lose money; for this reason I have given you the florin to hold in your right hand, it being the stronger." On giving the penny, you can say that "I would rather, for safety's sake, that it were along with the florin in the right hand, only, in that case, there would be no trick." In giving the coins into the holder's hands, it is highly essential that you close the latter rapidly, the coins being so covered by your own fingers during the operation that nothing is seen of them. Otherwise, it would be unnecessary to proceed further with the trick. The florin may be marked, but not so the penny, unless the audience insists upon it, as they sometimes will, at the instigation of Mr. Interference; in which case the pennies must be once more exchanged—a very simple matter—before the coins are returned to their owners.

(*i*) Borrow or produce (it is immaterial, save for appearance, which you do) six to nine coins, and lay them, apart from each other, on a table or slab. Have one of the coins marked by several persons in the room (use the "no confederate" excuse), and placed along with the unmarked ones in a hat and the whole shaken up so as to be well mixed. Whilst this is being done, have yourself blindfolded. Placing your hand in the hat, feel every coin, and you will at once detect which is the marked one, by its warmth. The heat is imparted to it from the many hands through which it has passed. It is always advantageous to have the other coins lying on as cold a place as possible; but never turn back a tablecloth for the purpose of allowing them to lie on the bare mahogany, or a clue to the solution of the mystery will be given. Sometimes some clever people will pretend to put the marked shilling into the hat without doing so. This you can easily detect by counting the coins. Of course, you would not count them until you failed to find the marked one, as the trick should be performed as quickly as possible. No sleight of hand whatever is required; but it is a trick which never fails to excite the greatest wonderment whenever successfully performed. By allowing the audience to arrange the preliminaries, you disarm suspicion. The blindfolding, which is an innovation of my own, I find a great improvement. Of course, make the most of it.

(*k*) Have a shilling palmed (Palm No. 1), and borrow another; also a handkerchief. Place the borrowed shilling in the handkerchief, which roll up very loosely, the coin from the palm being included in the folds, and as near the other one as possible without actually touching it. Place the whole in a hat, with one end of the handkerchief hanging out. Now borrow another shilling, which say you will pass invisibly into the handkerchief. Make a pass, and ask someone to shake the handkerchief into the hat, when the two coins will jingle together. This is a simple trick, and is capable of variation according to circumstances.

(*l*) The trick I am now going to describe, as a drawing-room experiment with coins, surpasses, for simplicity and effect, all others. But its simplicity must not lead the learner to attempt it without having attained some proficiency in the foregoing tricks, for considerable neatness is required to execute it effectively. Procure a piece of glass of the size and thickness of a penny, and have the edges ground smooth, but not polished. This is best obtained from a lapidary—not an optician. Have it palmed in either hand (Palm No. 1). Borrow a penny, and, whilst it is being marked, ask one of the audience to half fill a wineglass, which has been well examined, with water. Always let the audience attend to such matters as these, as it tends to disarm

suspicion, and also saves you trouble. You will, of course, not omit to make the most of there being no possible deception in the glass, which you will give a lady to hold by the stem or foot. Now borrow a white handkerchief, as coarse as you can procure it (do not ask for a coarse handkerchief, for that would be impolite, but say you want a gentleman's handkerchief, and then you can select which you prefer), and, taking the marked coin in the same hand as that in which the glass is palmed, spread the handkerchief over it. Approach the lady holding the wineglass, and affect to take up the coin, with the handkerchief, from the outside, by means of the disengaged hand, but in reality take up the glass, palming the coin (Palm No. 1). Now spread the handkerchief over the wineglass, with the supposed coin exactly above the latter, and within an inch of its rim. Let the holder of the wineglass grasp the coin (*i.e.*, the counterfeit presentment thereof) with the thumb and forefinger of the disengaged hand, and keep it in the same position, with the understanding that at the word "three" it is to be allowed to fall into the glass (see **Fig.** 13). Take great care that the piece of glass is held exactly over the wineglass, and utter the word of command only when there is a dead silence. The jingling of the falling glass will, of course, be assumed by the audience to be that of the penny. You will now express your intention of invisibly extracting the coin from the glass. Use any cabalistic form you may choose, and, with a flourish of the wand from the wineglass towards your hand, exhibit the coin, and give it to be examined. Let the lady withdraw the handkerchief from the wineglass, which at once seize and show rapidly round. The glass at the bottom will not be perceived, and you must take an early opportunity of extracting it. Some tricks "take" in various degrees at different times, but this one never fails to throw the audience into a state of bewilderment. Alway obtain possession of the wineglass as soon as you can after the completion of the trick, for people will sometimes feel to the bottom of it with their fingers, although without the faintest notion of what they are looking for. When you bewilder people, you must not be surprised if they do inexplicable things, and must prepare yourself for all emergencies.

My reason for directing the performer to borrow a *penny* for this trick is that it has, similarly with the circle of glass, no milled edge, and is of the size most convenient for the occasion. In extreme cases an eyeglass may be used, when, if it has a milled edge, as most of them have, it would be as well to borrow a florin; but in such instances there must be no dallying in showing the glass round after the trick, or the ribbed edge will infallibly be seen. I remember finding myself, on one occasion, without my piece of glass, and borrowed an eyeglass of one of the audience, under the pretext that the silken cord by which it was suspended was the very thing I required for a trick. I did some trivial thing with the cord, but forgot to return the glass for an hour or so, having in the interim forced it out of its frame (it was mounted in tortoiseshell), performed the trick, and replaced it. I knew that I should have to perform this particular trick, or have my reputation tarnished, so made a bold stroke for victory. Now I am never without the glass, and advise my readers to observe the same precaution. A port wine glass is the best to use, the piece of glass being liable to stick in the comparatively narrow sherry glass. Always give the wineglass to a lady to hold: ladies are less liable to attempt to conduct experiments after their own manner, or to make premature disclosures, either of which proceedings is embarrassing to the performer. The conjuring repositories supply a champagne tumbler, with a glass exactly the size of the interior of the bottom. This is an undoubted improvement, as the water may be poured out, if an examination be demanded, when the glass will still adhere to bottom of the tumbler, although the latter be turned upside down. This trick, when "worked" in conjunction with the nest of boxes, previously mentioned, makes an excellent combination. The nest can be used for any sized coin by the simple expedient of removing the very smallest boxes.

(m) Take a penny, in good condition, and make, or have made, by a competent person, a groove, quite $\frac{3}{16}$in. deep, all round the outer edge. This is very easily and most efficiently managed by means of a lathe; but, wanting that useful machine, a piercing-saw and flat needle-file will answer. When the groove is completed, with the piercing saw cut the penny into three pieces of equal width. Now take a very fine indiarubber band, obtainable at all shops where rubber goods are sold, and stretch it round the groove. The illustration shows the penny in three pieces, and also the band—actual size before being stretched. In putting on the band, commence with the centre piece, and then fit in the side pieces, the greatest care being necessary not to allow the band to get twisted. The result of these operations, when concluded, is that the penny can be folded up and made to occupy a space in width one-third of its usual diameter. When held at a little distance from the spectator, the incisions are not observable, especially before the penny is used for a trick,

Fig. 14.

the issue of which, being unknown, does not lead the suspicions of the audience into any particular groove. As the act of folding causes a sharp strain to be put upon the band at the junctions, the groove at those points must be carefully filed, so as to completely do away with anything resembling a cutting edge, or a disaster may very easily occur. Invariably, before using, the band should be minutely examined, and, if the slightest signs of wear manifest themselves, it should be changed.

The prepared coin (which need not necessarily be a penny) is generally used in conjunction with a bottle, into which it is made to pass, *viâ* the mouth. In order to make the trick at all satisfactory, a marked penny should be borrowed, and exchanged, by any of the previously described methods, for the prepared one.

A soda-water bottle has been previously handed round for examination, and this is taken in the left hand. With the right hand show that the penny is at least as broad again as the mouth of the bottle, and then, folding it up quickly whilst making a covering movement, and hidden by the body of the hand, let it fall through. Show the bottle round to the spectators, continually shaking it, as if to convince them that the coin is solid and real, but really to prevent the possibility of the slits being seen. The trick can now be finished in two ways, viz., the bottle may be broken, or the coin can be shaken out again. I fancy the breaking of the bottle is the more effective, as the shaking out method impresses too forcibly upon the mind of an intelligent company the fact that some mysterious, if ingeniously concealed, preparation exists in connection with the coin. But the performer in this instance, as in very many other cases, must be guided in his actions by the mental calibre of the spectators. To shake the coin from the bottle, the latter should be taken horizontally in the right hand, the fingers of the left hand closing round the mouth, leaving a hollow in the palm for the coin to fall into. A not too violent sweeping shake is then given, bringing the mouth of the bottle downwards, when the coin should pass into the left hand. Some little practice will be required to insure this operation being brought off at the first attempt. Having to shake the bottle three or four times looks unskilful, although it does not absolutely spoil the trick. I have directed the use of a soda-water bottle because it has sloping sides, which facilitate the operation of getting the penny out very considerably, and also because it is made of white glass. If a coloured bottle were used (which it must not be, if possibly avoidable), the spectators would suspect that a coin had somehow been concealed in the interior before the trick began. However the coin may be regained, whether by breaking the bottle or by shaking out, it must be immediately re-exchanged for the borrowed penny, which will then be returned. It is quite possible to have that coin palmed during the whole operation; but if the performer lacks the necessary skill for this, it should be carried in the ticket pocket of the coat. The conjuror should have every coat he wears (excepting his dress one) furnished with this ticket pocket, and it will be greatly to his advantage to have one on each side. It should not be too deep, so that coins and other articles may be speedily reached with certainty, and it should not have a covering flap.

The penny can also be prepared by omitting the groove, employing instead holes, made completely through, across the slits, through which elastic is passed, and fastened. As, for this purpose, flat elastic is immeasurably superior to any other form, some trouble is entailed in making suitable slits through; but, once accomplished, the article is far better than one prepared in any other way. The elastic should run quite freely through the centre piece, and be fastened with glue to the outside pieces only, first being slightly stretched, to insure the whole being brought closely together. The grooved penny can be purchased at a much less cost than would be incurred in making it, and, in addition, is more likely to be correctly constructed.

The following is a development of the use of the folding penny, which is even more startling than the foregoing, one or more pennies being made to pass into a bottle, which has been examined, and which has the mouth stopped by a large cork. In this case, the cork (Fig. 15) is a delusion and a snare. It is just 2in. long, and $1\frac{1}{16}$in. broad at the top, tapering to $\frac{15}{16}$in. at the bottom. Viewed from the exterior, it is a cork; in reality, it is made of brass, with a thin veneer of cork glued on the outside. The measurements given include the cork skin. The bottom opens, flap-like, on a hinge, but is kept normally closed by means of a fine spiral spring, running the whole length of the inside, and soldered on the top and bottom. Protruding through a hole drilled in the top is a pin, which also runs the whole length of the interior (carried inside a small tube), and, when pressed, pushes open the bottom flap, thus allowing any contents there may be to fall out into the bottle. When the pressure upon the pin is removed, the power of the spring closes it again. This cork is charged with one or more folding pennies (three or four are generally used), and concealed in the hand, a genuine cork being handed for examination. The latter is changed for the

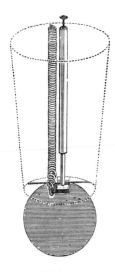

FIG. 15.

"property" cork, which is then placed in the bottle, which must be white, and, of course, have a very wide mouth. The performer now produces some pennies, which he may "pass" into the bottle in any way he pleases. A good method is to use the two boxes described in "Grand Magic" as then the performer's hands are free. But the pass shown at Fig. 11 may be employed, the bottle being taken in the hand in which the coins are actually concealed. When the coins are being "passed," the bottle must, of course, be held in one hand or the other, and pressure given the pin by a finger at the proper moment. Where one coin only is used, it may be simply palmed, which method would also apply where the performer is skilful enough to palm several coins at once. In this case, the coins would merely be held in one hand, and the bottle in the other, and the coins thrown into the bottle.

(*n*) A very pretty trick, though rather difficult to learn, is performed, with the aid of the Reverse Palm (Fig. 6), as follows: Borrow from two separate persons two coins of the same denomination. Take particular pains to have the marks quite distinct on each, so that the two are distinguishable from one another. There is no objection to the performer superintending the marking, in order to insure its being properly done. One coin, for instance, might have a single stroke marked upon it, or a cross, whilst the other could have a small circle or an initial. The numbers 1 and 2 could also be efficiently employed; and, for facility of description, I will now suppose them used. Palmed (Fig. 2), you have another coin of your own, similar to those borrowed. You place two chairs or settees a little distance apart, between yourself and the spectators. Take coin No. 1, and, standing behind one of the chairs, facing the company, act as though you tossed it upon the cushion. What you really do, however, is to palm the coin by the reverse palm, following the instructions on page 8, for throwing a coin away into the air; the coin that has been concealed in the palm being released, in its stead. This action must be assiduously practised until it can be performed with complete certainty and smoothness. Practise first tossing a coin on a chair from a distance of a couple of feet, and then imitate that action as nearly as possible whilst making the change. The toss must be made with a steady, smooth swing, neither too hurriedly nor too slowly executed. When the manœuvre is finished, the palm of the hand must, of course, be towards the audience. A half, or whole, turn of the body must now be made, to enable the performer to get the coin from the back of the fingers to the palm proper. The way to ensure the safe execution of this is to put the thumb over the first finger, so that it grasps the coin, assisted by the middle finger. The first finger can then be drawn out of the way. With coin No. 1 in the palm, take coin No. 2, and repeat the changing operation, at the completion of which the state of affairs will be: On chair 1, duplicate coin (supposed by spectators to be coin No. 1); on chair 2, coin No. 1 (supposed by spectators to be coin No. 2); in performer's palm, coin No. 2. Any fanciful form of causing a magical change to take place may be gone into, and the performer then asks a spectator to examine the coin on chair 2, which is found to be coin No. 1. As only two coins are known to the spectators, it is taken for granted by them that the one on chair 1 is coin No. 2; but it will be as well for the performer to incidentally remark, "And, of course, there is coin No. 2," and then at once proceed to show the trick over again, "for the general satisfaction of those present." For this purpose, coin No. 1 is taken from the person who examined it, and ostensibly replaced upon chair 2. Instead, however, coin No. 2 is placed there. Under the plea of placing the chair a little closer, so that a better view may be obtained, the performer takes up duplicate coin from chair 1, and, in apparently replacing it, substitutes coin No. 1. The coins have thus been made to regain their old positions, and may now, of course, be freely examined, the performer not touching them again. If the performer feels any confidence in himself in this rather difficult trick, he may use three marked coins, when, by skilful manipulation, he may make all sorts of changes. By working changes with only two of the three at a time, he always has one lying dormant, which is not liable to inspection, and may, therefore, be the duplicate one. It is not advisable for him to prolong the trick, unless it be going very well. He must keep his wits about him, however, or he may find that he has forgotten the precise whereabouts of his own coin. A very bold, but remarkably effective, way of bringing about the final change is to pick the coin from the chair, and, instead of moving that closer, toss the coin into a lady's lap. The lady should be sitting upon the extreme verge of the other spectators, or else must be shielded by some article of furniture, or the coin palmed at the back of the hand is not unlikely to be seen. The very boldness of this action is, however, its chief safeguard, only there must be no sort of hesitation in its execution.

A performer with large and muscular fingers can use half-crowns for the trick, but for the beginner shillings and half-pence will be sufficient. Copper coins are not so effective as silver; but an accidental exposure of a portion of them is not so readily perceived as is the case with the brighter metal—not that there is the least excuse for such exposure.

Before returning the duplicate coin to the pocket, the performer may produce one or two other effects with the reverse palm. Let him borrow a hat, and a coin similar to the one concealed. Standing sideways to the company, let him have the duplicate palmed reversely in the hand that is farthest from the audience. Say it is the left hand. With the right hand place the hat into the left one, the thumb on the brim, the fingers inside. As the company have seen the palm of the left hand open, not the slightest suspicion will be entertained that it holds anything. The borrowed coin is now made to perform an ærial journey, being palmed. The performer's eye follows its imaginary flight, and then catches it in the hat, the coin in the left hand being of course released, when it will be heard to fall. After showing this coin, reverse palm the other, under cover of the hat, and repeat the operation. To do this, the performer must be able to palm equally well with either hand. If the trick be repeated, it should be varied each time by some such device as finding that the coin had taken refuge in a gentleman's hair, lady's handkerchief, &c., on its way to the hat.

By the time the learner has proceeded thus far with success, he will have acquired a proficiency that will enable him to amuse a circle of friends for an hour or two by means of coin tricks alone, without much fear of detection, especially if the rule of rehearsing in private before exhibiting in public be adhered to. The security afforded by a good palm can scarcely be over-estimated, as it enables the performer to attempt the most barefaced impromptu experiments with comparative impunity. These impromptu interludes are always conducive to success, for the audience can generally discover originality.

But, before taking a temporary leave of coins, I must put my readers up to a few wrinkles in connection with the use of the sleeve—a portion of the conjuror's attire which is but rarely employed, notwithstanding the popular exclamation of " Up his sleeve," which is usually made use of when the operator has vanished some trifle in the shape of a cauliflower or rabbit, for the reception of which articles the sleeve of a dress coat is so admirably adapted. No; the sleeve is only used when its coadjutorship is unsuspected; and, in the case of coins, only when the palm is suspected of containing the coin. So many people have a misty idea of palming, that one frequently hears whispered, " In his palm." Should the whisperer be wrong, of course you will at once prove him to be so by exhibiting your palms empty; but should he be right, you will then feign not to hear the whisper. Sometimes, though, the announcement is not made in a whisper, but in the form of a challenge to you, and this you must be prepared to meet. Suppose the coin *is* palmed and you are challenged; you are close to or among the audience, and the challenger is importunate. Nothing remains but to sleeve the coin. This manœuvre is executed by shooting the arm straight out, the palm open and downwards, with such force as will carry the coin up the sleeve. Of course, you must not stand in middle of the room shooting your arm out, or the audience will either divine what you are about or will think you are taking leave of your senses. The action must be covered by an advance towards the challenger, which must be done as boldly as if you had never even seen the coin, much less concealed it in your palm. As you advance, say some-

thing; for example, " What! in my palm, sir? I don't understand you. How can anything be in my palm? If you don't
believe me, see for yourself." With this, make the shoot, and
turn the hand over. Care must be taken that the arm is
quite level, or the coin will slide gracefully on to the floor.
You must not stop here, but say, "Perhaps you would like
to see my other hand as well, sir" (show left hand, at same
time allowing coin to fall back in the right, where palm
it), "or maybe you think the coin is up my sleeve." Shake
both arms vigorously, which, as the coin is again in your
palm, you can do with impunity, and ask someone to feel
your sleeves. An extra effect is given by your asserting that
the cause of the gentleman's anxiety was that he himself had
basely pilfered the coin, and wished to pass the odium on to

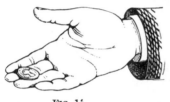

FIG. 15

FIG. 17.

you. With this remark, produce the coin from some part
of his person. Barring the disturbance to the equilibrium
of one's feelings of security whilst the performance is going
on, this little interlude, promptly carried out, is as good as
any set trick. Of course there must be no bungling. Should
the sleeves be turned back, as they often will be, they must
first be unrolled, with great deliberation. In such an
instance you would, of course, show that your sleeves are
guiltless of any deception, before exonerating the palm.
Practice will enable you at once to perceive the nature of
the objection about to be raised, so that ordinarily you can
anticipate, and turn down one sleeve at least. It is not often
that the exigency occurs, but it will infallibly do so at some
time or other, so one must be prepared to meet it, or be

looked upon as an impostor. A second method for sending a coin up the sleeve is to place it almost on the ends of the fingers (Fig. 16) palm upwards, and, turning the hand rapidly over, close it (Fig. 17). This will throw the coin up the sleeve, whereas the appearance is that it is enclosed in the hand. A third method is to hold the coin between the thumb and middle finger (Fig. 18) and "flip" it up the sleeve. A fourth method is to place the coin on the edge of the table and cover it with the ends of the fingers, which draw smartly back and shut, when the coin will be shot up the sleeve. This somewhat resembles the second method. A fifth method is to spin the coin high in the air, and as it descends make a "grab" at it as if catching, but in reality

FIG. 18.

allow it to fall down the sleeve, keeping the hand shut as though holding it. This is one of the most thorough deceptions I know of. It is so perfect that the operator himself cannot see the coin enter the sleeve. I am quite aware that it seems improbable, but a trial will be conclusive on the point. A pleasing variety of the first method is to place a coin (the heavier the better) on the palm of the hand. Turn the hand over briskly, at the same time thrusting it well forward, and the coin will slide up the sleeve. In performing any of these tricks be careful to have the shirt cuff pulled well up and out of the way, and do not wear large links or solitaires, against which the coin will infallibly clink, if only for the simple reason that it is not wanted to do so. No one but a bungler would use the sleeve in his regular performances, except when driven by necessity; but it is highly essential for a conjuror to be perfect in all the minutiæ of his art, and he must practise them as the pianoforte-player practises the scales which he never plays to the public.

In using marked coins, always take the greatest care that the marking is done in such a manner as to render it impossible for the coin not to be recognised on making its reappearance; and also let several people see the mark. It is very disheartening, when you have performed an elaborate trick, in which a Mr. Interference has given you no end of trouble, to hear the owner of the coin say that he cannot recognise his mark. I have seen people put some trivial mark on a coin in pencil, which would rub off immediately. It is also advisable to have a quantity of cheap coins by you. In such tricks as trick *d*, large, thin, and showy silver Turkish coins are the best. They possess every advantage; the milled edge gives a firm hold for the palm, whilst the substance of the coin allows of a large number being held in the hand. Besides this, thin coins give a good business-like clink; whilst a large coin is always more effective than a small one. Pennies plated over make very fair substitutes, and do not entail much loss of capital if kept aside ready for use, as they always should be, which can hardly be said to be the case with florins or half-crowns.

CHAPTER III.

TRICKS WITH COMMON OBJECTS.

I COMMENCE this, the second portion of drawing-room conjuring, with the decided hope that, before my readers
attempt to follow me, they will have attained some proficiency in the art of palming and other little matters alluded
to in my remarks concerning the treatment of coins. If
such skill has been acquired, although in a small degree
only, it will be of use in rendering the manipulation of other
objects much easier. The prevailing idea with the public is
that a conjuror moves things about from place to place before
one's very eyes, but with such extreme rapidity as to avoid
detection. This, I say, is the prevailing idea, and long may
it continue to be so, since it is the very thing an audience is
supposed to imagine. The learner, however, must, from the
outset, dismiss such an impression from his mind as unten-
able, even for an instant. If he has a lurking opinion that
a hand *can* be moved without the motion being detected, let

him practise at moving, say, a cork or a piece of sugar, a distance of only one short inch. Let him practise for a twelvemonth to begin with, and I will guarantee that at the end of that period he is no nearer the consummation of the feat than he was at the commencement. If time hangs heavily on his hands, let him go on practising, say, for five or ten years: the result will be precisely similar. No; conjuring is based upon more deceptive principles than mere rapidity of movement, although that, of course, enters largely into its composition. Articles are, indeed, transmitted from one place to another before the eyes of the audience, but it is always, as it were, *sub rosa*. This is the reason why conjurors say so much about the hand being quicker than the eye, &c. The audience is continually trying to detect movements which are never even attempted, the result being that other movements are conducted with impunity. The conjuror must start with the one principle firmly fixed in his mind that he is to deceive his audience in every way possible. At no time is he actually to do that which he says he is doing. Every look and gesture, besides every word, should tend to lead the mind into the wrong groove. MISDIRECTION is the grand basis of the conjuror's actions; and the more natural the performer's movements in this particular, the more complete will be his success. With each trick that requires it, I shall give hints for misdirecting the spectator's attention, although I am of opinion that every conjuror can best suit himself if he is only firmly impressed with the necessity for misdirection. The drawing-room conjuror must hold himself prepared to perform offhand with any article that may happen to present itself to view; although it is, of course, perfectly allowable for him to send for anything he may require. An article which one is tolerably certain to find in most houses is

Sugar.—Take four well-shaped pieces, of a medium size, and place them before you on a table, at which you will sit at your ease, in the form of a square, and about a foot from each other. Hatch up a long rigmarole about one piece being the Emperor of Japan, another his wife, another his daughter, and another his prime minister, or any other rubbish you please, so long as you bring it about that it is necessary that all four should assemble together in one place. In the country of which you are speaking, you will explain, it is the custom of Royalty to travel by telegraph, and invisible to the gaze of the "common herd." To illustrate how it is done, you will cover two of the four pieces, each with a separate hand, and, at the word "pass," make a slight movement as if throwing a piece from one hand to the other. On raising the hands, two pieces will be found under one, and none under the other. Repeat this operation (the minority always going over to the majority) until all four pieces are collected under one hand. The explanation of this really pretty, and, to the uninitiated, inexplicable trick, is, that you have a fifth piece of sugar palmed. If this piece be released, and that under the other hand palmed, the effect is the same as if an invisible journey had really been made. Supposing the five pieces of sugar to be represented by numerals, the various changes may be thus tabulated:

Left Hand.		*Right Hand.*
1.—Raise 1	and	Drop 5 with 2.
2.—Drop 1 with 5 and 2	and	Raise 3.
3.—Raise 4	and	Drop 3 with 1, 5, and 2.
4.—Raise both hands and pocket 4.		

The rough and adhesive nature of sugar renders it very easy to palm. In palming, avoid all contraction of the muscles of the back of the hand, which is visible to the audience, or a clue to the solution of the trick will be given. If going out to a place where you are likely to be asked to exhibit your skill, be provided with a piece of sugar, and then ask for the requisite four pieces. If you are unprovided, then you must secure possession of the sugar basin, and secrete the extra piece as best you can. The extreme simplicity of this trick is only equalled by the astonishment of the audience, who are straining their eyes to catch a glimpse of the piece of sugar as it passes. I need hardly remark that they never succeed.

Knives, I think I may say, are also tolerably common articles, and some good tricks are performed with them. Take a cheese knife and four tiny squares of paper. Stand facing your audience, however small it may be, and, wetting the papers separately, stick two on each side of the blade, taking care that the positions on both sides correspond as nearly as possible. Hold the knife before you in the fingers of the right hand (Fig. 19), and in such a position that

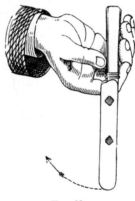

FIG. 19.

only one side of the blade is visible. With the thumb and finger of the left hand remove the piece of paper nearest the handle, and, putting your hand behind your back, make a feint of throwing it away, without actually doing so. Now, with a rapid movement, cause the knife to describe a half circle in the air *still with the same side uppermost*; but the position of the hand will be slightly altered (Fig. 20), which will lead the audience to think that the knife has been actually turned over. Barely before the movement is completed a finger of the left hand must be upon the spot recently occupied by the piece of paper, as if taking off a second piece from the opposite side. The first piece, which has all the time been in the left hand, is thus made to do duty twice. The second time, it is dropped on the floor in full view of the audience, accompanied by the remark, "that makes the second piece." Now remove the other piece of paper, and repeat the manœuvre executed with the first piece, taking the greatest care that only one side of the blade is visible, and that the finger of the left hand, with

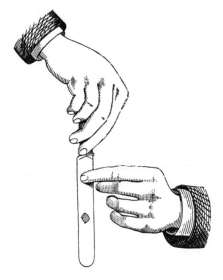

FIG. 20.

the concealed paper, is down upon the vacant spot before the spectators' eyes can rest there. Having ostensibly removed the fourth and last piece of paper, the knife is supposed to be empty, which you boldly declare to be the case, making a rapid backward and forward movement with the blank side to prove it. You then say you will cause the papers to re-appear upon the knife instantaneously. All you have to do is to put your hand behind your back and reverse the position of the knife so that the side of the blade with the two pieces of paper still remaining upon it is uppermost. Bringing the knife again to the front, make another quick backward and forward movement, saying, "Here are the papers back again on both sides as before," and then, without any further preliminaries, draw the blade through the fingers and cause the two papers to fall upon the floor. If this final movement is not executed, the audience will, when they have recovered their senses, point to the two papers which you dropped on the floor during the performance of the trick, and want to know why they are there and not on the knife. Continued rapidity of motion is what is required for the success of this trick. There must be no halting in the middle or hesitation of any kind, to avoid which practice in private will be essential, as, indeed, it will be with every trick worth doing at all.

Borrow a *light* penknife, and take care that it is not too sharp, and has a good deep notch at the haft. You are previously prepared with about two feet of very fine black silk, one end of which is attached to a button of your vest, the other end being furnished with a loop large enough to pass over a finger. This can either be wound round the button, or can hang loosely, with the free end looped up. I prefer the latter method, and have never found it lead to any inconvenience, which at first sight it appears extremely likely to do. Also borrow a hock or champagne bottle; pint size preferred. First send round the knife to be examined, and, whilst the examination is going on, get the loop of the silk over the end of one of the fingers of the left hand. When the knife is returned to you, and not before, give the bottle to be examined, and distract the attention of the audience by allusions to the "departed spirits" of the bottle, and admonitions to be sure and see that the bottom does not take out. By the time the bottle comes back you have slipped the loop over the blade of the knife and allowed it to catch in the notch, where cause it to remain. If the knife is a sharp one, extra caution must be observed, or the silk will be severed.

This actually happened to me on one occasion, so I speak from direful experience. By sending the bottle away to be cleaned, I gained sufficient time to tie another loop in the silk, and went on as usual; but the incident was not a particularly cheerful one taken altogether—there was too much " glorious uncertainty " about it.   Take the knife upside down, *i.e.*, with the sharp edge of the blade uppermost, between the finger and thumb, hold the silk sufficiently taut to keep the loop in position by means of the other fingers, and drop the whole into the bottle.   This must not

FIG. 21

be done with the bottle in a perpendicular position (in which case the loop will probably either break or slip off the knife), but with it inclined at an angle of about 45deg. (Fig. 21). This will allow the knife to slide down at a safe speed and yet reach the bottom with a good "thud."   Having satisfied yourself that everything is in order, hold the bottle perpendicularly in the left hand between the audience and yourself, and about breast high. Make use of any cabalistic nonsense you please, and then cause the knife to rise from the bottle by the action of moving it from you and towards the audience.

The action of raising the bottle must be but sparsely indulged in, if at all, as it is easily noticed; not so the horizontal motion. When brought to the mouth of the bottle the knife quietly topples over on to the floor, whence allow it to be picked up by a spectator, who will not require much admonition to examine it. Also send the bottle round again; and get rid of the silk as soon as you can after the trick is done. It will be noticed that I have directed the performer to use a hock or champagne bottle. The reason for this will be obvious after once trying the experiment with a bottle having an abrupt shoulder, such as an ale bottle. The knife catches in it, and a vigorous jerk, which is as likely to cause a breakage as anything else, has to be resorted to to free it. The sides of hock and champagne bottles presenting an even surface the whole way up, that class of bottle is therefore to be preferred. By means of the foregoing three tricks I have seen a room full of intelligent people utterly bewildered.

The following trick I have never known to be discovered if only properly performed. For it you will require another exceedingly common object, viz.:

Cotton.—Take a piece of any colour, 12in. to 15in. long, and see that one of the audience is provided with a very sharp penknife. Double the cotton once, and have the bend cut quite through. Double again and have it cut, and repeat the operation until it is nothing but pieces, each barely a third of an inch long. Rub the pieces together in the fingers, and, after a short time, quietly draw out the cotton again as it was in the first instance. That is what you must ostensibly do: now for how to do it. First of all, have concealed between your finger and thumb a piece of cotton about the length above mentioned. This you must roll up small, and deliberately hold between your finger and thumb, or, better still, if the fingers be sufficiently large, between the tips of any two fingers, as they are more naturally kept together. Nobody will notice it if the hand is engaged in negligently holding the lappel of your coat, the wand, &c. I need hardly mention that the concealed piece must be of the same colour as that operated upon, as the production of a white in place of a black piece would scarcely be satisfactory. To ensure the success of this preliminary, some considerable manœuvring has often to be gone through, and no small amount of tact exhibited. Where you are showing the trick for the first time, you can of course ask for any coloured cotton you please (always choose black when you have a choice), but it is such a fascinating trick that you will be called upon to perform it over and over again in the same house, or before the same people—which is quite as bad—and you will find that all kinds of ingenious devices will be brought to bear upon you. As a commencement, always carry in the corners of your waistcoat pockets two black and two white pieces, ready for emergencies. Each pocket will contain two pieces of the same colour, but differing in thickness, one in each corner. It is useless to carry other colours on the mere chance, as you are sure to be unprovided with the exact one required at the moment. When coloured cotton is produced, you must, by some means or other, get at the reel from which the cotton is taken. If driven right into a corner, you must go so far as to ask someone (always let it be the master or mistress of the house) to secretly obtain a piece for you; but this you will have to resort to on rare occasions only. Make all sorts of excuses so as to cause a delay, even going so far as to postpone the performance of the trick, but not before you have seen what colour you are likely to be favoured with. Your wits must do the rest. The reader must remember that I have taken extreme cases, and such as but rarely occur; but still they *do* occur, and if I did not warn the beginner of pitfalls ahead, he would not think much of my teaching. In the ordinary way, he will be able to ask for any colour he pleases, which will of course be similar to that with which he is provided. We will suppose that everything has progressed favourably. Take the cotton to be cut between the thumb and forefinger of each hand, by the extreme ends, and, doubling it, let one hand hold the loop to be cut, the fingers of the other hand holding the ends. As soon as the knife has passed through the cotton, give it a "twitch," and bring the ends, of which there will now be four, quickly together, as if you had performed some very intricate manœuvre. Of course, you have really done nothing at all, the movement being only a deceptive one to lead the spectators to believe that the secret of the trick consists in the way in which you twist or double the cotton. Have this in mind all through the trick, and keep up the deception. Continue to double the cotton, taking the greatest care that the ends all come neatly together, and that all the loops are cut through. Do everything with the greatest deliberation (except the delusive "twitch"), for there is no occasion for any hurry. When the cotton is cut so small that it will not double any more, commence to knead in the fingers, and gradually work the fragments behind the concealed piece, which must be brought to the front. This you will do without once removing the hands from the full view of the audience—in fact, under their very eyes. When you feel quite sure that everything is snug and secure, commence to unravel the whole piece, which will pass for the resuscitated original.

People who have seen the trick performed before will sometimes suggest that the piece of cotton should be measured before being cut up. Allow this to be done with all the grace in the world (when you find that you cannot do otherwise), but, before operating upon it, roll it up in the fingers, either absently, whilst engaging the audience in conversation, or for the purpose of seeing if it is of the proper dimensions, and exchange it, unperceived, for the concealed piece, which will be cut up instead. Although it is not advisable to have the cotton measured first, yet, when it is done, it invariably adds lustre to the feat. The pieces must never be carelessly thrown away, but secreted in a pocket on the first opportunity that presents itself, and afterwards burnt.

Rings can be made use of in many tricks, both in the drawing-room and on the stage. The following will be found very neat and effective: Procure a metal imitation of a wedding-ring, and have it cut neatly through. Pass this ring under a single thread of your handkerchief near one of the corners. Borrow a lady's ring, which palm, under pretence of putting it in the handkerchief. (The best method for palming a ring is to hold it between two fingers at the roots.) This you will appear to have done if you give the false ring (under cover of the handkerchief) to be held by someone who is not the owner of the borrowed article. It is immaterial whether

the genuine ring has a fancy head or not, as the back of it will usually be about the width of a wedding-ring. Take the wand in the hand, and, unperceived, slip the ring in your palm over it until it reaches the middle, still covered by the hand. Now ask two persons to hold the wand, one at either end, and lay the handkerchief containing the false ring (still held from the outside by the original holder) over it. If you now remove your hand, you will leave the ring on the wand still concealed by the handkerchief (Fig. 22). Take hold of the end of th handkerchief which hangs down below the wand, and instruct the person holding the false ring to leave go when you count "three." As soon as you are obeyed, draw the handkerchief smartly across the wand. This will cause the ring to spin round, and assist materially in inducing the audience to believe that it was actually conjured from the handkerchief on to the wand whilst the latter article was being held at either end by two people. A slight jerk will detach the false ring from the handkerchief, which you can send round to be examined. A hint I can give the learner is, never to ask a lady to lend you her wedding-ring or keeper. Many ladies are exceedingly superstitious, and feel embarrassed when asked, from not liking to refuse, and yet being unwilling to take their rings from their fingers. Always borrow a ring the back of which nearly, if not quite, matches your false article in substance.

Procure a metal ring, similar to the one used in the last trick, of very soft brass, and, when you have cut it through, sharpen up the two ends to points with a file, or any other way you please. Borrow a lady's ring, and exchange it, as in last trick, putting the false one in a handkerchief, which have tied with tape or string in such a manner that the ring is contained in a bag. If the borrowed ring is narrow all round, you may make use of your nest of boxes (described in trick g, Chapter II.), if it has not been previously utilised in some other trick; it being a golden rule among conjurors never to use the same apparatus twice during the same evening. An apple (a potato, small loaf, &c., will do as well) can be used instead with effect, if a goodly slit be made in it, and the ring pushed in while you are taking it from your bag or from behind the screen. Show the apple round, boldly saying that everyone can see that there is no preparation about it, at the same time taking care that no one has time to decide either one way or the other from the rapidity with which you pass it about. Place it in a prominent position, and then take the handkerchief containing the false ring by the bag, allowing the ends to fall over and conceal your hands. Quickly unbend the ring, and, working one of the pointed ends through the handkerchief, draw it out, and *rub the place of exit between your fingers, so as to obliterate all traces of it.* All this you must do very quickly, and, dropping the handkerchief on the floor, say, "Without untying the string, I have abstracted the ring, which I now pass into that apple." Here make a pass. Take a knife in the hand holding the false ring (unless you have been clever enough to get rid of that article), and, showing the audience that the other hand is quite empty, proceed to cut open the apple slowly. When the knife touches the ring, allow it to "clink" upon it as much as possible, and call attention to the fact, as it is a great feature in the trick. Do not cut the apple completely through, but, taking it forward (on a plate is the best way), allow the owner of the ring to take it out with her own hand. Of course, the audience must not be allowed to handle the apple, and so discover the old slit. This trick should not be performed with the preceding one, but on another evening. The principal effect of the trick is the apparent abstraction of the borrowed ring from its confinement in the handkerchief in an incomprehensible manner, and you must, therefore, allow the audience to see that the ring undoubtedly *is* tied up securely in the first instance.

Another trick with a ring is performed by aid of the wand only. Borrow a good stout ring, a signet for example, and, holding it near the roots of the fingers of the right hand, pretend to pass it over the wand, but, in reality, let it slide along on the outside of it, and still keep it in the hand. The deception is assisted if the ring be first carelessly placed upon the wand, and taken off again, two or three times. Say to one of the audience, "Will you be so kind as to hold one end of the wand with either hand?" and, in stretching the wand out towards him, allow the left hand momentarily to pass close under the right, and let the ring fall into it—of course, unperceived. If you look at your hands whilst doing this, you are a lost man. You must look the addressee boldly in the face, and thereby divert attention to him—not that there is the slightest excuse for exposing the ring during its passage from one hand to the other. When the wand is firmly held at both ends, say something about the futility of strength in certain cases, and eventually show the ring in the left hand, and remove the right from the wand to show that it is empty. If relinquished at this stage, the trick is very incomplete, as the audience usually divine, or affect to divine, that the ring never was put upon the wand at all. It is a peculiarity of this trick that this remark is almost invariably made, so the conjuror must be prepared with something still more " staggering." Return the ring to its owner, and call attention to the fact that you have not cut it in any way (not that anyone will ever think that you would do so, but you must assume that this idea is prevailing in the minds of the audience), and secretly take from your pocket, or wherever it may be concealed, a thick metal (or gold) ring, which keep in the left hand. Borrow the ring again, and slide it over the wand with precisely the same movement which you used in the first instance, when you did *not* put the ring on. This time you must appear to be very clumsy, and let the two hands come together so that everyone can see the action clearly, and snatch the left hand away sharply as if it contained the ring. You will doubtless see a number of heads lean towards each other, and hear a good deal of loud whispering, in which the words "left hand" will be conspicuous. Take no notice of this beyond looking as confused as possible, and the audience will think they have bowled you out at last. The strange part of it is that, in a trick of this kind, a spectator who fancies, rightly or wrongly, that he has discovered something, never attributes the fact to your want of skill, but to his own remarkable powers of perception. The effect of the ruse will be heightened if you allow a tiny portion of the false ring to catch the eye of one or more of the audience; or resort to any other artifice to induce them to believe that you really have the borrowed ring in the left hand, and have allowed the fact to transpire through carelessness. Now say that, the ring being securely on the wand, you mean to take it off as before, and give the two ends of the wand to be held. You will then appear to notice the incredulous looks and remarks of the audience for the first time, and stoutly deny that the ring is in the left hand, which, however, you decline to open. Allow the audience to argue the point with you, and, when one has said that he saw you take the ring in the left hand, and others have made a similar statement, pretend to give in, and say that you must admit that you are discovered; but, at the same time, you feel it incumbent on you to do something to retrieve your character. You will, therefore, pass the ring, now in the left hand, invisibly on to the wand. Make a pass with the left hand, and draw the right smartly away from the wand, causing the ring on it to spin round. The effect may be imagined. At the instant the right hand leaves the wand, the left should place the false ring (supposing one is used) in the pocket, as all manner of questions will be asked afterwards. The trick can be varied in many ways, by confusing the spectators. Peripatetic conjurors make a good deal of money by means of this trick, by betting that the ring is either on or off the wand. Manner has a great deal to do with the success of it.

CHAPTER IV.

TRICKS WITH CUPS AND BALLS.

THE variety of tricks performed with the aid of cups and balls take a prominent position in the repertory of every conjuror laying claim to any proficiency in pure sleight of hand. Three tin cups (or, rather, as they are always used in an

FIG. 23.

inverted position, covers), rather more than 4in. in height, and some 3in. across the mouth, with the bottom concave, and two or three little rings near the mouth (Fig. 23) will be required. Also make, to commence with, four cork balls, blackened, either by burning or by colouration, each about the size of an ordinary bullet. The audience know of the existence of three balls only, the fourth being concealed by the conjuror between the roots of the third and middle fingers. The very first thing the learner must acquire is the knack of slipping the ball rapidly from the exposed (Fig. 24) to the concealed position (Fig. 25) in a secure manner. The ball is partly slid, partly rolled, partly dropped into the position, the thumb, with a slight motion, which, in time, will become quite an unconscious one, pressing it finally home.

The action, which must be accompanied by the backward and forward swing used when palming coins, must be practised with both hands, the more awkward hand of the two being taught first. When tolerably perfect in this, practise

FIG. 24.   FIG. 25.

getting the ball down to the tips of the fingers at the roots of which it is held, care being of course taken that no portion of it protrudes. The object of getting the ball into this position is, that it may be placed under any cup, raised ostensibly for some other purpose, without detection. As the cup is placed on the table, the ball held in the fingers is slid quietly under it. All conjurors do not use this method, some grasping the cup as low down as possible, and jerking it up and down, thus getting the ball inside direct from the concealed position (Fig. 25). This latter method is exceedingly neat, but is the more difficult one to accomplish. However, the learner may try for himself, and adopt the method which comes the easier to him. The ball is not taken in the tips of the fingers until the hand is about to grasp the cup, the major motion shielding the minor one. With the two movements described under his control, the learner should proceed thus : Place the three cups in a row, with a ball in front (*i.e.*, towards the audience) of each, and explain that the cups are solid tin and are not provided with permeable bottoms. There is no objection to allowing an examination to be made, but it had better take place at the end of the trick, or much time will be wasted. Say that the tin cups are for the purpose of covering the balls, and place one cup over each to illustrate it. Now take up cup No. 1, and, whilst placing it down a few inches off, slip the concealed ball under it. Pick up ball No. 1, and vanish it by concealing it in the prescribed method (Fig. 25). You can pretend to throw it into the air, or affect to put it into the other hand (see Coins, Fig. 7), from which it will be "passed" by a rap from the wand, which article you will find a true friend when performing with the cups and balls, and which should be held in readiness under the arm. Repeat the operation with cups No. 2 and No. 3, each having a ball placed under it when shifted. Tell the audience that so well trained are the little balls, that, at your word of command, they will return from their invisible wanderings to their imprisonment beneath the cups, which you will then raise, and show the balls beneath. This is the first and simple phase.

In the next, cup No. 1 is placed over a ball, and the concealed one slipped in with it. Take up another ball, and pretend to "pass" it through the cup, which raise, showing two balls together, and then replace, slipping concealed ball under along with the other two; and then "pass" the third ball through, which will bring all three balls under one cup. On putting cup No. 1 down, after exhibiting the three balls together, slip concealed ball under it, and pick up one of the three, which vanish. Then say it is as easy for you to abstract a ball from beneath a cup as it is for you to pass it to the inside. Put cup No. 2 over the two balls, and

pretend to take one out by means of the wand, the concealed ball being exhibited as the one thus abstracted.
" Pass " this through cup No. 1, which raise, showing the
ball already there, and, on replacing it, slip under concealed
ball. Recall the ball you vanished previously, and show it
under cup No. 1, and then "pass" it back to cup No. 2, where
the two balls still are ; slip concealed ball under, and then
"pass " ball from cup No. 1 to cup No. 2. The ball "passed "
must in each instance be picked up and vanished, and not
merely told to pass from one cup to another. The changes
can be kept up for a long time if a ball be slipped under
a cup whenever it is raised; but the performer must keep
his head clear, or he will find himself getting into trouble by
showing four balls at the same time.

Phase 3 consists of piling the three cups one over the
other, and passing the balls into what I may term the storeys
thus formed. It is for this phase that the bottoms of the
cups are made concave to receive the ball. If the bottom
were flat, the ball would roll off at an awkward moment,
Place cup No. 1, with concealed ball underneath, on the table,
and, taking up a ball, " pass " it through. Put cup No. 2 over
cup No. 1, concealed ball being sandwiched between the bottoms
of the two. The slipping of a ball beneath a cup which is
placed on the table is a very simple matter, but it requires
considerable adroitness to slip one cleanly between two cups.
It is only to be done with a sharp jerk, the ball being thus
sent to the top of the cup, which is then rapidly placed over
the other. Considerable practice will be required to attain
this knack, but the pretty effect well repays any trouble.
Even when taking the greatest care, the ball is very liable
to become jammed between the sides of the cups instead of
their bottoms. The noise made by the rattling of the ball
in the cup is covered by that occasioned by one cup being
placed over the other. Repeat the operation with the third
cup, and then show the balls in their respective positions.
Should a cup cant over to one side, it will be because the

ball beneath it is not in its place, but is jammed in between the two sides of the cups. In this case, care must be taken in removing the uppermost cup. If adroitly managed, the errant ball can be brought back to its proper position on the top of the lower cup by the action of withdrawing the upper one. This should be practised in private, so that the emergency may be met without difficulty when it occurs.

The fourth phase consists in apparently manufacturing an inexhaustible quantity of balls beneath the cups. This is very easily managed by first covering each of the three balls with a cup openly. Take up cup No. 1, and put it down again a few inches off, with the concealed ball under it. Pick up ball No. 1, and pretend to put it in your pocket, but conceal it in the fingers; take up cup No. 2, and replace it, with concealed ball beneath it, and affect to put ball No. 2 into the pocket, but conceal as before. Repeat operation with cup and ball No. 3, and then recommence with cup No. 1. This phase can be prolonged at will. A number of balls can be carried in the pocket, and afterwards exhibited as the ones you have manufactured; but this is by no means necessary to the success of the trick.

A most startling and amusing conclusion to a display with the cups and balls is the introduction of large balls, potatoes, oranges, lemons, apples, &c., beneath the cups. Care must be taken that these larger articles will go into the cups easily, or a *fiasco* may result. The best balls are those made of fancy paper, as they are nice and light. A convenient place for keeping them ready for use is a shallow, oblong, open bag, made out of black silk or alpaca, and furnished with a bent pin at each end, and one in the middle. This bag you can affix to the tablecloth behind the table. In the absence of such a receptacle, the tablecloth can be pinned up, and so form an impromptu one; but this can hardly be arranged unperceived in front of an audience. In the absence of both cloth and bag, the articles to be conveyed inside the cups must be kept under the waistcoat, or in the pockets, but, in this case, the pockets must be side ones, and easily got at. The moment for introducing the large ball, orange, &c., into a cup is when the eyes of the audience are attracted towards any object just revealed to them. The orange, &c., must be taken by the left hand from its place of concealment whilst the right is engaged with the cup; and the instant the latter is raised, for the purpose of showing whatever may be under, it must be passed briskly—at the same time, in a manner not too marked—to the left hand, and the article slipped inside. The hands must remain together only sufficiently long to permit the completion of the manœuvre, when the cup must be again held by the right hand only; the article inside being prevented from falling by having the little finger placed beneath it. Sometimes, I press the paper balls lightly into the cup, and am so enabled to hold the cup by the top, and to raise it from the table, to show that there is nothing under it. By bringing the cup down hard on the table, the ball will become disengaged. This method should only be used as a change. Supposing that you have an orange inside cup No. 1, place it gently and unconcernedly on the table whilst drawing attention, by means of your tongue, to cup No. 2. By the time cup No. 2 is raised, the left hand will contain, say, an apple, which will go inside the cup, and public attention drawn to cup No. 3, which, in its turn, will be raised, and tenanted with a potato. You can now either knock over all three cups, and reveal their contents, which has a very good effect, or continue the manufactory as with the cork balls, pretending to put the potatoes, oranges, &c., into the pocket. It will be only necessary to have one of each kind of article, although the audience will be led to believe that your pockets are crammed with them by the time you have finished. It is best to have four kinds, as by that means each cup has something different under it every time it is raised. It is not advisable, however, to fill the cups more than twice by this method. The performer must not have his head filled with the idea that his movements are noticed, for the eyes of the spectators are sure to be riveted on the article last revealed. Any hesitation will be attended with disastrous results, so the thing must be done with dash, or not at all. Every conjuror should endeavour to become perfect with the cups and balls, as they not only amuse and astonish audiences, but afford great practice to the learner.

One very important thing in connection with this trick is the talk with which it is accompanied. The performer should be talking the whole time, explaining everything as he goes on; at the same time, he must not talk a lot of nonsense, which will only cause the audience to form a low estimate of his prestidigitatorial powers, but infuse his harangue with a little very mild humour. Something like the following, varied to suit the circumstances, will be to the point: "I have here three little tin cups, solid, and free from any trickery or deception, as you may see for yourselves." (Hand cups round.) "Kindly see that the bottoms do not take out. I have also three little cork balls, equally guileless with the cups. Madam, will you be so good as to squeeze one, and see that it is solid?" (Give a ball to a lady.) "Thank you. These little balls, ladies and gentlemen, are, you will be interested to hear, trained to a high degree of perfection, and are perfectly obedient to my will, as I will shortly show you. This cup, which you will perceive is perfectly empty, I place here on the table, and, taking up one of the balls, I simply say to it, 'Hey, presto! begone!' and it has vanished. The second little ball I take from beneath this cup, and command it to keep company with its predecessor. 'Fly!' and it has gone. The remaining ball I treat in the same manner. By the aid of my magic wand, I recall my little servants. See, here comes one, and, following my wand, it passes through into this cup" (tap a cup with the wand), &c., &c. It will be as well for the conjuror to study what he intends saying beforehand, in the early stages of his career, for he will find his wits sufficiently troubled to execute his tricks properly without requiring to think about his language.

A little sleight, which may be introduced with effect, is the apparent throwing of one cup through the other. This illusion is effected by holding a cup, mouth upwards, lightly between the thumb and forefinger. The other hand then throws a second cup sharply into it. The lower cup is allowed to fall, and the second cup caught by the thumb and forefinger, the appearance being that one cup has passed completely through the other.

CHAPTER V.

TRICKS WITH HANDKERCHIEFS.

BURNING A HANDKERCHIEF IN A SMALL WAY—HINTS ABOUT APPARATUS—HOW TO PULL A HANDKERCHIEF THROUGH THE LEG—THE KNOT UNTIED BY MAGIC—THE CONFECTIONER HANDKERCHIEF—FEATS WITH HANDKERCHIEFS.

WHAT conjurors would do without pocket handkerchiefs, I will not venture to suggest. Almost every trick has a handkerchief of some kind as a component part. Handkerchiefs are torn up, burnt up, tied into knots, made receptacles for money, and used in a variety of other ways; in fact, they are the conjuror's most faithful allies.

Burning a Handkerchief is usually made a stage trick, and belongs properly to Grand Magic; but there is a method which may be successfully tried in the confined limits of the drawing-room. I do not allude to the use of the "burning globe," which article entirely dispenses with the necessity for the display of anything approaching sleight of hand, with which I, in this book, have only to deal. By using mechanical tricks, many feats of sleight of hand are imitated; but then the apparatus cannot be shown round, and the audience goes away from the performance impressed with the idea that conjuring means exhibiting a certain number of cunningly-devised boxes, canisters, &c. I remember being present at an amateur conjuring entertainment, where tricks were exhibited that must have cost two hundred pounds, at least. The eye was perfectly bewildered with the array of electric clocks, drums, &c.; but every third trick failed at some point, which was not to be wondered at, seeing that the thing was got through as though against time. This sort of thing is not conjuring; although it would be bad for conjuring - trick manufacturers if everyone thought the same. Some apparatus one *must* have; but only what is absolutely necessary. The difference between an apparatus conjuror and an adept at sleight of hand is as great as that between an organ-grinder and a skilled musician.

To burn a handkerchief in what I may term a small way, be provided with a piece of cambric, or other material resembling a handkerchief, about four inches square. The best way is to cut up a cheap handkerchief that has been hemmed. Have this piece rolled up in the hand, and concealed by the act of holding the wand. Borrow a handkerchief, which carelessly roll up in the hands, as if judging as to its size, and get the piece mingled in its folds. Ask the owner if he or she has any objection to your burning the end of it. Say "Thank you," whether the answer be "Yes" or "No" (conjurors are often afflicted with a convenient hardness of hearing), and proceed at once to burn what is, in reality, your interpolated piece, but which will appear to the audience to be the handkerchief, at a candle. When you have burnt a tolerably large hole, put out the flame, and walk towards the owner of the handkerchief, as if about to return it to him, thanking him, at the same time, for the loan of it. If you had not permission to burn the handkerchief, the owner of it will probably now tell you so; and if he is at all testy on the point, so much the better for the success of your trick. Say that you really thought he said "Yes," are sorry for the mistake, which, however, cannot now be helped, &c. If, on the other hand, you had permission to do as you pleased, which a flattering, implicit faith in your abilities will frequently accord to you, you must affect to see in the person's looks an objection to take the handkerchief in a burnt state, and so, in either case, eventually set yourself the task of having to restore the injured article. This you can very simply do by rubbing it in your hands, and concealing the fictitious piece rolled up in the palm; or you can prolong the operation by folding the handkerchief in a piece of paper, omitting the burnt piece, and then pronouncing some cabalistic words over it, whilst it is held by someone in the audience. This is, perhaps, the better way of the two. If the beginner is afraid to trust to his own skill, and prefers using apparatus, he can procure many kinds of canisters, &c., for changing handkerchiefs, the working of which will be explained by the vendor, so there is no necessity to do so here.

To Pull a Handkerchief through the Leg.—This is a trick which will bear exhibition in any company. It recommends itself especially for drawing-room purposes. Take a very long handkerchief, and, seating yourself, pass the handkerchief (apparently) twice round the leg, just above the knee, and tie the two ends securely together, or have them tied for you. Take hold of a single thickness of the handkerchief, and jerk it sharply upwards, when it will appear to pass through the leg. The secret of the trick is thus explained: When you pass the ends below the leg, for the purpose of ostensibly crossing them, so as to bring them up on opposite sides, you rapidly make a bend in one, and pass the other firmly round it. By this means, a temporary junction is formed strong enough to bear a slight strain. By distending the sinews of the leg, the folds are compressed, and additional security is thus obtained. The ends are of course brought up again on the sides on which they descended, and the knot tied above the thigh—not beneath it. The formation of the bend and loop round it must be practised assiduously, for I do not know of any trick of the same magnitude requiring more skill in execution than this one. The hands should not remain an instant longer under the leg than one would require to merely cross the ends, and there must be no fidgeting observable. For performing this trick, Döbler (the original one) received a diamond ring from the Emperor of Russia.

To Untie a Knot by Word of Command.—Tie a knot with two ends of a handkerchief, but in such a manner that one end is always quite straight; in fact, one end should be tied *round* the other, and not the two ends tied together. If you take the extreme end of the straight portion, anyone may pull as hard as he likes at it from the other side of the knot without making it any tighter, although you must lead him to believe that he is doing so. When he has pulled to his heart's content, take the knot in one hand and cover it with the rest of the handkerchief. Whilst doing so, work, with the concealed hand, the straight end through the folds of the other, but do not destroy the folds, which give to be held, of course under cover of the handkerchief. Command the knot to come undone, and then shake the handkerchief out. This is the groundwork of a trick on a much larger scale, which will be treated of in Grand Magic. It is a very effective little trick, and should never be despised.

To Find Sweetmeats in a Handkerchief.—For this pretty trick the performer will require a conical bag, made of fine calico, cambric, or any other substance resembling a handkerchief. The length of the bag should be about 5in.; and it must be furnished at the apex with a bent pin—a black one. The mouth must be fitted with two pieces of flat watch or crinoline spring, sewn in the stuff in such a manner as to keep the opening closed. This bag must be filled with sweets, and suspended, by means of the bent pin, on the edge of the table—out of view of the audience, as a matter of course. Borrow a handkerchief, and say that you will now find something that will please the juvenile portion of the audience. Wave the handkerchief mysteriously about, and then spread it out upon the table. Wave your hands over it, take it up delicately by the centre with one hand,

and squeeze it with the other over a plate with which you will be provided. Naturally, nothing will come of it, so you repeat the operation, this time at a different part of the table. At the third or fourth attempt, the handkerchief should hang over that portion of the table where the bag is suspended, and when it is raised the bent pin should be included in the grasp. On squeezing the handkerchief this time, the hand should compress the ends of the springs, which will open, and allow the sweets to escape and fall upon the plate with a great clatter. Do not empty the bag at once, but give it two or three squeezes, allowing a little to fall out each time, which will greatly heighten the effect. When the bag is empty, the next thing to do is to remove it from the handkerchief. If a chair is handy, the bag can be dropped on it; but the best way is to boldly introduce the hand beneath the handkerchief, and, whilst calling attention to the sweets, hang it again on the edge of the table, which can easily be managed behind the handkerchief. The sweets used should be small round or oval ones, they being best suited for the purpose.

There are many little feats performed with handkerchiefs hardly deserving the title of tricks, in the way of tying bows and knots, &c., by entirely unorthodox methods. They are too insignificant for performance alone; but they look very well when worked in with more important tricks. Besides (and it cannot be too often stated), conjurors should endeavour to know *everything* connected with sleight of hand. In drawing-room circles, one is continually asked if one can do this, that, or the other; and it is quite as well to be able to reply in the affirmative, for it always tells detrimentally to fail in a little matter. The following feats will be found effective:

To Lengthen a Handkerchief —Having borrowed a handkerchief, great amusement is caused when the performer observes that the article is not long enough, and expresses his intention of stretching it. This is done by taking the handkerchief by one corner in each hand, and, whilst twisting it up, gathering an inch or two in each palm. Stretch the arms wide apart, so that the handkerchief lies across the chest, without allowing any of the gathered-up portions of it to escape. Now give the handkerchief a turn or two in the air, and again stretch it across the chest, this time allowing about half an inch to escape out of the hands. Twist again and stretch, allowing a little more to escape, and repeat the operation until the extreme ends are reached. Imply by manner, as much as possible, that a deal of stretching is taking place, and the audience will be led to believe that the handkerchief has been extended at least six inches beyond its original length.

To Appear to Tie a Knot that will not Draw Tight.—This feat is also exceedingly diverting. The performer, apparently, goes through all the necessary formulæ for forming a knot; but, lo! when the ends are pulled out, no knot is seen. There are three ways of doing this. One is to pass one end behind the other, instead of through the loop, as usual, which must apparently be done. To do this neatly, one end must be held in each hand, the handkerchief twisted sharply up, and the hands then brought quickly together, which will cause a coil of about two turns to be formed. Pass the right end quickly round the back of the left, and then draw out both, as if tightening the knot. As you pull, the coil will bunch in the middle, as if a knot were really there, and increased tension will pull it out quite straight. The second method is thus performed: Lay one end of the handkerchief across the right hand, the major portion of it being on the outside, and the short end held down by the little finger only. With the left hand, take the hanging end, and, bringing it round on the inside, lay it over the other. Pass the left hand through the loop thus formed, take with it the uppermost end, and draw it through; but, just as you pull the two ends out straight, slip the thumb of the right hand under the inside bend of the lower end, and hold it between the finger and thumb. In the third method, commence by taking one end of the handkerchief in either hand. Pass the right hand over to the left side, in front of the left arm, which is kept perfectly still in front of the body, so that the handkerchief hangs on the left forearm in the shape of a loop. The second end must now be placed in the left hand, which thus detains both for the time being. Pass the right hand, now free, through the loop from the inside, and, reaching up with it, let it grasp its original end just placed in the left hand, and pull it through. This must be done with great deliberation, as the beauty of the sleight rests in the extreme slowness with which it can be executed, the secret lying, not in any quickness of fingers, but in the fact that the handkerchief ends are never looped one over the other, as would be the case if the right hand were passed through the loop from the outside, which the learner may at once discover by experiment. In pulling the end out, as though tying the knot, if it be retarded by the left thumb, a more natural appearance is given. This method is to be preferred to the foregoing, which, however, are useful as changes.

To Tie a Knot Instantaneously.—Take an end of the handkerchief in either hand between the thumb and forefinger, the end in the left hand pointing inwards, and that in the right hand outwards, the hands being held so that their backs are towards the company, the thumbs on top and the little fingers below. Open the fingers of each hand at the first and middle fingers, and then bring the hands together until they overlap a couple of inches, the right hand on the outside. This will bring the end of the handkerchief in either hand between the opened fingers of the opposite one. The fingers close on the ends, and the hands are at once separated, when the knot will be found to be tied. This may be first practised with a piece of stout string, and the learner must not be satisfied until he can tie the knot by merely bringing the fingers together for an instant, the knot being tied apparently by means of the mere collision of the two hands. It is astonishing what perfection can be attained by means of practice, the knot at last seeming to appear on the handkerchief, instead of being tied.

To Tie a Knot on the Wrist whilst Holding an End of the Handkerchief in either Hand.—Jerk the right hand towards the left one, so as to throw a loop in the handkerchief, through which dart the left hand, still holding its end, and the feat will be accomplished. It should be done in a *nonchalant* manner, and without any ostentation. Practise first with a piece of string.

The performance of the foregoing feats will be facilitated by the use of a silk handkerchief that is not too new, and it should always be first twisted, rope-fashion.

CHAPTER VI.

CHINESE TRICKS.

A NEW MARBLE TRICK—FIRE-EATING—FINAL EFFECT—THE
BUTTERFLY TRICK—THE FAN—HOW TO MAKE THE BUTTER-
FLIES—HOW TO KEEP THEM IN THE AIR.

Chinese Marble Trick.—Some years ago, there came over to
England a few Chinese conjurors, who were seen by the
public but very little, but who favoured me on several
occasions with private views. Their skill lay chiefly in the
performance of such delectable feats as swallowing sword-
blades, tiny china cups, glass balls, and large leaden
plummets. Although appreciating such tricks, I respectfully
declined attempting to astonish my audiences by their means.
There was, however, one little trick performed with four
small marbles, which struck me as being something quite
novel and quaint. Of the four marbles (little ivory balls are
what I invariably use), one is concealed in the fingers, as in
the cup and ball trick, unknown, of course, to the audience,
who are supposed to know of the existence of three only.
These three the performer puts into his mouth—one at a
time, slowly, is the best way—to show that there is "no
deception." He now forms his left hand into a fist, and
holds it steadily in front of him, thumb upwards, as though
holding a sword at rest. With the right hand he pretends
to take a marble from the mouth, the concealed one being

exhibited. The action of taking a marble from the mouth must be imitated exactly; and this is best done by rolling it along the lips until it travels from the roots of the fingers to their tips. The sleight must be quickly done, for the eyes of the audience are full upon the hand. Place the marble on the top of the left hand, *i.e.*, on the doubled-up first finger, which, after a few seconds, open slightly, so as to allow the marble to disappear in the hand. With the right hand actually take a marble from the mouth, which will now contain two. Pretend to place this marble on the left hand, as you did the first one, but in reality conceal it. When the left hand is momentarily covered with the right, as it feigns to place a marble upon it, open the first finger, and, with the least possible jerk, bring the first marble again to the top. The audience will think that marble No. 1 is in the hand and marble No. 2 atop. After another short pause, allow the marble to again sink in the hand, thereby causing the idea that two marbles are concealed in it, and, with the right hand, affect to take another marble from the mouth, the concealed one being, of course, shown. Ostensibly, place this one on the left hand (deception as before), and allow it to disappear like its two supposed predecessors. At this stage, the state of affairs will be thus:—The right hand, presumably empty, contains one marble; the left hand contains presumably three, but in reality only one marble; the mouth, presumably empty, contains two marbles. The performer then proceeds as follows : Allow the marble in the left hand to sink until it is in the position for concealing at the roots of the fingers. If with the tips of the second or third fingers it can be pressed firmly home, so much the better, for the command to vanish can at once be given, and the hand opened—palm downwards, of course If the marble cannot be secured in this way, the thumb must be brought into use in the usual way; but the hand must be waved about a little so as to cover the movement. The three marbles are now supposed to be *non est*. The performer can proceed to find the first of them in whatever manner he pleases. He may pretend to pick it from the table cloth, break it from the end of his wand, or find it in the possession of one of the audience; how, is quite immaterial. As each hand conceals a marble, it is also immaterial which one is used. This first marble is placed on the table, and another one found. This second one, instead of placing on the table, the performer affects to pass into his ear, concealing it as before, and after a few seconds, it appears at his lips, the one thence protruding being, of course, one of the two concealed in the mouth. Allow it to fall from the mouth, and then proceed to find the third marble, which pass, say, through the top of the head. The remaining marble in the mouth is then exhibited, and the three wanderers are recovered. If the marbles or ivory balls are not small, their presence in the mouth, when they are not supposed to be there, will be discovered. I always conceal one on each side of the mouth, between the lower gums and the cheek. Ivory balls are in every way preferable, as they do not strike cold to the teeth, and do not rattle much, both of which disagreeable properties are possessed by marbles. Any ivory-turner will supply the little balls very cheaply. The performer must study to execute this trick with the greatest possible delicacy, or—especially before ladies — it will become repulsive. The method of finding the balls after vanishing them should be varied, each one being found in a different way. The portion of the trick requiring the most practice is that in which the left hand is opened. The knack of concealing the ball held in it unobserved requires some little address.

Fire-eating.—This was another trick performed remarkably well by my Chinese. It is, I should think, one of the best-known in England, for every country fair has its fire-eater; but it is not everyone who knows how it is performed. In the first place, prepare some thick, soft string, by either boiling or soaking it in a solution of nitre (saltpetre). Take a piece, from 1in. to 2in. in length, and, after lighting it, wrap it in a piece of tow as large as an ordinary walnut. Conceal this piece under a heap of loose tow, the whole of which is put on a plate, and so exhibited to the audience. The string will burn very slowly indeed, and the very little smoke issuing from it will be quite smothered by the tow. Show the mouth empty, and then put a little tow into it. Commence chewing this, and, after a little time, put in some more. Repeat this three or four times, taking the chewed portion secretly away each time you put any fresh tow into the mouth, and in one of the bunches include the piece containing the burning string. Do not chew this about at all, in reality, although you will make great gestures as if so doing. Take a fan, and fan the ears, and presently take in a good breath at the nostrils, blowing it out at the mouth. This will cause some smoke to be ejected, the volume of which will increase as the breathings are kept up. Always be careful to draw in at the nostrils, and eject at the mouth; otherwise you will be choked. Renew the fannings (merely for effect), and, by continued breathings, the tow in the mouth will be brought into a glow, and one or two sparks will issue from the mouth. When this has continued sufficiently long, take in more tow, and so smother the burning string again, extracting the piece containing it under cover of a loose bunch. There need be no fear of burning the mouth, as, directly it is closed, the light becomes a mere spark. The trick causes great effect, not to say alarm on many occasions.

A very pretty and laughable termination to the above trick is to pass, unperceived, into the mouth (under cover of a piece of tow, as usual) a little ball composed of a long band of coloured paper, about half an inch or so wide. Take this by the end, and draw it out through the teeth. Tightly rolled up, a ball may contain several yards of paper. It should be composed of three or four different colours, in lengths, each pasted to the other, for there must be no break. The end should have a piece of cotton attached to it, or it will be next to impossible to find it in the mouth. The cotton will adhere to some portion of the mouth, and so be easily found. These balls of paper are supplied at all conjuring shops, as is also an article known as the Barber's Pole. This consists of a spiral of paper, which shuts up into a very small compass, but assumes a great length on being merely twisted. A long pole appears to come out of the performer's mouth.

The Butterfly Trick.—Invisible at a short distance, very fine silk and hair are invaluable adjuncts to the conjurer's repertory, both in the drawing-room and on the stage. The celebrated and fascinating Japanese butterfly trick is performed with the aid of a piece of fine black silk or horsehair. The former is, in my opinion, immeasurably the superior of the two. Hair is most difficult to manipulate, from its springy nature, and requires a great deal of coaxing before it will condescend to be tied in a knot. In the butterfly trick, the performer sustains one or more butterflies, made from rice (or tissue) paper, in the air, by means of the current caused by the motions of a fan. When this trick was first brought out, "all the world wondered," for no one, even after long practice, could keep the paper butterfly hovering in a given space for a single moment. I tremble to think of the number of fans I destroyed in my early days over this trick, before I knew the secret of it. The fan used should be a very strong and large one, of the old shape—not the circular—and be composed of paper and wood only, so as to be free from superfluous weight. Affixed to the top waistcoat button, or any other convenient spot, have from 3ft. to 4ft. of the finest black silk floss or hair, with a knot at the free end. Have, also, a piece of crisp tissue (or rice) paper, and a pair of scissors. Let the audience examine the paper, and then proceed to cut out the rough form of a butterfly, explaining your action as you go on, giving the centre a twist or two, for the double purpose of forming a body to the insect, and concealing the knotted end of the silk or hair, which it is as well to have between the fingers before commencing operations, as it is not allowable to grope about for it in view of the audience. When finished, the butterfly's wings should have the appearance of being three parts extended, and should be slightly concave from beneath. A little care bestowed on its formation will be repaid by an increased steadiness when in the air. When all is ready, hold the butterfly in the air at the full stretch of the connecting medium, and fan pretty briskly with the other hand, not immediately underneath the paper, but from the body, and along the silk or hair, which must always be kept at a stretch, or nearly so, or control over the butterfly will be lost.

Notwithstanding the aid of a connecting medium, there is more skill required to perform this trick really neatly than is generally supposed. After a time, practice will enable the performer to cause the butterfly to settle on a flower or on the edge of another fan, and also to sustain two in the air at one time, which has a very pretty effect indeed. When two butterflies are used, it will be found almost necessary to have two fans, one in each hand, and each insect must, of course, have a separate thread. Some use wax at the end of the connecting medium, but this is a bad plan, as it deters the performer from giving round the butterfly to be examined after performing the trick. Whilst cutting out and twisting up the paper, it is as well to call attention to the fact that the trick is performed by some people with the aid of a thread—an assistance which you will say you utterly despise, as will be perceived. This will totally disarm those people who may have bought the trick (it is sold universally), and are yet only tyros at performing it.

There is a second method, in which two butterflies are joined by a thread or hair a few inches long. These do not require to be attached to the performer's person, the partnership being sufficient to enable him to keep them in mid-air.

Speaking of the Chinese, it is a most noticeable thing that their methods of vanishing and concealing articles are the same as those practised by ourselves, which fully demonstrates the fact that there is only one proper way ; for there is only one thing more highly improbable than that we learnt the *minutiæ* of the art of conjuring, practised by us for centuries, from the Chinese, and that is that the Chinese learnt from us. It is only during the present century that we have been sufficiently familiar with the Chinese to borrow their ideas on magic, did we wish to do so.

CHAPTER VII.

TRICKS AT TABLE.

To Vanish a Glass of Sherry. — When invited out to a dinner party, one usually leaves one's conjuring tricks at home; but in some instances, where, perhaps, one's fame has gone before, an unexpected call is made for an exhibition of skill. " Come, So-and-so, let us see some tricks," says the host, and "Hear, hear!" say the guests. You are, of course, quite unprepared, and beg to be excused, but in vain. You must acquiesce, or be voted a boor. In an absent manner, you place a glass of sherry to your lips, as though bracing yourself for the fray. The glass is half emptied (be careful about this), when a sudden movement is made as though you threw it up at the ceiling; but nothing is seen to ascend, though the glass, with the wine in it, has disappeared. After a short pause, to allow the general astonishment to take full effect, the missing article is discovered

inside the coat of your immediate neighbour, with the wine
in it unspilt. This startling effect is thus managed : Open
the legs just a few inches, and in the disengaged hand hold
a napkin or handkerchief. When the feigned movement of
throwing the glass upwards is made, the article itself is left
between the legs, and immmediately covered with the napkin.
It is, however, of the highest importance that the hand does
not dwell an instant in leaving the glass behind, otherwise
the movement will be discovered. The action must be swift,
clean, and noiseless. To find the glass on the person of
your neighbour, take it up, with the napkin with which you
have covered it, with one hand, and, bringing yourself quite
close to the party to be operated upon, whip it inside his
coat with the other. Produce it very slowly from its
supposed place of concealment, for extra effect. The success
of the trick is greatly enhanced by its total unexpectedness,
and the performer must take care not to reveal, by any
word or gesture, what he is about to do. He should, however, immediately preceding the vanish, draw attention to
himself by addressing the host, or otherwise engaging the
conversation, lest he perform the trick and afterwards discover that no one saw it, for it is a trick that will not bear
repetition. A tea· or coffee cup, small size, can be treated
after the same manner.

To Vanish a Plate. — This is considerably more ambitious
than the preceding, and requires some confidence in one's
powers. There are two methods, each differing only slightly
from the other. In the one, the plate, which should be
small, is taken in the hand, and apparently thrown up to
the ceiling, but, instead, adroitly grasped by one leg, purposely extended, behind the knee, between the calf and the
thigh. In the other method, the performer rises slightly
from his seat, as if to make an extra vigorous throw, and
the plate is slipped beneath him. Both methods are good;
but it is essential to the success of either that the performer sits on the extreme outside of everyone else. Under

any other circumstances, the requisite freedom of action cannot be obtained. So soon as the plate has disappeared, the conjuror should seize a napkin, wave it about, and find the plate in it. It must be distinctly understood that the leg which is to hold the plate during its concealment must be first brought round to the side of the chair on which the performer is sitting, and there doubled up slightly, so that there is just room to pass the plate between the calf and the thigh, which will then hold it tight. The learner must not expect to execute this vanish at the first attempt, but will require to practise considerably before arriving at anything like perfection of execution.

A primitive method for vanishing a plate is to place the left hand slightly behind the body, and with it receive the plate from the right hand. In this method, which can only be used when the performer is standing, the plate must immediately be found in someone's coat. Books, straw mats, knives, and other large articles can be made to disappear by any of the foregoing methods.

To Pass a Fork or Spoon through a Tumbler.—The foregoing successfully performed, take up a tumbler carelessly, and remark to the host that you notice that he has some of the "patent filter tumblers." Ignorance of the fact will, of course, be expressed, and you then proceed to show that the tumbler you hold has a hole through the bottom, by apparently passing the handle of a spoon or fork, or any other suitable article, through it. This diverting optical illusion is thus performed : Take the tumbler (empty) in the left hand, near the bottom, not in the ordinary way, as if about to drink from it, but in such a manner that it lies along the hand, the mouth towards the wrist. Take the article to be passed through the tumbler in the right hand, and, after thrusting it once or twice against the bottom, pass it between the hand and the outside of the glass, allowing two or three inches to protrude beyond the ends of the fingers. This simple action causes it to appear that the spoon handle, skewer, &c., has been passed through the bottom of the tumbler.

Permeable Plates.—Following up the idea of the patent filter tumblers, you can mention that you notice that the host has also the last new plate. Hold up a plate to the light and say, "Yes, I can distinctly see through it." Laughter will, of course, ensue, and you will offer to prove your assertion. To do this, make up three bread-paste balls about the size of those used in the cup and ball trick, of which this one is, indeed, only a variety. You will have an extra one concealed in the fingers, of course. Now take two plates, one in each hand, upside down, and held in such a manner that the ball in the fingers is concealed. Place them on the table, about a foot apart, and, by opening the fingers, allow the concealed ball to remain under one plate. Vanish a ball as in the cups and balls, and find it under the plate, repeating the process with all three balls, the one concealed being dropped each time the plate is replaced after raising it to show the one just passed through it. Now say that it is as easy to perform the feat with another plate, and take up the second one in the hand containing the concealed ball. Supposing this to be, as it generally will be, the right hand, it will now be taking up the plate on your left. Cross the arms, and, with the left hand, take hold of the plate on your right hand, allowing the fingers to extend well beneath it. Call attention to the fact that under the left-hand plate there is nothing, whilst under the right-hand one there are three balls; and then place the left-hand plate upon the table, with concealed ball under it. Then command one ball from the right-hand plate to pass under the left-hand one. With the fingers seize one ball of the three, and raise both plates. Now bring back the arms to their original positions, in order that the left hand, which contains one ball concealed, .may be brought to the single ball, which is supposed to have been transferred from the right-hand side. Replace both plates, allowing concealed ball to fall from the left hand, and take up another, in the fingers of the right hand. Command a ball to pass, and raise plates as before. Re-cross the arms, and repeat the operation, when all three balls will have apparently passed from one side to the other. Without crossing the hands this would not be possible, and the reason you give for so doing is to show that it does not matter which plate is used, both being equally permeable. The learner must bear in mind that in this, the second phase of the trick, the two plates are never relinquished simultaneously. The hand picking up a ball cannot quite quit all hold on the plate, or detection would ensue. The plate having a ball passed beneath it can be released for the time from the hand entirely. The ball remaining concealed at the end can be dropped in the lap under cover of the plate. It is always as well to have one's handkerchief lying carelessly in one's lap, as it comes in very useful for concealing small things. By taking some cork balls in his pocket, the conjuror will avoid the necessity for using balls made of bread.

Such occasions as the one I have now assumed are the ones favourable for the introduction of the previously mentioned tricks with sugar and knives; and, if the performer has taken my advice, he will be provided with his disc of glass for the performance of the glass of water trick, also previously described.

Changing Dice.—It is also useful, on such occasions, to have in the pocket a pair of dice, rather smaller than those in general use, for the performance of the following trick. Place the dice, side by side, between the finger and thumb. This will leave two sides, back and front, open to view. Ask the spectators to note the numbers at the front, and then those at the back. Show each side two or three times, turning the hand over each time, and then give a slight twist with the finger and thumb, just sufficient to cause the dice to revolve the extent of one square only. This will bring different numbers to the back, whilst the front ones have apparently remained unaltered, as you will show, taking care to twist the dice back again to their original positions. The twist must be given as the hand is turned over, when it will be quite imperceptible to anyone. This is the first and simple phase of the trick; the second is more convincing still. It very frequently happens that someone says, "Ah! of course you turn them over." This you stoutly deny, and proceed at once to prove the fallacy of the idea that the dice move in your fingers. To do this, give the twist backward and forward each time the hand is turned over in what the spectators consider to be merely the preliminary to the actual trick. Then say, "Now, I will turn my hand over as slowly as possible, and ask some one to hold my fingers firmly so as to render it utterly impossible for me to move them." Of course, as the positions of the dice have been changed each time you turned your hand over, you have now only to keep them still to effect an alteration. This ruse invariably silences sceptics.

The trick is also capable of further development if the dice be properly arranged. By placing the two fives face to face, the numbers will read one-three, three-one, six-four, four-six. Hold the dice in the fingers so as to cover one three-one and one six-four. The visible numbers will then be six-four and three-one. Suppose the six-four is on the top, the twist of the fingers will expose the hidden six-four at the bottom, and the hidden three-one at the top. The two numbers will then appear to have completely changed places. The fact that, in one instance, the four and the one are where the six and the three were previously will not be noticed if the performer is careful to always call the numbers the same, viz., "Here we have six-four on the top and three-one at the bottom; six-four" (turn over), "three-one" (turn back), "change" (turn over), "three-one on the top, six-four on the bottom." A fresh combination can at once be obtained by placing any other numbers face to face, so that they be the same unit. This variation will be found very effective and dumbfounding.

To Cut a Person's Arm with a Knife, through the Coat, without Injuring the Cloth.—Turning to his next-door neighbour, who, I need scarcely say, must not be a lady, the performer seizes a knife and asks him whether he would like to have his arm cut. A bloodthirsty slash in the air will add emphasis to the question. The person questioned will invariably decline, with thanks, and the performer then affects to think that the reason for the negative is an objection to having the coat cut, and not on the score of any pain to be inflicted. He assures his neighbour, with great emphasis and earnestness, that any injury necessarily done to the cloth will be immediately remedied, and that no traces of a cut will remain. When it is begun to be realised that the cloth is not to be cut, a joke is anticipated, and consent to the operation will soon be obtained, especially if the performer alters his manner, and becomes persuasive. It is necessary, in order to invest the trick with interest, to work up a state of apprehension to begin with, as it is but a small thing in execution, and requires filling out. When the necessary consent has been obtained, the performer places a napkin or handkerchief over the biceps of his neighbour, and, introducing the knife underneath, commences to saw away at the arm. Presently the patient will give a sudden start, and, if at all weak-minded, he will shout "Oh!" as well. On being questioned, he will explain that he distinctly felt the knife cut into his arm, which is, indeed, precisely the feeling communicated to him. The secret of the trick is simply a common pin, which, under cover of the napkin or handkerchief, the performer takes from his vest, or wherever it may be concealed, in the left hand. Both hands are introduced under the napkin, the right hand sawing away with the knife, with the blunt side against the coat. Great care must be taken to employ a new knife, as old ones frequently have their backs rather sharp, and the cloth might be cut in reality. Press pretty firmly with the knife, sufficiently to make the patient feel it, and then gradually push the pin through close beside it, pushing only when pressure is put upon the knife. In time it will work through the clothing—a quantity of which rather assists the illusion—and, entering the flesh slightly, will cause a sensation precisely as though the arm really were cut. The performer at once stops, and either sticks the pin into the napkin or in its former place of concealment, or else drops it on the floor. The trick may be repeated upon other patients; indeed, it is not easy to appreciate it unless it has been actually performed upon one. The pin need only be dropped when the performer notices looks of suspicion directed at his fingers. He has others concealed about him, naturally. Black pins should be used as being less likely to be seen, especially when dropped; although so common an object as a pin upon the floor, even if noticed, would scarcely excite suspicion. Still, it is always best to think of every contingency, and provide for it, or, haply, experience may teach the lesson in a harsh manner.

Corks are generally handy at a dinner table (at set dinners tricks would scarcely be introduced), and, being easily palmed, form excellent *media* for small conjuring. The cork should be held by the tips of the first and fourth fingers, lengthwise, and it then palms right across the hand, the sharp edges (do not choose a ragged edged cork) giving a splendid hold, especially as the article is so light. Corks are very easily swallowed, being either placed (apparently) in the mouth by the hand palming them, or else put into the other hand first. Houdin used to regale himself at friends' houses by a dessert of corks, brought on in a sauce-boat or soup tureen, especially chosen because it concealed the hand when thrust in. The performer continually took out corks, dropping the ones palmed as he did so, until he had apparently eaten a dozen. A good deal of natural chewing should be indulged in, and the changes continually rung upon the various palms and passes taught in this book. Finally, the performer says he can eat no more, as he is full up. As evidence of this, he extracts from his ear the last cork he ate, and, after (apparently) replacing this in the bowl, he is taken with a spasm, and another cork is taken out of his mouth, the supposition being that it had been unable to find room below. It is, of course, rolled into the partially opened lips from the palm. It is quite open to the performer to reproduce a number of corks from his person in this way, when the company will imagine that he really secreted those he pretended to swallow. This effect will be heightened if the performer has gone to the dinner with half-a-dozen corks in his pocket. As a *finale*, he says: "The rest are here in my pocket," and produces them all at once, throwing them carelessly into the bowl. If he has performed the rest of the trick properly, the company will think him quite capable of secreting half-a-dozen corks in his pocket without being observed, no one dreaming for a moment of any previous arrangement.

Swallowing a Knife.—Performed after the following method, this illusion can be carried out most effectively: Taking a large knife—a carving-knife is not too large—the performer lays it in front of him, right and left. He turns up his coat sleeves, as far as they will go, and then, squaring his elbows, so as to bring the forearms across his body, he places his hands along the knife, one hand overlapping the other, so as to completely hide the knife from view. In the case of a large knife, some parts of it—the ends—will be hidden by the wrists. Nipping it with the thumbs, or with one thumb only, it is raised from the table, the hands keeping their somewhat constrained position upon it. One hand is now brought to the mouth, the other being raised, and an apparent attempt made to swallow, the hands appearing to tilt the knife down the throat. The performer, however, suddenly begins to choke, and the attempt is relinquished, the knife being laid upon the table again. It is, however, immediately raised again, as before, but the second attempt is no more successful than the first. The knife is once more taken in the hands, and, in the act of picking it up, is brought just beyond the edge of the table, and allowed to fall into the lap. It must be barely raised from the table, or else the drop will be observed. The hands are, for the third time, brought to the mouth, as before, when, of course, the swallowing is successfully accomplished. The performer has taken the precaution to have a napkin lying loosely upon his lap, in which the knife at once becomes hidden. The illusion is a very complete one, especially if the performer takes care to make each of his three movements of the hands to the mouth precisely the same, the knife being brought beyond the edge of the table at each abortive attempt, and not at the last one only. If the performer pleases, he may refrain from turning up his coat sleeves, and, when the trick is finished, show them to be empty. Everyone will suppose that the knife has gone down the sleeve, and it, perhaps, provides an extra effect to show that it has not done so. As the position of the hands is somewhat unusual, the performer should be explaining, during the performance of the trick, that the true secret of knife-swallowing lies in the steadiness with which the knife is passed down the throat, this steadiness being better given with two hands than with one. As soon as the trick is safely accomplished, the performer should get his legs well under the table, and, taking the knife with one hand, place it under his knees, where it must be gripped, or else stick it in his boot. The hand is supposed to be placed below merely to procure the napkin, which is instantly produced, and the performer's lips carelessly wiped with it. He can then push his chair away from the table, and, leaning back, so as to expose his lap, join in the conversation, or, better still, at once commence a fresh trick. The thoughts of the company diverted, the knife may presently be brought to light from under someone's coat, or the performer may simply secrete it in his napkin, and place them together upon the table.

A smaller knife can be very effectively swallowed as follows : A cheese-knife is placed on the table, edge downwards, the left hand retaining it in that position by holding it near the point of the blade. It is then picked up by the right hand, the first and second fingers of which nip the back of the blade, close to the point, about half an inch of which is purposely left visible. The rest of the knife lies along the inside of the hand, the handle being concealed by the wrist. The handle is brought to the mouth, the knife being held upright, and the left hand, by means of gentle taps, thrusts it gradually downwards, until it wholly disappears down the throat. This illusion is managed within an inch or so of the end of a precisely similar knife to that supposed to be swallowed. This the performer has concealed between two fingers, and, when the knife is picked up, it is brought into position at the ends by means of the left hand, which is all the time busy helping the right one. The knife is, of course, at once dropped into the lap, the eyes of the company being fixed upon the little piece visible, which they naturally take to be the actual point of the knife. With the palm of the hand a few taps should be given the fragment, so as to cause it to slide out of sight, but still held between the fingers. The tapping is continued with the left hand, although it is performing upon nothing, the throat of the performer giving forth choking sounds, to assist the deception, until the knife may be fairly supposed to be swallowed. The fragment of knife is treated precisely as a coin held by the finger palm, and may be placed in the vest pocket, under the plea of getting out a toothpick. It should have its ragged edge nicely smoothed, so as not to cut the fingers.

CHAPTER VIII.

———

TRICKS WITH CARDS.

HAVING shown the beginner what can be done with the ordinary objects of everyday use, I will now endeavour to instruct him in the skilful manipulation of cards. By his success or failure in this particular branch of legerdemain will his reputation as a conjuror be made or marred. Card tricks, more than anything else, demand sleight of hand pure and simple, and success with them can only be attained by assiduous practice. To the learner some of the following directions will at first appear impossible of execution, owing to the unaccustomed positions in which the fingers have to be placed; but a little resolution will soon overcome all obstacles, and when once success, however trifling, has been achieved, greater results will speedily follow. In conjuring, as in most things, everything that is at all worthy of accomplishment requires some little trouble; and the learner must, therefore, not be disheartened if his early efforts are not crowned with success commensurate with his wishes. There is no disguising the fact that card tricks which owe their accomplishment to sleight of hand (and they are the only ones worthy of the conjuror's consideration) are difficult—in many cases exceedingly so; but this fact ought only to make one extra energetic in mastering them. Amateur conjurors of every grade I have met with, but those skilful with cards I can count upon the fingers of one hand.

Before everything, let me inform the reader of one fact, not by any means universally known, which is that the cards generally used by conjurors are considerably smaller than those in ordinary use.* I will not say that it is impossible to conjure successfully with ordinary cards, because I know of very clever conjurors who use the full-sized card, but they have strong hands; but the advantage of using smaller ones is so marked that anyone thinking seriously of practising

---

* Since this was written, a great change has come over the fashion connected with playing-cards, the large, heavy card giving way rapidly to a smaller and more flexible article, the American round-cornered cards occupying a prominent place.

sleight of hand should provide himself with some small-sized packs. Many use the French cards, but I find them far too flimsy for many things. The best are those made by nearly all the large English card manufacturers for conjuring purposes. Bancks Brothers, Glasshouse-street, London, are, perhaps, as good as anyone. Should the reader be unable to procure these small cards, he can provide very fair substitutes by having an ordinary pack shaved at the edges, and so reduced in size.

To enumerate every card trick individually would necessitate a separate volume, so numerous are the varieties of changes capable of being introduced. All the teacher can do is to instruct in the general principles, by means of which the results are brought about, and to give illustrations of the actions of the same. Accident or design will enable the performer to vary his tricks in hundreds of ways.

The chief things to be learnt at first are:

1. The pass.	4. The change.
2. The false shuffle.	5. The slide.
3. The palm.	6. The force.

THE PASS.

With the foremost of these, as the most important, I will first deal. The use of the pass is to transfer a given card from one portion of the pack to another. In nine tricks out of ten, a card is chosen and replaced in the centre of the pack, which is then shuffled. If this were in reality done without any previous interference on the performer's part, he would be at sea as to the position of the chosen card, and so rendered totally unable to find it when he wanted to do so. To avoid this *contretemps* he, by means of the pass, brings the card either to the top or the bottom of the pack, and executes a shuffle which, although it appears to mingle all the cards, in reality leaves the chosen one in its original position. If a chosen card is placed in the centre of a pack, it divides it into two portions, and the effect of the pass is to reverse the positions of these portions, the upper one becoming the lower, and *vice versâ*. It will therefore be seen that if the card is to go to the top of the pack it must, when replaced, and before the pass is made, form the uppermost card of the lower portion, and when it is to go to the bottom it must form the bottom card of the upper portion. Except in very special instances, the card is usually required at the top, and this, for the sake of uniformity, I shall assume in my examples to be the case.

FIG. 26.   FIG. 27.

For the purpose of learning the pass, it will not be necessary to assume that a card has been chosen, but let the learner take the pack in the *left* hand. The little finger is inserted in the centre of the pack, thereby dividing it into two portions, the upper one of which must be held by the fingers as securely as the unusual circumstance will admit (Fig. 26).* The right hand is now brought across the left hand, as in Fig. 27, the *lower* portion of the pack being held between the thumb at one end and the second and third fingers at the other. The state of affairs is now

* Some conjurors (myself included) use the third finger, but the little finger is the better one to employ, as it is more removed from observation. It is more difficult at the commencement, the digit being so weak ; but the better execution it ensures repays the extra trouble.

this: The upper hand holds the lower portion and the lower hand the upper. Now, in order to alter the positions of the two halves of the pack, the left hand must draw off, under cover of the right hand, the upper portion, and, working as though it were a hinge, replace it beneath the lower one, which is slightly raised by the right hand during the operation, so as to facilitate its execution. The cards should not be held in a horizontal position, but at an angle of fully 45 deg., or even more, the declension being towards the right hand. The movement should first be practised as slowly as possible, and with a few cards only. It will be time enough to increase the speed when a good action has been secured. One little point must be borne in mind, and that is that that half of the pack which was originally the lower one, and therefore held by the right hand, must always be kept hard against the root of the thumb of the left hand whilst the pass is being made, it working there as if hinged. At first the two halves, in passing each other, will make a scraping noise, sometimes very loud. This noise must be studiously avoided, as the pass must be noiseless as well as invisible. When making the pass before an audience, move the hands up and down or from side to side, to cover the movement. It is sometimes required to pass a single card from the very top of the pack to the very bottom. This can, of course, be done in the foregoing manner, but the quickest way is to simply press the fingers of the left hand (the hands being in position for the pass without the little finger inserted) on the top card, and then execute the hinge movement. This will pull the top card off and slip it to the bottom; but it is hopeless to expect to do this without some slight noise, although that can be almost nullified by immediately running the thumb sharply across the edges of the cards, and so causing a similar sound to be made. Such is the double-handed pass.

There are also various single-handed passes, one or two of which, at times, come in very handy. They are very difficult to master, and are best learnt with two cards only at the very commencement. The neatest, and in every way most effective, is the following : Hold the pack by the ends of the fingers and thumb, the first and fourth fingers acting as supports, by being slightly bent under (Fig. 28), and allow a portion of the cards to drop from below (Fig. 29). This

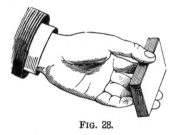

FIG. 28.

FIG. 29.

portion push back towards the thumb by means of the first and fourth fingers, until it will permit of the upper portion dropping down, and so becoming the lower (Fig. 30). The asterisk denotes the chosen card, which is passed from the centre to the top of the pack. Although three positions are

FIG. 30.

here shown, in order to make the action of the pass clear, it must by no means be thought that there should be three distinct movements. When the beginner can execute from thirty to forty passes in the minute, he may consider himself tolerably proficient. It will assist the action if the fingers are well raised and the thumb held a little low, thereby causing a better fall to be made; also considerable swing should be given to the hand, to cover the shifting which takes place. With practice this pass can be made without detection.

The pass shown at Figs. 31 and 32 is a fairly good one, but much more difficult than any other. The middle and third fingers are inserted in the pack, the bottom portion of which is held by the four fingers, two above and two below. The upper portion is held between the roots of the thumb and forefinger. The fingers draw out the lower portion and place it upon the upper one. This pass is useful

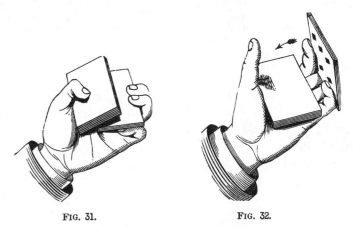

FIG. 31.   FIG. 32.

when it is required to pass a card from the bottom to the top. Under most circumstances, the pass first described (Figs. 28, 29, and 30) is preferable, except when the top card has to be passed to the bottom, when the following method is sometimes adopted. Push off the top card, which is the one to be passed, by means of the thumb, until it lies well over the ends of the fingers. Stretch the fingers out straight, and the card will be drawn completely off the rest of the pack, which is quickly raised by means of the forefinger, and placed over the card. A good backward and forward swing will assist the action considerably.

Experience has taught me, however, that the pass shown at Fig. 31, &c., is the best one for getting a card from the top to the bottom single-handed. The cards are so firmly gripped by the fingers that the pass may be executed, no matter what position the pack is held in, whether end on, sideways, or upside down. The beginner will find that the thumb has but little difficulty in dragging off the top card, especially if very slight pressure indeed be put upon it to commence with. If an examination is made of the root of the thumb, a line will be found to run half way round it, joining other lines on the inside, where the flesh is loosest.

FIG. 33.

The card should be held just there. Matters will be greatly facilitated if the right hand, whilst placing the pack in the left, holds it for an instant. The thumb of the left hand then draws the card off an eighth of an inch, which will be quite sufficient to enable the card to be seized by it at the root. But the aid of the right hand should be dispensed with as soon as possible. The passing of cards by means of one hand only is not suspected by the general run of spectators, who are, however, always suspicious directly the two hands are brought together.

The *learner* should always use the double-handed pass, practising the single-handed ones in private, until he has attained that confidence in his skill which is afforded by frequent exhibitions before his friends, &c.

An easy, but somewhat clumsy, single-handed pass is depicted at Fig. 33. The third finger is inserted in the pack, and the top portion held between it and the middle finger, the rest of the pack being between the first finger and thumb. The top portion is then twisted round in a semi-circle in the direction of the arrow, and so brought beneath what was originally the lower one. The objection to this pass is that it disarranges the cards a good deal. The best way of avoiding this is to move the hand towards the table whilst making the pass, so that the edges of the cards can be set square at once on its surface. The motion must be made as if it were merely intended to place the pack upon the table.

The Diagonal Pass.

This is a very useful variety of the two-handed pass, by means of which cards placed simultaneously in different parts of the pack are at once brought together. Say, three cards have been selected by various spectators. The performer presents the pack to each in turn, requesting to have the card chosen placed in any portion of it. The chooser thereupon pushes the card between the others, which are not opened out by the performer, but merely presented in a compact body. The card is not permitted to be pushed quite home, the performer withdrawing the pack in time to prevent this. The pack is presented to the two other selectors of cards, and, when the three have all been placed in it, the performer apparently pushes them home with the right hand. What he actually does is thus described: Nip the three cards by the still protruding portions between the thumb and middle finger, across their width, and, in the act of pushing them into the pack, turn them obliquely sideways sufficiently to cause the right-hand top corners to project

a quarter of an inch from the pack. The length of this projecting portion will be rather more than an inch, and is
easily hidden from the spectators by means of the first and
second fingers of the left hand. The top left-hand corner
must be pushed down out of sight, and it will then be found
that there are two considerable projections on the side and
bottom of the pack. The right-hand one is hidden by the
palm of the hand, and the lower one by the little finger.
The pack, as it appears at this stage of the trick, held in
the left hand (the right hand being removed for the sake
of clearness), is shown at Fig. 34.

As the cards are supposed to be pushed home along
with the rest of the pack, it is advisable to actually remove

FIG. 34.

the right hand for a short time, the performer commencing
to say what he is about to do with the cards. When he
subsequently brings the hands together again, for the purpose
of making the pass, the thumb and second finger of the
right hand should again nip the upper end of the pack. A
simultaneous twisting movement is made with both hands,
the right hand turning the pack to the right, whilst the left
turns the three cards to the left, until they are clear of
one another, when the motions are reversed, the three cards
being placed either on the top or at the bottom, as the
performer may desire. He will find it easier to place them
at the bottom, as they come more naturally there. The
position of the left hand remains the same throughout, the

three cards being held in position by the pressure of the little finger at the lower right-hand corner. The making of the pass must be covered by a slight swinging movement of the two hands in any direction. Some performers, finding it rather difficult to push home several cards into the desired position simultaneously and neatly, make the pass each time a card is placed in the pack. It is open to the learner to adopt this method if he so pleases, but he is more liable to detection; besides which, the feature of the pass is the showing the cards all in different parts of the pack, and then apparently pushing them home at one and the same time.

An alternative method is to push the cards down, with the projecting corner on the thumb side of the left hand, and then, by straightening the cards at once, leave half an inch or more of the whole width of the chosen cards projecting from the bottom of the pack, instead of having them diagonally across the pack, as is shown in illustration. A trial will show the learner that this method is an expeditious one, but my reasons against its use are twofold. Firstly, too much of the cards to be passed is exposed, and, secondly, the act of pushing them down is extremely likely to carry along with them indifferent cards intervening between two of them. This is especially likely to be the case with cards that are at all worn. The reason for this is that there is no stop to the body of the cards, which stop is provided, in the method shown at Fig. 34, by the little finger, during the whole of the operation. The act of pushing the cards transversely down, from the opposite side of the pack to that depicted, renders it impossible that the little finger can be in position on the lower side of the cards at the most critical time, the commencement, to prevent any but the desired ones from being pushed down. Its presence just at the corner seems to me to be very essential to the effective performance of the pass, combined with security from mishap.

THE FALSE SHUFFLE.

This the conjuror will find a very useful adjunct to the pass. There is nothing very difficult about it, but it is necessary to be somewhat bold in executing it. The two methods of shuffling in ordinary use are the perpendicular and the horizontal. The perpendicular is the most business-like, and I have no doubt that it is used by most of my male readers who are card-players. Ladies, I am aware, mostly patronise the horizontal shuffle, in which the cards are passed from right to left, or *vice versâ*, alternately over and under. To illustrate the perpendicular method, suppose the card to be at the bottom of the pack, just passed there, and it is desired to keep it in that position. By applying pressure with the fingers and thumb, the top and bottom cards will be retained in the left hand when the right hand draws away the rest of the pack, which is then shuffled over the two. The operation can be repeated hundreds of times without fear of a mistake. With the card at the top, the action is more complicated, though not difficult. The pressure with thumb and fingers must be made as before. This will bring the chosen card from the top to second from the bottom. Commence the shuffle a second time, and the card will be the bottom one of those held in the right hand, the one recently beneath it having been drawn off by the fingers of the left hand. It now remains to continue shuffling vigorously until the chosen card alone remains in the right hand, which then leaves it on the top of the pack in its original position. For this shuffle, which I prefer to any other, I have to thank myself. It is utterly impossible for the eye of anyone, be he the most practised conjuror, to follow the positions of the one card, even supposing that an opportunity for minute investigation were allowed, which it scarcely would be during a performance. When exhibiting before a select company of extra sharp people who have vague notions of false shuffles and passes, it is sometimes advisable to bring the chosen card to the top, with one card or more above it. You can then say, "Now, it is utterly impossible for me to know where the card is. You see it is neither at the bottom nor next to the bottom" (throw bottom card off), "nor is it at the top" (throw as many cards off the top as are above the chosen card). More than this the spectators can hardly expect you to do. In the horizontal shuffle, with the card at the top, draw the card off between the first and second fingers, and put all cards which are shuffled above it between the first finger and thumb. This will form two packs, divided by the first finger. The final movement in the shuffle is the replacing the lower half on the upper; but I prefer bringing this about by means of the pass. With the card at the bottom, one has merely to shuffle the cards in the ordinary way, just taking care that the bottom card is shuffled last by itself to the top, where it may be left; or it may equally easily be shuffled to the bottom again by simply retaining it in the hand last. This is the simplest shuffle of all, but it will not deceive enlightened people. I find it an excellent method to combine two methods of shuffling. Great rapidity of action should be studied; everything, however, being practised very slowly at first, until the proper method is secured. The false shuffle is very useful in covering the pass. The pass should be made, and the shuffle at once proceeded with, without allowing a fraction of a second to elapse.

Leaving the beginner to overcome at his leisure the various difficulties connected with the mastery of single-handed passes, I will describe some tricks performed by the aid of the pass, assisted by the false shuffle alone, commencing with the most simple. Lest the reader should say, "Oh! but no person in his senses would be deceived by that simple thing," I will observe that he should endeavour to suit his audience to his skill. The learner should commence by allowing a card to be selected from the pack, which he then cuts near the centre, and requests the person who selected the card to place it upon the lower portion. He then replaces the upper portion, taking care to allow the little finger to intervene between the two, so as to be ready for the pass, which must be made on the first opportunity, and the pack handed to a spectator to hold. Now say that you will cause the card chosen to rise from the centre of the pack, where it is supposed to be, to the top, and then let the holder of the pack show that such has actually been done. By inserting the finger beneath the card before making the pass, it will be brought to the bottom of the pack, whither you can afterwards command it to go. In these instances the effect will be spoilt if any shuffling takes place; but, in most of the following, false shuffling should be resorted to, attention being called to the fact that the cards are well mingled, and that you, therefore, cannot possibly know the position of the chosen card in the pack.

To Cause a Card to Show itself on the Top of the Pack.— Bring the card to the top, and, holding the pack in the right hand, push it off with the thumb of the left hand about half an inch, and then throw the pack violently on the table or floor. The resistance of the air will cause the uppermost card (the chosen one) to turn completely over, without losing its position. The effect is very good indeed.

The Attached Card.—Bring the chosen card to the top, and give the pack to be held by one corner tolerably firmly, between the finger and thumb. See that it is held neither too tightly nor too loosely, and then suddenly strike the cards upwards with the hand. Give a good strong blow, and all the cards, with the exception of the top one, will fly into the air, the chosen card remaining in the fingers. If the card is brought to the bottom, the cards must be struck downwards to the floor, which method certainly has the advantage of causing less litter. The effect is increased if two cards are chosen, one being brought to the top and the other to the bottom. The cards are then struck—only moderately hard in this instance—sideways, when the top and bottom cards will remain in the holder's fingers.

To Catch Two Cards in the Air, out from the Pack.—A better way with two cards is, after bringing one card to the top and one to the bottom, to take the pack firmly between your own thumb and fingers, and jerk it upwards. This will cause all the cards to fly towards the ceiling, except the top and bottom ones, in a bunch. Before the cards fall, you make a dash at them, and affect to catch the two chosen cards in the air out from the rest. This is a very finished illusion. The audience, having their eyes upon the pack, do not notice the two cards between the performer's fingers, but the dash at the pack must be made immediately.

The Congenial Aces.—Select from the pack the four aces (four cards of any other denomination would serve equally well, but aces are best for effect), and allow the pack to be thoroughly examined for the purpose of showing that there are no others contained in it. Give one ace to one person, another to a second person, and the remaining two to a third. Have the first ace placed at the top of the pack, the second at the bottom, and the third and fourth in what the audience will suppose to be the middle of the pack, but in reality between the top and bottom cards brought together by means of the pass. As you turn to the third person holding aces you pretend to open the pack in the middle, but in reality make the pass, but without bringing the two portions together again. The two remaining aces are thus innocently placed between the two already restored to the pack, which you instantly close up, whilst calling particular attention to the fact that you do so with all possible deliberation and slowness. Now command all four aces to join company in the centre of the pack. On the pack being opened, the command will be found to have been obeyed. The trick can be varied by placing a red ace in the centre and a black one on the top or bottom, and then causing them to change places by means of the pass. But the most startling change of all is when two aces of one colour are placed in the centre, and the two of the other colour, one on the top and one at the bottom, and then made to change places. The company cannot realise that this can possibly be accomplished in so brief a space of time; but it is simple enough. It should always be produced as a final effect, the performer saying, "Now I will show you something more remarkable still." He then places, say, the two red aces in the centre of the pack, and one black ace on the top and the other at the bottom. In order to convince the company thoroughly that things are as stated, the pack is turned over and opened slightly, fanwise. In showing the cards thus, it will be very easy to insert the little finger between the two red aces unperceived, and the double-handed pass is made in the act of turning the pack over. It is instantly placed in the hands of one of the company, who may be asked to blow upon it, or to perform any other operation equally unlikely to bring about any magical change, and then the cards can be examined without the performer approaching them again. But, in such cases, much depends upon how the pack is examined, and it should always be done under the performer's directions. For instance, he would say, "On the top was a black ace; will you please look at the top card now? — you will see that it is a red one. At the bottom was also a black ace; turn the pack over, please, and you will find a red one there also. In the centre were two red aces; kindly look there, and you will find the black ones." By this means, the whole of the company are informed of what has taken place, which would only be unsatisfactorily done if it were left in the hands of the temporary holder of the cards, who only thinks of satisfying his own curiosity.

The single-handed pass (Fig. 28, &c.) may be employed in this trick to great advantage, whenever it is required to bring cards from the outsides to the centre. Where cards, already in the centre, have to be brought to the top or bottom, the insertion of the little finger is necessary, and so the double-

handed pass has to be employed. In such cases, the employment of the pass depicted at Fig. 33 would be possible; but
the performer would have to execute it in a more masterly
manner than I have yet seen exhibited. For the first phase
described, the single-handed pass (Fig. 28, &c.) is perfect. Two
aces are placed, one at the top and the other at the bottom of
the pack, and as the performer turns to the holder of the two
others, he executes the pass, leaving the cards open, precisely
as depicted at Fig. 30, turning the hand slightly downwards,
so that the ace in the middle shall not be visible. It then
appears to the spectators as if he had merely opened the
cards slightly; and, when the two aces are inserted, the top
half is allowed to fall to, and the pack given there and then
into the hands of one of the audience.

The Reversed Card.—This is not at all a bad termination
to a trick. Bring the chosen card to the top, and then pass
it to the bottom with the two-handed slip pass previously
described; but, in passing, cause it to turn upside down. This,
it will be found on trial, is very easily managed by keeping
the face of the card always against the pack. Now make the
ordinary pass, and so bring the card to the middle, and then
throw the pack along the table, when the chosen card will
appear in the middle, face upwards. If you like, you may
ask the audience whether the pack shall be reversed and the
chosen card found face downwards, or *vice versâ.* It does
not matter which is selected, as it is only necessary to turn
the pack over before spreading it out, in order to bring about
a reversal of affairs.

The Travelling Card.—By attaching a hair to a waistcoat
button, and affixing the other end, by means of a tiny bead
of wax, unperceived, to the chosen card, it can be made to
walk out of the pack at the performer's command by a
slight motion of the body. The cards should be spread face
upwards upon the table, and the effect of one card disengaging itself from the rest is a very comical one. The
waxed end of the hair should be held in a finger nail, so as

to be at hand. Another method is to bring the card to the top, and then, holding the pack upright in one hand, with the faces of the cards towards the audience, pretend to pluck a hair from the head, and then to wind it rapidly round the pack with the disengaged hand. Pretend to pull at the imaginary hair, and, with the first and second fingers of the hand which holds the cards, work up the chosen card from the back. The effect is very comical. Two or three cards, selected by different people, may be treated in the same manner, when it is as well to come forward, after the first card has risen, and, making the pass, show that the chosen cards are not on the top. Before continuing, the pass must be again made to bring the cards back, the little finger having, of course, all the while divided the two halves of the pack. The trick should be practised before a looking-glass to ensure that the working of the fingers is not observed. It will be found necessary to allow the cards to well cover the finger roots. The performer should stand well away from the audience, and be certain that no one has a side view of his hand.

The Lady's Own Trick.—Say that you have now done quite sufficient yourself, and think it time someone else had a turn. Bring the card to any portion of the pack you please, so long as you know where it is. Take sixteen cards from various portions of the pack (you may have them selected if you please), taking care that the chosen card is included in the number, and arrange them in four divisions. Now, say that this trick must be done solely by a lady, and, giving your wand to one of the fair sex, ask her to point to any two divisions. The exact words you will use are, "Kindly tell me which two divisions I shall take." The word "take" is intentionally ambiguous, as, if one of the two divisions pointed at contains the chosen card, on which you are, of course, keeping a sharp eye, you will understand it to mean that you are to take those two and continue with them. If, on the other hand, they do not contain the card, you will assume that they are to be removed, and throw them aside accordingly. Two divisions will now remain, and you ask the lady to point to one of them, using the words, "Now, which do you prefer of the two?" This is, again, ambiguous, and you can do as you wish about taking or leaving the division pointed at. Four cards now remain, and you ask that two of them shall be selected, and, on two cards remaining, you repeat the request. If the chosen card is then pointed at, you allow it to be taken up; if the other, remove it, leaving the chosen card to be picked up by the chooser. You must endeavour to impress spectators with the idea that it is all sleight-of-hand, and *never do it twice*. Some tricks (not very many,

FIG. 35.

though) will bear repetition, although it should always be avoided if possible. If there is no help for it, endeavour to vary the method as much as possible.

Another very rapid single-handed pass is depicted at Fig. 35. As it is only useful for passing one or more cards from the top to the bottom, or, rather, from back to front, it is not in in general use, but forms almost a separate trick by itself. The cards, which should not exceed twelve or fifteen in number, should be held at the top corners by the first finger and thumb, and the third finger inserted beneath the card to be brought to the front. This card is then, by means of the middle, third, and little fingers, which hold it, brought from behind and passed round the others, care being taken to bring all together evenly. In executing this pass, the pack is first held up with the faces of the cards towards the audience, and is then turned downwards for a moment. When the pack is again held up, it is seen that the front card (the bottom one) has changed. The trick can be thus worked: Place secretly at the back of the pack three of any denomination of card, say, the fours. At the front, place the other four, which suppose to be the four of clubs, and request one of the audience to say into which other suite the card shall change. You will know the order in which the three fours at the back are placed, so you will only have to place the third finger beneath the one named and pass it to the front. If it is the actual top card, you will bring it forward alone; but if it is the second or third, those above it must come forward as well. As this pass cannot be effected without noise, it is always best to pretend to pass the card chosen as the one into which the original four is to change from some cards held in the other hand. Ruffle these cards with the thumb and say, "Did you not hear it go?" The slight noise heard will be accounted for by the cards passing from one pack to the other. If a duplicate four of clubs is held at the bottom of the second pack, it can be exhibited as the one changed in the other pack. But the best trick performed by means of this pass is by the aid of two duplicate cards, say, the knave of clubs and the ace of hearts. A pack must be held in each hand. At the top of the right-hand pack put the ace, and at the bottom the knave. At the top of the left-hand pack put the knave, and at the bottom the ace. The cards at the top are placed there secretly; those at the bottom openly before the audience. Hold the faces of the packs towards the audience, and, calling particular attention to the positions of the cards, say that you will make them change places. Turn the packs face downwards, with a flourish, executing the pass with both hands, saying, "Presto! pass. Did you not see them go?" On holding the cards up again, it will be seen that the knave has gone over to the left-hand pack, and the ace to the right-hand one. This is very effective indeed.

THE CHANGE.

This, as a sleight-of-hand feat with cards, takes precedence, for bare-faced daring, of, perhaps, any other. It consists in deliberately exchanging a card held in one hand for another in the pack held in the other hand, and this in full view of the audience. Such a feat may appear at first sight impossible, but, with a little attention and practice, it will become as easy as any other, although it will always demand some care and address in execution. There are various methods by means of which the change is effected, of which the following three are perhaps the best. For simplification of description we will suppose that the ace of diamonds is to be exchanged for the ace of clubs.

First method: Hold the pack, with the ace of clubs on the top, in the left hand, between the first finger and thumb. The other fingers should be so disposed under the pack as to leave a space between the first and middle fingers. This space, is for the reception of the card to be exchanged, in this instance the ace of diamonds, which is held between the first and middle finger of the right hand. To effect the change, bring the hands momentarily together, and place the ace of diamonds between the first and middle fingers of the left hand; the thumb and first finger of the right hand taking, at the same time, the ace of clubs from off the top of the pack. Just before executing the change, the thumb of the left hand should push the ace of clubs slightly off the pack, so that it may be in a favourable position for the finger and thumb of the right hand to seize. The action must, of course, be instantaneous and unaccompanied by the slightest hesitation or bungling. There must also be an auxiliary movement of the body from right to left, without which it is exceedingly difficult, if not impossible, to execute the change unperceived. The left hand must also be taken

away from the other, at the same moment, the feat being
practised until it can be accomplished in one movement,
the hands not dwelling together for the most infinitesimal
period of time. The learner should first practise by saying
to himself, "Now here I have the ace of diamonds, and, by
simply rubbing it on this table" (here give the body a half
turn from right to left, and execute change), "I will transform it into the ace of clubs." This form of address should
be used when exhibiting the change in this its most simple
form before spectators. The chief principle to be engrafted
on the mind is, that the first half of the change is performed

FIG. 36.

with the right hand and the second half with the left—the
two movements being interwoven, as it were, with the body
swing. On no account must the hands be brought suddenly
together and then parted as if something had been snatched
away. This method is the one in general use, and, for
ordinary purposes, I can scarcely recommend any other. By
its means, it is as easy to exchange two, three, or more
cards for others as a single card. The cut (Fig. 36) illus-
trating this change shows the two hands in actual contact.
It will be seen that the actions of leaving the one card
and taking the other are simultaneous.

Second Method: By the first method it will be seen that

the card first shown is left, after the change, at the bottom of the pack. This result is not always desirable. When the cards have to be, as is sometimes the case, changed back into their former positions, the card must be left at the top at each change. In this instance, the ace of diamonds must be held between the thumb and first finger of the right hand; the ace of clubs being, as before, at the top of the pack, and slightly pushed off by means of the thumb. On the hands being brought momentarily together, the ace of clubs is seized between the first and middle fingers of the right hand, the

FIG. 37.

ace of diamonds being left on the top of the pack. The thumb of the left hand is utilised in detaining the ace of diamonds, which, without its use, would probably fall on the floor. The first finger of the left hand must be kept well out of the way, or it will interfere with the smooth passage of the cards. Fig. 37 represents this change just as the hands are brought together. Noise is more likely to be made by this change than by the preceding one, so care must be taken to avoid it as much as possible. The "three card trick," so much in vogue amongst card-sharpers in wheedling money out of the pockets of greenhorns, becomes very amusing when worked by means of this change. The usual shifting about of the cards upon the table must be executed in the most childishly simple manner, which will not much matter, as you will take care to speedily change the card to be found, for one on the top of the pack. When the spectators have amused themselves for some time in endeavouring to find out a card which is not there at all, you will change it back again.

Third Method: Hold the pack in the left hand, with the ace of clubs at the top. Take the ace of diamonds in the right hand, between the first and middle fingers, and, bring-

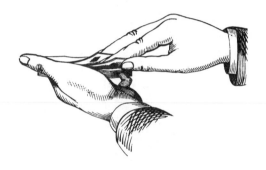

FIG. 38.

ing it briskly across the pack from front to back, take off the ace of clubs by means of the first finger and thumb, the ace of diamonds being left in its place. The little finger of the left hand should be curled up behind the cards, and so prevent more than the top one being removed, as will sometimes be the case if this precaution is not observed. This change is shown at Fig. 38.

Besides the part it takes in regular set tricks, the change is of the utmost utility to the conjuror in cases of emergency, especially when he makes, as he infallibly must at various times, a mistake. On eventually producing a card which turns out to be a wrong one, the performer must not

appear in the least discomfited, for that would commit him
at once, but ask the chooser of the card if the one now exhibited really is what he or she states it to be. Of course,
an affirmative will be received in reply, and the performer
must say, "Well, I would not for worlds contradict you, but
really I think in this case you are wrong. Will you, madam"
(here give the card, rapidly changed in the transit to someone else), "say if this card is the seven of diamonds, which
this gentleman says it is?" As it has been changed for the
ten of hearts, or whatever the desired card may be, a laugh
will ensue, and it will appear as if the climax of the trick
had been arrived at, and no one will know that you intended
doing anything else. One of the great arts in conjuring is
that of turning all mistakes and unexpected occurrences to
the best advantage, and a thorough knowledge of all the
various artifices and dodges is necessary to accomplish this.

THE PALM.

"Palm a card!" exclaims the reader, "how can one possibly
palm a card?" Not after the manner of a coin, certainly;
but, after the proper method, the palming of a card — *i.e.*,
the concealing it unnoticed in the hand—is not at all difficult. It is as important as, and, next to the pass, more used
than, the other sleights with cards, there being a continual demand for its assistance. To palm a card in the right hand,
take it in the left, across the middle, and place it in the
right, so that the top left-hand corner is against the inside
of the little finger, and the bottom right-hand corner against
the fleshy part of the thumb. This pressure is quite
sufficient to hold the card, but other parts of the hand and
fingers will render a slight assistance. This, unless one
possessed an enormous hand, would be impossible of accomplishment with the ordinary playing-cards, hence the necessity for using those of smaller dimensions. When the learner
can palm the card tolerably well, he should learn to secrete
it from its position on the top of the pack, under which cir-

cumstances the palm is mostly used. The right hand must press upon the pack, and when it is felt that the card is in postion it must be slid off sideways, not lifted. The hand containing the card should not be held unnaturally flat, but considerably curved, care being taken not to bend the corners of the card to any extent. The wand will, as usual, be of use here, as, if held between the finger and thumb, it will assist in disabusing the minds of the audience of the idea that anything is contained in the hand. It is not very likely that they will think so, for the idea that it is even possible to hold a card in the hand, without its being discovered, never occurs to anyone. The wand can also be held flat in the hand across the card, which is as good a way as any. Palming is not by any means confined to a single card, any number, up to a whole pack, being rendered invisible by this method. When two or more cards are to be palmed from the surface of the pack, they must be first slightly dislodged by the thumb of the hand holding them, and held a very little—not more than a quarter of an inch—above the others, just sufficient to enable the other hand to palm them rapidly without disturbing the pack. The palm is, of course, executed right in front of the audience, who never dream of what is going on. To entirely vanish a pack, take it in the right hand, across the back, lengthways, the thumb being at one end and the fingers at the other. Stand sideways to the audience, and, bringing the hands together, make a perpendicular swinging motion once or twice, as if about to toss the pack towards the ceiling. Make a final and vigorous toss, as if you had done so, and, with the left hand, press the cards into the right hand. The wand should be under the arm during this operation, in order that it may be at once seized by the thumb of the hand concealing the cards. If it be not handy, the lappel of the coat must be brought into requisition. It causes a good effect if the cards are afterwards found inside the coat of one of the audience, with whom you affect to be displeased thereat. You can also go down among the audience, and pretend to give someone the pack with the left hand, which must, of course, be so disposed as if it really contained the cards. To do this requires a little confidence, and care must be taken to hold the inside of the hand well towards the body, or detection may easily ensue when one is quite surrounded by eager, prying eyes. The simplest trick performed with the use of the palm is to ask someone to look at the top card on the pack held in your left hand, and to replace it. In the right hand you have a card palmed. Ask the name of the card just looked at, and, on being told it, affect surprise, and say that you fancy there must be some little mistake—you feel quite certain that the card is not what it is stated to be. Of course, the party who looked at the card, and who probably allowed it to be seen by others, will be positive, so you say that you will show that you are right. Bring the right hand over the cards in a similar manner to that employed when about to perform the third change (Fig. 38), and, with one movement, leave the one palmed on the top and pick it off again. The picking off will be done very slowly, to show that you really do take the top card. Finish up by palming the card originally looked at, and remarking that you cannot understand how the mistake occurred, "for here is the card in my pocket." Produce it from thence, the hand containing the card being merely plunged into the pocket, and slowly withdrawn, holding the card in the tips of the fingers.

Another very effective method is to stand sideways to the audience, and hold the pack perpendicularly (the length being horizontal) in the left hand, with the faces visible. In the right hand have a few cards palmed, with the faces towards the hand. Suppose the seven of hearts to be at the bottom of the pack in the left hand. Say that you can change it by simply passing the hand across it, which you then do, leaving one behind. If two or three are left by accident it does not matter, the chief object aimed at being smoothness. Care will have to be taken to have the end of the fingers of the left hand protruding well, so as to be in readiness to take the card thus left on the seven of hearts. The motion of passing the right hand over the left should be an upward one, and the performer should practise to dwell as little as possible over the pack.

The palm is also invaluable when anyone insists upon shuffling the pack, so as to make sure of mingling the cards well. The card secure in the performer's hand, the pack may be shuffled for a whole week without much harm being done. With the palm and the pass shown at Fig. 35 combined, a very pretty trick can be performed. It is somewhat similar to one already described. Take four cards of any denomination, and, cutting the pack into two halves, place one of the four at the bottom of one half. Place the remaining three at the top of the other half, which give to be held by a spectator, the three cards being previously palmed, and put on the top of the other cards, as you take them up to show the card at the bottom. Tell the person holding the cards, which are supposed to contain the three, to keep a very tight hold, and, tapping his pack with the wand, affect to take one of the cards away and pass it into your pack. Give a flourish, and pass one card to the front. The slight noise made by the pass will not signify if you say, " Ah! you heard it go ? " Repeat this operation with each of the cards, when you will show all four at the bottom of your pack, whilst the three will be found to have vanished from the one given to be held by one of the audience.

The Royal Marriages.—This is a very pretty variety of the foregoing trick. Take the four queens from the pack, and place them on the table, remembering the order in which the suits run. Take the four kings (in the same order as the queens), and have them put in one portion of the pack, which you have divided as before. If the kings are placed in the centre, you can make the usual pass, palm them, and put them, unperceived, on the top of the other portion of the cards, and then let someone shuffle till he is tired. The trick now proceeds very much as before, except that you commence operations by placing one of the queens on the bottom of the pack held by you, which has the four kings on the top. The lady is then supposed to call for her husband, who, as in duty bound, arrives with all despatch. Then place another queen at the bottom, and cause another king to arrive; and so on until all have appeared. The effect of this trick will be lost if the king of clubs arrives to console the queen of hearts, and so on. They must come together in suits.

As the pass employed in this trick becomes difficult to execute when many cards are held in the hands, eight or ten only should be taken up in the first instance, as eight will be added during the performance of the trick.

The Slide.

This is a very simple, but not, therefore, any the less useful, little deception, which deserves to be brought more into use by conjurors than it is. It consists merely in sliding back, in a particular manner, the bottom card of a pack, with the fingers of one hand, so that the other hand may

Fig. 39.

remove the one next to it, and yet appear to actually remove the bottom card. The particular method of holding the pack is shown at Fig. 39. The cards are taken, face downwards, in one hand, and the first and second fingers push back the bottom card to the extent of from half an inch to an inch.

Damp a finger of the other hand, and apply it to the bottom of the pack, drawing away the last card but one instead of the last. Thus, if, as in the illustration, the seven of hearts is at the bottom, and the seven of clubs next it, the red card will be exhibited to the audience at the bottom of the pack, which is then turned over. The seven of hearts is then ostensibly taken from the bottom of the pack (the seven of clubs being taken instead), and then made to change, whilst covered by the hand of a spectator, from the heart to the club suit. This is the simplest form in which the deception can be employed. It is very useful in demonstrating to the audience that a chosen card is neither at the top nor the bottom of a pack, when it is actually at the bottom. A card or two can be taken from the top, and then a few from the bottom, the actual bottom card being slipped aside. After taking off cards in this manner, always ask whether you shall take any more away, and so disarm the suspicion that you know the position of the card, and have only removed a certain number of cards so as to ultimately reach it. Should anyone not be satisfied, but demand to have the pack turned over, you must comply, making the pass as you turn the cards over. This will bring another card to the bottom; but, if you do not remove the finger from between the two portions, the pass can afterwards be repeated, and the cards brought back to their former positions. This is a ruse which will naturally occur to most conjurors when performing.

THE FORCE.

This is the last of the elementary principles to be learnt, and is a highly important one. It is hardly a feat of sleight of hand, although requiring considerable practice and determination to carry out properly. The act of forcing a card consists in inducing the chooser of a card to select from those proffered by you any particular card you please. As will hereafter transpire, it is highly essential for some tricks that a particular card, and none other, be chosen. The best method is as follows: Have the card which you desire to have selected at the bottom of the pack, in which the finger is inserted ready for the pass. As you advance for the purpose of presenting the cards, make the pass and allow the middle finger to remain under what was the bottom card, now somewhere in the middle. Spread out the cards, keeping them in constant motion, and as the chooser's hand is put forward to select a card, the middle finger should run the desired card into it. This action must be performed as naturally as possible. There must be no distinct motion of *pushing* the card into the hand, the cards being so manipulated that it always appears as if they were only just ready as the chooser's hand reaches them. Usually the difficulty of forcing a card is very small indeed, persons unacquainted with the ruse taking the first card that reaches their fingers with charming simplicity. In the event of a failure, do not appear in the least degree disconcerted, but "force" the card on some more tractable person, and then ask a third party to choose between the two cards selected. You will explain that your reason for having two cards chosen is to prove that you do not "force" any card, and then say, "Now, which card shall I take?" If the card you want is indicated, say, "This one, then, I am to use for my trick;" but if the other card is pointed at, then say, "This card I am to take away," and suit the action to the word. By this means you will appear to have given the audience a free choice, and at the same time obtained your own private ends. The beginner is sure to be nervous in forcing a card, and he must endeavour to overcome the feeling as quickly as possible. Some performers (I won't say conjurors) use what is called a "forcing pack," viz., a pack consisting entirely of cards of one particular kind, which will, of course, be that which is required for the trick. As, however, it is utterly impossible to allow such a pack to be examined, and highly disastrous to allow any number of the cards to fall or otherwise become seen, the conjuror should disdain to seek such adventitious aid as that afforded by a "forcing pack," the possession of which generally causes the appellation of "duffer" to attach itself to the owner.

With a command of the foregoing "elementary principles" the performer may attempt anything with the cards, taking care, however, always to rehearse any new combination carefully, lest it prove too much for him in the hour of trial. As previously stated, tricks with cards are without end, and the conjuror may vary his causes and effects at will. I give, however, a few of the most favourite tricks, so as to afford an idea of what may be attempted by the learner.

La Carte Générale.—This is, perhaps, as pretty a trick as can well be conceived. Force a card, say the eight of hearts, have it replaced in the pack, and re-force it on someone else so far removed from the first chooser that the possibility of their seeing that they have both selected the same card is avoided. Have the card replaced in the pack and reforce, repeating the operation four, five, or six, or even more times, according to the size of the room and number of the audience. Now and then it is as well to pass the card to the top, palm it, and then have the pack shuffled by one of the audience, or, at least, to shuffle it yourself. When you have forced the card a sufficient number of times, bring it finally to the top of the pack, from which select haphazard a card. Show this card to one of the choosers, and ask if it was the one selected. A negative will of course be given. Look neither surprised nor satisfied, merely exclaiming "No?" inquiringly. Show the card in turn to each of the persons who selected, asking if it belongs to them. When you have completed the round, turn to the first chooser, changing the card unperceived for the one (the eight of hearts) on the top of the pack, and holding it in front of the person, face downwards, so that no one can see what it is, say, "Well, since this card belongs to nobody, will you kindly tell it to go away?" As the words "go away" are uttered, run the thumb sharply along the edges of the cards held in the left hand, and "flip" the eight of hearts with a finger of the right hand, so leading the audience to believe that some miraculous change had taken place. Now hold the eight of hearts to the person whom you addressed, saying, "Is not that your card?" On receiving, as you will, a reply in the affirmative, turn the card face downwards and proceed to the next chooser of a card, and so on, until all are satisfied. As all are supposed to have chosen different cards it is imagined that each card is invisibly changed for the next one required. Commence another trick immediately, or otherwise divert the attention of the audience, or the drawers of cards will begin to "compare notes," and so discover that they all drew the same card. Although this discovery does not actually spoil the trick, it diminishes the effect immensely. It adds to the effect of the trick if the performer pretends to place each card, as chosen, upon a table, or other prominent place. Upon each occasion, however, he must change the forced card for an indifferent one. The last time the eight of hearts is actually placed with the rest. The supposed chosen cards are then held up, fanwise, together, and the choosers asked if they do not see their cards amongst them. As they all see the eight of hearts, they reply in the affirmative, and thus the idea that only one card has been selected is very unlikely to be entertained. To effect this valuable addition to the trick, great facility with the change is absolutely necessary, as it has to be so frequently executed.

The Sympathetic Cards.—Palm a few (say, four) cards, and ask one of the audience to take any number, without any reference to their specification, from the pack. Suppose eight are taken: how many is quite immaterial. Borrow a handkerchief; and after satisfying all that there is nothing whatever in it, ask for the eight cards, to which number add, unperceived, those you have palmed, and place the whole in the handkerchief with great deliberation. Fold the handkerchief up, and ask someone to hold it very firmly. Now have some cards drawn from the pack. "Any number you please," you will say carelessly, taking particular care that neither more nor less than four are chosen, the "force" being here brought into play. You now ask the person who selected the first batch how many are in the handkerchief, and the answer in this instance will be eight. "Eight, and four I have here, will make twelve, will they not? Now, sir," addressing the party holding the handkerchief containing the cards, "please to keep a firm hold whilst I pass these four cards into the handkerchief to join the other eight." Make a movement as though you threw the cards towards the handkerchief, palming them, and then have the handkerchief opened and the cards counted. The beauty of the trick is that the audience apparently selects the number of cards in each instance, the idea of any previous calculation on your part taking place being thereby precluded. Be careful to call attention to the number of cards in the handkerchief, and to the number to be passed into it, or the effect of the trick will be lost. This trick is sometimes performed without a handkerchief, the cards being given to be held in the hand only. Which method is the better is purely a matter of opinion, and the learner may follow which he pleases. Do not allow the drawer of the second batch of cards to examine the faces of them, or it will be noticed that they did *not* pass into the handkerchief, should anyone be 'cute enough to look for them. This possible *contretemps* can be avoided by having duplicate cards palmed in the first instance, in which case the faces of the cards should be shown to the audience, who will be asked to remember them. This is decidedly an additional feature to the trick, but it entails far more trouble. It is for the learner to try these little things, and then retain or relinquish their use as he finds it assist or trouble him.

Another way of performing this trick is to ask one of the company to count thirty cards from the pack, and then to cut them roughly into two parts. Taking one of the parts, ask a spectator to count them. Suppose the number is sixteen.

Taking them momentarily in the hands, for the implied purpose of describing exactly what you wish done, you place the four palmed cards upon the sixteen, and then instruct the spectator to hold them very securely. Now count the other heap. There will be fourteen cards, which number you announce to be quite correct, sixteen and fourteen together making thirty. Pick the cards from the table, and, in giving them to someone to hold, palm off four, taking the wand in the hand to cover the constrained position of it. Now you command four cards to pass from the heap last picked up to the one first given to be held, and, when the cards are counted, this will be found to have taken place. The trick may be reversed with success; the ten heap having the palmed cards secretly put back, and given to be held again, the twenty cards heap having four abstracted before being finally parted with. The cards are then commanded to go back to their original places. This method will possibly be found more difficult than the first one, in which a handkerchief is used.

The Permeating Card.—Have a card chosen, and, bringing it to the top, palm it. Ask someone who is seated to hold the cards in two hands, over the head, holding the pack in the desired position, and about six inches beyond the person's reach. This will cause him to rise slightly from his seat, when you instantly slip the card beneath him, saying at the same, "No, don't stand up; pray be seated," and allow the pack to reach his hands. The attention of the audience must be directed to the pack, or the action of placing the card beneath the holder will, perhaps, be perceived. The manœuvre requires a little care in execution, and it will be necessary to be as close as possible to the person operated upon, and at his side. Ask for the name of the card, and then command it to pass through the holder of the pack, who, on rising at your request, will find that he has been seated upon it. This trick usually causes much hilarity.

Divination of Thought.— This is an ambitious and daring

experiment. Hold the cards upright, and fanwise, before one of the audience (a lady for choice), and run them rapidly from right to left, or *vice versâ*, in such a manner that only a very small portion of each card, one excepted, is visible. The bottom, or front, card is carefully concealed by the hand, so that it cannot be seen. The cards are run so rapidly across that it is impossible to recognise any of them by the very small portions of them exhibited by you; but one you allow to be very much exposed, and on that one you place a finger, and continue pushing the rest over in a rapid manner. Whilst thus running the cards across, you ask the lady to kindly think of any one of the cards she sees. As you take good care to show only one card, you may rest assured that that is the one thought of, although it is advisable, on being told that a card has been thought of, to inquire if it were actually seen in the pack. Keeping the finger on the card, turn the pack over, and then make the pass. The card can then be produced after any method the performer pleases, but he should first ask the name of the card (at which he has taken a glance), as there is considerable uncertainty about forcing a card upon a person's notice in this manner. In the event of the chooser naming a card other than that manipulated by the performer, he must at once look through the pack for it, and first palming it, boldly declare that it is not in the pack, which he will give to be inspected. The card named can then be produced from someone's pocket, &c. The method of passing the cards fanwise from side to side, so as to expose the face of one card only, should be practised in front of a looking-glass until the learner is perfect. Perfection is the only degree in which it is allowed to exhibit conjuring tricks, especially those with cards.

To Cause a Card to Appear in any Position in the Pack, Counting either from the Top or from the Bottom.—This, a very favourite diversion in card tricks, is capable of being performed in many ways, the best of which are given here. The method of procedure is to bring the card either to the top or the bottom of the pack, after due shuffling, &c., and then to ask one of the audience to name the position in which it is to appear. If you have brought the card to the bottom, then say, "At what number from the bottom shall the card appear?" It will not answer to count it from the top. Suppose the fifth card is decided upon, all you have to do is to slide back (Fig. 39) the bottom card, which is the selected one, and draw away the next card instead. When four have been thus extracted, draw away the card itself, and the trick is done. This is the only method used when the cards are counted from the bottom. In counting from the top proceed as follows :

Method 1 : Bring the card to the top and then make the pass in such a manner that the two halves of the pack are facing each other, after the method previously described in dealing with a single card. This will cause nothing but the backs of the cards to be visible at both top and bottom. Hold the pack in the left hand with the thumb turned underneath it, and the fingers curled round the front side. The selected card is at the bottom, and it is required to produce it fifth. (For the sake of simplicity, I will suppose that the card is required in this position in each of the methods given.) Count off, one by one, four cards from the top, and then, whilst affecting to examine the last one, or to recount those taken off "to make sure," thus drawing attention away from the left hand, turn the pack rapidly over. This will bring the chosen card atop, and you have then only to take it off and show it. The reversion of the pack must be very rapidly and quite noiselessly made, and care must be taken that the cards set evenly at the edges, or the audience will perceive that one half of them are reversed : and although the elucidation of the trick will not of necessity follow, yet it is just as well to avoid the discovery if possible. If the pack be at the same moment handed to one of the company, with a request to have the next card looked at, to see if it be the right one, the action of reversing will be less likely to be remarked.

Method 2: Bring the card to the top, and hold the cards in the left hand as if about to deal them. Do not hold them quite squarely, but let the thumb push off the upper ones in such a manner that each card overhangs slightly the one beneath it. Now commence to take off apparently the top card, but in reality the one immediately beneath it. This is accomplished by exerting more power with the first finger of the right hand than with the thumb thereof, the thumb of the left hand at the same time putting sufficient pressure on to the top card to detain it in its position. The top card is taken off with much ostentation, when it is required for production. This deception is capable of immense development, if assiduously practised, it being possible to deceive those who actually know what is taking place. If the learner has this method at his command, he need never resort to any other, for he will never be discovered. This practice of dealing the second card in lieu of the first is a common dodge amongst card-sharpers, who are thereby able to retain all the good cards, which they have previously marked, for themselves. I strongly recommend the adoption of this method in preference to all others, but it must be well executed.

Method 3: Bring the card to the top, and count the cards off in regular order one by one. As the first card removed (now the lowest of those dealt off) is the selected one, the fifth will naturally be a wrong card. You appear surprised, and say that you must have made some mistake in the counting. Gather up the five cards, the selected one being at the bottom, replace them on the top of the pack, and ask the chooser of the card to count them off himself. This time, the card will, of course, turn up in its proper place. This is the simplest of all the methods, and is now and then seen through; but not often. On counting the cards off for the first time, they must on no account be turned face upwards. If this were done, it would be at once perceived that the chosen card was on the top in the first instance.

Method 4: Bring the card to the top, and hold the pack in

the left hand, in a position similar to that shown at Fig. 38, the little finger being in this instance not curled up behind the cards. Place all four fingers of the right hand well over the top card, almost covering it, and the thumb well under the bottom card. Draw the hand sharply away, bringing with it the bottom card by means of the thumb, which it will be as well to damp a little unperceived. The rapid motion will prevent the audience from noticing what has actually taken place. When the time has arrived for so doing, show the chosen card very slowly indeed, or even ask one of the audience to remove it, to show that it really is in the desired position. In counting off the underneath cards, use a fair amount of rapidity, and be careful not to draw away more than one card at a time. The action of drawing off the cards must be made towards the body, and not outwards.

Method 5: Bring the card to the centre of the pack, keeping the finger upon it, and, when you have counted off four cards, make the pass, thus bringing the card to the top. This method should only be used when some sharp person insists upon looking to see if the card is at the top or bottom of the pack.

After bringing the card to any number from the top or bottom, you can offer to perform the still more surprising feat of causing it to appear at any place indicated by the insertion of a pen or paper knife between two cards. To perform this feat, which, by the way, is a variation of my own, hold the pack as in Fig. 39, face downwards, and, presenting the end to one of the audience, ask to have indicated the place in which the card is to appear. When this is done, hold the bottom portion by the finger and thumb of the left hand, across the cards; and insert the first finger of the right hand, which is, of course, holding the upper portion, into the space made by the instrument of indication, from the front. Ask whether the person is quite sure that the place indicated is the right one, and whether another would not be preferred. This is to show that it really does not matter what position is indicated. On receiving a reply in the affirmative, draw off the top half rapidly, bringing with it, by means of the ends of the fingers, as taught in describing the "slide," the bottom card also, and hold the whole up to the audience. This manœuvre defies detection, and possesses the advantage of bearing a fair amount of repetition. Before commencing, it as well to show that the card is neither at the top nor the bottom. As it is at the bottom all the time, the slide will have to be brought into play, in order to enable another card to be drawn away from the bottom and exhibited. What lends great finish to the trick is the bringing the first finger over the ends of the upper cards, as by this means the slipped card can be immediately brought close against the others, and not allowed to stand out away from them, which would give the audience the idea that the trick had been clumsily performed, even if it did not afford a clue to the secret of it.

Card-boxes.—A well-known, but, when well executed, very effective, trick is performed with the aid of one or two boxes, known as "card-boxes." They are about half an inch deep, and sufficiently large to hold a card very easily indeed; that is to say, there is a good eighth of an inch to spare all round the card when it is in the box. The boxes are black inside, and are furnished with a thin piece of wood, also blackened, which is placed loosely within and fills up the entire interior space. This piece of wood is the secret of the box, for by its means a card is made to appear and disappear. Suppose that the box is wide open, and in the right-hand half is placed the card, whilst the left-hand half contains the piece of wood. If, on the box being closed (which movement must be rapidly executed, or the wood may unexpectedly fall out) the left-hand half is turned over on to the right-hand half, the card contained in the latter will necessarily be covered by the blackened piece of wood, and will appear to have vanished entirely when the box is re-opened. By simply turning the box over, the card will be made to appear.

The trick is performed by means of a duplicate card, which can either be forced, and, after being placed in the box, made to return invisibly into the pack whilst the latter is being held by one of the audience, or the box may contain one of the duplicate cards in the first instance. The other one can then be forced, replaced in the pack, brought to the top, and palmed. The pack may then be examined, after the card has been shown to be in the box, to prove that it really has gone from it. The proper time for replacing the card in the pack is immediately after the person has finished the examination. You take the cards from him, and, placing the palmed card on the top of the pack, make the pass, and so bring it to the middle; you can then perform the operation of passing it invisibly from the box back again to the pack, where it will, of course, be found. Opinion is divided on the question of handing the box or boxes round for examination. If this is done, the trick decidedly attains lustre thereby, but, of course, the false wooden bottoms must be concealed about the performer's person, and slipped in whilst retiring to his table. In showing the boxes round with the false bottoms in them, keep a finger on the latter, and knock the boxes about a good deal with the wand to show they are solid, &c. In "passing" the card, either from box to pack, or *vice versâ*, make a great show of taking it from either place by means of the wand, on the end of which you seriously declare you can distinctly see it. Conjurors are able to make great capital out of doing simply nothing at all; and as it is impossible, when performing with nothing, to make any mistakes, then is the time to do the most extraordinary things. The trick with the boxes can be varied by having two duplicate cards of different denominations, one of each kind being concealed in a box. Say the cards are the six of clubs and king of hearts. Force these cards from the pack and place the drawn king in the box containing the six, and the drawn six in the box containing the king. You have only to turn the boxes over to effect the change, although you of course affect to bring it about by magical means. You may then remove one six and one king from the boxes, leaving one of each still concealed, and, placing them in the pack, bring them to the top, palming them and proceeding as directed for one card only. This makes a very pretty trick. The boxes are best purchased from a conjuring repository, where they can be obtained cheaply.

To Throw a Card.—In a large room, throwing cards from one end to the other has a very good effect. It is astonishing how few people can throw a card, seeing how easy the feat becomes with a little practice. But I suppose it is just this practice which stands in the way. The card should be held across its end, the end of the first finger just turning the outside corner. When in position for throwing, it should rest upon the middle finger, which will be curved slightly for the purpose. Bend the arm back until the card almost touches the chest, and then throw it with considerable force from you, taking care to give it a spin with the end of the first finger. If this spin, the secret of the feat, is not given, the card will not travel three yards, whereas a good thrower can send one thirty or forty. For long throws, ordinary heavy cards should be used, but care must be taken to elevate the trajectory, as such cards hurt severely when they strike the face with full force, and serious injury might result if one struck the eye. Mehây used to place one card across the back of the left hand, and flick it off with the first finger of the right. People with strong fingers may try this method, which will, however, never send the cards farther than eight or ten yards. Some throwers merely seize a corner of the card between the finger and thumb, whilst others hold it between the first and second fingers—the latter being a favourite method.

The Revolution.—This, as an interlude, has a very pretty effect. Take a full pack of ordinary cards, and throw them obliquely on the table, so that they spread nearly across it, each card resting upon the one next it. Run the eye along the cards, and see they are all even, as a break will spoil the feat.   Place the hand well under the first (the lowest) card, taking care not to disturb the position of those immediately next to it, and turn it suddenly over in the direction of the other cards, which will, each in its turn, be made to reverse their positions on the table.   The first card must be more pushed than lifted over; indeed, that end of it which is towards the other cards must always remain on the table as if hinged there.   If they have turned over in good order, they may be turned back again by the same means.   The success of the feat depends upon the neatness with which the cards are thrown down in the first instance.   Simple as it appears, very few persons can execute it neatly, or with many cards.   When the line is very long, considerable force will have to be applied in turning over the first card.   The cards may also be spread in the shape of an arc, which has a still prettier effect, but considerable practice will be required in laying the cards out.   A more difficult method still is to lay the cards along the forearm, and turn them over there.   Many will be the spills, however, in practising this feat.

Prepared Cards.—Under the heading of "Sleight of Hand," the words "prepared cards" may seem out of place; but one of the chief articles in my creed is that a conjuror should know everything appertaining to his art.   Besides this, many tricks with prepared cards require considerable sleight of hand in their performance; and not infrequently their introduction is the means of defeating an antagonistic and inquisitive element which will sometimes introduce itself into an audience, members of which possess just that "little knowledge" which is said to be "a dangerous thing."

Cut Packs.—In some instances, it is very useful to have the edges of the cards shaved off obliquely, so that one end is broader than the other.   When a card is taken from the pack, the performer should watch and see if it is turned round whilst in the possession of the drawer.   If it be not turned, then he must reverse the position of the pack before the card is returned to it. The cards may then be shuffled any number of times, and the performer will always be able to find the card by the fact of its broad end being where the other cards are narrow. This ruse is but little known among amateurs It saves a good deal of passing, but it will not obviate the necessity for forcing.

Long and Broad Cards.—This, a most useful preparation, consists merely in having one or more cards in the pack a shade longer or broader than the others. I, myself, never use more than one card so prepared. When not forced, or otherwise actually in use itself, it is very useful to place over or beneath other chosen cards, which will, by its means, be easily found when wanted. My preference is in favour of a broad card, as opposed to a long one: it is more easily found by the finger when preparing to make the pass. As one cannot procure single cards longer or broader than others, it will be necessary to have the other cards shaved down a little, omitting, of course, those intended to be longer or broader than the rest. It is not necessary to go to a card manufacturer in order to have these operations of cutting and shaving performed; any stationer or card-plate engraver, who possesses a paper-cutting machine, will be able to do all that is desired.

Pricked Cards.—An excellent method for detecting given cards is to have them pricked in the corners, very nearly through, with a needle. The hole, or, more properly speaking, the indentation, should be made on the back of the card, so that the face presents a little mound to the touch. The card should be marked in each corner, so that it will not matter which end of it comes to hand first. When it is desired to mark more than one card in the same pack by this method, one card should have one hole in each corner, another card two holes, another card three holes in a triangular form, another card a line of holes along each end, and so on. It will, however, be seldom necessary to mark many. Card cheating is to this day often practised by this means, cards of value of a certain suit being detected by the dealer as he deals them out.

The Chameleon Card.—Have two cards chosen, and bring one to the top and one to the bottom. Take the pack, face upwards, and make the single card slip pass from top to bottom, reversing the card during the process. This will bring the two chosen cards back to back. Openly take them up by one corner, but show only one card. Ask the name of the other card, and, blowing on the two in the hand, turn them rapidly round, and thus show the one at the back. Replace the cards at once in the centre of the pack. Care will have to be taken that the cards are very even when back to back, or it will transpire that two cards are in the fingers, and not one only. This trick is sometimes performed with the aid of prepared cards, the two—duplicates of which must, in this instance, be "forced" from the pack—being gummed together back to back. Supposing the cards to be queen of hearts and ten of spades, the performer would thus proceed: Bring the ten to the top, and the queen to the bottom, unknown to the audience. Produce, as a single card, as if taken from the pack (you will, of course, have them concealed about you), the prepared cards, showing the audience the ten. In the left hand you will hold the pack, displaying the queen. Prepare for passing the ten (*vide* Fig. 35), which is at the back, to the front, and then say, "Hey, presto, pass!" Turn the prepared cards rapidly round, and at the time execute the pass, when the change will have been effected. Palm the prepared cards, and give the pack round to be examined. This method is useful when the performer is able to execute the pass peculiar to the trick with one hand only. As this is a very pretty effect, which may be introduced in all manner of emergencies, two illustrations are given (see Figs. 40 and 41).

A very excellent variety of this trick is that described by Houdin in his work on "Conjuring," and communicated to me by Professor Hoffmann, to whose research the conjuring

world is not a little indebted. Most of us have seen the
three cards forming a portion of the marvellous and heterogeneous pennyworth offered to the public by a versatile itiner-
ant vendor. When spread open one way, the seven of spades
only is visible, and on being shut up and opened the reverse
way, graceful female figures or donkeys' heads meet the view;
Houdin's trick is framed upon this model, but, of course,
very much elaborated and improved. Indeed, it was a
peculiarity of Houdin's that he never did touch anything
without improving it. The directions for the trick under
notice are as follows : Have a pack made with plain white

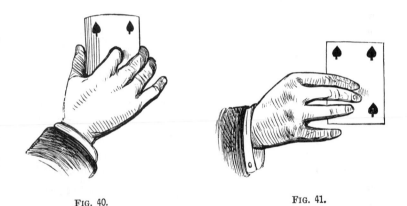

FIG. 40.   FIG. 41.

backs, each card being divided by a line diagonally from
corner to corner. Of the halves thus formed, one is to represent queen of spades, and the other the ten of hearts.
On the back of each card paint the ace of clubs. Have a
heap of cards near you, the three uppermost cards of which
are duplicates of those in the prepared pack, arranged in
an order which is known to you. If you prefer it, these
cards can at first be forced from an ordinary pack, and
then given to be held in the audience, which heightens the
effect of the trick. Take one of the three cards—for example,
the ten of hearts—and, after showing it to the audience, say

that the fact of placing it with those held in your hand (the prepared pack) will change them all into tens of hearts. Taking care that the ten of hearts halves are farthest from you when the cards are held faces downwards, as they must be, place the card at the bottom, and, after a little nonsense, spread them all out fanwise, with the faces towards the audience. Close them again, and remove the ten of hearts. Then take up next card, the queen of spades, and place that at the bottom, having previously taken care to turn the pack round so as to bring the court card halves to the fore. Repeat the operation of opening the cards as before, and reclose them, discarding the queen. Now take up the ace of clubs and place it at the bottom, or anywhere else you please. Give the cards a flourish, so as to enable you to turn them completely over, and then open them once more, this time displaying the backs to the audience. It is as well to have the top card of the prepared pack quite plain at the back, as it is not always possible to avoid showing it whilst performing the trick. When the aces are shown, this card can be passed to the middle, where the absence of an ace on its centre will not be noticed. The beauty of this trick is considerably enhanced if the prepared pack be palmed, and another ordinary one shown round for examination. When this pack is returned to you, you place upon it the hand in which the prepared cards are palmed, and, saying, "Now I take a few cards from this pack," affect to do so. This at once disarms all suspicion of any preparation. There is no necessity for using more than eighteen or twenty prepared cards, and that number can easily be palmed with a little practice. Some advise changing the packs altogether, but this method I cannot recommend, as it entails a deal of extra trouble, without a commensurate meed of effect. In "Grand Magic," a method for changing packs of cards will be described in its place, and the learner can then choose for himself. When well executed, there is no prettier trick than the one described above.

The Travelling Cards.—This is a pretty trick, and one that is always much commented upon by spectators who have seen it neatly performed. The performer has a couple of cards chosen, which he brings to the top of the pack; then, addressing the company, he refers to the notion that the sleeve of the coat is employed by conjurors for their concealment. He deprecates the attempt, made by many performers, to deny the immense aid afforded by this portion of the attire, especially for the effective concealment of eggs, pigeons, cannonballs, and other articles equally easy of manipulation (this as sarcastically as he pleases), and says he will now proceed to demonstrate, conclusively, in what way the sleeve is employed. " So far from there being any difficulty, ladies and gentlemen, in concealing cards, in the sleeve, for instance, it is a very easy matter to cause them to travel up or down with great rapidity, and invisibly. My waistcoat, as you see, contains nothing." The performer cannot very well unbutton and open his waistcoat before the company, so, to show it is empty, he places his hand inside, and performs the action of emptying sufficiently vigorously to dislodge anything that might be there. He next palms a dozen or more cards from the top of the pack, and then, extending the left arm, ruffles the edges of the remaining cards. This act, he explains, has had the effect of sending a card up his sleeve, and he affects to watch its progress. A jerk of the arm is made, the contraction being caused, the performer says, by the passage, by the card, of the elbow. Plunging the right hand into the vest, the cards palmed are dropped there, one card only, taken from the bottom, being slowly extracted. A second card is made to pass in the same way, and another indifferent card extracted. The performer now asks the choosers of the two cards on the top at what numbers they shall pass up the sleeve. This feat is easy of accomplishment, as the cards are taken from the bottom until the proper number has been reached. When the cards in the vest have been exhausted, more can be palmed, and the operation continued until all the pack has been employed; but this finish is by no means necessary to the success of the trick, which may be considered concluded when the two selected cards have been withdrawn, although it is as well to continue passing cards until no more are left in the vest.

The Assembly.—In this trick, four cards are laid separately on the table, in a row, and upon each card three more are placed from the pack, making four heaps of four cards each. The company themselves select one of the four heaps, which is found to consist entirely of the four cards that were only just previously laid upon the table, apart from each other, the remaining three heaps consisting of four different cards each. To accomplish this, the performer commences operations by picking out of the pack four cards of any one denomination, say, the knaves. This is far better than having four different cards selected, as the trick is one of startling effect, and four picture cards are better for the purpose, apart from the fact that no one in the company is called upon for an effort of memory. The performer gives the four knaves to one of the company, and seizes an opportunity for palming three cards. He now allows the four knaves to be placed upon the top of the pack, which he holds in the left hand, supplementing secretly the three palmed cards. He then proceeds to deal off the four topmost cards, one by one, placing them in a row, divided by a few inches, saying, as he does so, "Here I place one knave, here a second, here a third, here a fourth." After he has placed the fourth card, which will naturally be the only one of the four that is really a knave, upon the table, he pauses for a moment or two, and then turning it over remarks, pensively, "Ah! the knave of diamonds," or whichever it may be. This is really to let the spectators see the only knave there is, in order to convey the impression that all the rest are knaves also, they being led to fancy the performer looks at the suit of it for the purposes of the trick. The remaining three knaves are now, of course, on the top of the pack, the three palmed cards and one knave having been removed from above them. It is open to the performer to place these three at once on the top of the fourth knave, and this is generally done, but I do not at all advise it. Invariably make a pass at this point, so as to bring the three knaves to the centre of the pack, keeping the place where they are well defined by a finger, or by a break in the pack. I then place the three cards now on the top upon one of the three ordinary cards, emphasising the fact that they come from the top. I then open the pack a little lower down, and taking three cards from there, place them upon another ordinary card. The middle of the pack, where the three knaves are, is now reached unsuspiciously enough, and they are, of course, placed upon the fourth knave. Three more ordinary cards, from still deeper down in the pack, are placed upon the remaining ordinary card, as much deliberation being paid to this last card as to any other, or the conjuror's manner may reveal that he has accomplished what he wanted, however unknown its precise nature may be. The selection of a heap then proceeds precisely as described in *The Lady's Own Trick*, first two, and then one being removed. The four knaves are then shown together in the supposed selected heap.

A second method depends upon the neat execution of the pass, and is to be commended because, each time three cards are placed upon one of the four lying upon the table, they are first shown to be ordinary mixed cards, and not knaves. Three cards are palmed, and placed upon top of the four knaves, as in the first method, and the three ordinary cards and one knave are placed in a row, as before. Three mixed cards are then taken from any part of the pack, their faces shown casually, and they are then put upon an ordinary card. This is gone through three times, the knave being left till the last. As if by mistake, the performer places the three cards, which he has shown to be mixed ones, upon the cards in his left hand, instead of upon the knave on the table. At this instant the three are passed to the bottom, the right thumb at once taking off the three knaves, as though they were the cards just placed there by mistake. On no account must the performer make any apology; he need merely say, "Oh! that's wrong; they must go here," and place the cards upon the knave. One must be perfect in making the pass before attempting this method; but it is very easy indeed to pass so few cards as three from top to bottom.

A third method is also accomplished by means of the pass, and is preferred by many conjurors. The four cards are shown, and, as they are being put upon the pack, the little finger is passed between the third and fourth, three cards thus being above it. The insertion of the little finger is in all cases greatly facilitated if the cards are spread a little, fanwise, at the moment of placing them on the pack. The three topmost cards (knaves) are immediately passed to the bottom, leaving one knave on the top, and the little finger kept between them and the rest of the pack. This card is then placed upon the table, its face being accidentally (?) shown to the spectators, and three others (ordinary cards) successively laid beside it. Three ordinary cards, always taken from the top, are then placed upon each of the ordinary ones lying singly upon the table, the audience seeing their faces each time, and then the pass is made, bringing the three knaves from the bottom back again to the top. These three cards are then placed upon the other knave, which brings about the desired state of affairs. As these three knaves cannot be shown to be ordinary cards, as was each preceding set of three cards, I here recommend the conjuror to make use of a little ruse of mine. It is to take off from the pack four, instead of three, cards, the three knaves thus having an ordinary card beneath them. Holding the edges even, so that only the lowest card can be seen, the performer says, "Now I once more take three cards, and"—here he turns them over, and, spreading them slightly, discovers four cards, so he continues, "Oh! I see, I have taken one card too many." He then removes the underneath card, and places the remaining three upon the knave. To show the faces of three out of four heaps of cards and not those of a fourth, causes suspicion to be thrown upon the latter. By adopting the ruse described, this is ostensibly done; at any rate, sufficiently so to satisfy the spectators, which is all that is desired.

A fourth method is bolder still, and calls for a masterly execution of the change. Matters progress precisely as in the second method, except that the three knaves are always slightly pushed off the top of the pack, ready to be exchanged at any moment. It is just as easy to change three cards as one by the method illustrated at Fig. 36. The fourth time is perhaps again the most favourable for the substitution, as the performer may cover the action of changing by handing the pack to be held. Holding the pack, with the knaves on the top, in the left hand, and the three ordinary cards in the right, he should turn round suddenly to someone on his extreme left, and somewhat behind him, when every opportunity will be afforded for executing the sleight. Or the act may be gone through by giving the last three cards to someone on the performer's left to place upon the remaining uncovered knave, when the same facility for an exchange will be afforded.

Yet a fifth method remains, which is a very fine one indeed, if the performer should happen to be an adept at changing. To attempt this method, he must be absolutely perfect in this sleight. The four knaves are first thrown down upon the table, faces upwards. One is then taken in the right hand, and three cards put upon it from the top of the pack, held in the left hand. That is what the performer appears to do, but, in reality, as he approaches the pack with the knave, the change is effected, the knave being thereby placed at the bottom of the pack. As he executes the change, the performer says, "I will now take three more cards from the pack," and, under cover of the quite natural action of bringing the knave into proximity to the pack, the change, if only adroitly executed, will pass unnoticed. The three cards required are drawn off by means of the right thumb, and the heap of four placed at a corner of the table. A second knave is similarly treated, followed by a third. Three knaves are now at the bottom of the pack. The performer may now either make the pass, bringing the three knaves to the top, and then place them upon the fourth, or else he may say that he will take three cards from the bottom of the pack, to show that it is immaterial to him from whence they come. As the feat of changing three times in succession is materially assisted by some freedom of movement, it is as well to place the four heaps at the corners of the table, wide apart, the performer being thereby compelled, in the eyes of the company, to move about a good deal. The one great feature connected with this method is, that the four knaves are shown faces upwards, until the very moment of their being placed in a heap. In each of the last three methods, the selection of the knave heap proceeds as described in the first method.

The five methods described give the conjuror his choice according to his greater facility with the pass, the palm, or the change; and he will also find that they are capable of far wider application, in connection with other card tricks.

Thought-reading. — Give the pack into the hands of a spectator, and allow one card to be secretly chosen. Replaced in the pack, it is passed to the top (or bottom), and a furtive glance taken at it, the palm being employed, if necessary. Let three cards be chosen in this manner, a fourth being forced, consequently previously known. The object of this diversion is in order that the last card selected may be placed in the pack by the chooser, and the cards immediately shuffled, which will distract attention from the fact that this was not done in the other cases, which, however, could be done after the performer had glanced at the card, if necessary, which it is not, as it draws out any trick too long to have the cards frequently shuffled. The performer must be careful to remember the cards, and by whom drawn. Taking the pack in his hand, he presents one end of it to a card drawer, explaining that he is about to give an exposition of thought-reading. Although there is no reason for failing, it is as well not to make this announcement any earlier, in case of anything going not quite rightly. The performer makes a great fuss about the necessity for looking full in the eyes of the person drawing the card, and pretends to arrive at the designation of the card by slow degrees, saying to himself, but audibly enough to be heard, for instance, " A red card— hearts—one, two, three, four, five, six, seven spots;" and then, loudly, " The seven of hearts." Every incidental occurrence in the behaviour of the persons whose thoughts are being read must be taken advantage of; a want of alacrity in obeying instructions, for example, tending to make the read- ing more difficult, the subject being even left for the time being, and returned to after other cards have been revealed. This trick has the advantage of bearing considerable repe- tition.

A second method is as follows : The performer holds the cards in one hand, and presents them to a spectator to cut, with the injunction that the underneath card of the cut shall be removed, looked at, and remembered. It is im- material how many cards are thus chosen. As they are selected they are replaced in the pack by the person choosing, the performer turning his head away, if necessary, whilst this is being done; or they may be put back together, and the pack shuffled by the company. Simply by placing one end of the pack in the chooser's hand, whilst holding the other end himself, the performer is enabled to name the cards as before. This phase of the trick is accomplished by means of a " cut force." Glancing at the bottom card, the performer makes the pass, keeping the two packets apart by means of the little finger. The card which the performer has seen is now at the bottom of the upper half, and the pack is presented for cutting. As the four fingers are along one side of the pack, and the thumb along the other, the cut must be made lengthwise; and, as the little finger keeps the pack open at the back, it must be made there. The person cutting will notice nothing. Whilst the card is being examined, the performer glances at the fresh bottom card, and, when the upper half of the pack is returned to him, once more makes the pass, and presents the cards to another person to be cut. Four cards are quite sufficient for the effect; but, if the performer can remember others, he is quite at liberty to increase the number. The finish of the trick will depend upon the performer's ability to simulate the possession of thought-reading powers. If he has been showing any card tricks previously, with success, he may commence this one by saying, " I have an idea that many here fancy I have a method for forcing certain cards upon persons, such cards being previously known to me. Now, in order to render such a proceeding quite impossible, I will ask this gentleman to shuffle the cards thoroughly, so that I cannot know the position of any one of them, and then have the cards cut haphazard." This explains why the cut is used, and at once makes the trick appear stupendously difficult.

The " cut force " here described may be successfully employed for the purpose of reproducing cards that have been previously chosen, thought of, &c.; one of the company being made to cut the pack at the very spot where that card is situated, after shuffling, &c.

If the company appears still sceptical about the powers of mind claimed by the performer, he may give a final convincing proof. Placing the pack entirely in the hands of the company, he desires them to select two or three cards. These cards are gathered by a spectator, and given to another to hold, and afterwards placed by him in the pack. The performer then presents his hand to each chooser, and reads the cards as before. Unless the performer can execute the change with certainty, he must not attempt this method, or ruinous exposure may await him. About the first portion of the trick all is fair and above board, the company selecting the cards as they please. The performer, taking the pack in his left hand, then says, "Now, in order that I may not get a sight of the cards, will some gentleman kindly gather them in his hand?" Whilst this is being done, the performer must watch narrowly whose card is placed first, whose second, &c. Taking the three cards from the hand of the collector, the performer turns to a spectator on his left, requesting him to hold them between his hands. As he turns, he makes the change, the three chosen cards being left at the bottom, and three indifferent ones removed from the top, and given to be held. Great caution is necessary to keep the cards well covered by the upper hand, so that the performer shall not see them—his actual anxiety, of course, being lest any one else should do so. By this time he has glanced at the bottom card, and, making the single card slip pass, sees the next also, and the third soon afterwards. Affecting to see mistrust in the faces of the company, the performer says that perhaps it would, after all, be better to have the three cards in the pack. For this purpose the pack is handed to the person holding the three cards, who is directed to shuffle them with the rest. The trick then proceeds as before. If the change is properly executed, the effect of this trick is extraordinary, because the three cards have, apparently, always been in full view of everyone; and even if the performer had accidentally seen the face of the lowest one, the others have certainly never been visible to him.

A Game at Napoleon.—The performer forces five cards in succession, as quickly as he can, and remembering the whole five. Practice in the preceding trick will enable him to accomplish this, at first, rather difficult task, in public, it being simple enough to remember five cards when one has nothing else on hand at the same time. It is best to force all five cards on one person, who retains them. If forced upon different people, they must be afterwards collected in one hand. Giving the pack to another of the company, the performer asks for any five cards to be given him. This done, he tells the holder of the forced cards that he is about to play a game at "Napoleon" with him. For the sake of effect, he may allow one half of the company to see his hand, the other half looking over the hand of his opponent. In this way, universal interest is excited. Should the opponent have a poor hand, the performer may give him the choice of saying how many tricks he will declare. Should the opponent have at all good cards, however, then the performer must say, "I declare first.' What he declares will, of course, depend upon the cards; but, in nearly every case, he can go "Napoleon," one condition of the trick being, as he will explain just before playing the hand, that the opponent must play the cards as called for by the performer, who, of course, must not make his antagonist revoke. With this proviso, it is wonderful how often it is possible, even with the least promising cards, to win all five tricks; the cases in which four only are possible being very rare. A couple of sample hands will be instructive.

FIRST HAND.—The opponent's cards are:

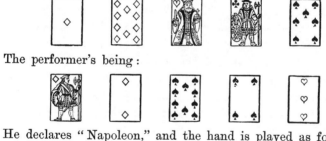

The performer's being:

He declares "Napoleon," and the hand is played as follows

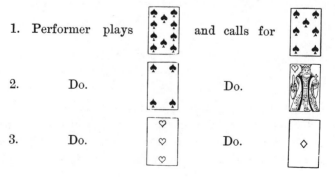

1. Performer plays   and calls for

2.   Do.   Do.

3.   Do.   Do.

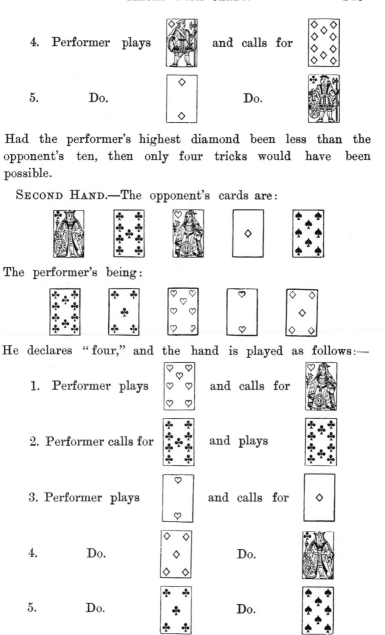

4. Performer plays   and calls for

5.   Do.   Do.

Had the performer's highest diamond been less than the opponent's ten, then only four tricks would have been possible.

SECOND HAND.—The opponent's cards are:

The performer's being:

He declares "four," and the hand is played as follows:—

1. Performer plays   and calls for

2. Performer calls for   and plays

3. Performer plays   and calls for

4.   Do.   Do.

5.   Do.   Do.

Should the opponent, by any chance, hold an overwhelmingly superior hand, such as, for instance, five high cards of one or two suits, and the performer low cards of the same suit or suits, the latter must say, as soon as he realises the state of affairs, "Ah! I see, I haven't the ghost of a chance against you with this hand; have I?" at the same time throwing down his cards, faces upwards, and demanding a fresh hand. Of course, the astonishing part of the trick to the spectators is the fact of the performer being able to call the opponent's hand, card for card, and no one cavils at the absurdity of permitting him to do so utterly regardless of the general rules of the game.

The performer can, of course, make sure of winning the whole five tricks every time, if he pre-arranges to give a poor hand to his opponent; but a great deal of the fun lies in the fact of good cards falling to insignificant ones. If the performer arranges to have five fairly good cards, three of them of one suit, with a big one at their head, on the top of the pack, it may be as well, as, when he asks for five cards, they are sure to be given him from that position ninety-nine times in a hundred. Should the five cards drawn prove, by accident, the masters of them, then, of course, shuffle the pack before asking for a hand from it. Personally, I like as little pre-arrangement as possible about the trick.

The Lightning Change.—This is an effective trick of my own, and the outcome of practice at the single-handed pass shown at Figs. 31 and 32. The performer has several cards selected haphazard. How many is not material, but four or five will be sufficient. These he has placed in the pack in the ordinary way, and brought to the bottom; an extra card, not one of those chosen, being added last of all. The order in which the cards were replaced in the pack should be noted. The performer stands sideways to the audience, with the left arm extended, the pack being held in that hand perpendicularly, and not horizontally—the faces of the cards, and not the backs, visible. The thumb should lie well across the centre of the undermost card, and the performer should ascertain by feel that he has it in his grip before continuing the trick. The card that is exposed to view is the added one, and it conceals the first card gathered in of the chosen ones, which is naturally the undermost. The chooser of this card is requested to name it, when the performer informs the company that, if they watch closely enough, they will see the one card change into the other. Anyhow, if they are unable to see it, they will infallibly hear it. As this pass cannot be made noiselessly, the latter is a very necessary remark to make. The change is not effected with the hand held stationary—no pass ever is—a rapid movement, some six inches in extent, and somewhat circular, being made towards the body and back again. It is only a fraction of a second in duration, but by the time it is completed the pass must be accomplished. Each card is made to appear in turn, the performer taking care not to attempt the pass until he feels the card well gripped by the root of the thumb; otherwise, a fiasco may easily result. The pass may also be effected whilst turning the pack face downwards and back again very rapidly, but I do not find this method quite as good as the partially circular movement towards the body, the cards sometimes flying out of the fingers in a body, which is destructive to the success of the trick, and highly disconcerting to the performer. The feat is ostensibly exhibited as one of skill, and, when properly executed, invariably affords astonishment; for, although the company are apprised of the actual moment at which the cards change, and even hear the movement, they can see nothing of what takes place.

This concludes the series of card tricks, and also the first part, Drawing-room Conjuring. I have not pretended to describe—and, indeed, the feat would be quite impossible—every trick capable of being performed with the various articles mentioned. Every conjuror who is what is popularly, if somewhat bluntly, termed "worth his salt," will find out little dodges and variations in the course of practice and exhibition; and I would advise no one who discovers a method for arriving at any given result which comes to him easier than any described by me, to follow my instructions in preference to his own ideas. This advice more particularly applies to card tricks. Conjuring, it must be borne in mind, is not like cricket, or rowing, or shooting, or anything else ; there is no *legitimate* means of arriving at anything through its medium. The wished-for result must be produced by fair means or by foul.

Many tricks included in the first portion may be successfully introduced on the stage. This is essentially the case with the more showy card tricks.

PART II.—GRAND, OR STAGE MAGIC.

CHAPTER IX.

GENERAL REMARKS.

PREPARATION—WHERE, AND TO WHOM, TO GIVE ARTICLES TO BE HELD—ON THE PUNISHMENT OF MEDDLERS—ON THE REPETITION OF TRICKS—REHEARSING—" PATTER "—ADDRESS —IMPERTINENCE AND AUDACITY—ON PLAYING THE BUFFOON.

THE learner has now arrived at that point where he will quit the humble drawing-room, understood in its ordinary sense, and essay to grander flights on the stage. It is true that this stage may, after all, consist only of the back drawing-room, the front one serving as the auditorium; but, in a conjuring sense, it is a drawing-room no longer. It is the exclusive domain of the performer, in which he will work his spells of enchantment unmolested by busybodies indulged in too close a view. In this exclusiveness consists the main difference between the two branches of conjuring. In what may be aptly termed impromptu conjuring, the performer is greatly at the mercy of his audience, who may at any moment, if so disposed, seize upon him and wring from him his secrets. He is beset with difficulties on all sides, and must exhibit a total invulnerability. In stage performances, he has matters much more his own way. To a great extent, he can control circumstances, to which he is constantly liable to fall a victim when exhibiting in a humble way. He can so arrange matters that one effect follows another in a most natural manner—a state of affairs which it is almost impossible to bring about under any other system of arrangement. So far stage conjuring possesses its advantages; but, unless the conjuror has gone through a course of training such as has been set before him in the preceding chapters, he would be quite unable to avail himself of them. The performer, with a limited amount of skill in execution, could never succeed in true legerdemain on the stage, where it is far more difficult —in most cases impossible—to cover a mistake or clumsy movement. Everything must be reduced to an absolute certainty. To ensure this, the learner must engraft on his mind the single but important word "preparation." Effective preparation is the great secret of success in stage conjuring of any magnitude: without it, things are tolerably certain to result in what is expressively termed a "bungle." The reader will discover, as I progress, what is meant by "preparation" quite speedily enough, so I will not now enlarge on what will sometimes prove a somewhat tedious operation. I once asked a well-known conjuror how he liked conjuring for its own sake. "As far as conjuring itself goes," he said, "I could perform all night; but what settles me is the everlasting preparation." I must say, that my ideas on the point are marvellously like his.

There are many axioms which belong equally to either branch of conjuring, and which it is well for the learner to bear in mind at the outset. By getting into the way of acting up to them from the first, they soon cease to be irksome, and so assist, instead of detain, when anything important is being undertaken. One important thing is to be careful to give borrowed articles to be held, when it is required to do so, in a part of the room as far removed from the owners of them as possible. This rule need not be observed when the article is not to be changed; but it is so seldom that this is the case, that the possibility of its occurring is hardly worth while considering. It can never do any harm to remove an article which is not to be changed far from its owner; but a great deal of harm may be done by substituting one article for another in such proximity to its lawful possessor that that individual is able to discover the fraud. If this care be not taken, the most perfect dexterity will be thrown away. In a large room, full of strangers, one can perpetrate the most barefaced deeds, such as giving a substituted ring, which is in every respect totally unlike the original borrowed one, to be held openly in the fingers. Neither the holder nor the owner of the ring will know that the article is not the one which was borrowed.

Where possible, always give articles, when they are not too ponderous or awkward, into the custody of members of the weaker sex. Ladies, as a rule, have much less self-possession than men during performances, and, besides, are naturally anxious (and not without some success) to do everything that is asked of them in the most graceful and effective manner possible. These causes conduce to the result which the performer so much desires, viz., an absence of that inquisitiveness which ultimately leads to a private and premature examination of the article in custody. This axiom applies only when an article is to be held passively. Under no circumstances must the performer cause a lady to rise from her seat; rather let the trick be shorn of some of its effect. When the assistance of one of the audience is required, select an intelligent-looking man, who will not be likely, from either incompetency or malice, to act exactly contrarily to your directions. Unfortunately, a large number of blockheads and malicious persons, with intelligent and winning expressions of countenance, do exist. On meeting with either individual in a dangerous shape, make him look ridiculous by giving him something big and cumbersome to hold above the head, in a conspicuous position (such as when standing on a chair), and let him remain there during the whole of the trick, or even longer, if he will put up with it, selecting someone else to render you the assistance you require. Be careful not to allow it to be palpably seen that you are hoaxing the person, or offence may be given to more than one: and conjurors must always strive to keep their audiences in the best possible humour.

Never perform a trick twice. If the performer is weak enough to give way on this point, he must expect to have the secrets of half of his tricks the common property of his audience in a very short time. Such interludes as swallowing an egg, orange, &c., and finding it at the elbow, point of the toe, or other unexpected place, one may repeat with tolerable frequency, although it is as well to vary the precise method a little each time. The reason such feats are comparatively safe to repeat is, that they come unexpectedly. If people knew that it was intended to vanish any particular article, they would keep a sharp look-out, and endeavour to discover what really became of it; but, as the performer is particularly careful not to warn his audience of what is about to be done, the movement is executed before anyone has had time to think. I wish to lay particular stress on the suicidal policy of performing the same trick twice during the same evening, as I know it is a weakness to which young beginners are much addicted.

Conjurors must never fail; that is to say, they must never allow the audience to see that they have failed in arriving at any desired result. The surest method of avoiding this is to practise and rehearse everything, down to the minutest detail, in private, so as to be able to present it in its perfect form to the audience. The beginner feels a little awkward and stupid in rehearsing at first, but when he discovers, as he soon will, the necessity for it, he will soon become used to it. The great thing is to begin well, and this is best done if two persons commence studying together, in which case one will act as a critic to the other. My plan—and I recommend everyone else to adopt it—during the first six months, was to write down everything I had to do or say, accompanied by the most minute stage directions. Each hand and foot had its proper position at a given moment. Book in hand, my fellow-student would take up his position as audience, and keep me rigidly to my stage directions, besides giving such hints as seemed to him to be necessary. At first, this kind of thing feels somewhat irksome, but the good results derived will soon make themselves manifest, and compensate for all trouble. I have frequently spent a whole evening in getting perfect in a single trick, which would perhaps be rehearsed ten or twelve times. The properties of each trick should be written on a separate card.

One thing of paramount importance is the talk to be used with each trick. At the outset, this should invariably be written out beforehand, and committed to memory, if not word for word, very nearly so. By this means, one is best able to avoid a repetition of any well-marked points, which would pall upon the audience, and cause them to fancy the performer before them to be a man of limited ideas. At the same time, great care must be taken to avoid making anything approaching a speech, which is even worse than saying nothing at all. People come to conjuring entertainments expecting to see sleight of hand performed, and not to listen to speeches, however beautiful they may be in themselves. What is wanted is something to accompany the trick, just as a pianoforte-player accompanies a singer. If this simile be borne in mind, the learner will not go far wrong. The only occasions on which nothing should be said are when some feats of dexterity—corresponding to the runs and scales of the expert vocalist—are being performed: a verbal accompaniment would only spoil them. On the other hand, a very poor trick can be made a good deal of by the introduction of a few lively sallies, mingled with allusions to topics of the day, which will be made to appear to bear upon the matter in hand. I shall give but very few examples in my descriptions of tricks, for I think that a conjuror should be, before everything else, original; and this he would not be if he only repeated what other people had to say. I hope the reader is impressed with the absolute necessity of being as well up in "patter" as in sleight of hand.

Address in execution is another thing which cannot be too attentively studied. It is not enough that an orange is successfully vanished; the operation should be performed with all possible grace. This will naturally be impossible if the performer is not well up in his trick; but this he must not fail to be. The learner must study to acquire a manner that is neither hurried nor slow. Some tricks it is necessary to do with extra dash and rapidity; but the extra speed will never require to be sustained. As a general rule, audiences prefer a suave and easy style — one which appears free from the slightest exertion. Being in a hurry is the way to forget many little but telling points; whilst being too slow is the way to weary the audience. The worst possible style to adopt is that which impresses the audience with the idea that conjuring is nothing but a mere cheat—a swindle—from beginning to end. This impression is given when the performer wishes to appear extra sharp, and endeavours (to use a common idiom) to thrust everything down people's throats, whether they will or not. Always endeavour to impress spectators that they are being deceived by skilful manipulation, and not "bamboozled" by talk.

Be careful not to substitute impertinence for impudence. Too many beginners err in this respect. They mistake the precise nature of the impudence required by the conjuror. A better name for it would be audacity. To be successful out of the ordinary way, the conjuror must be audacious and venturesome now and again, although it is as well not to tempt Fortune too much or too often: the jade may fail at an awkward pinch. The warning not to play with edged tools should be taken to heart by the conjuror.

On no account play the buffoon, as I have seen conjurors do before now. When a laugh is raised, it should be with, and not at, the performer. Also, on raising a laugh at anyone's expense, let it be done in a polite and inoffensive manner, unless, of course, it be a punishment for previous misbehaviour.

CHAPTER X.

———

THE TABLE AND DRESS.

OF very important assistance in Grand Conjuring are the
specially prepared tables, of which one, two, or three will
be used, according to the size of the room. These tables
differ from ordinary ones, in the first place, by being considerably higher, their height being from 2ft. 10in. to 3ft.
This is to render it unnecessary for the performer to stoop
when taking anything from or placing anything upon the
table, as the action would take away a great deal from an
effective execution of many things. The next important
difference (unknown, however, to the audience) is that the
body of the table is a hollow box, of which that side which
is unseen by the spectators is perfectly open, and is furthermore provided with a protruding shelf, technically called the
servante. This shelf is one of the conjuror's most invaluable
assistants. It is always at hand to receive any article which
it is desirable to get rid of, and is a patient holder of others
which it may be required, at a particular moment, to produce

from an invisible source, but which are too large to be concealed about the person. This shelf should be about 5in. or 6in. broad, and should have the ends either rounded or cut off obliquely. If this is not done, the shelf will be noticed by persons standing or seated at the extreme sides of the auditorium. The edge should be furnished with a small raised beading, to prevent articles from falling off. The depth of the body of the table should not exceed 6in., or it will excite suspicion and remark. If the shelf is fitted to the body of the table by means of hinges, it will be found a great convenience. It will never become mislaid or knocked about, and so be either missing or useless when most required; and it also enables one to use the body of the table as a means for conveying the bulk of the conjuring apparatus. The legs should be made to screw on and off, so as to increase the portability of the whole; but see that the worm of the screw is long and deep, or the table will be unsteady.

But, if the back of the table is mysterious, the top of it is still more so. For the speedy, easy, and complete vanishing of objects, particularly solids, it has been found convenient to fit the tops of tables with spring traps, which, yielding to certain pressure, resume their position when it is removed. Judiciously used, these traps are very useful, and the results attained by their use are most bewildering. In a table 36in. by 18in. (a very convenient size) there should be a round trap, 3½in. to 4in. in diameter, in each front corner, and an oblong trap, 9in. by 5in., in the centre. These traps are made of zinc; but I would recommend no one to attempt manufacturing them at home whilst they can be purchased so reasonably at conjuring trick repositories. I would certainly recommend having the table itself made, under personal supervision, by a carpenter, who will let the traps into the top of the table. The ordinary price for a 4in. trap is about 7s. 6d. There are many elaborate mechanical traps devised for changing articles, but I have never found them of much assistance in

the hands of amateurs, so cannot conscientiously recommend
them.   There are also several methods for arranging piston
rods, which work up and down by means of a string drawn
by a confederate at the side or rear, or by electricity.   But
such assistance is so seldom required by the amateur conjuror,
that I cannot recommend him to encumber his table with
more than three traps.   Everything beyond this he will find
an unnecessary expense.   The amateur will also find that his
sphere will be continually changed, one day performing at
this friend's house and the next day at another's.   Hence he
will be unable to produce the results which are attainable
only by those who, like professional conjurors, have sole
dominion over their stage and its surroundings at all times.
As these chapters are written solely for the edification of
amateurs, and not for the purpose of training up professionals,
I shall not launch out into descriptions of things impossible
to the great majority.

   When the size of the room permits of it, the performer
should have, besides his oblong table in the centre, one or
two small round tables at the sides.   These tables should be
of the same height as the large one, but only about 18in. in
diameter.   They should be provided with one round trap
and a small *servante*.   The border should have a deep fringe.
The tops of all three tables should be covered with a check
pattern, in order to hide the lines of the traps.   On a perfectly
plain surface these might be noticed.   Do not forget to provide
the smaller traps with bags to receive the articles passed
through.   An egg would make an unseemly mess inside the
table, whilst an orange or a lemon would descend with a thud
sufficiently loud to reveal to the audience what had taken
place.   The centre trap, being used almost exclusively for
vanishing live stock, need not be furnished with a bag.

   Whilst on the subject of traps, I will describe the method
for passing articles through them.   Supposing an orange has
to be made to disappear.   After showing that it is a real
orange and perfectly solid, &c., place it upon the trap, the

spring of which must, of course, be strong enough to bear the weight without giving in the least. Turn up your sleeves very deliberately, and then place the hands around the orange as if about to take it up in them. Screened by the front hand, the rear one presses the trap down quickly, and the orange falls through, the hands being brought together as though holding it. Advance towards the audience a step or two and commence rubbing the hands together, gradually making the circumference of the hollow smaller and smaller until the orange appears to have been rubbed away. The action of vanishing the article must be assiduously practised, for the hands must not dwell perceptibly on the table, but appear to actually take up whatever they are supposed to. When pretending to rub it away, the eyes must be directed attentively to the hands as if interested in the experiment. When passing one article into another, as an egg into a lemon, place the lemon just in front of the trap, and, holding the egg in the rear hand, pass it down the trap under cover of the front hand, which will at the moment be just closing upon the lemon. The two hands then take the lemon, and, after rubbing it about a little, show it *minus* the egg, which you will say is inside. In the drawing-room, without the table, the same results would have to be arrived at by means of "vesting." The present instance affords an excellent illustration of my remark that drawing-room conjuring is more difficult than grand conjuring.

Another method for vanishing articles through traps is to fix a cord to the under side of the trap, and, by means of a tiny pulley and staples, bring it to a hole in the end of the table, on the outside of which a knot is tied. The article can be then placed upon the trap and covered with a hat, &c., and made to disappear by pulling the cord. It is better to have the cord belonging to the right-hand trap coming out at the left-hand side, and *vice-versâ*; otherwise the audience would be likely to notice the action of the hand pulling the cord, from its close proximity to the hat. By standing at that end of the table which is opposite to the hat, the performer can turn sideways, and point with his wand to the hat or tap it, when the action of pulling the string will be concealed by his body. In covering any article with a hat, be careful that the front or back part of it is towards the audience. The arch formed by the side brim of the hat of the present day enables one to see anything placed underneath it, and it must be admitted that it would be rather awkward if any of the audience saw the article suddenly drop into the body of the table. The uses of the large trap will be dilated upon at another time and place.

The uses of the *servante* being to hold things as occasion requires, they will make themselves manifest in due course.

Dress.—The conjuror's dress will command a great deal of consideration, the disposition and capacity of the pockets being of considerable importance. I will first take the coat, which will, of course, be a dress one. The whole of the inside of each breast of this should be one huge pocket, the opening of which is perpendicular instead of horizontal, and about two inches from the edges, so as to just escape observation. This enables large objects to be concealed, and yet easily got at. The tail pockets are not used in performing, so can be either entirely absent or else made in the usual way. One tail, however, should have a large pocket about five inches deep at the bottom, and right across its width. This pocket should be made very loose so as to be always open to a slight extent, for it will often have articles dropped into it at all sorts of odd times. Some conjurors have copper wire in the edge to keep it open when required.

The vest is extremely important. It should be split right up the back and then re-joined by three bands of broad elastic. This is to enable one to put large articles in the breast without causing any unusual wrinkles or bulging. For vesting purposes, some have a strip of thin leather, about two inches broad, sewn round the bottom, inside, but I do not find this sufficiently safe. I usually have some fine elastic run in the hem by means of a bodkin. It should be tight enough to hold an egg (a heavy, slippery thing, and awkward when dropped) securely; but it must not pull the vest out of shape. The only extra pockets required in the trousers are one at each hip, covered by the tails of the coat. They should be about three inches long by one and a half in depth, and constructed so as to be always partly open. They are very handy for receiving such articles as coins, little balls, rings, pocket-knives, &c., which it is desirable that the audience should not see. Little pockets, of a similar nature, are sometimes used behind the lappel of the coat; but those in the trousers are far superior, as they are got at by the perfectly natural action of dropping the arm. The inside turn-up of the sleeve of the coat I have also seen similarly employed, but have not noticed any particular advantage to be derived therefrom.

Starting now with his prepared tables and mysterious suit, and armed with a fair amount of manipulative skill, the learner ought to be able to bid defiance to the world, and to boldly attempt anything within his particular scope or province that he has seen anyone else do.

Before commencing, always say a few words, to the effect that you are there to conjure, and not to make speeches; so you will not detain the audience with a history of conjuring from the year 1, but proceed to show them what can be done in the present year. In family circles, more talking should be done than in public places, where an impressive style should be cultivated.

Introductory Tricks.—Besides, by means of the few words the performer addresses the company before commencing, it is quite in order that he should introduce himself to the spectators magically; that is to say, give them at once some little evidence of his skill, without any formality of explanation. A well-used trick for this purpose is that of causing a flower to appear instantaneously at the button-hole. Just as the performer is about to step forward, he perceives that he has forgotten his flower, but explains that the omission is very soon rectified, as he notices a bouquet in the hands of a lady, or some flowers in a coiffure, or about a costume. Asking permission, and taking it at once, the wand is waved in the direction of the visible flowers, and the button-hole then touched with it, when instantly a flower appears. The flower is an imitation one, and is attached to a piece of elastic, which passes through the button-hole, and inside through the one next below, so that it may be fastened to a vest button, or elsewhere. When the performer comes on, the flower is concealed under the left armpit; so that, when the button-hole is touched with the wand, all that is necessary is to raise the arm slightly, when the flower, being released, flies instantly into position.

Another common, but very effective, practice is to come on the stage with the gloves on. As they are taken off the hands, they melt away, apparently, for nothing more is ever seen of them. Elastic is again at the bottom of this, one end passing round the wrist of the glove, whilst the other is fastened round the biceps of the arm, or attached to the brace. The glove is removed, care being taken not to let it slip too soon, and, when held between the two palms, is allowed to go, when it flies, unperceived, up the sleeve. The performer must not dwell at all upon the fact that he is doing anything magical, but act as though his gloves were merely performing their usual evolutions on being taken off for the day.

CHAPTER XI.

SLEIGHTS AND PROPERTIES FOR GENERAL USE.

HOW TO PRODUCE ARTICLES FROM THE WAND—ARTICLES PRODUCED FROM THE PERSONS OF THE COMPANY—VANISHING OBJECTS FROM THE HANDS—EXCHANGING ARTICLES—MESMERISING A DOVE—MARKING A CARD IN COURSE OF PERFORMING—PASSING HANDKERCHIEF OVER FLAME OF CANDLE—THE CONJUROR'S SHUFFLE—THE DEVIL'S HANDKERCHIEF — COIN HANDKERCHIEF — FLYING RING — MAGICIAN'S EGGS — PRODUCTIVE EGGS — COIN-VANISHING TUMBLER—MAGIC PLATEAU.

Sleights.—Often, in the description of a trick, the learner is told that a handkerchief, coin, egg, orange, or other article has to be made to disappear or appear by sleight of hand. In the descriptions here given, my own methods naturally appear in preponderance over those of others; but it is a mistake for conjurors to confine themselves arbitrarily to any such, whosesoever they be, or whatever their nature. The peculiar means for magically vanishing or producing an article which has seemed to me to be most convenient under the conditions governing the particular trick under notice, I have always laid the most stress upon; but it is very likely that, were half a dozen experts to write upon the same tricks, they would each vary more or less in the precise means by which the same results were arrived at. This is only as it should be, the success of a conjuror, like that of an actor, depending, in a very great measure, upon his originality or individuality. The reader will notice that I frequently describe a trick, and then give one or more alternative ways of doing it, the last-named being usually methods I have seen adopted with success by other conjurors. In order to save endless repetition, I give here a few sleights which the learner should be incessantly practising, just as he would the pass or the palm. Some of the feats actually form small tricks in themselves, but are only introduced by the performer as suddenly inspired interpolations in the course of a trick, of which they may, as a fact, really form part. For the disappearance of a coin or coins, the various palms provide; the method described in connection with the cups and balls (page 55) suffices for the evanishment of marbles, nuts, and articles of that size; whilst the palming of cards has been specially treated. The other sleights which I have found most necessary are as follows:

To Produce an Egg, Orange, &c., from the Wand.—This daring feat is certainly one of the most wonder-inspiring description. The performer says, " I now require, for my trick, an egg. I presume none of the company happen to have such an article about them; and, as I have forgotten to provide it myself, I must make an appeal to my wand, which rarely fails me in such cases." Standing sideways to the audience, the performer holds his wand in the fingers, at arm's length, and then, suddenly running his hand along it, upwards, as though squeezing it, he produces, from the very top, the egg. As his sleeves are turned well up, and nothing has been visible in either hand, the mysterious appearance of the required article is quite inexplicable. It is thus managed. The egg may be either upon the shelf at the back of the table, or under the vest band. I prefer the latter place of concealment, because the performer is better able to carelessly show his hands quite empty just previous to the production of the article; whilst a longer time must elapse between the secretion of the article in the hand and the moment of its appearance on the top of the wand, if it be placed upon the shelf. Apart from this, going behind the table should always be avoided where possible. It is the easiest thing in the world to get down the article from the vest in the act of turning round. It should find its way at once to the very centre of the hand, the root of the thumb gripping it, and the fingers should either seize the coat flap, or the wand should be put into it. The *modus operandi* may be simply described as follows: The wand is lying upon the table and the performer comes forward, showing, by rubbing them together in the act of speaking, that his hands are empty. When he has uttered the words "in such cases," he wheels round *to the left*, for the purpose of fetching the wand from the table, and when his back is fairly towards the audience, he gets down the egg in the right hand, which then seizes the coat flap. A very important matter must here be observed. The article vested must always be placed on that side of the body which is opposite to the hand that is to bring it down. If, in the present instance, the egg were upon the right side of the performer's body, taking his vest buttons as a central line, the act of getting it into the right hand could not be achieved without sticking out the elbow, which would at once reveal to the company that the performer was carrying out some manœuvre with that hand, and, when he turned round, they would immediately fix their eyes upon it, and keep them there, to the serious detraction of the proceedings following. The golden rule must be followed of glueing, as it were, the upper arm and elbow to the side. Then the forearm and hand may do as they please, with impunity. The getting down of an article from the vest need occupy only a half-second of time, so the performer turns briskly to the table, his every visible action and look being, of course, concentrated upon the matter in hand—the fetching the wand from the table. With the right hand, containing the egg, holding the coat flap lightly and naturally, the wand is picked off the table with the left, the performer's right side being towards the company. Holding the wand for a few moments in the left hand, and looking at it amusingly, as though wondering quite as much as the company how it is going to accomplish its task, the right hand is brought boldly to the front, and the wand placed in the fingers. The back of the hand is, of course, towards the company. The fact of its containing a bulky article will naturally cause it to be somewhat curved, so it is necessary to cause it to look as flat as possible. This is best managed by straightening the fingers and bending the wrist outwards, the whole length of the fingers being thus presented to the view of the company. It will be found that the wand, pressing against the article in the hand, assists towards keeping it in its place there. In the case of an egg, care must be taken not to put on too much pressure. The wand must be held by its middle portion, and should not remain in the right hand for more than a couple of seconds, at the outside. It is then re-taken by the left hand, but by the lower end, the right hand simultaneously making the upward "squeeze;" the article being produced at the tips of the fingers, when they reach the top of the wand, it being allowed to drop from the palm into the bent fingers just previously. The illusion is complete when the sleight is performed with neatness and dash, the article appearing to actually come out of the wand, although everyone knows how impossible it is for it ever to have been there. An article so mysteriously produced should, by all means, be given for examination. It is surprising what very large-sized oranges can be produced by this means, when the performer has once acquired sufficient boldness. Audacity is the chief ingredient in the sleight, and the learner will acquire it by beginning with small-sized articles. Brilliantly-coloured articles, such as oranges, or perfectly white ones, as eggs, make the best appearance.

To Produce Articles from the Persons of the Company.—Here audacity plays a very important part indeed, as the performer goes in amongst the spectators and finds such oranges, eggs, lemons, &c., as he may want, in their hair and apparel. In the *Gant de Paris* (page 228), I have seen a performer use an orange, a lemon, an egg, and a walnut, all of which he has found upon the company within a very few seconds of time. A description of how this is done will suffice as a guide to the learner how to proceed in all similar cases. The walnut should be palmed, and the lemon held in the same hand, the other hand holding the orange, both hands of course seizing the coat. The egg is vested. Coming on to the stage from behind, the performer proceeds rapidly into the very midst of the company, and says, " Can any one lend me a kid glove for a few minutes ?" then, turning suddenly towards a male spectator—with long hair, if such a one be handy—" I beg your pardon, sir, but I see a something in your hair; what is it ?" Whilst this is being said, a rapid dash is made at the addressee's hair, the orange being slid to the ends of the fingers, and produced with all slowness. It is given a second spectator to examine, who is discovered to have a lemon in his hair, or inside his coat. Whilst the lemon is being produced, and all eyes are intent upon it, the empty hand gets down the egg. This is found in the hair of a third person, whilst the walnut is discovered on the tip of the nose of a fourth. When the performer afterwards collects all four articles into his hands, it will never occur to the company that so much bulk could have been deliberately palmed by him in their very midst. As a matter of fact, it is easier to do these sort of things in the midst of a numerous and rather closely-packed company, than in the presence of a meagre and widespread one, and the performer should always go where the spectators are thickest.

How to Cause Large-sized Objects to Appear to Vanish from the Hands.—By large objects are meant eggs, oranges, ladies' handkerchiefs, gloves, small birds, &c. The sleight-of-hand conjuror should embrace every opportunity for a display of his skill, handkerchiefs being swallowed and reproduced elsewhere, and other articles thrown away or made to pass imperceptibly from out of the hand into thin air, nothing being left of them when the hand is opened. In order to bring about these things, all that the conjuror has to do is to adapt, to the altered circumstance of having larger articles to deal with, what he has been taught in connection with the palming and passing of coins. Take, first, the apparent placing of an article in the mouth, and swallowing it. The method adopted will vary, according to the size of the article. If it be a comparatively small one, such as a walnut, then the action depicted at Fig. 7 must be followed, the article being palmed in the right hand, the back of which must necessarily be turned towards the audience more than is shown in the sketch, by reason of the more bulky nature of its contents, and the fingers of the left hand rounded in a way suggestive of containing the article supposed to be put into them. The right hand then takes the wand, which, in these cases, must *always* be carried under the right armpit. Should the article not be swallowed, the wand strikes the closed fingers of the left hand, which are simultaneously opened and shown to be empty. The success attending this method will depend solely and entirely upon the neatness with which the palm is executed, and the article apparently placed in the left hand. It must not be ostensibly thrown there, as is the case with a coin, but deliberately put in, the fingers of the right hand, after the execution of the palm, forming as though they actually held the article, those of the left hand closing around them, as if taking it firmly in charge. It is always as well to actually place the article in the left hand at least once, thereby silently impressing the company with what is to be done with it. The palming of a walnut is quite as easy as that of a coin, and the pass must be regarded as a very simple one to learn.

Eggs, oranges, lemons, and solid articles of that size, must be treated according to the action shown at Figs. 8 and 9, facility in executing which will render the accomplishment of what is now described very easy. As the article is not a coin, it must not be held between finger and thumb, but made to rest upon the very tips of the fingers of the left hand, which is held perpendicularly for the purpose. It is thus very conspicuously in sight of everyone. It is allowed to rest there for a few seconds, when the right hand is rought suddenly in front of it, and the action gone through of taking it. At this instant, the orange (say) falls into the hollow of the left hand, which is immediately dropped to grasp the coat flap, whilst the right hand apparently puts the orange into the mouth, a muffled noise being made indicative of the mouth being full. Before the hand is removed, the mouth is closed, when it is as well to bulge one of the cheeks out with the tongue, and then make three or four desperate attempts (ultimately successful) at swallowing, accompanied by choking sounds. A smile should then illumine the face of the performer, who appears to have enjoyed the operation, and the orange, if it is wanted again, may be produced at the right elbow, or brought round from the back of the neck, rolled along by the tips of the fingers. A very effective sleight with which to quickly follow the foregoing is as follows: Place the wand under the left armpit, and hold the orange in the fingers of the left hand, as above described. Open the legs slightly, and then apparently take the orange in the right hand and smash it into the right leg, just above the knee. The orange must be apparently vigorously snatched out of the left· hand, which at once mechanically finds its way to the wand, that article being grasped by the thumb only, the fingers and palm concealing the orange. The performer allows a second to elapse, and then, briskly taking the wand in the right hand, rolls the orange from behind his left thigh to the front. It does not in the least signify what the company fancy actually happened with the orange, so long as they are not allowed to suspect that it never left the left hand. Obliged to account for the phenomenon, the theories formed will be various, the majority polling for a tubular communication between sleeve and sleeve, *via* the performer's back. As the orange is apparently smashed into the leg, the performer will find it necessary to stoop slightly. This sleight should follow the preceding one before the spectators have begun to recover from their wonderment at seeing the orange apparently swallowed and then reproduced. A cigar, or article of the like shape, can be similarly treated if it be held in the left hand between the tips of the middle finger and thumb, the broad end being against the thumb. As the right hand covers it, in the act of apparently taking it, the broad end is allowed to fall against the root of the thumb, and the hand turned slightly over and then allowed to hang down at the side. A very little pressure on the part of the middle finger will suffice to keep the cigar in position. The right hand must conform itself as closely as possible to the shape it would assume if it actually contained a cigar. This sleight will come in handy in conjuring at table.

A more complete method of vanishing is as follows: Take the article in the right hand, and hold the waistband of the vest by the left. Toss the orange, &c., twice or thrice in the air, and then whip it swiftly beneath the vest, which will be partly raised by the left hand. The two hands thus brought together should be closed one over the other, as if they contained something, which something you will then proceed to gradually rub away. As you have nothing whatever in the hands, you will be able to execute this portion of the deception with great confidence and ease. When you slip any article beneath the vest, the body should be partially turned from the audience. Quickly done, the movement will never be noticed, and it is one of the most perfect deceptions practised. The vest is never thought of by an audience as being a place for the concealment of articles, and so it escapes notice, and everyone wonders where the vanished article can have gone to. The vest is also an excellent place in which to carry such things as eggs, lemons, &c., which may be required during any trick.

To Change an Article.—This is executed very much after the manner of the preceding, with this exception : the left hand contains the article concealed, which is to be exchanged for whatever is held in the right. Say, for example, that the right hand holds an orange, which the audience, of course, examines. The left hand conceals, say, an apple. The orange is vested in the orthodox manner, and the hands brought together as directed, but this time they contain the apple. Rub them a little, and exhibit the apple, which can be brought back to its original shape—an orange—if the performer pleases. On no account must the conjuror inform the audience what he is about to do, or he may find the ideas of the spectators anticipate his actions, which is, to say the least, awkward. These actions of vanishing or exchanging can be done when one is actually surrounded by people; but the hands must be quick and must appear natural : for instance, when supposed to contain an orange they must not be compressed so as to barely leave space within them for a walnut. Nothing but careful practice will ensure a satisfactory result, for the least bungling will lead to detection. I need hardly say that it enhances one's reputation greatly if one can be said to have "changed a real orange into a real apple under our very eyes" without the aid of any gaudy boxes or canisters. By all means allow the orange to be squeezed and the apple to be eaten.

To Vanish Handkerchiefs.—Not being solid bodies, hand-kerchiefs will require different treatment, and present the greatest difficulties, which are fully compensated for by the superior effects produced. In the first place, the performer must be careful to borrow a lady's small handkerchief, if for the purpose of vanishing. In performing *The Knots* (page 218) a small handkerchief is generally included amongst those borrowed. It is not used for the trick; but the performer says he is very fond of such handkerchiefs, and forthwith rolls it up in his hands, pops it into his mouth, and swallows it. Whilst the company are wondering, he suddenly pulls the handkerchief out of his leg. This is a most wonderful sleight, and one the conjuror must endeavour to become perfect in. He should begin with a small piece of muslin, which rolls up very tight and easily. This he takes between the two hands, the left hand below, with its back turned somewhat towards the company, and rolls it sharply round and round, until he feels that it is well balled. Then, with the right hand, he apparently takes it up, the left hand really retaining it by means of the thumb, and grasping the coat-flap, as in other cases, or the wand under left armpit. The right hand apparently conveys the handkerchief to the mouth, where the choking and swallowing performance is gone through. After a pause of a couple of seconds, the conjuror looks curiously down at his leg, and, pouncing at a spot in the rear of the thigh, just above the knee - joint, presses the handkerchief there, to enable the fingers to obtain a hold of a very small portion of it. It is then at once jerked forcibly away, when it will appear to the spectators precisely as though it had been pulled out through the cloth. The different movements must all follow one another with regularity and swiftness, and yet the performer must not appear to be hurrying himself in the least. If the handkerchief experimented upon be large, some risk is run of a portion appearing from the left hand. Even with small handkerchiefs this will, at times, occur; but if the performer carries out the movements of the right hand properly, the eyes of the company will be directed solely to that.

The same sleight is employed in feigning to throw back a handkerchief to its owner, the action of throwing being employed instead of affecting to place the article in the mouth. In this case, it is as well to pivot round at once, vesting the handkerchief in so doing, and then at once inquiring, with empty hands, if the handkerchief arrived at its destination all right. It may be afterwards produced from the interior of a spectator's coat, by being whipped quickly in and then produced very slowly and at extended length. If this reproduction is to follow quickly, then do not vest, which is only done for the purpose of showing the hands empty. If the performer pleases, he may plunge his hand into his breast, and produce the handkerchief; but it will cause less wonderment, and no amusement at all.

Small birds present considerable difficulty, the object being to conjure with the bird without injuring it. A bird cannot be palmed, like a walnut, nor can it be rolled up, like a handkerchief. But, strange to say, the very difficulty of the feat assists the performer. In the first place, the company never suspect that the bird is about to be made to disappear, unless the performer is weak enough to forewarn them; and, secondly, never having experimented, they do not suppose for an instant that the bird will be simply retained in the hand all the time, as it really is. All the conjuror has to do is to hold the bird in the right hand, outside the wings, and head downwards, the tail pointing up the wrist, and then affect to put it in the left hand, which is bulged so as to appear to hold it. The wand must be under the right armpit, and the right hand seizes it at once, the left hand being struck and opened, showing the bird to be flown. The sooner the bird is reproduced the better. The most unlikely, and therefore the best, place to produce it from is the bottom of the trouser—a lively course of speculation as to how it got there being thrown open to the company. If it be desired to get rid of the bird altogether, the performer must pivot round and vest. There is not much chance of the bird moving in that position, but, of course, it will be better for the performer to make an early exit, and relieve himself of the encumbrance.

Doves are made to disappear by means of the shelf at the back of the table, or the pocket directed to be made at the bottom of the coat-tail. The shelf vanish is more open to suspicion, but I have, nevertheless, found it enormously successful, when-properly managed. The performer, in the first instance, must not announce, by word or deed, that the disappearance is about to take place. Standing to the left (*his* left, facing the audience) of the table, and slightly to the rear of it, he takes the dove in the right hand. Walking briskly past the table, at the back, he casts his eyes upwards, and just as he reaches the extreme corner of the table, makes a movement of tossing the bird into the air. It is, instead, placed gently (not dropped, or thrown) upon the end of the shelf, the brisk pace of the performer carrying him at once a good yard beyond the table, from which spot the dove is apparently cast into the air. The success of the sleight depends very much upon the exactness with which the performer imitates the actual throwing of a bird into the air, and the fearlessness with which it is conducted. Any symptom of a glance at the shelf would be fatal. The bearings must be taken whilst stationary, and the rest carried out with the eyes fixed earnestly on the ceiling. Rabbits and guinea pigs may be similarly treated; but large-sized rabbits are unsuited, since it is not easy to place them upon the shelf. When the pocket is used, supposing it to be in the right coat-tail, as it probably would be, the performer should stand with that side away from the audience, and ascertain, by means of the right hand, if the mouth of the pocket be open. Lean slightly over to the right, and then, taking the dove in the right hand, make a movement of casting it into the air, straight upwards, whither the eyes are directed. It is, of course, left in the pocket, head downwards. An attempt to place it there tail first would be likely to lead to disaster. As this sleight may be performed away from any table or chair, it is, of course, to be preferred. It is, undoubtedly, more difficult of accomplishment than the shelf vanish, requiring more neatness in depositing the bird; for, if the downward sweep be too vigorous, it will have the effect of disturbing the coat-tail, which will be momentarily seen, pushed out behind the performer, by the company, and the place of concealment thereby betrayed. It need hardly be pointed out that, in either case, the hand must grasp the bird firmly by the body, clasping the wings tightly down. If it be felt struggling in the pocket, the performer should bow himself off at once.

Mesmerising a Dove.—The apparent mesmerising of a dove makes, of itself, a capital effect, leading the audience to pay high respect to the necromantic powers of the conjuror. Also, it makes an admirable introduction to the vanish. The bird is taken in the right hand, outside the wings, and laid upon its back on the front edge of the table, so that the head just projects over. The beak is now taken in the left hand and the head turned backwards, as far as it will go. When held in that position for a few moments, the hands may be removed, when the bird will lie perfectly still. It will not always do this at the first, or even the second, attempt, but perseverance will always be rewarded with success. The performer must be as gentle as possible, and go slowly to work. We need not stay to discuss the reason for the singular phenomenon, it being sufficient for our purpose to know that the bird will lie still when placed in the proper position. The performer waves his hands over the bird, as though mesmerising it, and then he may take one of the feet in his fingers and actually raise the bird, by one of its legs, completely off the table. This will require the greatest delicacy and patience to accomplish, operations being discontinued the instant the bird shows any signs of fluttering. Anything approaching a jerk will rouse the bird, so the lift must be made as gradual and as imperceptible as possible. The reader will, doubtless, be able to appreciate the sensation that will be caused when, the mesmerising accomplished, the bird immediately afterwards vanishes from sight, no one knows whither.

To Exchange Borrowed Rings for Dummies.—With a single ring, and in a small way, this may be done by means of the finger palm (Fig. 3), the dummy being already held in the left hand, between the roots of the fingers, and a feint made of placing the borrowed one into it. (See " Tricks with Coins," *b*, p. 11). This does very well for the drawing-room, in which domain the following method may also be adopted when two or more rings are borrowed. Have the dummies screwed up in a piece of paper, which hold in the left hand, and cover with a precisely similar piece of paper, open. Into this latter place the borrowed rings, and screw up. All that is now necessary is to reverse the positions of the two parcels, the left hand carrying away the borrowed rings, the right taking the dummy ones, the paper containing which is, of course, not opened again during the trick. The same method should be adopted with large audiences when a borrowed watch and chain have to be exchanged; but the following method is far away the best to adopt on the stage with rings.

For the purpose of collecting rings borrowed from the audience, the conjuror should provide himself with an ebony wand, rather thicker than an ordinary penholder, and about eight inches in length. If he be performing with an assistant, that person should do the collecting. Upon the wand are already placed the dummies, covered by the hand holding it by one of its ends. The wand is presented the persons lending the rings, who slide them on. The performer remains well up the stage, and, the assistant, turning towards him, changes the wand from one hand to the other, securing the borrowed rings under the latter, and spreading the dummies along the wand. This can be quickly effected, and the assistant at once turns round facing the company, presenting the wand, with dummy rings, to the performer, who takes it; the borrowed rings remaining in the assistant's hand, dropped at once to his side. The performer at once draws attention to himself, and the assistant makes off with the rings for whatever purpose may have been previously arranged. An assistant must be something of a conjuror to possess the necessary *sang froid* for effecting the exchange without drawing attention to his movements, so the performer may have to execute it himself, in which case he would place the dummy rings in some conspicuous position, and pass behind the scenes momentarily on the strength of some plea, which would suggest itself according to the trick in course of performance.

How to Show the Hands Empty whilst still containing Coins.— In many tricks with money ("Hold them Tight!" for instance) it may be advisable, or even compulsory, by reason of the doubt of a spectator, to show that the coins are not in the hand, whilst they really are so. With a single coin to manage, the reverse palm will suffice. When two or more are in the hand the coins must be slid inside the doubled up fingers which hold the wand, placed across the hand. The really empty hand is opened, and the one containing the coins also, as far as the performer dare. Now, if he held the fingers doubled up without the wand in the hand, the spectators would know where the coins were; but, seeing the wand, the partial closing of the hand seems natural enough. Of course the hands are boldly thrust out, the performer saying the while, "It is pretty plain that I haven't the coins, for here are my two hands both wide open. Now sir, what have you done with them?" &c. Unblushing audacity is again the order of the day. A capital effect is made if, after showing the hands apparently empty, the coins are abstracted from the hair or beard of a spectator. One never knows when such a sleight may be wanted. When it is, it is as well to know what to do, so as to prevent exposure.

To Mark a Card, in the Course of Performing, so as to be able to Recognise it again.—This is a very useful little dodge, as by its means the machinations of the obnoxious person in this book denominated Mr. Interference may be defeated. It is only requisite when it becomes absolutely necessary to convince the company that you do not know the position of the card in the pack. It is necessary to get at least a portion of the card in the hand, when, from the upper side, an indentation is made in the card with the thumb nail, one of the fingers, on the under side, performing the office of pressure pad. The card need not be removed from the hand of the chooser, the performer merely touching it momentarily whilst explaining what he wishes done. It is as well to make the mark near the centre of the card, as then it is more easily found. After it has been made, the pack may be given the company, the card placed in it, and the whole well shuffled by anyone. The card will at once be recognised by the slight projection that has been made on the under side. Should a repetition of the ruse become necessary, the performer must either leave the card originally marked out of the pack, or else make two marks on the next; but it is better to leave the first one out. As the whole of the pack is not used—at least, not under my instructions—some spare cards are always lying unused upon the table. This spare heap is always exceedingly useful, as cards such as the one under notice may be placed in it, whilst others, which may be presently wanted, can lie upon the top, ready at hand.

To Pass a Handkerchief over the Flame of a Candle without Burning it.—This is a remarkable effect, which only requires confidence to ensure its successful execution. The performer has a lighted candle standing upon the table, and when in possession of a borrowed handkerchief for a trick, he introduces the sleight as an interlude. Grasping the handkerchief by one corner, in such a way as to spread it somewhat with the fingers, he holds it in front of the candle, and then draws it upwards and backwards, right over the flame, almost extinguishing the latter in so doing. The handkerchief should be an ordinary white one, and the flame will be seen by the spectators to be eating into it, apparently. There is not the least necessity to be in any hurry, the action of drawing the handkerchief over the flame being a steady and deliberate one. It may be repeated as often as the performer chooses, but not made anything of by him, the impression to be conveyed being that the power of placing a handkerchief in the flame of a candle without injuring it is one necessarily possessed by him, as a matter of course. This sleight will come in particularly *à propos* if it precedes a trick in which a handkerchief is burned. It is not advisable to try the feat with a scented handkerchief, it being just possible that the spirit contained in the perfume might ignite.

The Conjuror's " Shuffle."—Nearly all good conjurors preface their card tricks with an exhibition of shuffling, a process always conducted in the showiest manner possible, although, by the time it is completed, it is possible that the position of the cards has not been interfered with in the least. As the term " shuffling " is only employed for want of a better one, and it is merely a question of exhibiting skill, this does not signify. When a conjuror wishes to shuffle the cards, he adopts the specious method generally in use—if he can. According to whether he be a genuine adept, or only a performer of an inferior order, so will the phenomena exhibited to the spectator in this connection vary. In the one case, the performer, holding the cards in the two hands, suddenly opens them very wide apart, the cards spreading, after the manner of a comet's tail, from one hand to the other. For an instant they form an aerial arc, when, before they can fall to the ground, the hands are brought smartly together, collecting the cards by the action. This movement is repeated twice or thrice. This is what the genuine man does. The impostor ostensibly does a very great deal more, for he begins by parting and bringing the hands together again, as one does in playing the concertina, several times, the cards acting the part of the concertina perfectly. He then tosses the cards about from hand to hand in the most *nonchalant* manner, the cards invariably following one another in an unbroken stream which assumes serpentine and other shapes, at the will of the performer. They are spread along the conjuror's arms, and over his chest, and are invariably gathered in again without a single one being allowed to fall. The feats performed appear to be nothing short of marvellous, until one becomes possessed of the interesting fact that the cards are all sewn together, so that the whole thing is merely child's play. Now, although I have seen conjurors with good reputations using these prepared cards, I entirely disagree with their use myself. In order to deceive the public, one must not be particular about the means employed; but here it is a question of one conjuror setting up to be vastly superior to others, the facts of the case being precisely the other way. As a matter of fact, these prepared cards are only used when the performer is so wanting in skill that he cannot execute the genuine shuffle. Looking, as I do, upon the use of these cards as being unworthy anyone but a music-hall performer, I never hesitate to expose the fraud whenever it is perpetrated. I shall, of course, describe nothing in connection with it, but pass on to the genuine article, which may be at once recognised by the noise accompanying its execution, the fraudulent method being quite noiseless. As the feat is really difficult of accomplishment, its study must be conducted by easy stages. The pack, which should be composed of small cards (the large English ones being very unsuitable), thirty or so in number, is held lengthwise in the right hand (left hand if the performer is very decidedly left-handed) by the thumb at one end, and the first, second, and third fingers at the other end, the body of the hand making an arch over the cards. The left hand is held out, a little lower than the elbow, in front of the body, with the fingers spread out, and slightly curled upwards, the first finger a great deal more than the rest. Now, if the cards be squeezed by the fingers and thumb of the right hand, they will bend thus, ‿ ; but if, just as the pressure is put on, the fore finger of the left hand pushes the centre of the pack from below, the opposite curve will be taken, thus, ⁀, which is the one wanted. With the cards thus bent, they must be held over the left hand, and more pressure then applied, when they will "squirt" into the left hand, their foremost ends striking against the up curled forefinger, and so being prevented from falling to the floor. In making the squeeze, it will be found that the middle and third fingers use more influence than does the first finger, which is merely an auxiliary at the commencement. The greatest power of all must be exerted by the thumb, which is always pushing the cards forwards with considerable force. The learner must content himself with merely "squirting" the cards from the right hand into the left, at a distance of two or three inches only. When he can do this easily and smoothly, and without dropping any on the floor, he may increase the distance to six or eight inches. This is about the greatest distance he will be able to attain by simple "squirting." In order to make a more effective show, he will have to give to the right hand an upward movement at the moment the cards are pouring from it. This will tend to increase the distance between each card, but as, at the same time, it kills the forward *momentum*, the cards would simply fall to the ground were they not prevented from so doing. To accomplish this, the left hand must follow them up quickly. For an instant of time they will poise in the air, and then commence to fall; but, at that moment, the left hand comes upward with a rapid sweep, bringing the cards together against the right hand. By not attempting too great a distance at first, the learner will progress more rapidly; and he should not be satisfied until he can compass a distance of two feet. Great experts can accomplish very much more than this. As proficiency is attained, the "shuffle" should be made more across the body, the direction being from the left hip towards the right shoulder, this being more showy. A very difficult, but highly effective, method is to make the "shuffle" the reverse way, *i.e.*, downwards. The left hand is held nearly shoulder high and the cards "squirted" into it, the right hand sweeping downwards in the direction of the right hip. The performer must always direct his practice towards making the cards remain as long in the air as possible. To this end, the movement of the right hand must be exceedingly rapid, so that all the cards are visible to the spectators at once; and the longer the left hand dallies, the more rapid must be its motion towards the right hand. It must be distinctly understood that the two hands do not move simultaneously, there being two decided movements, one following the other. Old cards are useless for this feat, as they come off in batches, and have no spring. American cards are a trifle too thin, and are only good when new, whilst the regulation English whist card is too thick; therefore a medium thickness must be chosen. The finest quality cards will be found the cheapest to use, as they stand the strain better. Inferior cards soon become demoralised by the rough treatment to which the " shuffle " subjects them. After using a pack faces downwards for some time, turn it over, and use with the faces upwards, changing back again when the spring of the cards becomes weak.

PROPERTIES.—Besides the auxiliary articles mentioned in connection with various tricks, there are some that are of general application which the conjuror should always have in readiness. They are here enumerated and described:

The Devil's Handkerchief.—The peculiar use of this article is that anything wrapped in it is made to disappear when the performer desires, by simply shaking out the handkerchief. The secret lies in the fact that there are two handkerchiefs, three of the four sides of which are sewn together, the fourth being left open, so as to form a bag. The article to be made to disappear is apparently placed under the handkerchief, but really into the bag, and it is usual to give this to be held by one of the spectators. Later on, the performer takes the two upper corners of the handkerchief, and, asking the spectator to loosen his hold, gives it a vigorous shake. The company look in the air, or upon the floor, expecting to see the object there, but of course it is at the bottom of the bag. Cards are successfully vanished in this manner, as also watches, eggs, and articles not more bulky than they. The handkerchiefs should be of a sombre colour, and have a decided pattern. This will tend to conceal the contour of the article inside the handkerchief after it has been made to disappear, although the performer invariably retires with it to the stage, out of harm's way. Some performers use handkerchiefs sewn up on all four sides, and having merely a slit, from four to six inches long, made in one handkerchief.

The Coin Handkerchief.—This is an ordinary coloured handkerchief, into one corner of which, by means of a small extra piece of stuff, is sewn a piece of metal (to avoid unnecessary sinking of capital) resembling a coin. The performer should have on hand three handkerchiefs prepared with pieces of metal to represent sixpences, shillings, and half-crowns. For the latter, a penny will do admirably, and it will also act for florins and pennies, the public not being able to appreciate the slight difference in size when felt or seen through the folds of a handkerchief. The shilling handkerchief will answer admirably for halfpennies. A borrowed coin is apparently folded in the handkerchief, which the performer has drawn carelessly from his pocket, and not had lying in state upon a table, but palmed instead, the dummy being presented in its place. and given to be held. The palmed coin is then secreted in the place to which it is presently to be magically transported. To cause the coin, supposed to be wrapped in the handkerchief, to disappear, the performer shakes it by one or two corners, as in the case of the *Devil's Handkerchief*. Each of the three prepared handkerchiefs should be of the same pattern, so that, if more than one are used on the same evening, no remark will be excited as to the appearance of a new property upon the scene.

The Flying Ring.—This is a dummy ring, attached to a piece of elastic passing up the sleeve, with the other end fastened to the brace, or elsewhere. On a ring being borrowed, it is apparently placed in a handkerchief, the *Flying Ring* being substituted, and held by a spectator, of course through the handkerchief. At a given signal the ring is released and at once disappears up the performer's sleeve.

Magician's Eggs.—These are merely blown eggs, which should always be used when the employment of solid ones is not imperatively necessary. Their lightness enables the performer to palm them with considerable ease, and the same peculiarity renders them less liable to break; and, when they do, by chance, crack, no disconcerting emission of glutinous contents ensues. Besides this, a stock can always be kept on hand ready for any performance, which cannot be done with real eggs. Imitation eggs are made in indiarubber. These are of everlasting wear, bodily, but the exterior paint wants renewing occasionally, in order to maintain the resemblance to the real article, at no time any too exact.

Productive Eggs.—These are blown eggs containing lengthy slips of coloured paper, rolled up tightly. The introduction of the paper is thus managed. The egg blown and dried, a slit is made along one side with a piercing saw or fine file. A wire is then passed longitudinally through both thick and thin ends, one end of the paper inserted through the slit, and rolled up by means of the wire, twisted from the outside, until the egg is full. A piece of cotton is attached to the loose end of the paper, and the slit and holes in the ends of the egg closed up with plaster of Paris. At the conclusion of any trick in which real eggs have been used, one can be exchanged for a prepared egg, which is then broken, and the paper extracted, the piece of cotton at once showing where the loose end is to be found. Into a good-sized egg some fifty or sixty feet of paper may be secreted. The paper may be purchased at conjuring shops in large rolls; and the conjuror will find it better to prepare a quantity of eggs at a time.

The Coin-vanishing Tumbler.—This is an ordinary tumbler, with a horizontal slit at the side, on a level with the interior bottom, large enough to allow of the passage of a half-crown. If the tumbler be held in such a manner that a finger closes the slit, liquid may be poured into it. This should be done casually, and not professedly for the purpose of showing that there is nothing peculiar about the tumbler, such a suggestion being unnecessary and dangerous. The company would naturally say, "If there be really nothing wrong with it, why does he not place it in our hands for examination?" A coin placed in the tumbler may be got into the hand at any moment *viâ* the slit, the top being covered with cards, &c., to prevent the exit of the coin that way: as if coins were in the habit of leaping out of tumblers into which they have been placed, and deceiving audiences! Nevertheless, an audience is invariably satisfied when inanimate articles are covered up, and so supererogatorily prevented from performing acts which are not possible to them.

The Magic Plateau.—This is a glass plateau, in form like a school slate, there being a broad fancy wood border, glass taking the place of the slate. The plateau is held like a tray in the hands of the performer, and coins are placed upon it, which disappear when it is waved in the air. The secret lies in the fact that the wooden border is undermined, and, when a sideways movement is given to the plateau, the coins disappear underneath. The plateau is then carried with that side in which the coins are concealed, downwards. It makes a trick of itself, but is more useful as an adjunct to other tricks. As it is advisable to have a very narrow frame, shillings should be used: in no case coins larger than a florin. The plateau is also of great use when the performer is desirous of changing several borrowed and marked coins for some of his own. Taking the plateau, with the marked coins upon it, in the right hand, he pretends to pour them off into the left hand, where the conjuror has his own coins concealed. The marked coins disappear under the frame, and the concealed ones are exhibited. When the reappearance of the coins on the plateau is desired, they may be shaken out of the frame as easily as they were sent there; but I do not advise this addition, as it is very likely to give a clue to the mystery. The article is not difficult of construction, and the fact of the greater part of the material being transparent glass, lends it a desirably innocent appearance.

CHAPTER XII.

TRICKS WITH CARDS.

HOW TO VANISH AND RECOVER A PACK—THE EGYPTIAN
POCKET; HOW TO MANUFACTURE CARDS—THE MISSING
LINK—ASCENDING CARDS; VARIOUS METHODS—THE CARD-
HOLDER—WHAT APPARATUS NOT TO USE—THE SALAMANDER
CARD—A LEGITIMATE USE FOR "FORCING" PACKS—HERR-
MANN'S BOUQUET—A HUMAN HEN—THE HATCHED CARD
—THE WAND, AND HOW TO MAKE IT—MORE ABOUT AP-
PARATUS.

NEARLY every modern conjuror of any pretensions to skill
commences with a card trick. There is something about a
good card trick well executed that always takes with an
intelligent audience. When a performer does not commence
with the cards, it is generally because he does not possess
skill enough to do anything effective with them, although he
will generally make a virtue of necessity (at which conjurors
are particularly apt), and give some totally different reason.

Vanishing a Pack.—When the time is limited, none should
be wasted in preliminaries; but, when possible, the performer
should always vanish the pack, by palming it, and find it
either at the elbow or sole of the boot, or else in possession
of one of the audience; or he can pretend to give it into the
hands of a spectator, and then discover it some distance off,
with someone else. To execute this properly, the cards

should be palmed in the right hand, which affects to put them into the left hand. The right hand should take the wand or lappel of the coat, and the left be disposed, palm downwards, as though it held the pack. Such a little exhibition of skill makes a good impression at once, and puts the spectators on the alert from the very commencement.

The Egyptian Pocket.—One of the very best sleight-of-hand card tricks is that introduced by Herrmann, who, a few years ago, was such a favourite throughout Great Britain. He called it the Egyptian Pocket, though, for all the name implied, it might as well have been called the Nubian, Chinese, Japanese, or Brazilian Pocket. One of the audience took a pack round, and allowed four cards to be drawn from it. These cards were afterwards gathered in by the same person, who, after mounting the stage, placed them in the pack, which was then well shuffled. The pack he placed in his breast pocket, and then drew out, one by one, three cards of those selected in the audience as they were called for. The fourth card, however, he failed to find, and was told to search the pack for it. The search proving fruitless, he was told to maufacture the card, and, on expressing his ignorance of the proper method to pursue, was directed to blow into his pocket, where the missing card was then discovered. He was found, however, to have blown too hard, for his vest contained a perfect avalanche of cards; whilst his nose, on being squeezed, gave forth a stream of them, amidst roars of laughter. The method for performing this trick is as follows: Place upon your centre table two bulky packs of cards, and step forward with a third pack in your hands. Ask someone to assist you, and give him the pack in the shape of a fan, directing him to ask certain ladies, four in number, whom you will indicate with your wand, to select one card each. On this being done, take the pack from his hand, and direct him to receive the four cards, faces downwards, on the flat of one hand. Whilst this is being done, step on the stage, but never take your eye off the operations that are going on, for you must notice whose card is placed under-most, whose next, and so on. Request your volunteer as-sistant to kindly step on the stage, and, opening the pack in the middle, ask him to place the four cards inside. Close the pack, keeping the finger inserted where the cards were placed, ready for the pass, and inquire if the person on the stage with you possesses an inside breast pocket to his coat. If it is outside, it does not much matter, but the inside one is better for the trick. On receiving an answer in the affir-mative, ask to have the pocket emptied. Whilst this is being done, sometimes amidst much amusement, by reason of the miscellaneous character of the contents of the pocket, make the pass, bringing the four cards to the top, and, opening the pack slightly, carelessly run the eye over them. It is always as well to know them, in case of an accident occurring. Palm them, and give the rest of the pack to your assistant to shuffle. Taking the pack back, replace the palmed cards upon it, re-palming the top card only, and bid your assistant place the' pack in his pocket. Feel the outside of his pocket, under the pretence of seeing that everything is all right, but in reality to give the cards a bend, cross-wise. This bend will cause the back of the uppermost card to be the first met with by a hand entering the pocket. Now inquire of the chooser of this said top card—which, as you have palmed the original top one, will be the third one gathered in—what the name of her card is. You will affect to do this haphazard, and not as though you selected that particular person to inquire of. On receiving a reply, desire your assistant to put his hand quickly—" very quickly indeed, sir "—into his pocket, and draw out a card. If you have arranged everything properly, this will be the desired card. Now ask the chooser of the second card what the name of hers is, and repeat the operation. Do the same with the first card, and then with the fourth. By thus apparently dodging from one lady on one side of the room to one on the other side, it will still more appear that you are indifferent whose is asked for. This last card will not, of course, be forthcoming, and after a few fruitless attempts to produce it, plunge the hand, in which the card is palmed, into the pocket, and draw out the pack, leaving behind the palmed card. The assistant looks through the pack, but does not find the card, and you say, "Well, sir, you must make one, I suppose." On hearing that he does not know how, say, "Oh! it is as simple as possible. Take this wand in your right hand, and open your coat with the left. Good. Now blow into your pocket." The card will be found there, and your assistant, thinking it is all over, will be about to retire, when you, having just palmed one of the packs from the table, detain him with the remark that, "Although you did the trick very well, sir, for the first time, yet, owing to your inexperience, you unfortunately blew a little too hard. See here, sir, what you have inside your vest!" You then plunge the hand containing the cards rapidly inside his vest and draw out one card only, then another, another, and so on, and finally say that, as you do not know how many more there are, he had better take them out himself. Whilst he is doing this, palm the other pack, and say, "Have you any more cards, sir? No! Excuse me, but will you allow me to finish my experiment?" You then place your hand to his nose, and, compressing the hand, cause the cards to shoot forth in a stream on to the floor. Immediately it is over, shake hands with your assistant, and say you are extremely obliged. This will ease his mind of the idea that you meant to make a fool of him.

Sometimes, in drawing the cards from the pocket, the assistant will accidentally take them from the bottom, instead of from the top. In this case, they will be wrong cards, and you must say, "Ah! you don't do it quickly enough; this is the way," and, plunging your hand in the pocket, draw out the desired card, giving the pack, at the same time, a good bend, when you can allow the assistant to try again. About thirty cards will make the best pack for this trick, and great care must be taken that it does not contain two cards of a kind, for if one of these duplicates is chosen, and it is the fourth card, *i.e.*, the one which is missing at the last, it (its duplicate) will be found in the pack when it is gone over, and all your blowing in the pocket performance, which is the great feature in the trick, will be knocked on the head. I have actually seen this occur. All the performer could do was to palm the card and pretend to pass it into the pocket, where, of course, the duplicate was found; but it was a very weak finish.

The Missing Link. — This is another very telling card trick, and one that has made the fame of more than one amateur conjuror. A card is chosen from the pack and torn into shreds. The pieces, with the exception of a single one, which is given into the custody of a spectator, are then put into a little box, piece of paper, &c., and made to disappear. The card is then found restored in some part of the audience, but it is noticed that a small portion of it is missing. The single piece, which was given to a spectator to hold, will be found to be of the very size and shape required, thus proving that the performer restored the actual card that was destroyed.

For this trick, some slight prearrangement will be necessary. In the first place, a card (say, the six of hearts) must have a small piece torn out from one of its sides. This mutilated card must then be secreted in some out-of-the-way place in the auditorium, or, what is still better, in the pocket of one of the audience, of course some time before the performance begins. I once had it sewn up in the lining of a coat, and on another occasion inserted in the sole of a boot: but, in such instances as these, care must be taken that the article containing the card is to be worn on the evening of the performance, or a fiasco will result. It is, however, always worth while to run a little risk for the sake of increased effect. The small piece torn from the card is carefully kept, and, whilst the trick is being performed, should be on the table, concealed by any trifling object that may be upon it at the same time.

"Force" (see instructions for "forcing") a card, exactly similar in every way to the one you have previously mutilated and concealed, and then ask the chooser to tear it up. Whilst this is being done, go to your table for your box or piece of paper, according to which you may elect to use, and bring with it, concealed in the fingers, the little piece of card. Then have the pieces, which should be reduced as nearly as possible to the size of your secreted piece, placed in the box or paper and, putting your fingers among them, affect to take out one piece, but, in reality, show the one you already had in your hand, and give it to a spectator to hold very tightly, or if he likes, to put it into his purse. If you have plenty of time on your hands, and wish to make extra fuss, you can have it put into an envelope and sealed by the audience, which certainly improves the effect. A very pardonable joke here comes in well. On giving the portion of the card to be held, say to the gentleman, "Will you kindly keep the piece, sir?" and then, affecting to notice reluctance in his looks, "No! then I must apply to a magistrate, who will, I have no doubt, bind you over to keep the *peace* for six months or so, whilst I shall only trouble you for a bare six minutes." If you have had the pieces put in paper, you can roll it up into a ball and vanish by palming in the right hand, whilst affecting to place it in the left, after the manner previously described for vanishing objects. A box can be treated in the same manner, or you can give the trick extra finish by having two boxes exactly similar, one being filled with chocolate creams or other comfits, and exchanged for the one containing the torn-up card. The box should be a small round one, and can then be treated exactly as if it were a coin, and palmed.

The pieces are then commanded to pass to wherever you have originally concealed the torn card, which will be found in due course. You exhibit it triumphantly, not affecting to notice the absence of a portion of it at first and, when you do make the discovery, you must appear overcome with bewilderment. Then suddenly remember the piece you have given to be held, and have it fitted to the card, which it will naturally make quite complete. Then, if you have used boxes, have the box supposed to contain the pieces opened by the lady who chose and tore up the card, and present her with it and its contents. Most conjurors leave the trick here, but, if the performer pleases, he can go still further, and render the card quite complete again. This is easily managed with the use of a card box (see p. 127), which can have a perfect card concealed in it. The incomplete card and piece are put in, and the box turned over. This latter phase is not absolutely necessary for the success of the trick. When, as is sometimes the case, it is found to be impossible to conceal the mutilated card satisfactorily in the audience, the card box will have to be used in the first instance.

This trick is best introduced in the middle of a performance, when the production of the card from the person of one of the audience will look more genuine than it would if it took place at the commencement.

The Ascending Cards.—For this trick some little preparation is also necessary, and a certain amount of apparatus will be required. Three, four, or more cards are chosen, and then shuffled up in the pack, which is put into a metal or cardboard receptacle of the size of a pack of cards. At a word of command, the cards ascend, one by one, from the pack, without any apparent agency.

The apparatus required for this trick consists of the case, which can either be made to conceal the cards entirely, or may have the front cut out so as to show the face of the foremost card, a small border being left for the purpose of preventing the cards from falling out. This case is divided into two divisions, the rearmost one being much smaller than the other, and just large enough to hold about ten cards. To the top of the dividing partition affix a piece of fine black silk, which allow to hang over the smaller division. Into this smaller division now introduce a card, which, as it is put in, must have the silk under it. Now introduce a second card, but pass the silk over this one instead of under it. Put in a third card with the silk under it, and a fourth with the silk over, continuing the operation according to the number of cards you intend performing with. When the silk is pulled, it will cause those cards which have it passed beneath them to ascend. The same effect would be caused without the intervention of intermediate cards, but then they would all rise at once, whereas the trick is to make them do so singly. The performer must have all this arranged before commencing, and also have the silk passed out either at the back (which is to be preferred, where possible) or the side of the stage, where an assistant is stationed, holding the end of it. If at the side, then a small staple or pulley must be fixed in the back of the table and the silk passed through it, otherwise a direct pull will not be obtained. The case holding the cards can either be made to fit in the neck of a decanter by means of a cork on the under side, or can be permanently fixed to a tall stand. I prefer the decanter myself, as an opaque stand always causes suspicions of mechanical assistance to arise in the minds of the audience. The decanter should be given for examination.

The performer must force duplicate cards of those arranged in the small division of the card-case, of course taking no notice of those over which the silk passes, as they will never be exposed, and, asking the audience to remember the names of them, have them put in the pack and shuffled. The rest of the trick follows as a matter of course. The pack is placed in the larger front division of the case, and, as the chosen cards are called for, the assistant, who must have a view of the cards from his place of concealment, pulls the thread. A very commonly practised piece of humour is to include a knave in the forced cards, and to place two in the small rear division of the card-case. The one that is to appear first is put in upside down, court cards with one head only being used. It is upbraided for thus making its appearance, and it is replaced in the pack—still upside down—but in the front division. The second time, the other knave appears, right side up. The marvel of the audience is how the card managed to reverse itself in the pack. These card-cases can be procured from any of the vendors of conjuring apparatus.

A better arrangement is the following, which enables the performer to have his case examined by the audience—always a great advantage. It will require a little construction on the part of the performer himself, unless he is more fortunate than I ever was, and can find someone to carry out his ideas for him.

Instead of having the tin case made with partitions, let him have it quite plain, and just large enough to take from thirty-five to forty cards. This will bear any amount of examination, and a pack of cards should always be put in it before the audience, to show that it is entirely filled therewith, and so cannot possibly be made to contain any mechanical contrivance. The performer's little arrangement lies in a few cards, which, with others, are lying carelessly upon his table. These cards are pre-arranged with the silk exactly as just described for the small partition of the case, the end of the silk being affixed to the top of the undermost card. When the performer returns to his table with the pack, he should place it, whilst arranging his case in the decanter, with the loose prepared cards, which should then be picked up with it, the pack being undermost. The trick can then proceed as usual, and the case be handed round for examination afterwards. Great care must be taken not to disarrange the silk whilst picking up the cards, as any fault in this respect cannot possibly be remedied. The more simple and free from apparatus the method of performing this trick, the better it will be appreciated.

A third method, quite original, which I have adopted with unvarying success, the performer, will, I expect, prefer to any of the foregoing. It is the only method which does not call for the forcing of the cards; and its general surroundings are so simple that I find conjurors themselves sometimes puzzled to explain how the result is brought about. The performer has the usual bottle, which it is, perhaps, as well to open before the company. It should be of perfectly clear glass, and some fluid should be left in to give it steadiness during the performance of the trick. The card-holder should have the front side open, a quarter-inch flange being left on each side, to prevent the cards from falling out, and the inside coloured black. The silk, by means of which the chosen cards are to be made to rise out of the pack, has a small round cloth-covered button attached to the free end, and this button must be lying upon the table, in a convenient position. The performer first comes forward, and gives the bottle and card-holder into the hands of the company for examination. The examination concluded, he takes the articles to the table, and, as soon as possible, drops the button into the bottle. He next fits the holder into the neck, taking care, as he does so, to cause the thread to pass over the top of it. He now brings forward his pack, which he gives up entirely into the hands of the company, who select three cards. As many people nowadays have some idea of the "force," this at once disarms suspicion in a remarkable manner, and puts off many knowing ones, who are sure to have seen the trick before, otherwise performed, it being a very favourite one with conjurors. The performer now takes the pack back to the table, getting a picture card to the front, as he does so. If he chooses, he may ask the selectors of the cards to mark them with pencil, and whilst this is being done, he goes with the pack to the table, where he places it carelessly into the holder, taking care that the thread passes over the top of the cards.

It also passes over the front of them, but, as a picture card is in front, it is not seen, as it would be if a card with much white showing were there. For this same reason, the inside of the holder is coloured black. The three cards are now fetched from the audience, faces downwards, so that the performer, as he will explain, cannot see them. It will not assist him in the least if he does; but audiences invariably think an immense deal attaches to the fact of the performer seeing a card, and it is as well for all conjurors to conspire to keep up the delusion. Laying the cards first upon the table, he takes up one, and places it amongst those in the holder, some three or four from the front. As the card is pressed down, it takes the silk with it, care being taken to keep the latter as near the middle of the card as possible. The second card is now placed a few cards farther in the rear, and the third still farther back. It will be necessary to keep a finger of the disengaged hand upon the top of the card or cards in front of the one being placed into position, or the downward pressure will cause a corresponding, but premature, upward motion to be imparted to those already in position, which would spoil the trick at once. Whilst the cards are being thus placed in the pack, the performer must be careful to keep the company engaged in conversation. The trick then proceeds as usual; but, at the conclusion, the performer, seizing the bottle in one hand and the holder in the other, separates them, and comes rapidly forward to give them and the cards for examination. The assistant keeping firm hold of the thread, the button is drawn out of the bottle, and no trace remains of the medium by which the ascension was accomplished. I take some pride in this little arrangement, which, I need scarcely say, is not elsewhere made public.

To force three or more cards, pass them all from the bottom to the centre together, and not one at a time. Always be very particular about showing round the decanter or bottle, the most innocent portion of the whole apparatus. Where convenient, it causes a good effect to have a bottle of champagne opened on purpose. Give some of the wine away, and use the bottle half emptied, saying that you must keep some of the spirits in it for your trick.

The Salamander Card.—A card is chosen and torn in halves. One half is given into the custody of the audience, and the other placed in a cleft stick or crayon-holder, and burnt over a candle. The ashes are put into a piece of paper, which is rolled up and made to vanish by sleight of hand, the method used being one which ought, by this time, to be familiar to the performer. A letter here arrives addressed to the performer, brought in by an attendant at the door by which the audience has entered. The performer asks one of the audience to open it for him, as he cannot stop in the middle of a trick. Inside the envelope, which is sealed, is found another, and, inside that, another; and so on until a fifth or sixth is reached. Inside the innermost of all that half of the card which was only an instant before burnt before the eyes of the audience is found, as is proved by fitting it to the portion in the custody of a spectator.

This trick is thus managed : The cleft stick, which is an ordinary piece of firewood rounded and smoothed a little, has a cleft at each end. A metal crayon-holder, with double ends, also serves the purpose admirably. In one end, the performer has fixed the half of a card, which must be one of the pack from which the card is to be chosen, doubled up tolerably small. This end he conceals in his hand, and then has the half of the card which is to burnt doubled up and placed in the cleft in the other, retaining the stick in his hand all the time. On turning round to his attendant (who must know his part, and have rehearsed it once or twice) for a candle, he reverses the ends of the stick, and, removing the piece of card just placed in it, gives it to his attendant whilst in the act of taking the candle. If the attendant is not very proficient, the performer may go to the side and stretch the hand containing the abstracted piece of card behind the screen or curtain, and so effect the transfer. The attendant should stand with one hand open and the candlestick in the other (of course, out of sight). The performer will call out for the candle, but, receiving no answer, will go quickly to the side, where he will obtain it. The stick, with fictitious card in it, he must have in the other hand, which must be outstretched all the time, and never for an instant removed from the view of the audience. If this is not done, no suspicion will be attached to the fact of his going to the side. The instant the attendant receives the piece of card, he must slip it inside the small envelope, which will be arranged, in order with the others, beforehand (the outside one being already addressed, as a matter of course), and either take it round to the front himself or deliver it to the servant who is to take it into the room. Too much rapidity cannot be exercised in executing this portion of the trick. When once the letter is delivered, the performer has nothing more to do in the way of exerting his skill, but has merely to do a little talking, and eventually have the letter opened. Indeed, in this trick there is but little sleight of hand to be exhibited; but a bungler would nevertheless make an egregious muddle of it. It requires great neatness of execution. For instance, in turning round for the purpose of reversing the position of the stick in the hands, great care must be taken that no movement of the elbows is visible. The movement made must be confined to the arm below the elbow, or even to the wrists only. This movement of the wrists must be practised, as it is a highly essential one and has to be brought into use frequently. If any of the audience see the arms moving, they know, or surmise, that something is going on, even though they cannot divine what it is.

Although not absolutely necessary, it is as well always to force a card for this trick. The card can then be doubled up with the pips outwards if the prepared end of the cleft stick contains a portion of a similar card. For frequent performances of this trick and *The Missing Link*, it will be advisable to have what I have previously described as (but condemned the open use of) "forcing packs," viz., packs the cards of which are all of one denomination and suite, as it will not do to tear up cards from ordinary packs. They are easily obtainable at conjuring repositories or card manufacturers.

This trick is also exceedingly effective when a borrowed letter or other document is used instead of a card. In large public audiences, a bank note or other paper of value may be borrowed. It is easy to have a piece of a note of the "Bank of Elegance" in the concealed cleft, in imitation of a bank note. On important occasions the performer should always have three or four sticks prepared with various coloured papers, so as to be ready for any emergency. The preparation is trifling, and the sticks not used will do for another time.

It is quite immaterial which way it is done, but sometimes I tell the person to whom I give the stick and candle not to burn the paper, but to "put it in the candle." When I notice that it is in a fair way to be burned I look in another direction, as if not noticing what is going on, and am horrified on turning round to find the paper destroyed. This answers best when the material burnt is a borrowed paper.

Most conjurors perform this trick with the aid of a square wooden ladle, which possesses a movable flap similar to that of the "card box," and worked by twisting the handle round. This flap releases a fictitious paper, whilst it covers up the borrowed one. The excuse given for using this ladle is that the performer does not want the audience to suppose, as they would do if he handled it, that he changes the paper. This excuse is poor and weak, as it puts the idea of fictitious substitutions (the heart and soul of stage conjuring) into the heads of people who would otherwise never have dreamed of such a thing.

The arrangement of the premises very often makes the employment of the envelopes one within the other impracticable. As a substitute method, I here give one of my own, which, whilst it is not as amusing as the first one, is far more wonderful and inexplicable to the company.

Subsequently to borrowing a piece of paper or bank note from one of the company, the performer shows round a piece of glass tube, say four inches in length, having both ends hermetically sealed by being melted up. This piece of tube is folded in a piece of paper, and given into the custody of one of the company. The trick is gone through, as above described, except that the burnt paper is found restored inside the tube, which, of course, has to be broken before the contents can be recovered by their owner. This, on the face of it, is, of course, an utter impossibility; but it is thus accomplished. Glass - blowers, and those who have studied practical chemistry, know that to construct such a glass receptacle as that above described, all that is necessary is a piece of tube and a spirit lamp. The tube is held in the flame by the hands, and, as the glass melts it is drawn asunder, the result being that the two new ends thus formed collapse, and, cooling, take the form of points. Behind the scenes the assistant is provided with a piece of tube, eight or ten inches in length, one end of which has already been melted up. So soon as he receives the piece of paper from the performer he folds it up small, and pushes it down the tube as far as it will go. Then he melts this tube some three inches up, which will be far enough removed from the paper to keep it from being burned, and by this means the paper has become hermetically sealed inside a glass receptacle. If the assistant has had the necessary practice, the operation should not take long. When it is concluded, the assistant brings the glass on, and, under pretence of fetching away the candle, which the performer has placed upon the table, leaves it upon the shelf. The empty tube is upon the table, and the performer, in fetching it, takes with him, secretly, the one with the paper inside. This is very easily concealed in the hand if one end be pressed against the root of the thumb, the other end being pressed by the middle finger. The empty tube is shown, as also a piece of paper, in which it is ostensibly wrapped, the one with the paper inside being substituted. This substitution is effected by having the one tube concealed in the left hand, the empty tube being apparently transferred to it, but really palmed, as above directed. The right hand at once seizes the paper, and covers the tube in the left hand with it, and the wrapping-up is immediately proceeded with, as no further exposure may be permitted. If the performer prefers it, the assistant may wrap the prepared tube in paper, similar to that used by the performer, who then conceals the parcel under his vest. In this case, the empty tube is wrapped up by one of the company, the performer giving the parcel the necessary resemblance to the other (each should have twisted ends), and the exchange may be made subsequently. After the parcel has been opened, for the purpose of showing the tube with the paper inside, the performer must not approach it until the owner of the paper has broken it open with a hammer (the use of the wand for this purpose has less appearance of premeditation about it), and identified his property. I do not recommend the use of a card for this trick, as therein the spectators might find some explanation of its wonderful character. By employing a piece of a letter belonging to one of them, complete mystification is secured.

The restored card may be reproduced from a candle, by way of variety. The performer has on his table two or more candles; on no account brought on purposely for the trick. It will not matter in the least how long they have been burning, so that a good portion of them be remaining. As though struck with a sudden inspiration, the performer suggests, in his happiest manner, that the destroyed article be found inside one of the candles. The company not objecting (spectators, anticipating amusement from them, never object to the conjuror's suggestions in these cases), the owner of the paper or chooser of the card is requested to say which candle shall be employed. One being pointed out, and extinguished, it is taken out of the candlestick and put upon the table, where the performer proceeds to cut it in two with a knife, affecting great pains in making the portions exactly equal. He now asks which half he shall take, and, when the person asked says, "the right" (or left) half, he must inquire, "Which right [or left]; mine or yours?" The chosen half is again cut in two, and one of the portions chosen, that portion being again divided. The pieces remaining will be an inch or so long, and one is selected of these. This the performer gives to the person most interested amongst the spectators, on a plate, along with a knife, and, when it is cut open, the paper or card is found inside.

The way this is done is simplicity itself. The candles are all ordinary ones, so it really does not matter to the performer which is chosen, although he will do well to exhibit anxiety on the point, by way of effect. Neither does it matter to him which portion of the cut-up candle is eventually chosen, he having previously given off the piece of paper or card to the assistant, who has placed it in a small piece of candle, which the performer has safely secured under his vest whilst he is cutting up the chosen candle. When the last stage of the cutting is finished, the prepared piece is got down and exchanged in the usual manner for the innocent piece. It is then brought forward on the plate, and the remainder follows, as a matter of course.

The Obliging Bouquet.—This trick resembles to a great extent *The Ascending Cards*, and was one of Hermann's many masterpieces. As performed by him, it outshone, in exquisite neatness and effect, all other card tricks; but the amount of skill and daring necessary to carry it properly through is considerable, and persons of nervous or uncertain dispositions had better consider well before they attempt it. At the same time, those with the requisite skill and nerve may earn incalculable glory by including this trick occasionally in their programmes. The description of it (never before made public) is as follows: A bouquet of real flowers is handed to a lady in the audience, and three or four cards are then chosen from the pack. These cards are made to disappear. One by one they are then seen to rise from the bouquet, which is still held by the lady.

As in *The Ascending Cards*, a case for holding cards is required, but in this instance it is made of zinc, and just large enough to take about eight cards. The outside is painted dark green. This case must be prepared beforehand, with cards, as described in *The Ascending Cards*, with the exception that human hair is substituted for silk. It is also as well either to have the intermediate cards, *i.e.*, those over which the hair passes, fixed permanently, or else to have partitions of the same material as the case. The loose end of the hair should have a tiny bead of wax on it, and the case must be placed in the centre of the bouquet, in such a position that, although it is not visible from the outside, yet the cards will have a tolerably free passage for their ascent. If possible, bring the mouth of it just beneath two buds of roses, which will give to the slightest pressure, and allow the card to come up between them. The hair should hang down between the buds, passing between the stalks. The greatest care must necessarily be taken in arranging all this, and the trick rehearsed within an hour of its performance, to make sure of everything being safe.

Bring the bouquet on, and, selecting the lady least likely to interfere with your arrangements (this selection should be made whilst you are on the stage performing other tricks), ask her to kindly hold the bouquet for you, calling attention to the fact that the flowers are real ones. If possible, always have the bouquet held in the front row of the audience, and take care that the hair is towards you all the time. Now "force" duplicate cards of those in the bouquet, and then cause them to vanish as you please. As looking the most skilful, I prefer palming to any other method, on all occasions. If, from knowing the cards as you "forced" them, you are aware who took particular cards, you can ask the person who chose the duplicate card of the first in the case, the name of it, and then desire that one to rise from the bouquet. On hearing the name of the card, or just before, advance to the bouquet, and ask the holder of it if she saw the fairies bring the cards to the flowers, or any other fanciful question you please, and then, under the pretence of having it held a little higher or lower, or a little more to the right or to the left, advance the hand to the bouquet, and so obtain possession of the end of the hair. A good deal of deceptive action must now be introduced, the wand being put into the hand holding the hair, which must then be pulled very slightly indeed, and if the card rises the strain can be continued. Just before the card shows itself, say, "No! I am afraid the fairies have been disobedient to-day." This will momentarily remove the interest of the audience from the bouquet, and attention will be directed to you, as if inquiring what will be done next. This is the opportunity you must seize for causing the card to rise, and then exclaim, "Ah! there is one, after all." Run the card up quickly, and take it out of the bouquet, or, if it appears to be very loose, allow the holder of the bouquet to remove it. If, at this juncture, you fancy your temporary assistant is at all suspicious, at once take the bouquet to someone else; but on no account take this step if all is going on well. Ask the name of the next card, which cause to rise in the same manner, and repeat the operation with the remaining card or cards. As the hair becomes gradually longer, you will be enabled to stand a little further off on each occasion. You must contrive to alter your attitude as often as possible, and also endeavour to look quite unconcerned. The best way to assume this by no means easy appearance, is to affect to be rather more amused at the ascension of the cards from the bouquet than the audience itself. One ticklish point is in ascertaining whether everything is in order. This never reveals itself until the first pull is made, when, if there is anything wrong, a jerk will be felt by the holder of the bouquet, and, in all likelihood, a clue to your secret will be given. If you only so much as fancy that anything is wrong, take hold of the bouquet with your disengaged hand, without taking it away from the holder of it, and have it held a trifle higher or lower. This will enable you to give a precautionary pull without allowing any strain to be felt. Such a thing as a hitch ought not to take place, for the previous arrangements should be so perfect as to do away with all possibility of such an occurrence. The cards all out of the case, inquire, for the sake of effect, if there are any more chosen ones that have not appeared, and then take the bouquet round, allowing people to smell at it, &c. This is really to enable you to remove the case from the bouquet, but ostensibly to show that the flowers are real. The best way of removing the case is through the stems of the flowers, and for this purpose it is made of zinc, it being a weighty metal. As it is a small affair, it can easily be palmed. The bouquet should be then presented to the lady who held it during the performance of the trick, with the request that the flowers should be examined to see if there be any preparation about them.

Taking into consideration the difficulty in performing the trick, the desirability of having as small a case as possible, and the usual shortness of hair, it is advisable to force only three cards, although three or four hairs may be employed. When I first saw Herrmann perform this trick, I was simply appalled at the audacity required to perform it successfully; but experience has taught me that, with practice, it is as easy as many other tricks which are not one quarter so effective. The difficulties to be overcome are causing the first card to rise without being discovered, and removing the case. It will be found that if the bouquet is held a little lower (only a few inches) than the hand holding the hair, there will be less likelihood of any strain taking place. If the performer pleases, the chosen cards can be torn up or burnt in the first instance, but the destruction is a needless one.

The Hatched Card.—A chosen card is destroyed or made

to disappear, and on an ordinary egg (selected from a number) being broken, it is found inside.

Before describing the trick itself, I will give a unique method (Herrmann again) for obtaining the eggs. A rehearsed assistant will be required, and he must have in his mouth an egg, and, besides, either a portion (either end) of the shell of, or a wooden or porcelain imitation of, one. Under the vest band, and sustained by the elastic thereof, you have four more eggs concealed. You come on with your assistant, whose mouth is then empty, and, telling the audience that you will require an egg, ask him if he has taken the egg powder you gave him, and whether he thinks he can give you any eggs. On receiving his reply in the affirmative, tell him to fetch a plate. This he does, and, at the same time, pops the egg and real or imitation portion of shell into his mouth, all done in an instant, so as to avoid suspicion. He now takes up his position in the centre of the stage, a little "up," with the plate held before him and elbows close to his sides. You stand beside him, and place your rear hand upon his head. He then slowly exhibits the egg, which, with the forward hand, you then extract with seemingly immense difficulty. Whilst the forward hand is thus engaged, the rear one takes an egg from the vest, and you cross over behind the assistant, and are just about to take the plate from him when he exhibits the shell, which, to the audience, appears to be another egg. You exclaim, "What, another! you must have taken too much powder," and then advancing the forward (late the rear) hand, you slip the egg palmed in it half into your assistant's mouth, and then proceed to drag it forth with the same difficulty which attended the abstraction of the first one. The rear hand has by this time another egg in it, and you go round behind the assistant, only to find him exhibiting another egg, which you extract, as before. The process is repeated until all the eggs are gone. It is not advisable to use more than five eggs, for precautionary reasons, and that number is quite sufficient to excite wonder. The assistant must be careful not to allow the shell inside his mouth to be seen whilst you are removing an egg just "laid." If you can find anyone with a mouth capacious enough to contain two eggs (small ones will do), secure him as an inestimable treasure. No trick being more conducive to laughter than this one, extra care must be taken with it. The performer should move about in an easy and unostentatious manner, and endeavour, by word and mien, to keep up the impression that the whole of the trick lies in the assistant's mouth. The use of the extra egg end is not absolutely necessary, for the palming can begin with the first egg, the one originally in the mouth being kept there till the last, when it may be allowed to fall out into the performer's outstretched palms. Either method is effective. Show the eggs round on a plate, and have one selected with which to perform the succeeding trick. For that, the following apparatus will be necessary.

Make, either of wood or metal (tin, brass, zinc, &c.), a hollow wand (open at one end, and closed at the other), painted or varnished on the outside, so as to resemble in every little particular the wand you ordinarily use. If the latter has ivory or brass tips, then your imitation wand must have the same. There is not the least necessity for running into any expense, for, by going to a working tinman or walking-stick maker, the thing can be obtained for a shilling. I much prefer wood to metal, and would recommend its use. This imitation need not be made of real ebony, although it should be of tolerably hard wood. Fitting inside there must be another piece of wood, an inch shorter than the interior of the wand itself, which should move up and down pretty easily, but not loosely. Commencing exactly 2in. from one end, cut a slit 1in. long, and, making a little peg of wood, or providing yourself with a small brass round-headed nail, which must be afterwards coloured to match the wand, drive it into the sliding piece of wood, which must be pushed up against the closed end of the wand at the time.

By holding the wand at the closed end, and placing the thumb on the little peg, the sliding piece of wood can be made to move up and down as easily as can the pen or pencil inside an ivory holder. By making the slit the same length as the space left at the open end of the wand, the sliding piece will not protrude when the peg is pushed down by means of the thumb. The sliding piece should also be blackened all over, as, if left white, it might show through the slit or at the exposed end, which, however, should never be turned full towards the audience at any time.

It is now open to you either to force a card or to have one selected haphazard. If the card is to be forced, then you can have the wand loaded beforehand. This is done by doubling up the card until it is only 1in. wide, rolling it up, and putting it into the wand, which you can then leave on the table handy. If the card is not to be forced, the wand must be behind, and the card chosen before the egg-laying performance (supposing you find your eggs in that way) takes place. Have only about twenty cards to select from, and let your assistant know what they are. They can be arranged in sequences or suits, for greater convenience. When your assistant retires, after producing the eggs, he takes the pack of cards with him, and whilst you are showing the eggs round he looks through the nineteen cards and finds out which one is missing. He then takes a duplicate of this, and puts it into the wand. For the sake of expedition, you should have a duplicate of each of the twenty cards in readiness. I remember once finding myself without a duplicate of a selected card, and I had actually to go forward and, under the plea of placing it in an exposed position, "where everyone could see it," effect a change. I left a dummy card on the chair (the " exposed position,") face downwards, and carried off the chosen one in triumph, feeling very much relieved. This method of having a card or cards chosen from a pack, the cards of which are known, does not belong particularly to this trick, but can be used in many others. It is only worth while to take the trouble when your audience is a particularly sharp one, and not likely to be imposed upon by a "force." The egg and card both chosen, you may do what you please with the latter, so long as you get rid of it, and, taking the egg, which you have previously had minutely examined and held up to the light, to show that it is empty, upon a plate, give the plate to be held by a spectator, and then break the shell by means of the open end of your prepared wand. Immediately you are well through the shell, push the peg along by means of the thumb, and the rolled up card will be forced into the egg, whence have it extracted by a spectator. If you please, one of the audience may hold the egg whilst you break the shell. I need hardly mention that, before you bring your wand into play, you should make a fuss about passing the card into the egg. The reader, by this time, will take that as a matter of course. Always have a cloth or handkerchief handy in this trick for wiping egg and fingers.

The preceding six card tricks, used judiciously, that is to say, not too frequently, should, with those described in "Drawing-room Magic" (*La Carte Générale*, for instance), last a conjuror a lifetime. They are the very best I have seen performed, for they combine sleight of hand with a minimum amount of apparatus; indeed, the articles I have directed to be used are hardly worthy of the name, the nearest approach to it being the card-cases and the hollow wand. There are a number of tricks sold in which cards rise from demons' heads, imitation plants, and pedestals ; but these are all exceedingly expensive, and are nearly all worked by electricity. Besides this, there always seems to be an artificial effect about such things. For all the audience know, there may be a small boy concealed in the demon's head, or in the huge flower-pot in which the "Magic Rose Tree" is generally stood. At any rate, the idea of "sleight of hand" is not conveyed, and, if for that reason only, I will have none of them.

CHAPTER XIII.

TRICKS WITH HANDKERCHIEFS AND GLOVES.

THE RESTORED HANDKERCHIEF: ITS VARIOUS MISFORTUNES
—THE CONJUROR'S PISTOL—SUN AND MOON: A TOTAL
ECLIPSE—THE DISSOLVING KNOTS—THE DECANTED HAND-
KERCHIEF—THE MELTING HANDKERCHIEFS—THE ELASTIC
GLOVE: HOW TO ACCOMMODATE ALL SIZES.

The Restored Handkerchief.—This title will doubtless apply
to many tricks with handkerchiefs, so, if the performer thinks
it too general, he can find another of his own for this particular trick. Herrmann called it Le Mouchoir Serpent, from
the fancied resemblance to a snake which the handkerchief
was made to take at one stage of the trick. For it the performer must have prepared a lemon, with a small handkerchief
inside. The way to operate on the lemon is as follows: Cut
off one end—the apex is the best—and then, by means of a
spoon, take out the whole of the interior, being careful to
remove the inner white skin. Push in the handkerchief,
replace the portion of lemon which you cut off, and sew it
carefully on with yellow cotton or silk. The first lemon or
two are rather tiresome to prepare, but after a time the job can
be done very quickly and neatly. The method of sewing which
should be adopted is that known as "under-sewing," and it
will be necessary to guard against including the handkerchief
itself in the stitching. As the handkerchief placed inside is

meant to be subsequently destroyed, it need be of the very commonest description only. It can be obtained for three-halfpence. On the centre table have a small scent-bottle, with methylated spirits, a lighted candle, a common plate, and a knife. Concealed in the palm of one hand are about ten pieces of cambric, each about three inches square, and properly hemmed. Under the vest is a piece of cambric two inches broad and about four feet long, doubled, not rolled, up. Behind the scenes are a couple of pieces of thin wrapping paper about nine inches square. In the hand not occupied by the pieces conceal the prepared lemon, and advance to the audience. Pretend to see something in a gentleman's hair, and, after fumbling in it, produce the lemon. Let several persons smell at the fruit, taking care to present the better-looking end, in case your sewing has not been very successful. Of course, the lemon must not leave your hand, except to be tossed once or twice in the air, to show that it is real. Place this lemon on a side table, and there leave it, with the sewn-up end from the audience.

Now borrow a small handkerchief, the smaller the better but do not take one that is much ornamented with lace Turn to a gentleman, and, whilst asking him to stand up, roll the handkerchief up carelessly in the hand, and, working it round the bundle of pieces which you have concealed, bring it underneath and let the pieces appear at the top. This can be done in an instant whilst you are talking with the person whom you wish to assist you. Give the bundle of pieces, which the audience will think is the handkerchief, to him, with instructions to rub it gently in the hands. You have, in the meantime, taken care to keep the exchanged handkerchief well concealed in the palm. Retire to the stage, and, whilst mounting it, vest the handkerchief and take in its place the doubled-up long piece, which keep concealed by means of the wand. Ask your assistant how he is getting on, and explain that you wish him to rub the handkerchief so small that it can be passed inside the lemon. After a little rubbing has taken place, ask him to open the handkerchief out, to see if it is any smaller. Of course, when he attempts to do so, it will drop about in pieces, to everyone's astonishment. Affect great annoyance, and advance, saying that the trick is now spoilt all through the handkerchief being *rubbed the wrong way.* Collect the pieces together, and, rolling them up, exchange them in the hand for the long piece. This exchange may at first seem very daring and difficult, but, if care is taken always to have the piece or pieces concealed well down in the hand before the substituted article is removed, there need be no fear of detection; only the performer must go right at it, and not falter in the least. Give the long piece to your assistant, and tell him to rub it this time with the left hand. Whichever way he rubs you must say is the wrong one, and finally ask him to give you one of the pieces that you may show him what you mean. In his attempt to give you one of the supposed pieces, he will unroll the long piece amidst much laughter. After suggesting that the gentleman pays for the destroyed handkerchief, rub it up in the hands and "pass" it into the lemon. For this purpose, it may be rolled up on the table, and passed down a trap.

Instead of "passing" with the hands, it is in every way neater and more effective to use a conjuring pistol, which is loaded with the handkerchief and then fired. This pistol will have to be provided with a large tin funnel, so constructed that the tube portion, which must fit the barrel of the pistol closely, extends for a long way inside the funnel. When a handkerchief, or similar article, is rammed into the funnel, care is taken that it goes around the tube so that, on the pistol, which has been previously loaded, being fired, the flash passes harmlessly down the tube. The mouth of the funnel must never, by any chance, be seen by the audience. These pistols, which are exceedingly useful at all times, can be purchased at conjuring repositories; but it is easy for anyone possessing an ordinary pistol to have it fitted with a funnel by a tinman.

Suppose the long piece either "passed" or fired out of the pistol, take the lemon and cut it open with the knife, and pull out the handkerchief that was already in it. Pretend to advance for the purpose of returning it to its owner, but suddenly discover that it smells of lemon. Say that you will put some scent on it, and, placing it upon the plate, saturate it with spirits from your bottle. Whilst advancing a step or two, to inquire if it is enough, your stage attendant enters and quietly sets light to the spirits with the candle. You turn back and nearly burn your fingers, and start aside horror-stricken.

A slight scene now takes place between you and your attendant, who insists that you told him to set fire to the handkerchief. Run down to the audience with the plate and its blazing contents, asking the owner of the handkerchief to take it in its present state. Turn back and drop it on the floor of the stage, and then go behind the scenes, where quickly take the original borrowed handkerchief from the vest, and wrap it in one of the two pieces of paper (it will add to the effect if you scent the handkerchief a little), which hold in the hand covered by the second piece of paper, open. During your absence your attendant has been dancing about, affecting to burn his fingers, &c. When the handkerchief is nearly burnt out, snatch up the remains of it quickly and pop it into the open piece of paper, roll it up rapidly and exchange for the real handkerchief in paper, vesting it at once, or a severe burn may ensue. This is done whilst hurrying towards the owner of the handkerchief, to whom you say that you have done the best you can, and are sorry that you have only the ashes of the handkerchief to offer ; but that if she will leave her address, you will forward a new one in the morning, &c. Finally, you have the supposed ashes blown upon, and then tear open the paper, revealing the handkerchief. If you have scented it, call attention to the fact.

If I wanted to test a conjuror's ability, I should give him this trick to perform. No duffer could ever get half way through it; and yet, by attention to the rudiments of palming, &c., it becomes easy enough. There can be no two opinions about the effect produced. The principal portions should be rehearsed with your attendant.

A very amusing variation to this trick is the following: Purchase two cheap sunshades of a precisely similar pattern. They should be small, and the covers of light alpaca. From one carefully strip the cover, so as to leave the ribs bare, and, at the end of each rib, fasten a piece of cambric exactly similar to those used in the rubbing-away episode. This sunshade have lying upon the shelf at the back of the table, rolled up in paper. In one of the large side pockets have concealed the cover, rolled up and tied with very fine thread, that may be easily broken. Upon the table have lying a piece of paper similar to that in which the sunshade upon the shelf is wrapped. At the opening of the trick, show this sunshade round, and then proceed to wrap it up in paper, on the table. You will always have some extra sheets, and behind one of these the one sunshade is exchanged for the other. Give it to be held in the company. Then borrow a hat, and secretly introduce the cover, placing the hat on a side table. When the trick has proceeded as far as the discovery of the small pieces in the hands of the spectator who is rubbing the handkerchief, place them in the pistol and fire at the sunshade held in the company. Great amusement ensues when the bare ribs are discovered, with the pieces of cambric flying from them. These are then taken off, and the trick proceeded with, as before described, the cover being discovered in the hat at any convenient period. Break the thread, and shake it out well before bringing to view, so as not to suggest any idea of its ever having been rolled up tightly into small bulk.

Sun and Moon.—This is another amusing trick, in which handkerchiefs are destroyed and restored in a most lavish manner. Beyond the preparation of a couple of handkerchiefs, and the use of a conjuring pistol, no apparatus is required, if the trick be performed after the following method, which is according to my own arrangement, and in keeping with my belief in sleight of hand as opposed to apparatus.

Purchase three common coloured cotton handkerchiefs, all of precisely the same pattern, and from the centre of one of them cut a circular piece some three or four inches in diameter. Replace this with a white piece, so that you have a coloured handkerchief with a white centre. Take a white handkerchief, and cut from its centre a circular piece just a trifle smaller than that from the coloured handkerchief, which latter then sew in the centre of the white handkerchief. A friend of yours in the audience should have the second of the coloured handkerchiefs in his pocket, and receive instructions to the effect that, when you ask for a handkerchief in a particular manner (you can easily arrange a sort of by-word between yourselves), he is to offer this particular handkerchief, which you tardily accept. This is one of the very rare occasions on which I permit myself to have a confederate in the audience; and I only do it because (1) a really capital trick would otherwise be impossible of performance, and (2) because it is not at all necessary that your confederate should know anything about the trick. I always say that it is necessary for me to have in such-and-such a trick a coloured handkerchief, *merely for effect*, and it is rarely that people bring coloured handkerchiefs with them, so, to avoid disappointment, &c., &c. If the person who officiates be a dullard, he will be none the wiser, and if he be a relative, as he should be, he is tolerably safe. Coloured handkerchief No. 3 you have rolled up in a piece of paper and placed in your capacious breast pocket. Besides these, you must have in the palm of one hand an ordinary white handkerchief concealed. The two prepared handkerchiefs already described are done up in paper in the shape of a ball and placed upon the shelf at the back of the table, on the top of which are lying a few loose sheets of paper similar to that in which the handkerchiefs are wrapped. Also on the table are two plates, some methylated spirits, a lighted candle, two pairs of scissors, or else two sharp knives, and a funnel pistol. Advance to the audience, with the white handkerchief concealed in the palm, and borrow two handkerchiefs—one a white one, at hazard, except that you endeavour to let it be one somewhat similar to your own, and the other, the coloured one, from your friend. Exchange the white handkerchief for your own, as in the preceding trick, and vest it, and then give both white and coloured handkerchiefs to be held by separate persons. Each handkerchief should be held horizontally by the two hands, one holding the very centre of it, and the other grasping it a few inches away. Give the scissors or knives to two other persons, and bid them mark the handkerchiefs. At first some hesitation will be shown at cutting the handkerchiefs, but you must say there is no fear. From the position in which each handkerchief is held, it will be incumbent on anyone cutting between the hands of the person holding it to take a piece clean out of the centre. When this cutting is over (you might do it yourself, only it looks more genuine and creates more fun to have it done by the audience), say that there will be no mistaking the handkerchiefs now, for they are marked with a vengeance. Now take the mutilated coloured handkerchief and the white piece, and put them on one plate, the the mutilated white handkerchief and coloured piece being put on the other. Pour spirits on both, and set fire to them. When they are well ablaze, pretend to discover that you have made the mistake of mixing the colours, and endeavour (fruitlessly, of course) to take out the burning pieces. Remark that it is a very bad job, as you had hoped to have shown a specimen of your skill, but now everything is spoilt through your forgetfulness. Your stage attendant can attend to the burning of the handkerchiefs, if you so please, in

which case you can give him a good blowing up, and threaten
to discharge him on the spot. The more penitent he can
manage to look, the better it will be for the effect of the trick.
Take the ashes, and put them in a piece of the paper which
is on the table, and, whilst affecting to put this in a second
piece, exchange it for the prepared handkerchiefs in paper on
the shelf. This method is very easy, and is thus performed:
Stand at the end of the table, and, with the hand that is
nearest the audience, raise a piece of paper partly from the
table, but not so much as to enable the audience to see under
it, and behind this temporary screen the exchange can be
effected by means of the rear hand with impunity, providing
it is done quickly but not hurriedly, and with the eyes
turned towards the audience, to whom the performer is im-
pressively descanting on the many vicissitudes which chequer
a conjuror's career. Directly the two parcels are safely
exchanged, go forward and give the paper to be held by one
of the audience. An ordinary pistol can now be let off, or a
word of command given, and the paper then opened. Affecting not to notice that there is anything wrong, you proceed
to return the handkerchiefs to their respective owners.
Laughter will, of course, ensue, and you will then appear to
be overwhelmed with confusion. Borrow a hat, put the handkerchiefs in it and take them out again, and finally drop one
on the floor. The action of stooping to pick it up will enable
you to bring the opening of the hat against your breast, and
you must seize this opportunity of slipping the roll from the
breast pocket into it. Go back to the table and place the
hat upon it, and then, taking up the funnel pistol, ram the
handkerchiefs into it, with the remark that you may as well
get rid of them altogether. Fire the pistol, and then ask if
anyone saw anything pass into the hat, as you fancy you did.
Go to the hat and produce the roll, which open, and show
the coloured handkerchief. Spread this out, to show that the
centre is perfectly restored, and, whilst going forward with it,
take the white handkerchief, unperceived, from the vest, and

roll it up inside the coloured one. Then say, "Ah! but we have not the white handkerchief yet; well, perhaps we shall be able to find it." Rub the coloured handkerchief in the hands, with the white one inside, and, finally, open both and return to their owners. This finale is, perhaps, the most difficult part of the trick. Take care when the funnel pistol is fired that you either stand it upon its broad end, or else place it upon the table with the mouth from the audience. Although, to the audience, an enormous amount of destruction appears to be going on, such is not really the case, as two handkerchiefs only are destroyed in the trick.

The Knots. — I call this trick by a simple name, because

FIG. 42.

extreme simplicity is its prevailing feature from beginning to end. The last few tricks described have all had apparatus, to some extent, as a component part; this one is all sleight of hand. In "Drawing-room Magic" (p. 65), I gave directions for untying a knot by word of command, and noted at the time that an enlargement of the trick would be given in "Grand Magic." We have now arrived at the enlargement. In the minor trick, the knot is tied in a peculiar fashion by the performer himself; now the knots are to be tied by various members of the audience, and it is this which gives the trick such a marvellous appearance.

The performer advances, and begs the loan of several handkerchiefs. He takes two of those proffered, and, advancing towards one of the audience, presents just four inches (on no account more) of one end of each handkerchief, one being crossed over the other, with the request to have them tied together in a knot. The reason for crossing one end over is to induce the tyer to make either a "granny" or a reef knot, which are the knots easiest to undo — that is, after the conjuror's method. Fig. 42 shows a "granny" knot. The general appearance of a reef knot is somewhat the same, so it does not require a separate sketch, and the mode of proceeding will be in both cases similar. For convenience of description, I have depicted a dark-coloured and a white

FIG. 43.

handkerchief, and the performer will do well to take this hint, and always, where possible, borrow handkerchiefs varying in colour or texture, in order that the sinuosities in the knots may be easily followed by the eye. As the performer wants a knot that is tied neither too loosely nor too tightly, he must keep his eye upon it whilst it is being tied. If it is loosely done, he must say, "Don't be afraid of tying it up tight, sir [or madam]; pull as hard as you like." In the event of a too literal acceptance of his words, he should take the handkerchiefs at once. Even when the knot is tied as hard as a stone, the performer takes it in the hands, and, with the remark, "Oh! this is not half tight enough yet," pretends to pull it up with all his force. What he really does is to take the small end of one handkerchief in one hand, and the body of the same hankerchief on the other side of the knot in the other. By pulling at these hard, and, where they do not give easily by wriggling them as well, the end of the handkerchief will be pulled out quite straight, as in Fig. 43. It will there be seen that the white handkerchief has been manipulated upon, and that the dark handkerchief is now really only tied *round it*. In some cases, the greatest difficulty arises through some malicious person tying an extremely hard knot. If the performer pulls too hard, he will, in all probability, rend the handkerchief without making things much better. In this case, he must endeavour, whilst borrowing another handkerchief, for the continuation of the trick, and under concealment of the same, to loosen the knot a little in the ordinary way, and then he can straighten the end openly· later on, as though trying if all the knots were secure. It is not often that the amateur will, at the outset of his career, find much difficulty of this kind, for his audiences will not be of the antagonistic class. Suppose everything has gone favourably, the performer then takes another handkerchief, and has that tied on also, of course to a disengaged corner, and so goes on with four, five, or six, each knot being operated upon as soon as it is tied. If he notices that anyone is tying a reef knot, he should at once audibly remark upon it, as the public has a great idea that a reef knot is the most difficult to untie, whereas it is really the easiest of all. When anyone goes in for a multiplicity of twists, one end being wound round the other several times, let the performer rest easily in his shoes, for he has only to pull that end round which the other one is coiled, and five or six coils will make no difference; at the same time, he must appeal to the audience whether it is fair, &c., for effect. When the required number of handkerchiefs have been tied together, and all the knots have been operated upon *secundum artem*, the performer retires to the stage, and, taking a chair or low table (the chair for preference), proceeds to place the handkerchiefs in a pile upon it after the following manner: Knot No. 1 is held between the tips of the finger and thumb in such a manner that the main body of the straight end lies along the palm of the hand. The loose portion of the handkerchief is then opened out by the left hand and covered over the knot, which is placed, at the same time, upon the chair; whilst, under cover of the handkerchief, the little finger of the right hand is drawn up by a contraction of the hand as closely to the knot as possible, and there grasps firmly the main body of the straight end. By straightening out the hand again, the end will be pulled right out, and the handkerchiefs parted. All this must be done quickly. If the end, as it often will, requires two pulls to draw it clear, it is best to lift up the handkerchief, and exhibit the knot again, to show there is "no deception," or on any other plea, before giving the second pull. Proceed after the same manner with all the knots, each one being covered with a separate handkerchief, taking great care that none of them slip off the chair during the operation, or it will be shown that the knots are already undone. The handkerchiefs should either be trailed on the floor or hung over the back of the chair, where they will not become confused or get under the performer's feet, and so receive an undesired tug. For the purpose of diverting the attention of the audience during this operation, the performer should make some jocular remark concerning each knot. He should say something about having at length come to the "knotty point," and then describe each knot, whether correctly or incorrectly will not much matter. One, he must say, is the reef knot, another the Gordian knot, and another a weaver's knot. The last made will generally be a true lover's knot, about which the performer may remark, before small audiences, that it was a *knotty* (naughty) person who tied it. The performer has only to wave his wand over the heap, or to blow upon it, and then lift off the handkerchiefs one by one. The beginner will do well to try only three knots as a commencement, and to have them tied by ladies, who, as before explained, are always the best to fly to in risky cases. Whilst the knots are being tied, hang the handkerchiefs already joined over one arm, where they will be out of the way of danger, and in the way of assisting the performer by concealing any covert proceedings on his part in untying obstinate knots. The knot depicted at Fig. 44 I have christened the *bête noire* knot, and such the performer will find it whenever it is tied for him. If he does not put the ends of the handkerchiefs crossed into the hands of the person whom he requests to tie a knot, he will find the *bête*

FIG. 44.

noire appear with marvellous rapidity. When it or any other difficult knot appears, the only thing to be done is to untie it covertly, and do it up again after the matter described in "Drawing-room Magic." This may seem a very cool direction to give, but is the only one appropriate to the occasion, and the performer must make the best of a bad job. I have often untied a knot whilst mounting the steps of the stage, and had everything done up again by the time I reached the chair. The performer must practise by tying for himself the most intricate knots imaginable; or, if he learns with a companion, let the two tie knots for each other. Silk handkerchiefs are, as a rule, the best; they slip easily and do not tear readily, which latter quality is not the lesser advantage:

it makes one very uncomfortable to have to return a handkerchief with one end hanging by a thread. This trick is one of the few which it is impossible to purchase. Let every conjuror be careful in his performance of it, and only give it " by request," or on special occasions, for it is worth half a dozen apparatus tricks put together.

Although very good indeed, the following method, in which one handkerchief only is used, is not so effective as when several are employed. The performer takes a large handkerchief, and ties a single knot in it, near the centre. He does not pull this knot tight, but leaves a loop large enough to receive his hand, or, at least, several fingers. Holding this loop in one hand, and presenting the two ends, side by side, with the other, he has another knot tied upon the first one. Whilst passing to another person, one end is pulled out straight, of course whilst ostensibly tightening the knot, and another knot is then tied; the end before straightened is again pulled at, and another knot tied, and so on until the handkerchief is all knots. The performer takes a pull at the straight end to ensure its running easily, and also pulls it through as far as it will come without actually untying. He then covers the bunch of knots with the loose centre of the handkerchief, and gives the whole to be held in the hands of a spectator. As the trying of many knots will have caused the centre of the handkerchief to become tightened up, it will be necessary for the left hand to take some time in opening it nicely. The time thus gained is just sufficient to enable the right hand to work out the straight end through the many folds, the movement being naturally screened by the open portion of the handkerchief in the left hand. Ask the person to whom the bundle is given to hold, to feel that the knots are still there. He will feel the hardened folds, and will mistake them for the knots. Always borrow a handkerchief for this trick, or the audience will infallibly think that the knotted handkerchief is rapidly exchanged for another. If anyone starts tying a *bête noire*, you can stop him at once by saying that there will be no room for anyone else to tie a knot. This method is much easier than its forerunner, but, as before stated, it is not half so effective.

The Decanted Handkerchief.—The performer comes forward with an empty decanter, which is examined, and then completely covered with a cloth and given to a spectator to hold. The performer takes a second decanter, and places in it a handkerchief, also previously examined, and stands upon the stage. At the word of command, the handkerchief vanishes suddenly from the second decanter, which is not covered, and, on the cloth being removed from the first decanter by a spectator, the handkerchief is found inside. This pretty trick is thus performed : Procure two toilet water-bottles — by courtesy called decanters—with as wide necks as possible ; also two silk handkerchiefs, precisely similar. Scarlet is a serviceable colour for the purpose; and the handkerchiefs should be of very fine material, in order that they may be rolled up into a very small space, and not more than 15in. square—rather less, if anything. Behind the scenes the performer folds up one of the handkerchiefs small enough to be concealed under the fingers when they are holding the neck of the bottle. If three fingers are sufficient, so much the better ; but even if four are used no uninitiated person would ever suspect that anything would be concealed in so audacious a manner, especially as not the least clue has been given by the performer as to what is to be subsequently performed. The bottle shown round, a cloth is produced and covered over it, the handkerchief concealed in the fingers being popped into the bottle during the process. As it should at once spread out, it is not advisable to "double" it up tightly in the act of folding, but rather to "bunch" it, as it will then spring open the more readily. The bottle should be completely wrapped up in the cloth, bottom and all, and the spectator into whose custody it is placed must be enjoined to place one hand on the top and another at the bottom.   The performer now proceeds with his other bottle and the visible handkerchief.   Around his left wrist he has attached a thick eyeglass cord, which passes up the sleeve, round the back, and down the right-hand sleeve, where it has a short hook attached.   In order that it may be readily found, this hook should be fixed in the inside of the coat cuff.   The performer shows round the handkerchief, leaving the second bottle on the table, and, as he turns to fetch that article, the hook is got down and fixed firmly into the *centre* of the handkerchief.   It is then pushed down the neck of the bottle by the performer, the pushing down being conducted in such a way as to suggest the extreme difficulty of getting the handkerchief into the bottle.   The wand may here be used with effect to ram it down.   Standing with his right side towards the audience, the performer holds out the bottle, and announces his intention of causing the handkerchief to fly from it into the one held by a spectator, the holder being enjoined to keep a good watch, &c. At the word " three " (counting " one, two, three," slowly, always adds to the effect, by preparing for a climax), the performer thrusts out both hands to their fullest extent, when the handkerchief will fly out of the bottle up the right sleeve, its passage being shielded by the right hand, which must, of course, be disposed preliminarily so as to afford a free course to the handkerchief.   If the performer, holding the bottle in the right hand, presented his left side to the company, many spectators might be able to see the handkerchief fly up the sleeve.   With the right side towards them, they only see it disappear suddenly from the bottle.   The length of the cord will require adjustment, and it should be as short as the conjuror can conveniently manage without cramping the movement of the arms.   Some performers use a piece of stout elastic, which certainly has the property of causing a self-acting, rapid disappearance ; but when once the hook is in the handkerchief, and the latter in the bottle, a constant hold must be kept on the elastic to prevent a premature flight, which would at once destroy the trick.. The spectator holding the bottle is asked to remove the cloth and examine the bottle as much as he pleases, and the performer then hands the second bottle for examination, which has not been done before. A trick so very easy of management, and yet so effective, should be a favourite one with amateurs.

The Melting Handkerchiefs.—The performer comes forward with a soup-plate in one hand and two silk handkerchiefs in the other. The plate, after being shown empty, is placed upon the ground, inverted, whilst the performer takes the handkerchiefs in his hands, and commences to roll them

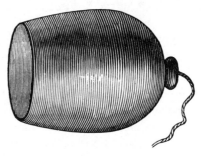

Fig. 45.

up in them. He rubs his hands together, and, on opening them, the handkerchiefs are found to have melted completely away. The soup-plate is then raised by one of the company, and the handkerchiefs are found beneath.

The soup-plate portion of the trick is thus easily managed: The performer has balled up under the fingers of the hand holding the plate duplicate handkerchiefs of those he holds openly in the other hand. They are of very fine silk, and so are easily concealed. As he boldly shows the inside of the plate, where the fingers are, the spectators never suspect the presence of the handkerchiefs, or of anything else. As the plate is laid carelessly upon the floor, it is drawn a few inches towards the performer, the side that is towards the company scraping the ground. In this way the handkerchiefs are got underneath. The melting away of the handkerchiefs is accomplished with the aid of the plain-looking implement depicted at Fig. 45. It is constructed of wood, is hollow, and is blackened on the outside. Through the end is a hole, and through that is passed a piece of stout elastic, having a knot on the inside. On the side seam of the vest is sewn a ring, and the end of the elastic, after being passed through this, is brought round the back and left side, and fastened securely to a button in front. This great length is necessary for the facile performance of the trick. When at rest, the wooden holder rests against the ring on the vest. After the performer has finished placing the plate upon the floor, he retires to the stage, and stands sideways to the company. Supposing the holder to be on his right side, that side would be nearest the company. First of all, the sleeves are turned very far back, and then, under cover of the right forearm, the left hand seizes the holder, and, drawing it out of concealment, places it in the right hand, where the handkerchiefs are being held. The performer may get out the holder before this, if he pleases—the proper time for so doing being whenever a favourable opportunity presents itself—and keep it palmed in the right hand. The arm will always prevent the elastic being seen by the company. With his arms outstretched, and the hands together, the performer proceeds to gather in the handkerchiefs by slow degrees, the fingers of the left hand pushing them into the holder. When they are all pushed home, the hands are opened slightly, the left hand only being moved for this purpose, and the holder, thus released, flies back until stopped by the ring. The performer continues rubbing away the handkerchiefs, still supposed to be in his hand, and he must act as though they were being rolled into an ever-decreasing ball, the final kneading being done by the tips of the fingers of the right hand, working in the palm of the left hand. All that now remains is to have the plate lifted. The trick may be prolonged and varied if the performer has a second holder on his left side containing handkerchiefs of other colours to those first used. By getting this holder out and rolling up the handkerchiefs from under the plate, the new handkerchiefs may be got out and the old ones substituted. Or the trick may be done the other way round, and the change executed first, the second handkerchiefs being found under the plate. There is no reason why this trick should not be even more elaborated, and further changes of handkerchiefs made. This may be done by means of a holder, some four inches in length, open at each end, and connected with the elastic by a metal fork-shaped piece, upon which it swivels by means of a pin passing through the centre. Each side can contain handkerchiefs of different colours, the pin through the centre preventing their becoming mixed with one another, and a variety of changes made, which will be intensely bewildering to the spectators, especially as the performer each time gives the handkerchief for examination, and shows his hands empty. The perfect simplicity and completeness of the method of vanishing permits of its being repeated any number of times, each successive change or disappearance causing fresh wonderment. Care must, however, be taken, in each instance, that the handkerchiefs are pressed well home in the holder, as an exposed portion might be seen as it flashed under the coat; whilst there is still greater danger of its subsequently working out and becoming slowly visible to the company. If the great length of elastic which I have recommended were not employed, the performer would not be able to stretch his arms out to their full extent in front of him; and it is highly essential for effect that the hands should be as far removed from the body as possible. The ingenuity of the performer will enable him to employ the holder in many tricks in which handkerchiefs take part.

Le Gant de Paris.—For this trick, which will bring the

performer's utmost skill into play, the following articles will be required: An orange, a lemon, and a walnut, all embowelled. The walnut contains a small kid glove, the lemon contains the walnut, and the orange the lemon.   Besides these, the performer has a whole orange, lemon, and walnut, which he can either bring forward, or, for preference, find in persons' hair or on their noses.   He has, also, concealed separately under the vest, a tiny glove, not more than three inches in length, and another quite ten inches long.   These will be best manufactured at home under personal supervision, and they should be well made.   The three fruits, produced or discovered, are placed in various positions on the table, or tables, care being taken that the lemon is situated conveniently near a trap.   Opportunity must be taken for exchanging the orange for the prepared one.   There are many ways for doing this.   One, which is as good as any, is to give the perfect orange to the stage attendant, telling him to place it upon the table, and then at once engage the audience with something else.   In going towards the table, the attendant effects the exchange.   Other methods, such as having the prepared orange on the shelf, and exchanging it with the other whilst calling attention to the lemon—carrying it in the breast pocket, and exchanging it when the back is turned to the audience—will readily suggest themselves. It is impossible to set down any hard-and-fast rule for such *minutiæ* as these.   Sometimes the disposition of the stage, or of the audience, will necessitate the adoption of a method that would, under other circumstances, be impossible of introduction.   The small glove is now brought down and kept concealed in the palm, and a kid glove, of the same colour as the one inside the prepared walnut shells, borrowed. Express your intention of making it pass inside the walnut, and observe that it is a little too large. Saying that you will make it a little smaller, proceed to rub it in the hand, and eventually exchange it for the tiny glove, which produce, and give to a gentleman to fit upon the hand.

Of course, it will be too small, and you will inquire what size glove the gentleman wears. You affect to misunderstand him, and clap on ten sizes more. Thus, if eight and a half is said, you exclaim, "Eigh*teen* and a half! That's a very large size, sir. But perhaps you think I can't make one so big. I will show you." It is sure to be explained that eight and a half, and not eighteen and a half, was the size mentioned, but you affect not to hear the correction, and proceed to rub up the small glove, having previously got down the large one. Make a great fuss of stretching, and finally produce the large glove, allowing the small one to drop inside it. The original borrowed glove in the meantime vest, if you have not done so already. Now proceed to the table, and, rolling up the large glove, with the little one inside it, tightly, pass it down a trap, and affect to rub it away into the walnut. Take up the walnut and vanish it by sleight of hand, pretending to pass it into the lemon, which get rid of, along with the nut, down a trap, and finally cut open the orange. Take out the lemon and cut that open, and produce the walnut. Ask one of the audience, on that side of the auditorium which is opposite to where the owner of the borrowed glove is seated, to open the walnut, at the same time getting down the borrowed glove from the vest. Take the glove from the walnut in one hand, and, pretending to place it in the other, whilst advancing towards the person from whom it was borrowed, effect an exchange. This must be done with all possible neatness and skill, or, at the last moment, the trick will fail. Supposing that you take the glove from the walnut with the left hand, the right should contain the borrowed glove. The left hand then makes a rapid movement towards the right, as if placing the glove in it. The glove in the left hand is in reality concealed, and the one in the right hand revealed. Half an hour's practice will make a wonderful difference in the execution of this pass, which will often have to be used, sometimes in cases of great emergency. On cutting open prepared oranges, lemons,

&c., always be careful to throw the skins behind you, or elsewhere away from the view of the audience, who are not likely to be deeply impressed in favour of your skill after a close examination of the remains of the prepared articles. If the triple combination of orange, lemon, and walnut is at first too difficult, try the dual one of lemon and walnut only. It is still very effective, and there is far less to think about. If the performer is limited as to traps, the large glove can be fired at the walnut from the pistol tube. The variation is quite unimportant.

CHAPTER XIV.

TRICKS WITH COINS.

The Invisible Transit.—This is a remarkably effective coin
trick. Several coins are inclosed in a little box, which is
stood in a position close to the audience. An empty tumbler
is placed upon a chair or table far away on the stage, and
the performer, abstracting the coins one by one from the
box, "passes" them into the distant glass, into which they
are heard to fall. On the glass being brought forward, the
coins are poured from it, and the box into which they were
put is found to be empty.

The tumbler used should be coloured and opaque, or semi-
opaque. Into it is fitted a zinc plate, depicted at Fig. 46.
This plate is, it will be seen, divided into two unequal portions, which are then hinged together. B is an arm which,
in the position shown in the sketch, prevents the flap C
from opening; and E is a tiny pin fitted into C for the
purpose of preventing the arm B going too far, and so

becoming difficult to control. At D is a pin which, first connected with the arm B, runs through the plate, and then through the bottom of the tumbler. Underneath, it is provided with another arm (A, Fig. 47), the position of which should correspond with that of B. The pin D should be considerably larger than the holes (they should be round ones) in the glass and zinc plate, and those portions of it which are to pass through the said holes must be filed down to the necessary thinness. By this means two shoulders will be formed, which will prevent the plate from coming down too far, and thus keep a space clear between it and the bottom of the tumbler. This space should be about three-

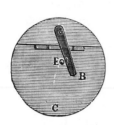

Fig. 46.   Fig. 47.

quarters of an inch in depth. The best method for fixing A to D is to have a tiny hole through the protruding end of the latter, through which a cross-pin can be passed. It will be seen that so long as the arm B is kept against the pin E, or anywhere near it, the flap C cannot possibly open, even though the tumbler be inverted. The shifting aside of the arm A will cause a simultaneous and equal movement on the part of B, and, when the glass is again inverted, whatever has been concealed in the space beneath C will fall out.

The performer will also require two little boxes, resembling each other in every particular. If nothing else be at hand, then little fancy cardboard boxes may be used, but it is by far the best to have a couple turned out of some light wood. The turner should receive directions to turn them both out of the same length of wood, which should have some slight imperfection running through it, as this will cause each box to be naturally marked in a similar manner. Should one lid have a little knot in it and the other be without such a blemish, it can be faithfully imitated by making a hole in the wood and running a little shellac into it. The boxes should be turned as lightly as possible, consistent with strength, and should just admit a half-crown. The interior depth should be that of six half-crowns. One of these boxes the performer conceals under the vest band. The tumbler he loads with four or five half-crowns, placed in the space under C, and the arm B is turned into position against E. This glass is placed upon the table. In one outside trouser pocket is a half-crown.

The preparations made, the performer advances with five other half-crowns and one of the little boxes, and gives the whole into the hands of a member of the audience, with the request to have the box examined and the coins placed in it. Whilst this is being done, the concealed box is got down from the vest into the left hand. The box, with the money in it, is taken by the right hand, and apparently put into the left. It is, however, palmed, and the empty box shown instead. The performer executes this movement as he is passing to another portion of the audience, to whom he will explain matters briefly. This passing about the room is highly essential in concealing many movements, and the conjuror's actions should be well mapped out beforehand, and not left to accident. As I am describing the trick, the money should be put in the box by someone on the conjuror's right. It then becomes natural for the performer to place the box in his left hand, in order to exhibit it to those on that side of the room. The learner will find, as he progresses, how highly important it is to pay attention to these apparently small, but by no means insignificant matters.

The performer's motions should balance, as it were; and his great study should be to make actions that are absolutely indispensable to him appear to be perfectly natural, if not the only ones that could be suitable to the occasion.

The empty box is then placed in the fingers of the right hand, in which the box containing the half-crowns is still concealed. The performer brings a chair close to the audience, and places upon it the empty box, first shaking the hand once or twice to show that the money is still inside. The coins rattling in the hidden box will appear to be in the one which is really empty. Care must be taken to keep the back of the hand towards the audience, and to allow it to hang down considerably, so as to do away with any possibility of an accidental exhibition of the palmed box.

The performer now proceeds to his table, pocketing the box with coins as he does so in as noiseless a manner as possible. He then takes the tumbler in one hand, and, rattling it hard with his wand all the time, turns it upside down to show that it is empty. On turning it back again the rattling must be repeated. This rattling, the reader will readily comprehend, is for the purpose of covering the slight clinking of the coins that are confined within. It is a good plan to have a piece of baize or cloth on the bottom of the tumbler, inside. This will deaden the sound of the clinking when the tumbler is being replaced upon the table The performer now returns to the little box, previously getting the half-crown from the pocket into his palm, and feigns to abstract one coin from it, the palmed coin being shown. This, with appropriate explanation, he "passes" into the tumbler, into which it is distinctly heard to fall. The whole of the coins are, one by one, abstracted from the box, and made to pass into the tumbler. The methods of extracting them should be varied. One can be taken out by means of the wand, another caught in mid-air, the next be found at the tip of someone's nose, and the next in somebody else's hair, whilst the last will probably be found attached either to the performer's elbow or to the sole of his boot. This variety of movement keeps the audience amused, and, consequently, distracts their attention, which might, perhaps, be employed in watching other matters somewhat too narrowly. The same system of variation should be observed in " passing " the coins, three or four different passes being brought into use. The last " pass " may be effectively made with the reverse palm, by the method described on page 8 for throwing the coin away. The palm can then be shown perfectly empty, the coin being recovered as the performer proceeds towards the glass.

The mystery of the coins being heard to fall into the tumbler has yet to be explained. The explanation is, that the conjuror's stage assistant is concealed behind the scenes, in a position as proximate to the tumbler as possible, with another glass and some coins. The performer and assistant must have an understanding between them, and when the assistant hears the word given he drops one coin into the glass, allowing a short time for the supposed journey. The word " pass " is the one commonly used, and is the best, for the conjuror is using it all through the performance, and it does not, therefore, excite any particular attention. It is as well to vary the speed with which the coins travel. The first two should occupy from a second and a half to two seconds in travelling from hand to tumbler. The next the conjuror should say will take a little longer, it being a very old coin and, consequently, weak. Five seconds will be quite long enough for this, and the next can be despatched with the command, " Presto, pass ! " This should arrive at its destination in half-a-second. If no arrangement on this head has been made beforehand, the performer must take care to speak loudly and distinctly. This co-operation of performer and assistant has already been explained in connection with *The Shower of Gold.*

Sometimes, with the view, I imagine, of making the trick appear still more difficult, the tumbler is covered with a borrowed handkerchief, pocketbook, programme, &c. When this is done, the assistant must cover his glass with a handkerchief, and so cause the sound of the falling coins to be muffled. I have seen an assistant commit an absurd error of using only one coin. The sound caused by one coin falling upon others in a glass is very different to that of a coin falling into an empty glass.

The use of the two little boxes in this trick is an idea of my own. Other conjurors invariably use a box with a hinged lid, which has a horizontal plate on a level with its upper rim. This plate has four slits in it, and into each slit is placed a half - crown. By an exceedingly ingenious mechanical arrangement, a coin is made to drop into the body of the box each time the lid is shut down. The performer affects to abstract one in the manner just described. The chief objection to this box is its great expense; otherwise, it is a very good piece of apparatus.

Another piece of apparatus that is also frequently used in conjunction with the trick is what is called the Half-crown Wand. This is a hollow tin wand, with a sliding piston inside it. One end is divided into two parts, which are hinged. A half-crown, that has been cut into three portions, is concealed in this opening top, and by means of a complexity of hair springs, and the action of the piston, moved by the thumb from the outside, the three fragments are pushed out, and, ranging themselves side by side, cause the appearance of a half-crown on the end of a wand. All I can say about this piece of apparatus is, that it is a pity the inventor's ingenuity was not directed towards making something else. I believe, though, that the article sells well, as it does away with the last piece of sleight of hand left in the trick, and so gives lazy people and duffers a chance.

The Banker. — In "Drawing-room Magic," a method for collecting coins from the air, &c., and passing them into a hat through the crown, was explained. Before larger audiences, the trick is capable of being much more elaborated. Going down amongst the audience, the performer collects quantities of coins from the heads and persons of the audience. There are various methods of executing this. One is to keep a coin palmed, and then produce it from the hair, whiskers, beards, sleeves, elbows, &c., of different spectators, a motion of throwing it into the hat being made each time it is produced, and the hat shaken, to cause the resemblance of a coin falling into it. Another method, which I hardly like as well, although successfully adopted by some good performers, is to dip the hand into the hat, and gather some coins quickly in it. These coins are kept in the palm of the hand, and concealed by the two outside fingers, and the thumb pushes one forward as it is required for production. The coins, in this instance, are actually tossed in the air and caught in the hat, which is of itself a great advantage, but the chances of detection are considerable. Nevertheless, the effect is very fine when the conjuror moves rapidly about, picking coins indiscriminately from everyone around. It is possible to hold a great number of large coins in the hand without detection ensuing. The third method is somewhat similar. The coins are gathered in the hand from the hat, but, instead of being reproduced singly, they are all swept from the head of a spectator into the hat. Coins invariably drop on the floor when the latter method is adopted, and the conjuror is enabled to take a fresh dip into the hat unperceived, whilst busying himself about the recovery of his property. What I recommend is a happy mixture of all three methods. Whichever is adopted, the performer must be exceedingly rapid in his movements, never stopping in one place, and accompanying his movements with a running commentary, such as, "Ah, one more on your nose, sir. Thank you, sir, just a few in your hair. Madam, a little one hiding itself under your bow, and, I declare, another in your fan." A lady's muff, when handy, can be well employed. It should be taken in the hand containing the coins, which are allowed to run through into the hat. A good variation, too, is to snatch a hat from a person's head or elsewhere, and dropping a few coins into it, immediately toss them about, and then pour them into your own hat. The larger the audience, the better this money collecting will succeed. It is a great feature in a performance, and always takes well.

A little piece of apparatus which, although I never use it myself, many find very useful for the magical production of coins, is what is known as the "money tube." This is a long flat tube of tin, japanned on the outside. It is just wide and deep enough to admit of the coins in use passing easily through it, and no more. At one end, on the outside, it is furnished with a broad flat hook, for the purpose of suspending the tube from a buttonhole or slit in the interior of the performer's vest or coat. The bottom end is furnished with a lever arrangement on the outside, which for half-crowns would be thus constructed : In length it would just exceed the width of a half-crown, and each end be furnished with a peg about a quarter of an inch long. In the centre is drilled a hole, and on the tube is a bifurcated projection, also with a hole through it. The lever is placed in its position, and a pin passed through it and the projection. A joint will thus be formed very similar in appearance to the centre joint of an umbrella rib. In the tube (exactly underneath the pegs, which must be towards the tube) pierce two holes, and under the upper half of the lever fix a small piece of spring, tolerably strong. The apparatus is then complete. The spring causes the upper half of the lever to rise, and, as a natural consequence, the lower half to be depressed. The lower peg thus prevents anything that may be in the tube from passing out at the end. So soon, however, as any pressure is put upon the upper half of the lever the lower peg rises and allows the coin to escape. The upper peg, descending at the same time, prevents the escape of any other coins that may be in the tube. The method for using the tube is to fix it securely under the vest or coat flap, with the bottom end all but exposed. When the performer requires a coin, all he has to do is to curl his fingers under the mouth of the tube, and press the upper portion of the lever, when a coin will fall into his hand. As the operation is invariably accompanied by a slight clattering, however careful the performer may be, the hat should always be shaken for the purpose of smothering the sound made by the tube. A small band of elastic on the coat or vest will serve to keep the tube steady. The lever lies transversely across the tube, and not straight along it. This enables the little pegs to pass into the triangular spaces left between two coins, the edges of which are touching. It is not advisable to produce many coins in a short space of time by this method, as the frequent repetition of the movement of the hand might easily be noticed.

An effective continuation is to apparently cause the coins to pass through the crown the reverse way, i.e., from the inside to the outside. For this purpose, the performer must retire well up the stage, concealing, as he does, so several coins in the palm of the hand, one being shown at the ends of the fingers. The hat is held out, crown downwards, in the other hand, and the coin in the fingers then tossed high in the air. Whilst it is descending the thumb gets another coin in readiness, and as the coin in the air falls into the hat the one brought from concealment is put against the crown and instantly pulled sharply away from it. The effect is as if the coin thrown in the air had passed through the crown of the hat, and was caught by the performer as it came through. Considerable practice must be undertaken, as it is indispensable that the fall of the descending coin into the hat and the production of the fresh one at the crown be precisely simultaneous, otherwise the effect will be weakened, if not altogether spoilt. The hat must contain some coins at the commencement, otherwise the accumulation of those thrown into the air and subsequently caught in the hat, would, of course, be noticed. The effect is improved if the crown of the hat be turned slightly towards the audience at the moment when the coin is supposed to come through it. As the eyes of the spectators always follow the coin in the air, the slight motion of the thumb in getting a fresh coin in readiness is never perceived. Large coins tell best, and about six should be used.

When the performer has sufficiently amused the audience in this way, he can proceed with the trick under notice. For it he will require—at least, he will find it advisable to have—an oval tray of japanned tin. To all appearances, the tray is only an ordinary one, but it has a double bottom, the space between the two bottoms being a little more than the thickness of a half-crown, or whatever coin the performer may be in the habit of using. The rims of the two bottoms are joined all round, with the exception of a portion at one end, which is left open to the extent of a little more than the width of the coin in use. Two strips of tin, soldered firmly in their places, extend from each side of this opening, in parallel lines, to the other end of the tray, and so form a passage between the two bottoms capable of receiving a quantity of coins, ranging in number according to the length of the tray or the will of the performer. When the tray is tilted to any extent, the open end being the one that is depressed, the coins will naturally slide out one after the other. If the space between the double bottoms is too deep, the rearmost coins will overlap those in front, and so cause an obstruction. The tray is loaded with (say) five coins, and so brought on. Fifteen (a few more or less will not matter) coins are then taken from the hat, and placed upon the tray, which is then put into the hands of a spectator, who must be enjoined to rise for the purpose, and to keep very steady, so as not to upset the coins. A boy's cap is then borrowed, and put into the hands of another spectator, who is placed in a position close to and facing the holder of the plate. In the absence of a cap, a handkerchief, held in the form of a bag, will answer as well, if care be taken to arrange it so that none of the coins can escape and fall to the ground. The performer retires to the stage, and explains that, when he counts "three," the holder of the tray is to pour, as rapidly as he can, the fifteen coins into the cap, the holder of which is directed to close the cap immediately this is done. As the performer has taken care to place the tray in the assistant's hands, with the opening from him, it follows that, when the fifteen coins are poured from the surface into the cap, the five from the concealed receptacle will accompany them. A very distinct mark should be made upon the tray so that the performer can readily distinguish one end from the other. When the cap is closed, the performer counts five more coins into his hand, and "passes" them into the cap, the holder of which is then requested to count out the coins upon the plate, to show that the number has been increased by five. All counting of coins should take place both before and afterwards, or the audience may fail to perceive what has been done. The trays sold at conjuring repositories are nearly always round; this is a bad shape, as there is nothing to induce the holder of the tray to tilt it as the performer desires. When it is oval, it is only natural to pour the coins off the narrow end. It is also impossible to notice from any distance if a round tray has been shifted, accidentally or otherwise. A couple of inches difference will cause the trick to fail, for the coins will not pour out; and some people who are in the secret are malicious enough to be capable of wilfully turning the tray round for the purpose of spoiling the trick. The name of "The Banker" is given to the trick, because the performer supposes the holder of the cap to be the banker, and he then shows how he pays in his money. The great effect of the trick is derived from the fact that the performer never approaches the custodians of the money after once giving it into their hands.

Hold them Tight!—The performer takes a few coins—four half-crowns or florins will be found the most suitable—and also a strong white cotton handkerchief. He then asks the assistance of one of the spectators, stating his predilection for a very strong man. The more burly the volunteer, the better he will suit the conjuror's purpose. Seat him on a chair a little on one side, and facing the audience. Place the coins in the centre of the handkerchief, which then invert, and grasp the coins through it from the outside. This is done openly and deliberately, and the assistant is requested to hold the handkerchief firmly between the two hands a few inches below the coins. He is then asked if he thinks it possible for the performer to pull the coins through the handkerchief without making a hole, or to get them out without interfering with the assistant's hand. The answer will invariably be a negative one, and the performer then says, "Very good; that is your opinion. I will now see what the audience think about it." With this, the performer steps forward with the coins and the handkerchief, and explains to the audience that it is a trial of Strength *versus* Skill between the strong man on the stage and himself. He then requests someone to place the coins in the handkerchief, so that there shall be fair play, the handkerchief being spread over the performer's left hand for the purpose. When the coins are placed in the handkerchief, they should be grasped through it by the thumb and first and second fingers. The performer then turns suddenly to the person on the stage, and says, "I trust you are not nervous, sir; you look very pale." This will cause everyone to look at once at the person addressed, who will, if under the glare of footlights or other strong gas, infallibly bear a pale appearance. But whether he looks pale or not will not matter, the diversion being made for the purpose of distracting the attention of the audience from the performer for a moment or two. Whilst all eyes are directed towards the assistant, the performer turns the coins over twice in the handkerchief, a fold of which is taken at each turn, and the coins thus enveloped. The coins are then grasped in the right hand,

and a good shake given to the handkerchief for the purpose of straightening it as much as possible. The result of this manœuvre is that the coins are simply hidden in a couple of folds on the *outside* of the handkerchief, the supposition indulged in by the audience being that they are *inside*, and that the handkerchief has been merely inverted as before. This folding and turning is not easy to accomplish quickly and neatly. The coins must be held firmly, and the fingers then turn them over inwards, the thumb being raised to allow them to be pushed well under it. Before the fingers are removed, the thumb descends and nips securely that portion of the handkerchief pushed over with the coins by the fingers, and retains it whilst the second turn is being made, the same process being repeated. With the fold well made, the performer may venture to allow that portion of the handkerchief containing the coins to hang downwards, and even give a slight jerk to cause the coins to jingle, This will totally disarm suspicion. It is much easier to hold the handkerchief, with the coins, in one hand and make the folds with the other, but the proceeding is unbusinesslike and provocative of suspicion.

The handkerchief is then put into the hands of the seated assistant, as before, the performer holding that portion containing the coins. A tremendous mock struggle ensues, the performer allowing himself to be pulled nearly over once or twice, which will cause him to remark that he has made a mistake this time, and has met with someone a little too strong for him. All the time he is working a finger into the folds, which he quietly undoes, and, under cover of the left hand, gets the coins out into the right. With this hand he takes his wand, which is held under the armpit during the trick, and continues pulling with the left. After a while, he says that it is no use, and, relinquishing his hold, asks to have his money given back to him. Of course, the assistant knows nothing about it; but the performer points out the fact that there is no hole in the handkerchief, consequently *he* cannot have the coins. Under the plea of finding out where they are concealed, the performer taps with his wand on various portions of the assistant's person. When he reaches either the elbow or the knee, he allows the coins in the hand to rattle against the wand at each tap, and it will appear to the audience that they are concealed up the assistant's arm or leg. Grasping the sleeve or trouser, the performer turns it up a little, and rattles the coins out on the floor. If found in the trouser, the assistant should be asked to place his foot upon a chair. It is very easy to jerk the coins a few inches up the sleeve or trouser leg as it is being turned up; they will then fall out naturally. The reason I give directions for using a strong pocket handkerchief is because the continued pulling will sometimes cause a sharp-edged coin to cut through. I never use any but my own handkerchief, for this reason.

There is another method of folding the coins in the handkerchief, which surpasses the one above described for neatness, and it may be executed in full view of the audience, with their eyes specially directed upon the performer's hands, instead of momentarily diverted. The coins, in this instance, are taken between the finger and thumb of the left hand, and held perpendicularly. With the right hand, the handkerchief is thrown over them. This the performer does close to his temporary assistant upon the chair; upon which he says, "That is all very well: you know that the coins are safe inside the handkerchief; but I must also convince the rest of the company." Suiting the action to the word, the performer advances a few paces, performing, as he does so, the following manœuvre : With the right hand inverted, *i.e.*, the palm turned upwards, the coins are seized between the first and middle fingers. Simultaneously the left hand is shifted a couple of inches backwards, and the right hand, turning over in that direction, places the coins once more between the left finger and thumb, but this time there are two thicknesses of the handkerchief intervening. That half of the handkerchief which is hanging on the side nearest to the company is now raised by the right hand, when the coins will be exposed to view. The act of shifting the left hand back a couple of inches has caused the fingers of the left hand to be covered by a false fold of those dimensions. The company, therefore, cannot see the said fingers, the performer making doubly sure by holding his hand as low as possible, without exciting suspicion. Now, after having shown the coins, if the performer merely turned back the half he had lifted, no par-

Fig. 48.

ticular result would be arrived at; but the learner, who is, of course, following me with coin and handkerchief in hand, will at once see that, if that half of the handkerchief which is hanging on the side nearer the performer be turned over along with the one that has been raised to show the coins, in the direction of the company, the result achieved is that the coins are on the outside of the handkerchief, but enveloped in the 2in. fold. This turning back of two halves, instead of one, being the vital part of the whole thing, must be done with great carelessness. Indeed, the action of turning the rear half over with the right hand is a mistake : all that is necessary is to drop the left hand with a good shake, when both halves will fall on the same side, as naturally as possible. These little things require a good deal of explanation, but it is a really very simple manœuvre, which I divide into four distinct movements, viz. : First movement—placing the coins under handkerchief, in left hand ; second movement— turning over coins with right hand, and seizing again with left thumb and finger (see Fig. 48) ; third movement—dropping left hand and raising front half of handkerchief with right hand ; fourth movement—releasing handkerchief with right hand and shaking two halves over with left. When the fourth movement has been completed, the right hand should seize the handkerchief just below the coins, which can then be struck upon the left palm, carelessly, but hard, so as to indirectly convey the idea of their being contained in a bag, made by the handkerchief. There need be no fear of the fold becoming loose if the handkerchief be gripped firmly ; and the boldness of the act will disarm suspicion. The very security of this fold renders it more difficult to work the coins out when the " trial of strength " comes on, and the assistant must be made to hold the handkerchief some distance away from the coins, so that the performer's hands have plenty of space to work in. Whilst the assistant is thus holding the handkerchief, it is a good plan to allow that part in which the coins are folded to hang down—whilst the sleeves are being turned back, for instance. This will keep up the impression of their being enclosed in a bag.

The Money Changer.—This trick is accomplished by means of the first deceptive fold described in *Hold them Tight !* Its simple nature may cause it to appear easy of execution ; but let not the learner foster this delusive idea, for the slightest bungle will spoil the trick, which depends entirely upon sleight of hand.

In the left hand the performer has three pennies concealed. Three half-crowns and three pennies, all marked by various members of the audience, are then borrowed. The three half-crowns are first collected in the right hand, and given into the custody of one of the audience. The pennies are next collected, in the right hand also, and then the performer begs the further loan of a couple of handkerchiefs. Just as he is stepping forward to take the proffered articles, he says to one of the audience, " Would you kindly hold these pennies for an instant ?" and, making a " pass" (Fig. 11) towards the left hand, exhibits and hands the coins therein concealed. The idea conveyed by the performer is that, the coins being in his way whilst borrowing the handkerchiefs, he wants to be rid of them for a short space of time. This covers the action of the pass, which might otherwise appear suspicious, as being unnecessary and meaningless. Take the first handkerchief in the right hand, and let the second hang over the left shoulder. Now go at once to the holder of the half-crowns, and, taking them from him, place them in the centre of the handkerchief, previously spread over the right hand, which contains the marked pennies. Turn briskly to another member of the audience, executing as you do so a single turn only of the coins in the handkerchief with the fingers of the right hand, the coins that are in the hand itself going over as well. Take that portion of the handkerchief which contains the coins in the left hand, grasping the whole securely. Remove the right hand from underneath, and with it grasp the handkerchief some four or five inches from the coins, and then reverse the positions of the hands, handkerchief and all, the right being above and the left below. The pennies which were recently in the right hand will now be in a bag, as it were, formed by the handkerchief. The half-crowns are still on the outside, hidden by one fold of the handkerchief, and held by the fingers of the left hand. Request the person to whom you have advanced to stand up, and inform him that you wish his right hand to take the place of yours, and that he is on no account to relax a firm hold for an instant, or to allow any coins either to enter or escape. As you say this, dance the coins two or three times up and down in the left hand, which hollow as much as possible, and the half-crowns will fall into it. Their clinking will not signify in the least, as it will be attributed to the coins in the handkerchief. Then give the handkerchief into the custody of the person selected, the left hand simultaneously finding its way to the handkerchief hanging from the left shoulder, which it takes. The same manœuvre is then repeated, the handkerchief being spread over the left hand with the half-crowns in it, and the right eventually securing the substituted pennies. All that remains to be done is to command the coins in the handkerchiefs to change places, which feat is apparently accomplished. The great peril of the trick lies in the necessity of repeating the action of folding. To avoid detection, the performer must be always on the move, and endeavour by gesture and speech to continually direct the general attention of the audience to the persons whom he is addressing. The most dangerous person is he from whom the coins are taken before being put into the handkerchief. The best method for disarming him is to be very profuse with thanks for his kindness. By the time you have done thanking him, your object has been accomplished. It is strange what a trivial thing is required for the purpose of distracting the attention of the audience, whether collectively or individually, if the performer can only assume an appropriate expression of countenance. On the other hand, the least appearance of anything approaching to bewilderment only tends to make the audience doubly sharp. "Hallo!" they will think, "he is in a fix," and forthwith the minutest action is devoured.

In this trick, the effect of manner will make itself manifest in a marked degree. It is evident that, if anyone in the audience fix his eyes intently upon the performer's hands from the commencement of the trick to the finish, never removing his gaze for an instant, he is bound to notice the turns that are made. Now, it is impossible for a conjuror even to keep his eye upon every member of his audience for the purpose of noticing who is and who is not watching him. The utmost he can do is to make such diversions as are best calculated to accomplish his ends in a general way. If any-one in the audience be particularly sharp, and will not be taken in, it cannot be helped.

I make these remarks in this place because a good opportunity presents itself: they are of universal application. It is only another sermon on the old text, misdirection.

It is as well to borrow either very thick handkerchiefs or else coloured ones for this trick. Thin white handkerchiefs will reveal the nature of the coins contained in them under certain conditions of light. The person who temporarily holds the substituted pennies should be enjoined to close his hand. This is to prevent him from whiling away the time by seeking for the marks. A person might do this merely out of curiosity, and without any malice whatever. When practising, it is best to commence with a single coin of each sort, then two, and finally three. Four coins would only make the trick more difficult, without increasing the effect. With one coin only, the trick is very poor; besides, it naturally appears to the audience to be more difficult for the performer to transmit a number of coins from one spot to another than to perform a like feat with a single coin.

The Crystal Plateau.—This is a very pretty, but almost unknown trick. Hanging by a couple of cords at the back of the stage is an oblong plateau, composed simply of a frame and a piece of glass. The performer borrows three marked florins or half-crowns, which he can either hold in his hand, or place in the little box described in *The Invisible Transit*. He calls attention to the plateau, the transparent nature of which seems to render any examination unnecessary, and announces that, not only will he cause the coins to invisibly

leave his hand (or the box), but they shall do so one at a
time, and affix themselves to the glass of the plateau. This
is done, the coins appearing one after another upon the face
of the plateau, from which the performer removes them, and
hands them back to their owners.

This fine effect is thus managed: The plateau (Fig. 49) is
composed of two pieces of glass, one behind the other. The
front piece is fixed firmly into the frame, but that in the rear
is only loosely fastened. An indiarubber band, passing across
the lower portion of the latter, keeps the two glasses close

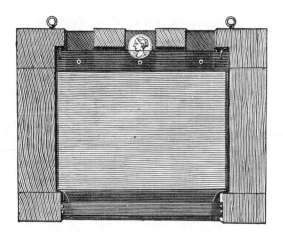

Fig. 49.

together at their lower edges, but at the top they are kept
apart to the extent of about twice the thickness of a half-
crown. From the upper part of the frame three spaces are
cut out, wide enough to admit a coin, and deep enough to
cause a coin dropped in from that point to fall between the
two glasses. To keep the coins temporarily suspended, three
holes are drilled through the rear glass, just below the places
for the coins, and little pegs inserted therein. To each of
these pegs is attached a thread, held in the hand of the assistant behind the scenes. The latter should be immediately

in rear of the plateau, in order that he may get a straight pull. When the performer cries "Pass," one peg is pulled out, and the coin it supported falls between the two glasses. As these approach each other by degrees, the falling coin sticks fast about mid-way, appearing to the company—and, for that matter, to the performer, too, so perfect is the deception—to be stuck on the surface of the front glass, supposed by the company to be the only one. When all three coins have thus made their appearance, the performer proceeds to the plateau, and, placing a hat beneath it with one hand, opens the rear glass slightly out from the front one, the coins thus falling out. The marked coins have, of course, never left the performer's hand, three of his own having been placed in the little box, if that was used; and it is very easy for him to palm these in the hat, and produce the marked ones, as though taken from it. To pass them, one by one, from the hands, they must be held in the left hand, and palmed singly with the right. If the performer is skilful enough to palm them one over the other, so much the better, otherwise the palmed coin must be got rid of in the little trouser pocket each time, whilst the contents of the left hand are being exhibited.

The Money-producing Candle.—The performer commences by stating that the next trick will be performed with a quantity of shillings. He will want so many that the company can scarcely be able to supply them, so he will not put them to any trouble, especially as he has perfected a new invention by means of which money can be manufactured out of candles. He either borrows a hat, or takes a plate, which should be given for examination, and then approaches a candle, which has been burning for some time on the table. Turning up his sleeves, and indirectly showing both palms to be empty, he places his thumb on one side of the candle and the fingers on the other, near the bottom, and draws the hand upwards, as though squeezing the candle. Two or three quick movements are made, and then

a shilling appears in the performer's fingers as though it had
been taken out of the very flame. The coin is placed in the
plate, or hat, and, after the palm has again been shown empty,
a second shilling is squeezed out of the candle, *via* the flame.
This is repeated a great number of times, a quantity of
shillings being produced, with which a trick should be sub-

FIG. 50.

sequently performed, the candle experiment, in itself, being of
insufficient length.

The secret lies in the candle. This is a brass cylinder,
covered with white paper (Fig. 50), a piece of candle being
introduced into the top, and lighted. This introduction must
be neatly done, and some wax from the candle scraped
over the junction, so as to hide it. Inside the cylinder is a
spiral spring arrangement, precisely similar to the cylindrical

sovereign - holders sold, from which one coin at a time is extracted by a simultaneous pressing and drawing action. Such a holder, placed inside the imitation candle, with the opening downwards, would be the very thing (for sovereigns), provided an opening were made just below it sufficiently large to permit the insertion of a finger with which to withdraw the coin. The spiral spring continually presses the coins from above, keeping the lowest one always at the opening, it being prevented from falling by a narrow projecting rim inside, which leaves a large portion of the central space of the coin free to be acted upon by the inserted finger. The side of the candle upon which the opening is situated is, I need not say, turned away from the spectators, and, as the performer slides his hand slowly upwards, a finger brings away a coin—the movement being, of course, continued evenly, and no stoppage made at this particular moment. With a little practice, the coin can be extracted with wonderful facility. Before commencing, the performer should show that there is no preparation about the candlestick, by turning it upside down, and banging it upon the table. The candle is grasped by the hand, for the purpose of removal, over the spot where the opening is, and it may then be shown on all sides; but I do not advise that the performer should draw attention to the candle. No hint of a prepared candle should be given the spectators, who are not at all likely to think of such a thing unless it is suggested to them, particularly if the performer advances boldly, candle in one hand and candlestick in the other, and exhibits them. It will be found that an imitation candle to take shillings will have to be a fairly large one, so the conjuror must use his judgment, and have one for sixpences only, if his exhibition of an abnormally large candle be likely to draw suspicion towards it. For large stage performances a candle capable of taking florins might be used. The candle can be profitably used incidentally to vary the collection of money in the air (see page 14, &c.), a coin being now and again placed visibly into the hat, instead of "passed" magically through the crown, and a fresh one obtained from the candle, just as would be done from the money tube (see page 239).

The Flight.—This is a method for causing five coins to disappear. It is a very useful interlude when the performer is hard up for something to do, and when it is desirable to lengthen out the entertainment.

Take five well-worn half-crowns (your own or borrowed; marked or not), stand sideways to the audience, right side to the front, and extend the left hand, palm upwards. Hollowing the hand slightly, place one coin upon the tip of each finger. Place the right hand upon the left, the corresponding fingers of each hand meeting at the tips, so that the coins are held firmly between them. Give the hands a half turn, so that the back of the right hand is towards the audience, and hold them in this position for a few moments, the eyes being directed upwards, as though the remainder of the trick were to be in connection with the ceiling. Give the hands two upward and downward sweeps, increasing in vehemence, and at the third bring the points of the fingers together. This will cause the coins to lap one over the other in tolerably good order, when they must be pushed firmly between the root and first joint of the right thumb, breadthwise (see Fig. 5). The action must be executed as the hands descend for the third time, and with such speed that the coins must be secure in position when the hands are brought up again, when they will affect to toss the coins hard up at the ceiling. This takes some little doing, as there must not be the slightest pause in the upward and downward swing. The coins can be reproduced from the person of the performer or from the audience, or they need not be reproduced at, all.

The feat is capable of being introduced into tricks where five coins are made to disappear. Unless each finger has an occupant, it does not look complete, so it is not advisable to introduce the variation where four coins, or fewer, are employed.

Coin and Worsted Ball Trick.—A very good trick indeed is performed with a ball of worsted and a coin. Have a flat metal tube broad enough to admit with ease the coin intended to be used, and wind round one end of it a quantity of worsted, so as to form a large ball, completely closing up one aperture, the other end being left open and protruding half an inch or so. Place this in a pocket or a bag, or behind a screen. You must have a duplicate coin palmed, which change with the borrowed one, and give to be held in a handkerchief. The coin would, of course, be marked. When the worsted ball is in a bag, or behind a screen, the coin must be dropped down the tube, which is then withdrawn, and the ball compressed in the hand so as to obliterate all traces of an opening. It is, however, a much neater way to have the ball and tube in the pocket (it will have to be a side pocket); another ball being sent round to be examined before anything is done. When the coin is in the prepared ball, and the tube withdrawn, it can be exchanged with the other. When this has been successfully accomplished, give the ball to be held high in the air, and, taking the substituted coin, "pass" it inside. Now have the ball placed in a tumbler, which is held by one person, whilst another pulls at the end of the worsted, and so unwinds it. In the centre will, of course, be found the borrowed article.

CHAPTER XV.

MISCELLANEOUS.

ON APPARATUS, AND ITS USES AND ABUSES—HOUDIN'S DIE—
ADDITIONAL EFFECT—NEW METHOD—THE GOLD-FISH TRICK:
PISCICULTURE EXTRAORDINARY—THE BOWLS AND COVERS
—THE CLOTH—WHERE TO CARRY THE BOWLS—HOW TO
PRODUCE THEM—BAD AND GOOD INNOVATIONS—HOW TO
CAUSE THE BOWLS TO DISAPPEAR—MISHAPS—GOLD FISH
AND INK—THE GLOBE—THE LINING—THE LADLE—HOW
TO FILL IT—THE CARD—THE TRICK IN A SMALL WAY—
TRAVELS OF A GLASS OF WATER—GOLD! GOLD! EVERY-
WHERE—THE HEN FOR EVERY HOUSEHOLD—THE BEST
BREEDS: NO. 1, NO. 2, AND NO. 3—HOW TO HATCH YOUR
EGGS WITH DESPATCH—DECAPITATION NOT FATAL TO
FOWLS—" KLING, KLANG "—HOW TO STAND FIRE—THE
INTERCEPTED BULLET — THE WANDERING GINGER-BEER
BOTTLE—THE PLUME AND THE SEED—COOKING MADE
EASY: HAT VERSUS SAUCEPAN—A LITTLE ACCIDENT, AND
HOW TO RECTIFY IT—THE FLAGS OF OLD ENGLAND—A
NUT FOR BLACKSMITHS TO CRACK—THE DRAWER BOX—
HOW TO MAKE IT — WHEN TO USE IT, AND WHEN NOT
—THE CONE—BACCHUS' DOVECOTE—HOW TO PREPARE THE
BOTTLE—HOW TO MESMERISE AND CAUSE A DOVE TO
DISAPPEAR—THE WINE-DRINKING CRYSTAL BALL—BACCHUS'
MAYPOLE—ON PROGRAMMES AND TITLES—HOW TO MAKE
THE BOTTLE — THE ACCOMMODATING BOTTLE — HOW TO

"WORK" IT SUCCESSFULLY—ANOTHER METHOD—THE MES-
MERIC SUSPENSION WAND: TWO METHODS—THE MAGI'S
BRAZEN ROD—THE BALLS—HOW TO CHANGE THE RINGS
—THE SHOWER OF PLUMES—THE FAIRY FLOWER—THE
VASE.

HOWEVER great the respect which one may have for sleight
of hand pure and simple, it is quite undeniable that a set
performance is greatly improved by the occasional introduction of some neat-looking, but not gaudy, apparatus. Under
this head need by no means be included self-acting machinery,
during the performance of which the performer acts as a
mere puppet. All the apparatus mentioned in this work will
require adroit handling; and the conjuror will do well to
practise as thoroughly with each article as he would towards
the acquisition of a feat of sleight of hand. Apparatus seems
to have a malicious pleasure in going wrong, always on the
most critical occasions, and, for this reason, the majority of
skilful performers feel most happy when using very little of
it. One thing may be taken for granted, viz., that apparatus,
exhibited without the assistance of sleight of hand, and
plenty of it, causes the performer to degenerate into a mere
showman—opening a box here, and taking off a lid there.
In introducing apparatus, the performer must lay a very great
deal of stress upon the sleight of hand portion of the business, as though therein lay the whole of the trick, the apparatus being a mere necessary evil in connection with it. By
engaging the attention of the company with sleight of hand,
it is drawn away from the apparatus, the spectators being so
convinced of the performer's skill that they do not so readily
accuse him of trusting to gaudy boxes and canisters for his
effects.

Some of the apparatus described can be made at home,
but, as a general rule, it is cheaper and more satisfactory to
buy it at a conjuring repository. Low prices are the order
of the day; and, as the articles are made by experienced

men, they must be superior to those manufactured by persons new to the business.

Houdin's Die Trick.—Although this trick, sold everywhere for a shilling, must be as well known as any, I have found it appreciated by certain audiences, which have, by the way, invariably been drawing-room ones. Before a boys' school, or large public audience, it would not be advisable to exhibit it. The trick consists in placing a die upon the uppermost of two hats, covering it with a cover, and causing it to pass through into the lower hat. The secret lies in a hollow false die, which has five sides only, and which fits over the real die like a cover. The actual cover used in the trick fits over the dummy die. The method of performance is extremely easy. Place the dummy die in the breast pocket, in a handy position, and give the real one to be examined with the cover. Whilst this is being done, borrow two hats, and take them to the centre table, slipping the false die from the pocket into one of them when your back is turned. Place the hat containing the dummy on the table, crown downwards, and invert the other one over it. Now take the die and place it upon the uppermost hat, and explain to the audience as follows : "Ladies and gentlemen,—You have all kindly examined the die and cover, and found that both are genuine and free from trickery. I now take this solid die and place it upon this hat; but before doing so I will show you that the hat has no hole through the crown. [Take up hat, and hold it before the light, and bang it about a little, then replace and put die upon it.] The trick I shall perform will be to cover the die with this cover, and, on again removing it, it will be found that the die will have passed through the hat into the one underneath, thus [tilt the top hat so as to cause the die to fall into the lower hat]. Now that I have explained what is to be done, I will proceed to do it." Take the dummy die out of the hat (being careful to keep the open part from the audience, and leaving the real die behind), and place it, with the opening downwards, upon the upper hat, which you have replaced. You can pretend to cut through the hat, all round the die, with a penknife, making a noise with the nail to imitate the sound of cutting, and then, placing the cover over the die, give it a rap with the wand. Grasp the cover very tightly near the bottom, and raise it, bringing away the dummy die as well. Hold it up to the spectators, and rattle the wand inside, and then turn out the real die from the hat on to the floor. Whilst doing this with one hand, the other should be passed behind the table, and the dummy allowed to slide out of the cover on to the shelf. This latter effect is invariably omitted by conjurors, and the trick, in my opinion, spoilt, as attention to it enables the performer to hand round the cover for inspection after the trick is performed, thereby totally upsetting those who, having purchased the trick, fancy they know all about it. I have frequently been asked by such people how I do the trick, they little thinking that the apparatus I use is exactly similar to their own. The die, cover, and dummy can be purchased so cheaply that it is scarcely worth while for the conjuror to manufacture his own. If he wishes to exercise his ingenuity, let him try the following method, which is an improvement on Houdin's old one only inasmuch as it is not so well known.

Procure a die some four inches square, with dummy and cover complete. A smaller size can be used, but I give the most effective for the trick. Now take five pieces of cardboard, each the size of one side of the die, and join them together with hinges of linen, not all in a row, but with one in the centre and the four others on either side of it. Lay these upon the centre of a large coloured handkerchief, and place another handkerchief, of a precisely similar pattern, over it. Sew the two handkerchiefs and cardboard together through the centre piece of card only, and then sew the edges of the handkerchiefs together all round. The two handkerchiefs are made to pass as a single one only. Before commencing, the dummy must be placed, opening downwards,

upon the shelf, and the handkerchief should be lying carelessly upon a chair or side table. Show the die and cover
round, and borrow two hats. Take the cover and hats to
the table, and whilst one hand is placing one hat over the
other, as in the first method, the other should place the
cover over the dummy die on the shelf, which must thus be
picked up. Show the inside of cover (*i.e.*, the inside of the
dummy), and place it upon the uppermost hat. Now take
the die and place it upon the table, a few inches only from
the back. Spread the handkerchief over it, and whilst taking
hold of the centre piece of card of the internal arrangement across the middle, with one hand, from the outside,
pass the other hand underneath the handkerchief, and, under
cover of the same, place the die upon the shelf. The hand
holding the handkerchief will all the time appear to be
holding the die in the air a few inches from off the table.
Fold the handkerchief carefully up, and the five pieces of
card will give an exact resemblance of a die folded up in
a handkerchief, which idea is what you wish to convey to
the minds of the audience. Place this carefully upon a side
table, and then explain that you are about to pass the die
from the handkerchief invisibly under the cover. Raise the
cover — and, along with it, the dummy die — once more
rattle the wand inside, and replace it. Then take the handkerchief carefully by two corners and suddenly give it a
hard shake in the air. The die that is supposed to be inside
will not, according to the expectations of the spectators, roll
upon the floor, but you will show it to be on the top of the
hat by raising the cover only, and revealing the dummy.
Remove the dummy from the hat to the table with two
hands, as if it were solid, and act as if you were about
to return the two hats. You, however, take one of them,
opening downwards, and, bringing the brim on a level with
the top of the table, but overhanging the shelf considerably,
pop the die inside it with the other hand, which instantly
takes up the second hat, and you advance with both. Before

you have progressed very far, however, you say that, perhaps, after all, the audience would prefer seeing the die back again; and it is very evident that so large an object must be somewhere. Of course, no one will object, and you replace the hats one over the other, the one containing the die being naturally the lower one. The trick then proceeds as before described, the dummy die being carefully lifted with two hands upon the uppermost hat, and the cutting operation gone through. The difficult portion of the trick is getting the die from the shelf into the hat. This should be well practised.

The Gold-fish Trick.— Of the first three questions asked a conjuror by a new acquaintance, one will infallibly be, " Can you do the gold-fish trick? " When it was first exhibited, it caused intense excitement, and, the secret being fairly well kept, the trick is but little known even now. The performer advances with a shawl or large handkerchief, and, after waving it about, he produces from it a large glass bowl full of water, in which gold-fish are complacently swimming. I have heard the wildest suggestions made in explanation of the trick. One says the bowls of water come up a trap door, regardless of the fact that the cloth does not reach the ground, consequently anything coming up through the floor must infallibly be seen at once. Another explains that the performer has the bowls empty about him, and has an indiarubber reservoir of water up his back, with a pipe coming down the sleeve. Where the fish come from is not explained. No one seems to be able to think of the real secret—an indiarubber cover. The bowls are flat, not more than two inches deep in the centre, resembling gigantic saucers made of glass. The indiarubber covers are made exactly the size of the rim of the bowls, and have a broad turn-under edge besides. The bowls are filled with water, the fish put in, and the covers are then stretched over. To put them on neatly and with dispatch two persons are required, as some force is necessary to pull the indiarubber out sufficiently far to enable it to go on the bowl. Deep, round-bellied bowls should be avoided, as the covers cannot get a good grip upon them. As, with ordinary care, there is no possible chance of a leakage taking place, the bowls can be placed anywhere the performer pleases, and in any position. The favourite places about the person are inside the vest, which will distend sufficiently if prepared with elastic behind, and inside the large breast pockets of the coat. Some conjurors, however, prefer placing the bowls simply under the armpits, inside the coat, and it is surprising how remarkably safe they are in such a position. They are certainly less liable to cause any extraordinary distension of the performer's person, and are far more easily got at. But this is a matter entirely for the consideration of the performer. Some go so far as to put a bowl up the back, which to me seems making the trick as difficult as possible. Wherever the bowls are put, they must be pushed well back, so that all the distension takes place behind, and the performer must necessarily always face the audience during the trick. A bowl is also sometimes placed upon the shelf of the table; but a far better place than this is the back of a chair, made opaque on purpose, where the bowl is held by means of two large wire hooks. As three bowls are generally sufficient for most audiences, one can always manage to carry a sufficient number about one's person. I usually have one in the vest and one in each breast pocket.

To produce the bowls, the performer takes a cloth by two corners, and, after waving it about a short time for effect, he throws it over one shoulder, allowing it to hang well down in front of him. If the bowl is to be taken from the left side, then the cloth must cover that side most, and the left arm must be held out so as to allow the right arm room to work. With the right hand, take the bowl from its hiding place, and hold it horizontally under the cloth, which then draw off the shoulder by means of the other hand, and let it hang over the bowl. Now, with the disengaged hand, grasp the indiarubber cover firmly on the edge of the bowl, through the cloth, and remove it from the bowl with a backward motion. This wants some little doing, as, although it greatly heightens the effect to spill a *little* water, it looks clumsy to three parts empty the bowl. Lay the cloth carelessly aside and take up a fresh one for each bowl. Some conjurors, Dr. Lynn amongst them, use only one cloth, which is provided with pockets, into which the covers are stowed away; but this is a totally unnecessary innovation, and often obliges the performer to fumble about before he can get the covers into the pockets. The idea that the audience think more of the trick if the bowls are all produced from one cloth is erroneous, for in most instances the fact is not noticed; and when the performer uses a fresh cloth for each bowl the spectators, when they give the subject any thought at all, attribute it to the cloths becoming wet and so disagreeable to use a second time. By using several cloths, greater freedom of action is obtained.

An innovation by Herrmann was calculated to make the trick even more wonderful that it is in its ordinary form. Herrmann, after producing no fewer than four bowls, used to go right amongst the audience, and there, from a borrowed handkerchief, produce a fifth. This bowl was carried either in the vest or in a breast pocket, and its production was the more extraordinary by reason of the handkerchief being held across the performer's breast by one of the spectators. It may be safely asserted that no such feat of daring has ever been performed by any other conjuror. Few men possessed such indomitable pluck and nerve as Herrmann, who, during a performance, was to be deterred by nothing. He took the precaution of using a very shallow bowl with sharp sides and a very thin cover. The instant the cover was off, the handkerchief containing it was rolled up in the hand and carried off along with the bowl as if by accident, to be immediately returned to its owner, *minus the cover*.

The most recent addition to the trick is causing the bowls

to disappear after production. The simple method for doing this is to have a double handkerchief, as described in the die trick, with a circular piece of cardboard, the size of the bowl to be made to vanish, inside. The bowl is placed upon the table, and the handkerchief spread over it. As one hand raises the card the other hand places the bowl upon the shelf. The handkerchief is then brought forward with great care, and then shaken out in the midst of the audience. A piece of wet sponge is kept on the shelf, and this is squeezed when the performer goes forward with the supposed bowl. A far better method than this is to use a bowl the top of which is entirely of glass and made in one piece with the bowl, the water and fish being put in through a hole underneath, which is stopped with a cork or plug. It must not be quite filled with water, and when produced the surface must be held a little from the audience, so that the glass top cannot be noticed. When the bowl is to be vanished, all the performer has to do is to cover it with the cloth, and thence quietly put it back into his pocket or vest. It must, of course, be done quickly.

Some ludicrous mishaps have occurred with carelessly covered bowls. One celebrated conjuror produced two bowls with the contents of a third distributed impartially about his person, saturating his clothes and filling his boots. Another performer, a very skilful amateur, accidentally threw the whole of the water from a bowl into a lady's lap, much to the discomfiture of both parties. Had due care been taken, these accidents could never have taken place.

The bowls and covers can only be obtained at conjuring repositories.

Gold-fish and Ink Trick. — This is another instance of astonishing and inexplicable effect produced by most simple means. A large globe (not a bowl, such as is used in the foregoing trick), full of ink, is produced. The performer ladles out some of the ink and sends it round on a saucer for examination. He also dips a white card into the globe, and brings it out dripping with ink. After this, he merely spreads a handkerchief over the globe, and instantly removes it, when the ink is found to have disappeared and its place supplied by pure water and gold-fish.

The preparation for this trick is as follows : Procure a piece of black silk, in width about four-fifths of the height of the globe, and sufficiently long to go once round it on the inside. Sew the two ends together, so that a broad band is formed. To any part of the top edge fasten a piece of thin wire, which blacken. With this silk line the inside of the globe, and then pour in water exactly to the height of the top of it. The wire must be turned over the edge of the globe a little, so as to be easily found. When the globe thus prepared is brought on, it is impossible to tell it from one full of ink. The ladle, which will be best procured at a conjuring repository, is not an ordinary one, but has a hollow handle communicating with the bowl by means of a tiny hole. This hole is made where the stem joins the bowl, and at the upper end of the handle is another small hole. The hollow handle is filled with ink, and a finger or thumb placed over the uppermost hole, thus preventing the fluid from running out. When the performer puts the ladle into the globe, as if dipping some ink out, the thumb or finger should be removed from the upper hole, and the ink will then flow from the handle into the bowl of the ladle. The methods for filling the handle with ink are various. One way is to fill the bowl of the ladle with ink, and then apply suction to the hole at the other end. This is a very simple method, but, unless the person who applies the suction has a decided taste for ink, it is not a pleasant one to adopt. Another method is to exhaust the air from the handle by means of suction, and then put the ladle in ink; but this is even worse than the other. The way I get over the difficulty is by making the upper hole, which is never seen, large enough to admit the nozzle of a very small syringe, by means of which article the ink can be injected into the handle with cleanliness and dispatch. In purchasing a ladle, care should be taken to procure as plain a one as possible. A fancy ladle excites suspicion. If the conjuror does not mind a little expense, he will possess a most perfect article if he purchase a cheap plated sauce ladle, and then have the handle and stem fitted with a hollow back. This will be entirely free from suspicion. The card which is dipped in the supposed ink is simply a piece of card, about an inch and a half wide and a few inches long, with about half of one side of it blackened with ink or paint. The white side is shown to the audience, and it is then turned over with the peculiar twist illustrated in "Drawing-room Magic," Figs. 19 and 20. It is then actually dipped into the water and brought out with the blackened side towards the audience. The water dripping from it will appear to the audience to be ink, and the deceptive twist can be again given to show that both sides are blackened.

In apparently taking out ink with the ladle, and dipping the card in, care must be taken that the manner of the performer does not too forcibly impress upon the minds of the audience that he is over anxious they should believe there is actually ink in the globe. The ladling out and dipping the card in must be done tolerably briskly; for, if the audience have time, some of the members may suggest, what is only reasonable, that the performer should show the bowl round bodily. The trick is finished by a large, dark-coloured cloth or handkerchief being thrown over the globe, and instantly removed, the performer taking care to grasp the wire, which will, of course, be on his side of the globe, through the cloth, and so cause the silk lining to come away inside the cloth or handkerchief. I do not believe in introducing rock work into the globe, as it gives the audience the idea of something fixed, and they thus obtain a groundwork to start upon. Water and fish are enough to manufacture from ink, in all conscience. The trick is also very effective when performed in a small way with a tumbler.

The Ubiquitous Glass of Water: First Method.—Procure two

small tumblers, exactly similar in size, shape, and appearance. Fill one with water, cover it with a tight-fitting indiarubber cover, and place it in the breast pocket or inside the
vest. These little covers are easily procurable, as they are
universally sold as covers for jam-pots. They cost about
sixpence each. Have a small double handkerchief or cloth,
containing a circular piece of card, the size of the mouth
of the tumbler, with a few stitches through it to keep it in
the centre. Show the empty tumbler, and then fill it with
water. Cover it with the handkerchief, and affect to take it
up, but place it on the shelf. Advance very carefully with
the supposed glass of water, and either stumble on the floor
and drop everything, or else pretend to place the glass in
someone's hands. If you stumble you must take care to
avoid injuring the concealed tumbler. The glass and water
vanished, it is now your business to find them again. For
this purpose, you call in the aid of a spectator (a youth
preferred), whom you request to stoop. Over his back spread
the cloth or handkerchief, and, grasping that portion containing the card, raise it gently. Hold it a short time in the air,
and then say that you will throw it into someone's pocket,
indicating the particular person. Shake out the handkerchief
or cloth again and then desire the person indicated to examine
his or her pocket. Of course nothing will be found, but you
borrow the handkerchief, which will have been taken from
the searcher's pocket during the examination, and, waving it
about, get the tumbler into it from the pocket, according to
the directions given for producing the bowls of water and fish.
Remove the cover and produce the glass and water, saying
that you knew you had passed them into the indicated pocket.
The cover being small, it can be easily removed and the
handkerchief returned. It improves the effect a great deal
if a small piece of wet sponge can be introduced beneath the
cloth whilst the glass, presumably found in the youth's back,
is being held, and then squeezed in imitation of the spilling
of water from the glass. The sponge can be carried at the

mouth of one of the large breast pockets, and, if carefully disposed, need not make the performer uncomfortable by wetting him. I have even seen the sponge attached to the under side of the prepared cloth or handkerchief, which is an excellent plan if the performer is careful not to expose that side, as the sponge is always at hand, and there is no necessity to introduce the hand under the covering, compression from the outside being equally effective in exuding the water.

Some performers think it necessary to go through certain actions for the purpose of convincing the company that the handkerchief does not contain a card or other shape. I must confess that I regard such actions as being decidedly supererogatory, for there is not the least foundation for assuming that the audience suspect the existence of any such thing; and for the performer to do anything indicative of an anticipation on his part that the company are likely to divine what is the true secret of the trick is highly suicidal. However, all are not of my opinion, so, if any beginner thinks he would like to be able to draw the handkerchief through the fingers previous to using, he can easily do so. All he will have to do will be to run a couple of stitches from two adjacent corners to the centre of the handkerchief, and inclose his card in the triangular space thus formed. As it is now loose, when the handkerchief is held by one of the opposite corners, the card falls to the extreme border, and the bulk of the handkerchief may be drawn through the hands. When the handkerchief is held by that side which forms the base of the triangle, the card falls at once into position in the centre. A copper or brass wire ring, being heavier than card, is perhaps more serviceable, as it more readily falls into position.

Second Method.—For this a special tumbler will be required. It is a large one, with perfectly straight sides, and is furnished with an outside cylindrical shell, also of glass, which is not discernible from the glass itself when in position. This outside shell must be sufficiently large to slip over the hand of the performer, so it will be seen that it is of considerable dimensions. This fact is always of value from the point of view of effectiveness: the larger the article the performer can manage to successfully manipulate, the better. The performer advances with the glass and shell together, and fills the former to the brim with water. He then places the whole on the rear edge of the table, and covers with the cloth. Grasping the shell, from the outside, with one hand, and placing the other hand below, the glass is slid gradually off the table, when it will drop through the shell into the hand of the performer, which places it upon the shelf. The more rapidity there is employed, the better. The performer comes forward with the shell inside the cloth, and allows the audience to feel its shape, and also taps it with the wand, to make the glass ring. He cannot allow the shell to be actually seen, as the absence of any water would be at once noticed; but the satisfying of the senses of touch and hearing will be sufficiently convincing. Retiring to about the centre of the stage, the performer thrusts one of his hands through the shell, from the bottom, and, whilst supporting the card shape with the fingers, allows the shell to glide down the arm, inside the coat sleeve. The handkerchief is then shaken out, and shown to be empty. In this case, the glass is not reproduced, the trick depending for effect upon the apparent bringing of a very large glass, full of water, amongst the audience, and causing it to vanish before their eyes. In the first method, there is no tapping of the sides of the glass when in the handkerchief, or any feeling of its shape, which is, of course, a very great feature of this method. The cuff must be gripped by the third and little fingers, when the arm may be dropped without any fear of the glass shell falling to the ground.

Third Method. — This method is, in every way, vastly superior to either of the preceding, and, in clever hands, becomes perfectly marvellous to the uninitiated. Only one tumbler is employed. This should be of a substantial character, and requires to be fitted with a flat glass top, exactly the size of the top of the tumbler. To the under side of this should be cemented a slightly smaller circular piece, the size of the interior circumference of the mouth of the tumbler. The glass top cannot now possibly shift from its position. This top the performer has concealed under his vest or in his breast pocket, so that it is readily at hand. Without so much as approaching a table or chair he has the tumbler filled, and, as he covers it with the cloth, he gets out his top and places it into position. With the supposed object of, say, placing the tumbler upon a chair, so that some plea be instituted for bending the body, the tumbler is removed from the cloth and put into the pocket at the bottom of the coat tail. The performer now goes through any performance he pleases with his shape and sponge, and, at the proper moment, produces the tumbler again. In doing this, however, he must get both hands under the cloth, so that he may secrete the top in one of them. It would not do to lift this off from the outside of the cloth, as its extra presence would be noticed. Its size enables it to be readily nipped between the joints of the fingers and root of the thumb.

As the performer does not approach the table, it is impossible for the audience to imagine what has become of the glass, filled, as it is, with water. There is no doubt that this method calls for more skill in execution than does the first, but the effect is immeasurably superior.

To Invert a Glass of Water. — This is an effect which may either be accomplished separately, or may follow the third method of the preceding trick. The performer places the tumbler upon the table, fills it with water, and, in the act of shifting its position, places the lid, unperceived, upon it. He is provided with a half-sheet of note-paper, which he places upon the tumbler, and then, covering the whole with one hand, inverts the glass upon it. He then addresses the company, remarking that they are, no doubt, familiar with the schoolboy trick of holding an inverted tumbler of water, with merely a sheet of paper to keep the contents from falling to the ground. To illustrate this, the performer holds the tumbler by the base in the disengaged hand, and removes the one below. In the ordinary way the paper would fall to the ground; but the performer has taken care to allow it to become slightly wetted, so that it adheres to the glass top. The performer now proceeds: "This any schoolboy can do; but I dare say you do not think it possible for me to remove this paper and yet retain the water in the tumbler. However, I will show you that such a feat is possible." Taking the paper by an edge, the performer gradually removes it, all the time affecting to hold the tumbler with the greatest steadiness, and keeping his eyes rigidly fixed upon it, as though momentarily anticipating some catastrophe, to avert which a concentration of all his energies is necessary. If he pleases, the performer may swing the tumbler into an upright position and back again, repeating the action three or four times. The paper may be eventually replaced, and the top removed inside it, or that article may be got rid of without the aid of the paper at all.

A slight objection exists in connection with the use of the glass top, from the fact that it is liable to "talk," i.e., make a noise, as it is being placed in position. This does not signify on the stage, but, when performing before small audiences, it may be as well to use a piece of mica. As this has no sunken edge, it is not quite as secure as the glass top; but, with ordinary care, no mishap need be apprehended. In removing the paper from beneath, it will be necessary to adopt great caution in avoiding all approach to a sideways sliding movement, which would probably have the effect of shifting the mica, when a deluge would immediately follow. The paper must be boldly peeled off away from the mica. Mica may be purchased in sheets, and the conjuror should cut several sizes, both for tumblers and wineglasses, and carry them in his pocket-book.

When at a house, if even only for the evening, where he is likely to be called upon, he can soon obtain an opportunity for fitting the various glasses in use, by carrying a mica in the palm. Performed with a wineglass, the trick makes a very valuable addition to the few applicable to the table. In turning the glass back to the upright position, always place the hand beneath first, as, in removing it, it is then an easy matter to take away the mica.

The Shower of Gold.—The conjuror can perform this trick with the same tumblers and prepared cloth. One tumbler must be filled with imitation sovereigns (which are sold cheaply as whist counters) and placed upon the shelf. The empty tumbler is handed round, and then covered with the cloth, and apparently placed upon the table. It is instead rapidly exchanged, under cover of the prepared cloth—which, when held by the circular card, will sustain the idea that the tumbler is inside it all the time—for the one containing the coins. The performer now goes down to the audience, and continues to find in various ways either single coins or three or four of such at a time, which are "passed" into the distant tumbler by the various methods described in "Drawing-room Magic." As coins thrown from a distance would not in the ordinary way fall into a glass receptacle without causing any sound, it behoves the conjuror to imitate such sound. This is easily accomplished by having an assistant behind the scenes, stationed as close to the table as possible, and provided with a quantity of coins and a tumbler. When the performer "passes" any coins towards the tumbler, the assistant should, after a short lapse of time, allow some to pour into his tumbler. The attention of the audience is so riveted on the covered glass that the deception cannot be detected. Indeed, it is difficult for anyone who knows exactly what is going on behind to notice anything at all suspicious. The deception is a very perfect one, and is used

in many ways by the best conjurors. Of course, performer
and assistant must be *en rapport* with each other, the one
being careful to state loudly at each "pass" how many coins
are being transmitted, and the other paying strict attention
to what is going on. Supposing the performer finds a single
coin, he will exclaim loudly, "Ah! madam, here is just *one*
coin on the edge of your fan! Permit me." And, on finding
several, he will say, "Ah! in your head, sir, quite a quantity
of coins. One, two, three, four, *five!*" Sometimes, too, it is
as well, for effect, to vary the speed with which the coins
perform their imaginary aerial journey. "This one," the
performer will say, "is, I see, a very old coin, so will go
very slowly indeed;" or, "quite a new one, I declare; see
how quickly it will travel." If the assistant be not listening,
the effect will be absurd. The tumbler into which he drops
the coins should be covered, or the sound will be too sharp.
It should be a muffled sound.

The Egg Bag.—This is a bag which, although repeatedly
shown to be quite empty, continues to give forth eggs. In
its smallest form, it consists of a square bag, made from
chintz, or similar material. One of the sides is double,
and thus forms a secret compartment, the mouth of which
is at the bottom of the bag, inside. The bag can be taken
and turned inside out, to show that it is empty, and yet
have an egg inside the compartment. The bag, on being
turned back again, can be held upside down and shaken
without the egg falling out, for it will still be sustained by
the inner lining. To produce the egg, all the performer
has to do is to put his hand inside the bag and take the
egg out of the compartment. He can then replace it, and
cause it to disappear. Sometimes the inner lining covers
only about three-fourths of the real side of the bag, but
it is best to have it almost the same size. If, in turning
the bag inside out, the double side were accidentally shown to
the audience, they would infallibly notice the mouth of an
inner bag, if it were placed about three-fourths of the way

down one side; but if it came on a level with the bottom of the bag itself, it would rarely be noticed.

The larger egg bag, for the production of many eggs, is a very different affair, and requires some making. There are various patterns, the best of which I give: No. 1 is a chintz bag, about two and a half feet long, and of proportionate breadth. There is no double lining to it, but it is barefacedly provided with as many little pockets, each just capable of containing an egg, as one side can be made to take. These pockets have buttons, and the eggs are placed in them, and they are then fastened, their mouths being, of course, downwards when the bag is held in its proper position. The performer brings on the bag; and, after explaining that he has simply an ordinary chintz bag in his hands, proceeds to show that it is quite empty by turning it first upside down and then inside out. In performing the latter operation, that side which is provided with the pockets must naturally be always turned towards the performer. The bag is then turned back again, and waved about, and, saying that he fancies something has been put into his bag by the fairies, the performer puts his hand inside, opening one of the pockets rapidly as he does so. The egg thus released is produced, and the bag again waved about. The operation of producing the eggs is continued until all are exhausted. It is perhaps better to open the pocket sometimes as the hand is withdrawn with an egg. This will enable the performer to compress the material round the egg, thereby released from the outside, before inserting the hand again to extract it, and exhibit its contour to the audience, who will then see that the egg is not placed into the bag by sleight of hand just previous to being withdrawn. No. 2 is made of any opaque material, a soft one for choice. Besides the ordinary mouth, it has two smaller ones, each some sizes larger than an egg, at the bottom corners. They are best made by simply cutting the corners off. The double lining is very small, it being only of sufficient breadth to take an egg. It is situated at the mouth of the bag and runs along the entire length of it. It has only one opening, a slit across the centre, and the eggs are put in through this. For safety's sake, it is as well to have the opening secured with a button. After the bag has been duly turned inside out and back again, and the slit (if closed) opened, the fingers are run along the top of the bag, where the narrow strip of inside lining is situated, and an egg squeezed out through the slit. This egg falls into the bag proper, which is then tilted sideways over a plate or a basket, or even a hat, and the egg thus caused to roll out of the open corner. No. 3 is similar in principle to No. 2, but has a net underneath, into which the eggs drop with very pretty effect. The corner openings are dispensed with, and the hand is inserted into the bag when an egg is to be taken out.

What puzzles audiences as much as anything is that so many eggs are manipulated and yet not broken. The secret of this is that the eggs used are, with the exception of the one first produced, which is broken on a plate as a specimen, guiltless of the possession of any interior, the performer having taken the precaution of blowing them. This enables the performer to throw the bag carelessly on the floor and then to trample on it. Of course the trampling would be equally fatal to both blown and unblown eggs if the performer did not carefully avoid that portion of the bag which contains them; but the mere act of throwing a bag full of eggs in their original state on the floor would alone be disastrous to many of them. The method for holding a bag for the purpose of taking out an egg is to hold one corner between the teeth and the other in one hand stretched out. This leaves the other hand free for operation. Ordinarily, conjurors do not produce more than eight eggs. If the amateur wishes to perform the trick in really good style, he should have a bag made capable of producing at least two dozen eggs. For this, a large-sized chintz bag is recommended.

Incubation by Magic.—A very amusing trick can be per-

formed when an entertainment is given in the country, or
anywhere where a few very young chickens are procurable.
Take four or five of these, and put them in a black alpaca or
silk bag, the mouth of which is tied with cotton, and is easy
to open. Place the bag on the shelf. Be provided with a
blown egg, not too large, which palm. Borrow a hat, and
find the egg in any way you please, and then retire to the
stage. Place the hat on its side on the table, with the crown
towards the audience, and the brim over the back edge, just
where the bag is placed on the shelf. Do not place the hat
in the desired position at once, but try it in various places
first, and finally decide that the position in which you place
it is the only secure one. Stand at the end of the table (R),
and place the left hand on the brim of the hat, to hold it
steady. With the right hand take the egg, and, after one or
two feints, make a pass at the crown of the hat with it.
Palm the egg and rub the hat, as if the egg had gone
through it. This process of palming is not difficult when
the egg has been made light, by blowing out the inside; the
small end fits nicely between the two fleshy portions of the
hand. Find another egg (*i.e.*, the same one), in your leg,
wand, or elsewhere, and pass it through the hat as before,
and repeat the operation as often as you have chickens inside
the bag. This bag will have to be introduced into the hat
with the left hand, and the best time for doing this is when
the right hand is engaged in finding another egg on any part
of your person. It is not advisable to do it when the hat is
first set down, as the eyes of the audience are full upon it.
This is an illustration of misdirection. When you have
"passed" the requisite number of eggs through the hat, raise
it and bring it forward, remarking that not only have eggs
passed through, but they have all become hatched. (The
hatching can, of course, be done over a candle.) Great
astonishment and amusement will be caused when you produce the chickens one by one. Before removing the last one
secure the bag in the hand, for it will never do to allow the

audience to see that. The egg you, of course, vest before commencing to reveal the contents of the hat. This trick is but little known, which is a pity, as it is a very simple one, and invariably causes great amusement. It also serves to vary the conventional list of tricks performed with hats.

There is a capital method for collecting the eggs for this trick in place of finding each one with the hand, and "passing" it through the crown of the hat. The hat is loaded, as before, with the chickens in a bag, and placed upon a side table, as being the least suspicious, brim upwards. The performer now takes a handkerchief, which is lying carelessly about, and opens it out. It is then doubled lengthwise, perpendicularly, and, held by opposite ends; one end is tilted over the hat, when an egg slides out. The handkerchief is then opened out to show that it is perfectly empty, is taken up by two corners, folded, and once more emptied of an egg into the hat. This process is repeated as often as necessary, when the handkerchief is put aside and the trick proceeded with, as before described.

The secret of the handkerchief is that on one side is suspended a blown egg, by means of a piece of black silk thread. A very thick, or, at any rate, opaque handkerchief, must be employed, so that by no possible chance can the shape of the egg be seen through it. The length of the thread will require nice adjustment, as will also its position on the handkerchief, for naturally it must not be long enough to allow the egg to appear below the lower margin of the handkerchief, when that article is held up by two corners, but must still have an inch or two to spare, to enable it to fall into the hat without being jerked backwards in the least, for so unnatural a movement imparted to a falling egg would at once undeceive the company. The position for the thread to be sewn to the handkerchief is about half way between the centre and a corner. The folding of the handkerchief must be done in a very easy manner, but without imparting a wavy motion to it, for the least lifting of the lower portion will expose the egg. When the handkerchief is folded the performer may go with it to various parts of the room, seeking where he can magically find an egg. The egg found, one of the company may be allowed to feel its contour through the handkerchief. The opening out of the handkerchief, after the egg has been poured from it, requires some attention. The lower end is released, and then the two upper corners are seized, one by either hand, and the handkerchief thrown wide open, showing the side to which the egg is attached. It is then thrown forward, so as to spread over the hat. By this act it has been turned completely over, the audience having seen both sides of it, whilst the egg has been peacefully resting inside the hat, the thread not being sufficiently prominent to become observed. The two corners nearest the performer, originally those belonging to the lower end of the folded handkerchief as the egg was tilted into the hat, are then taken, and the handkerchief drawn off from the hat towards the performer, with an oblique upward motion. The handkerchief is then in the position for refolding, and right for the discovery of a new egg.

One defect which always struck me as being apparent in this method was the fact that the handkerchief could never be given round for examination. This difficulty I surmounted by the following method: The egg and thread I keep apart from the handkerchief until the actual moment for performing the trick arrives. At the loose end of the thread, the length of which has, of course, been previously adjusted to a nicety, I fasten a bent black pin; that is, a very much bent pin—a hook, in fact—with the head end very short and the pointed end very long. The egg lies in my capacious breast pocket, and the hook is fastened in a convenient position in the edge of the coat flap. The handkerchief is given round for examination, and returned to the performer, who, as he retires to the stage, fastens the hook into it. Before he turns for this purpose, he must have fixed his eye upon the place where the hook should go, and

have grasped the handkerchief there, so that afterwards he
may be able to conclude his movements without turning his
eyes upon the immediate scene of operations; not that this
need take very long.   The pin hook must not be merely
stuck through the handkerchief, such a hold being very in-
secure, but it must be put through and brought back again
immediately.   This will effectually prevent its slipping out
during the manipulations to which the handkerchief is subjected.   So soon as the pin is fixed, the performer faces the
audience, if otherwise ready, and, taking the handkerchief by
the two upper corners, stretches them out, when, by putting
his hands away from him in front, the egg will be drawn out
of the side pocket.   The trick then proceeds precisely as
before.   If the performer deems it necessary to allow the
handkerchief to be again inspected, which is a matter of
fancy, he must, prior to commencing, place a white handkerchief in the hat, "in order that the eggs may fall soft,
and not make an omelette," he will explain.   When the
requisite number of eggs have been found, the pin is un-
hooked, and the egg allowed to remain in the hat, from
whence it is removed, folded in the white handkerchief.   If
the performer observes a suitable handkerchief amongst the
company, he may borrow it, when, of course, the egg must
be got rid of; but it is not often that this circumstance will
occur.   It must be admitted that connected with the whole
of this trick there are a style and a neatness which are very
different from the general run of conjuring tricks.

The Resuscitated Fowl.—This can either follow the trick
just described, or it can form a separate trick altogether.   It
is very old, and has formed a portion of the stock performance of conjurors for hundreds of years.   The head of a fowl
is concealed in the hand, and a live bird seized.   The conjuror engages in a mock struggle with it, endeavouring to
seize its head, the object of the disturbance being to enable
the real head to be turned down under one of the wings,
and there held with one hand, and the loose head to be held

on with the other hand, in its place. The stage assistant now advances with a large knife, and cuts off the imaginary head. The performer must make the deed as realistic as possible by causing the fowl to appear to struggle vehemently, and twitch its legs if possible. The head is then taken, and applied to the neck, the conjuror remarking that nothing is easier than to cause it to grow on again. Palm the loose head, and, at the same time, allow the real one to escape from its confinement, when it will at once appear to have suddenly grown on again. Release the fowl for a short run, to show that there is no mechanism about it. This trick is frequently performed by the very best conjurors, sometimes with a pigeon. The loose head must match the real one as nearly as possible, or the deception may be noticed.

"*Kling-Klang.*"—This is a pretty little trick, and does not take long to perform. Take a fancy coloured silk handkerchief, of a small size, not more than a foot square, at the utmost. To the centre of this attach a *blown* hen's egg by means of a piece of thread 2in. to 3in. long. The end of the thread inside the egg is attached to the centre of a tiny piece of wood, such as a portion of a match, which can be pushed in, end foremost, through the hole at the end of the egg, but which, when once inside, will steadfastly refuse to be pulled out again. This method is far better than all other devices with cobbler's wax and glue. Two other silk handkerchiefs, quite opposite, in point of colour, to the one attached to the egg, will also be required, as will a toddy glass with a foot, and an ordinary egg, not blown. The last-mentioned article must be vested. One of the two handkerchiefs of a like colour fold neatly in the palm, and in the same hand take the blown egg, and, as a natural consequence, the handkerchief attached to it, which arrange neatly around the egg, so as to conceal the handkerchief in the palm. Place the other handkerchief in the toddy glass, and, with the wand under arm, emerge thus laden from the secrecy of "behind the scenes." Give the glass and handkerchief to one person, and ask him to examine them both, and then take from him the glass, to be held by another person. Then say, " I have here another silk handkerchief and an egg. The egg I will place in this glass, and then cover it with the handkerchief." Proceed to do this, taking care to slip in the concealed handkerchief *under* the egg, and then retire to the stage, taking with you the second of the duplicate handkerchiefs. As you go to the stage, bring down the egg from your vest, and take the handkerchief in the hand which contains it. Turn to the audience, and ask the holder of the glass to shake it gently to show that the egg is still inside. The peculiar " kling-klang " made by the egg against the glass gives the name to the trick. A caution from you not to shake too strongly, as you do not want an omelette inside the glass, is sure to amuse. Now bring both hands together in front of you, and commence to draw in the handkerchief little by little. At intervals have the glass shaken. When a few inches only of the handkerchief protrude from the hand, draw near the holder of the glass, whom desire to cease shaking. When you have drawn the handkerchief completely into the hands, and feel that it is perfectly concealed, ask a spectator to hold out his hand, and suddenly produce the egg, which give to him. Without losing a moment, raise the handkerchief from over the glass by its centre, thus removing the egg at the same time, taking care to continually tap the glass with the wand during the operation, otherwise an accidental knock of the egg against the side of the glass would be heard, and the whole trick spoilt. Call particular attention to the fact of the egg which you produce being a genuine one, and then get away with your other properties as fast as you decently can. The trick is mostly performed with an imitation egg, instead of a real one. The egg is hollow, and has a great opening in one side. Into this the handkerchief is forced. There is no sleight of hand about this, and the egg cannot be given for examination, which is fatal.

The Harmless Shot.—Procure a substantial-looking muzzle-loading pistol, the larger the better, and get a tinman to make a tube that fits neither tightly nor loosely inside. One end of the tube must be closed, and the open end be furnished with a turn-over rim, which you colour or polish, so as to resemble as nearly as possible the muzzle of the pistol. If it comes easier, by all means reverse the process, and make the muzzle of the pistol resemble the muzzle of the tube. The tube should be at least two-thirds the length of the interior of the pistol barrel, and not about an inch and a half only. Now make a wooden ramrod, which will fit rather tightly into the tube—tightly enough to bring it away from the interior of the pistol when withdrawn after being rammed into it. The exterior of the tube should match the ramrod in colour and appearance, so that the fact of the one being within the other when held in the hand in that condition will not be detected.

Advance to the audience with the pistol, ramrod, powder, caps, paper, and bullets. The tube is concealed somewhere about you. Give round one or more bullets to be marked by the audience, and, at the same time, give the pistol into the hands of someone for examination. If the pistol takes to pieces, so much the better, as it is highly advantageous for the audience to be quite convinced that there is no mechanical preparation of the performer's own devising connected with the implement. Have a fair charge of powder put in, and give the ramrod for ramming the charge. Whilst this is being done, get the tube into the hand, and, when the ramrod is returned to you, pass it into the tube, and then at once say earnestly, "I hardly think you rammed it sufficiently, sir." Without taking the pistol yourself, hold the muzzle in the fingers of the left hand, and ram with the right. The left hand must pinch the rim of the tube, which will thereby become disengaged from the ramrod, and remain inside the pistol. By this means the tube has become inserted in the pistol without any occasion for the pistol leaving the possession of the person assisting. The bullet

or bullets are then dropped in by such of the audience as
have marked them, the pistol being handed round by the
volunteer assistant, who is also asked to put a piece of paper
in as well. This piece of paper is very small, and is rolled
up by the performer himself, who will, of course, take particular care that it is not bulky enough to jam in the tube.
The performer now, without taking the pistol, puts in the
ramrod and presses down the bullets—apparently. He, however, takes good care to avoid pressing them at all, but
brings the hand holding the ramrod over the muzzle of the
pistol, and so secures the tube. There is nothing in the
action to excite the least suspicion ; still, it is best to have
the ramrod of such length that only an inch or so of
it protrudes from the muzzle. If this particular be observed, then the hand must approach the muzzle on every
occasion of ramming down a charge, and so no suspicion can
possibly be excited by the action. The imaginary ramming
is, of course, continued, the tube being moved up and down
inside the pistol vehemently. Withdraw the ramrod and
tube, carefully concealing the junction of the two, and have
the pistol capped. Having secured the bullets in the tube,
the next thing is to get them into the hand. As it is impossible to withdraw the rod from the tube in full view of the
audience (it can certainly be done behind the table; but the
unavoidably lengthened absence of both hands for the purpose would be fatally suspicious), the performer must necessarily retire behind the scenes. The best excuse is that of
requiring a plate. Whilst fetching this, the rod is withdrawn
from the tube, and the bullet or bullets shaken out. The
paper ought not to stick, but it might; and so it is always
as well to have a piece of wire with a sharp hook at one
end in readiness. This abstraction of the bullets could be
managed whilst the performer retires up the stage, and it
would be advisable to do so if the bullets were certain to
drop out, which, however, they are not. When the performer has a stage assistant, as he always should have when

possible, the matter becomes much easier. The assistant holds the box of caps on or near the stage, and the performer goes to him for them, and gives him the wand with the tube on it in an offhand manner. The assistant then manages all the abstraction whilst the capping of the pistol is going on, and stands, just removed from sight, with the plate in one hand and the bullets in the other. The performer then has only to stretch his arm behind to receive the bullets first and the plate next, both in one hand. The bullets are held under the fingers, which are on the inside of the plate. The performer now holds the plate either in front of his face or at arm's length, and requests that the pistol may be fired at it. When this is done, the bullets are allowed to roll on the plate, which is brought simultaneously into a horizontal position, a kind of "grab" being made with it, as if catching the bullets in the air. I like this method better than catching the bullets in the mouth, as the performer can at once run forward with them on the plate, and the audience will be thus enabled to see for themselves that no substitution has taken place during transit.

The difficulty of extracting the bullet or bullets I finally mastered, after various trials, by using a tolerably thick piece of cork for the purpose of closing the one end of the tube. When the performer retires up the stage, he holds the closed end in his hand and presses the ramrod against his body, thus forcing out cork, bullet, and paper with one vigorous push. The operation does not occupy a second, and, when the performer turns facing the audience again, the ramrod is in his hand as before. It will naturally occur to everybody that, if the ramrod fits tightly into the tube, the whole arrangement will be neither more nor less than a popgun, and the cork will be blown out as soon as the ramrod is inserted into the tube. To avoid such a startling result, the ramrod must, although fitting the tube at certain places, be made out of truth, so as to admit of an escape of air, or else the cork must have a hole burnt through it by means of red-hot wire. Piercing a hole through the cork will not suffice, as the nature of the material will speedily cause the opening to close up again. If this cork arrangement be used, then the performer need never leave the stage.

I have given the learner what I consider to be the best method for performing the trick. A method which differs only slightly from mine, the principle being the same, is to use a tube barely two inches in length. This tube is dropped into the pistol by the performer, who takes the pistol entirely in his hands, for the purpose of ramming down the powder charge. As it lies secreted a long way down the pistol, it, of course, can never be seen. In pushing the ramrod down, it becomes fixed in the tube, and brings it away, the ramrod being the least bit tapered, to insure its going into the tube. It should be tapered at each end, so that there may be no bother about looking to see which end is the graduating one. The rest of the trick is performed exactly as in the other method. My objections to the use of the short tube are that, in order to get it into the pistol, the performer must secure actual possession of the firearm, and he must repeat the manœuvre when he wishes to take it out again. Again, it is very difficult to conceal the point of junction of a short tube on a long ramrod. If the performer does not use the utmost caution, the tube will be noticed sticking on the rod as they are withdrawn from the pistol. The rim of the long tube is covered with the hand before the abstraction is made, and added to this is the fact that the pistol never leaves the hand of the volunteer assistant, which is a great feature in the trick. The only objection to the long tube I found to be the difficulty sometimes arising in abstracting the bullets; but my cork has now removed that difficulty. I have given both methods that the learner may choose for himself. Although I have said "bullet or bullets," because some conjurors employ one only and some three or four, I should, myself, never think of using more than one. The effect is the same, whilst the trick is made immeasurably easier to the performer. People may, perhaps, be a little more satisfied at seeing several bullets marked by different people, but it is just as easy, and quite as effective, to have one bullet thus treated. It will not matter in the least to the performer how many people mark it.

Another method for performing the trick is to substitute for the marked bullet a blacklead one. This, on account of its lightness, the performer must himself drop into the pistol and see that it is so rammed that it is broken up. I would never advise anyone to adopt this method, although Houdin caused consternation amongst the Arabs by allowing himself to be fired at from a distance of a few paces. With his usual completeness he finished the trick by firing another pistol at a whitewashed wall, on which appeared a large splash of blood. This was managed by means of a ball of black wax, the inside of which was filled with blood. The Arabs were duly impressed.

There are some pistols made with spring openings in the barrel, through which the bullet falls into the hand of the performer; but, in this case, the pistol cannot be examined, which fact is quite sufficient to taboo the method. Unless the pistol is given to be examined, and left in the hands of the spectators the whole time, there is, in my opinion, nothing in the trick.

A Bottle of Ginger Beer.—The reader will scarcely require to be told that one of the great deceits practised by conjurors is that of duplication. In order to apparently execute the impossibility of conveying a large solid body invisibly through space, the conjuror has to cause the article itself to disappear by any means at hand, and to produce another similar article, or counterfeit thereof, at the spot to which the original one is supposed to be magically transported. In the case of Houdin's die trick a counterfeit die was made use of, and in many of the coin tricks duplicate coins were employed. Whatever the article used, the method is almost invariably the same ; and the public are often invited to witness the exhibition of a new wonder, which is in reality only a variety of what has been done in hundreds of ways before.

One very effective variety of this particular deceit is the transposition of a ginger-beer bottle from one paper cover to another. The trick and its explanation are as follows : The performer brings forward a ginger-beer bottle and a glass, on a tray. If he pleases, he may have two ginger-beer bottles, and ask the audience to choose between them. He should ask them to select between the one on the right and the one on the left. If "right" is said, and the one with which the trick is to be performed is on the left of the audience, then the performer must say, "On *my* right. Thank you"; and instantly take up that bottle without more ado, and uncork it. He then pours out the ginger beer, to show that it is genuine—so he says, but the real object is to keep the spectators from suspecting that there is anything "uncanny" about the bottle itself. The peculiarity of the bottle is that it either never had a bottom to it, or else that portion of it has been forcibly removed. Some few conjuring trick makers supply bottles without bottoms; but any lapidary will perform the desired operation should the performer himself be unsuccessful in accomplishing it with a hammer. The chief thing is to obtain two bottles that match exactly in colour. Height is not of much consequence, as that is not so readily retained by the eye as is colour; still, it is as well to have them match in that even, but colour stands first in importance. One of these bottles is placed upon the right-hand side of the shelf behind the table, and the other is fitted inside with either a piece of thick cork or gutta-percha. Whichever it is, it must fit very tightly, and be situated about an inch from the foot of the bottle. The cork must be left out until the last minute, or the fermentation of the ginger beer will cause the false bottom to come out unexpectedly with a "pop." This prepared bottle is the one that is brought on on the tray, with or without another genuine one, as the performer pleases. When two are brought on, the second one should always be left with the audience for them to open if they be so minded. It is sure to be examined with strict minuteness, and its unblemished innocence will reflect upon its late companion.

Under his vest band the performer has a small apple, a walnut, or little ball. This he gets down as he retires to the table, and slips it in the lower cavity of the bottle, holding it there suspended by means of the little finger. He then places the bottle upon the left-hand front corner of the table, and on the corresponding corner he places a duplicate of the article which he has secretly introduced under the bottle. This duplicate will have been lying on the table all the time, and can, of course, be examined. The performer now takes two cardboard or paper covers, each just large enough to cover a ginger-beer bottle easily, and shows them round. These covers can be made with very little trouble, and the plainer they are the better, in my opinion. Spectators think no more of a trick because of a cover of many colours covered with gold or silver stars. A fancy paper on the outside is all that is required, for it will not do to look " beggarly." These two covers are now taken back, and the performer goes behind his table. With the left hand he places one cover very slowly and deliberately over the bottle, and calls very particular attention to what he is doing. The cover in the right hand is meanwhile being placed over the bottle on the shelf. The conjuror's whole attention, eyes and everything, must be engrossed on what he is doing with the bottle which is visible. Any glance which he may want to take for ascertaining the exact position of the bottle on the shelf must take place as he goes behind the table; any downward look after this would be fatal. Directly it is felt that the hidden bottle is safe in the cover, the latter must be brought into view again; and care must be taken that it is held a little obliquely, the mouth being towards the performer. As an additional security, it is always as well to have the inside of the covers blackened, or lined with black paper, and the inside and base of the second bottle treated likewise. Any accidental exposure will then not be so likely to be attended by serious results.

When the first cover is fairly over the bottle, the second one, containing the other bottle, is placed over the little ball, or whatever it is. The performer next takes up his wand and says, "Now, what I am about to do is to cause the ginger-beer bottle and the little ball to change places. This, I am aware, anyone can do by simply lifting off the covers and altering the positions of the articles with the hand; but I shall do nothing so transparent. I will show you that the articles are still where I placed them, and that I have not already moved them from their positions." (The covers are alternately lifted, care being taken not to prematurely expose the wrong article.) "My method of procedure is as follows: First, I take out the little ball" (on the shelf there is a third article, similar to the other two, and this the performer palms in the left hand) "in this manner. You see, I simply run my wand up the side of the cover, and here I have the little ball in my hand." (Strike left hand with wand, and open it and put the ball on table.) "This cover is now empty. By means of my wand, I remove the ginger-beer bottle, large and cumbrous as it is, from the cover—here it is, see, on my wand!—and pass it gently, for fear of breakages, into the empty cover. This little ball I take thus, and pass into this cover, where the bottle was, not five seconds since." (Perform any pass with the ball, and put it back upon the shelf.) "On raising the covers, it will be seen that the change has actually taken place." Raise the left-hand cover first, grasping it firmly so as to ensure the bottle from slipping, and then show the second bottle on the right, bringing the left hand, at the same time, over the shelf, upon which the first bottle is permitted to drop, very gently, from the cover. Both covers should be afterwards shown round, although the trick can be repeated, *i.e.*, done backwards, if the performer desires. If he does so, he should say, "Ah, I daresay everybody did not see how that was done, and, as I always like the method of my tricks to be understood by everybody, I will do it over again. There is no fun in a trick if one does not see how it is done." On removing the bottles at the close of the trick, care must be taken that the hidden ball, &c., is not knocked down on the floor, as is sometimes done by accident. This is a genuinely good trick, the opening of the ginger-beer bottle before the audience serving to throw that body off its guard.

The Flying Plume and Seed.—This is another trick in which duplicated representations play an important part, but the articles and methods employed are so totally distinct from those used in the preceding trick that one might follow the other in a performance, and yet both appear to be totally distinct in every way. There is a little simple apparatus in connection with the trick. First of all, a tin tube, 18in. long, and at least 1½in. in diameter. It is provided with a cap at each end, fitting inside, and not over, as is usual. The tube also possesses the peculiarity of being divided longitudinally, by a tin partition, into two portions. This partition does not run down the centre of the tube, but takes a transverse direction from one side of one end to the opposite side of the other end. By this means, both ends are open to their full extent, and the tube can be shown briskly round, with the cap off, without anyone being able to detect anything wrong. Of course, only one end will be given for inspection, the audience not suspecting the existence of more than one opening.

Then there is a vase, also of tin, but painted on the outside or japanned. This vase has a foot about 3in. high, which is hollow, and is connected with the body of the vase by means of a very large hole. This hole is hidden by a large domed cap on the end of a pin, which runs through the foot, and is furnished with a button underneath. A spiral spring inside keeps the cap down on the hole, but pressure on the button under the foot causes it to rise, and any seed that may be in the body of the vase will instantly run down into the foot. Two plumes of exactly the same colour and length will also be required. These plumes can be obtained at a cheap rate at any plumassier's. One of the compartments of the tube is secretly filled with seed, and the end opening that division is closed with the cap. This cap should bear a distinct mark to distinguish it from the other. In the vase there should be an egg, orange, lemon, or apple, &c., which must not be seen by the audience, and on the table there should be another similar article. Up the performer's sleeve, or in his side pocket, one of the plumes is secreted. The other plume is handed round and then thrust down the tube, which, to all appearances, it entirely fills. Place the tube on a chair or on the floor, and then take the vase, and into it pour a quantity of seed, going forward so soon as the article at the bottom is covered. Show the vase round full of seed, and then place it on another chair, the button being pressed and all the seed allowed to run away in transit.

Now borrow either a hat or a handkerchief. If the plume is up the sleeve, then a handkerchief is required. Spread the handkerchief over the hand, as if showing there is nothing in it, and seize the end of the plume through it with the other hand. Draw the handkerchief smartly away with the plume inside it, and throw both on the floor. If the plume is in the pocket, then borrow a hat and slip the plume into it. The plume will curl round inside the hat, and remain firmly fixed, so the hat can be turned brim downwards without fear of the plume falling out.

These preliminaries concluded, proceed as follows : Touch the tube with the wand and say you have taken out the plume, which you then "pass" into the hat or handkerchief, as the case may be. Now touch the vase with the wand, and say that you have removed all the seed, which you then command to go into the tube. Vanish the egg, or whatever it may be that you use, down a trap, and "pass" it into the vase. Nothing then remains but to open the tube, and to show the vase and handkerchief or hat. Millet is by far the best seed to use. It is light, and its spherical shape causes it to run smoothly. A conjuror, who was experienced enough to know better, persistently used rice for this trick. The result was extra delay, for the rice generally managed to clog somewhere, and always made a tell-tale rattling as it trickled into the foot. It made one tremble to look and listen. The trick is very easily managed, and creates a remarkably pretty effect. The conjuring shops supply the apparatus.

How to Make and Cook a Pudding in a Hat.—Procure a large size gallipot with nice thin sides. Have a tin lining made to fit the inside of this, and divide the lining into two portions by means of a horizontal division across the middle. The inside of a gallipot being somewhat narrower at the bottom than it is at the top, the lining will be taper, and consequently one partition will be larger than the other. Into the larger partition put a plum pudding, or cake, hot, and stand it on the shelf, without the gallipot. Borrow a hat, and, whilst busy about putting some paper at the bottom of it, and explaining that it is to prevent its being spoilt, take an opportunity of slipping the tin containing the pudding into it. Now take some flour, eggs, plums, sugar, and water, and mix them all up in the gallipot, to the accompaniment of some facetious remarks about your being a first-rate cook. Next pour the paste from the gallipot into the empty division of the tin, and, putting the pot momentarily into the hat, press it down well over the tin. which it will bring away, leaving the pudding alone behind. Now hold the hat over a spirit lamp (a candle would spoil the hat), and profess to be cooking the contents, which presently take out close to the audience and distribute. Some conjurors make omelettes and pancakes, which certainly make a good show, and are suggestive of being cooked on the crown of a hat. Some address is required in executing this trick, especially in getting the tin into and out of the hat. The knack of putting things into hats from the shelf neatly is one of the most difficult things to acquire, and the performer must never be nervous at the moment, or he will be certain to allow himself to be discovered. Sometimes the egg is first broken into the hat (*i.e.*, the tin), and the flour and water afterwards mixed up in the gallipot. The effect of the contents of an egg dropping into a hat is certainly good.

An amusing interlude, when borrowing a hat, is to apparently push the forefinger through the crown and then restore the hole supposed to be made by the act. This deception is managed by having a cast of a human fore-finger made in either wax, guttapercha, or plaster, and provided with a pointed wire at the thick end. This finger is concealed in the right hand, and the left hand put inside the hat. The right hand is then brought on the outside of the crown, and with the remark, "I fancy you have a hole in your hat, sir," an apparent effort is made, and a finger shown protruding through the crown. All that is done is to pass through the wire, which is held on the inside by the left hand. After making a few sharp movements simulating a finger in the act of being shaken, bring the right hand on to the crown again, and make as though considerable exer-tion were required in order to get the finger back again. The dummy is, of course, merely secured in the right hand, and the hat immediately shown ostentatiously round, so as to keep attention away from the right hand. The imitation finger must naturally be coloured to resemble the performer's flesh. The trick must not last long—a quarter of a minute is ample. If the finger remains through the hat for any length of time the audience will soon realise what the nature of the deception is. It should appear as if the finger had been just pushed through, shaken derisively, and then withdrawn.

The Flags of Old England.—Without any visible preparation, and from no conceivable source, the performer produces hundreds of flags with the hands. The flags, which can, of course, be of any colour, but, for obvious reasons, should be red, white, and blue, for preference, are thus made quickly: Procure some sheets of tissue paper, and cut them into slips of equal dimensions. A good size to commence with is 3in. by 1½in., three of which will make a flag of 4in. by 3in., a very nice size. For rapid pasting, place, say, the red slips one over the other, each one permitting just a quarter of an inch of the one beneath it to be seen. With one sweep of the brush a large number can be thus pasted. Perform the same operation with the blue papers, and the white ones will not require any paste at all. Join the three together, and, when dry, paste them on either very thin sticks or wire, or else on bass. The latter is far preferable to any other substance, and can be easily procured. Now make some flags about 6in. by 4in. in the same manner, and, if you choose, a few even larger still. Roll them all up very tightly in two or three bundles, and secrete them about you. I always place a bundle of small flags up each sleeve, the larger ones being either in the vest or in the large breast pocket of the coat. Take a little flag in each hand, and advance with them. Wave them about, and, lowering one hand, allow the bundle to slide into it from the sleeve, care being taken that the back of the hand is towards the audience. Bring the hands together immediately, and continue to wave them about for a few seconds, when commence to unroll the flags, and cause a few to appear first at the top, and then to fall on to the floor. Continue this, all the time moving about, until you find the supply getting low, when, with a downward sweep of the hands, extract the bundle from the other sleeve. This movement will be perfectly concealed by the numerous flags flying about. It will also be perfectly easy to obtain possession of the other bundles from the vest or pocket, if care be taken to raise the flags that are being exhibited, so as to conceal the motion of the hand. When the larger flags are being unravelled, the waving should increase. The effect of a quantity of flags coming from apparently nowhere is always very bewildering to an audience, and this is heightened when the larger ones appear. I remember producing one quite 8ft. in length, with a complimentary motto, allusive to the season of the year, elaborated upon it. There is, however, no necessity to go to such a length as this. Buatier, instead of two flags to commence with, takes a bundle of coloured paper, which he rolls up, and then pretends to transform into flags. This is not at all a bad method, and, if the performer prefers it to my own, there is no harm in adopting it. Buatier decidedly makes a mistake, though, in producing the original paper after he has manufactured several hundreds of flags from it. This is not consistent.

The Chinese Rings.—Whether originally Chinese or not, is of little moment: the trick has received the name, and is known by it only, so I adhere to it. The trick consists in apparently accomplishing the evident impossibility of linking strong metal rings, that have no break or opening in them, one within the other. The secret of the trick lies in the fact that one of a number of rings is provided with a slit or opening, which is kept carefully concealed by the performer's fingers. As, however, one ring with an opening would not alone suffice to link several others together in a continuous chain, the rings are made in sets of three and two welded together, besides three or four single ones. The set of two I always dispense with as useless. There is not the slightest necessity for going to a conjuring repository to obtain the rings, for an ordinary smith can produce a much more serviceable article. My idea of a good ring is one made of iron wire fully ⅜in. in thickness and 9in. in diameter. Let the metal be well burnished, and see that the welding is properly done. The opening in the one ring should be $\frac{7}{16}$in. wide so as to admit the other rings freely. Some rings have a slit merely, whilst others have the ends springing one into the other. These precautions are quite unnecessary, for the secret ring is never given round for examination. When the performer comes on, he has the open ring concealed either under his armpit, in his breast pocket, or in the vest; or he may have it hanging behind a chair, if he has one with an opaque back on the stage. The other rings he has in the hand, and gives them round for examination. Unless this examination takes place, there is nothing in the trick, for the audience would justly argue that all the rings have secret spring-bolt openings which are invisible at a short distance. To abstract the concealed ring without detection requires, at times, considerable address. A good way is to allow some of the others to fall, and whilst stooping quickly for them, get out the concealed one. Turning the back upon the audience, and deliberately taking the ring out from its place of concealment whilst walking towards the stage, is the method I usually adopt. When it is hung at the back of a chair, the bulk of the rings should be placed upon the seat, and two or three taken up in one hand; say, the right. In stooping to pick up some more rings with the left hand, the right, naturally enough, finds its way to the top of the back of the chair, and, as the ring will be suspended half an inch down, the end of one finger will be sufficient to obtain it.

I lay some stress upon this recovery of the open ring, for in its neat execution lies the whole secret of the trick. If the performer feels that he has accomplished the feat without being observed, he may boldly assert that he knows that other conjurors perform the same trick with prepared rings—he does nothing so mean and despicable. As a rule, I disagree with any hint whatever that may give a clue to the secret of a trick; but this particular one is so widely known that I doubt if an audience of ordinary size could be found with everyone ignorant of its secret. Under these circumstances, the conjuror who wishes for success must be different to everyone else. If he is not " prepared to do or die," let him leave the Chinese rings alone.

The method of "working" the trick is to first take up the open ring and one of the single ones, one in each hand. Unless the performer be left-handed, or ambidextrous, it is always advisable to hold the open ring in the right hand, the opening being between the finger and thumb. Stand at the front of the stage (if there are side boxes, then a little back), and let the open ring hang carelessly on the thumb, only broadside on to the audience. By turning up the point of the thumb ever so little, the opening is rendered quite invisible to spectators, who will think that two perfect rings are being held before them, they having no possible reason to suspect even that an open ring is anywhere about. Bang the two rings together several times, and pretend to make two or three attempts to fit one into the other, by what precise movement does not matter in the least.

Presently slip the solid ring rapidly through the opening of the other, without ceasing for an instant the movements you have hitherto made, which continue as if the two rings were still apart. Soon you will work the two close together, and, by degrees, bring round the solid ring to the bottom of the open one, and then allow it to hang from it. Be careful, however, that the opening is never so much as approached by the solid ring after the latter has been passed through it. By a reversal of the proceedings, the ring must be taken off again, the two rings being held touching one another, and worked about as if still linked, long after the actual detachment has taken place. The audience are supposed to actually see one ring pass through the other, and the performer must cause this to appear to be done at the lower half of the open ring. Performers always make a grand mistake in hurrying over this, the opening part of the trick, which is really the most important part of it. Within reasonable bounds, the linking of the two first rings cannot be much too long drawn out. If he be possessed of sufficient daring, the performer may advance to one of the audience with the two rings linked, and give him one of them (the solid one, of course) to hold. Just as the ring is put into his hand, the disconnection should take place. This is an interlude, which the performer may use or not, according to how he feels in spirits, for conjurors are like race-horses, and are at times "in" or "out of form." Two loose rings can then be put on the open one, one at a time, and then removed and held together. The open ring can be passed over the arm out of the way, the opening being, of course, concealed, and some "business" can be gone through with the other two, which, as they never were together, can be separated without much difficulty.

Some conjurors become breathless at the bare idea of allowing the open ring to leave the hand, whereas, when properly managed, there is not the least danger to be apprehended. When the ring is passed over the arm, the hand does not leave the opening until it is well embedded inside the elbow joint. It is bad policy to hold one ring continually in the hand, as the fact is extremely likely to be noticed. When a few evolutions have been performed with the single rings, including throwing one in the air and catching it on the open ring on its descent, the triplets should be taken up, and, after plenty of shaking about and turning round and over, an end one should be linked on. By linking up the other end as well, a square is formed. Give two rings of this to be held by different people, and tell them to pull. Give one or two jerks yourself, and at one of them disconnect, and then gradually appear to unlink the square, bringing, at last, the four in a single chain. Make a lot more flourishes, but merely bring the four side by side in one hand, hanging. Hold the open ring firmly, and allow the others to drop steadily. This they will do in two distinct stages or jerks, at each of which you make a movement with the disengaged hand as if controlling them. As a finish, it is usual to put all the rings in a bunch on the open one. When this is done, one of the solid rings should be made to sustain the rest for a short time in place of the open one, which may be allowed to hang down in the rear of the others, where it will not be seen. The solid ring thus temporarily used should be held alternately in several places, so that the audience, and especially such as know the secret of the trick, may see that there is actually no opening it. This is an excellent *ruse* to adopt. When performing with the rings, always make a deal of clatter with them; it adds to the effect. An effective *finale* is to grasp the open ring by the solid part immediately opposite the opening, and, turning the whole bunch rapidly over, shake the other rings loose upon the floor, dropping the open ring amongst the rest. The apparent recklessness of this goes still further to disarm suspicion as to an open ring.

It will be seen that, beyond obtaining the open ring, everything is what is understood as "hankey-pankey"—in fact, downright humbug—but it is humbug of a superior order. The performer who introduces it injudiciously and unskilfully will have reason to regret any imperfect study of this trick. There is not much true sleight of hand in it, but the perfection of "address" will be required.

The Drawer-Box.—This is not the name of a trick, but of one of the most useful pieces of apparatus which a conjuror can possess. I have purposely refrained from making any mention of it before, because I wanted to make the beginner an adept at vanishing and producing with his hands before I gave him an article that would save him the trouble at the loss of a large amount of effect. When a person is able to do considerable execution with his hands alone, there need be no anxiety about giving apparatus into them. It is only with the beginner that the danger lies, for he will say, "Oh! this box does all I want—at least, quite well enough for me—so why should I take the trouble to learn to do it without?" The expert is never too anxious to use apparatus, and invariably manages with as little of it as he can.

Now, the drawer-box is an article of such peculiar handiness on so many occasions, that the temptation held out to beginners to use it frequently is too great to be resisted. It will bear a cursory examination, and yet, although crammed with any kind of article to its fullest extent, it is made to appear quite empty, by merely being shut and re-opened, and this in the midst of the audience; or the operation may,

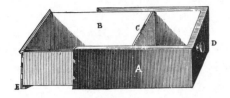

FIG. 51.

with modifications, be reversed, and the box shown first empty, and then full.

Most of us must have seen the little cigar-case which is so handy to smokers who wish to keep a good brand of cigar to themselves. The drawer-box is made on exactly the same principle as this, only, of course, in an enlarged form, and in wood.

The appended sketches (Figs. 51 and 52) show the appa-

FIG. 52.

ratus. I give a minute description of it here, as it is only in very large towns that the article is procurable, made in the manner it should be, so the conjuror can either get a cabinet maker to make him one, or, if he be anything of a carpenter, make one for himself.

A (Fig. 51) is a lightly-made drawer, without any back end,

and fits somewhat easily into F (Fig. 52), which should be made
of ⅜in. stuff, and strongly put together. B is another lightly-
made drawer, smaller than A, into which it fits. A has a
narrow combing all round the upper surface of the front end
and sides. This serves to conceal the presence of B, which
in reality looks like the inside of A. To perfect this deception, the open sides of A are, as depicted in sketch, made
with mortises, and the end of B being allowed to extend a
little each side, and also mortised, the two dovetail one into
the other, and present a most innocent appearance. The
knob D is not fixed, but has a slight perpendicular play. It
is connected with a piece of flat metal, which extends from
the knob to the upper portion of the wood, inside the combing, where it is furnished with a catch, which can be made
by turning over the end of the metal and sharpening it a
little. In B there is a slight incision made at C. When B
is pushed home into A, and the knob D pressed downwards,
the catch fixes itself into C, and thus keeps the two drawers
firmly together. The action of shifting the knob up and
down is very slight indeed, a ¼in., or, at the outside, ⅓in. play
being ample. When the two drawers are thus fixed, they may
be shown round, and no one not in the secret will suspect
that there is more than one drawer. The more care and
attention that is paid in fitting the drawers nicely together,
the better.

At the lower part of the back end of B will be noticed
a protruding piece of wood, E. This fits closely against A
when the two are closed together, but it plays an important
part in the working of the box. In the body, F (Fig. 52),
is cut a square hole, immediately under the point where the
thumb is seen to be pressing. G is a flat spring let into
the bottom of F, and fixed at the end farthest removed from
the square hole. A square piece of wood, the same thickness as the bottom of the body F, and slightly smaller than
the hole, is glued firmly on the free end of the spring, so
that it is always in the hole. The exterior of the box should

be painted or French polished, and the bottom covered with baize or cloth. The material should be glued on, the space covering the spring, and half an inch all round it, being left free. The apparatus is then ready for use, and is thus "worked": We will suppose that it is required to cause several apples to disappear. The drawer A, with B inside it, and the knob pressed firmly down, is shown in one hand, and the body F in the other. The apples are then put into A (really into B), which is then pushed into F. After the performer has pretended to extract the apples by magical means, he takes up the box with both hands, one hand grasping one end, with the thumb on the spring G (Fig. 52), and the other hand seizing the knob D, which it presses upwards, thus removing the catch from the slit C. With the thumb pressing as hard as possible on the spring, the drawer A is pulled out. The square piece of wood on the end of the spring G, being pressed inside the box, causes an obstruction to the inner drawer B through the medium of the protrusion E, and B is consequently held back in F. The drawer A, which is, after all, merely an outer shell, is shown instead, and the audience, not knowing of the existence of a double drawer, imagine that the one shown them is the one which they saw filled with apples. When the box is opened, it should be held sideways, with the top turned towards the audience, and when it contains such articles as apples, which easily shift in a very audible manner, it should be placed in this position on the table, before the contents are made to disappear. It would be stupid to pull out an empty drawer and then cause a rumbling to be heard. The audience would at once divine that the articles were kept back in the body of the box by some means.

When the box is made so large that the hand cannot grasp it in the manner shown at Fig. 52, the closed end should be furnished with a knob matching that on the drawer A. This can then be held by the fingers, and so enable the thumb to find a purchase.

A very good box is one made without the spring acted upon by the thumb. In its place is a loose metal peg, which drops in and out of the hole in the double drawer by the mere tilting of the box. This style of box is best made with both ends of the cover open, an increased appearance of innocence being thereby secured.

With such a handy article at command as the drawer-box, which will vanish or produce anything at will, it will be easily understood that the beginner is extremely likely to be tempted into using it with too great a frequency. Let him beware of this, and, at the outside, use it not more than twice in the same evening, and then only under completely differing conditions, and after the lapse of a good interval of time. In a number of the foregoing tricks the drawer-box could be used with success, I grant, but not with any very great effect. In the trick with the large die and the handkerchief, it would be handy for causing the die to vanish. It could be used in *The Sun and Moon*, *A Bottle of Ginger Beer*, and in a dozen others, but the temptation to do so must be resisted.

Popular usage has assigned the drawer-box the position of a regular "property" in a very effective trick performed with a large solid block of wood, familiarly known as the Cone. It can be made of any size, but it is as well to have it as large as possible, that is, not less than 6in. in height. When large, it is just as easy to manipulate, and is much more effective. The only desideratum is that it should go comfortably into the drawer-box. It should be well tapered from the base to the summit, which may be simply flat or fancifully turned. Over this block fits a thin shell, the *fac-simile* of it—the die and dummy repeated, only in a different shape. The dummy shell is usually turned out of a piece of wood similar to that of which the block is made, and both are polished to match. It is essential that they be very smooth. All else that is required is a very tall paper cone, which passes very loosely over the shell, and a couple of apples, oranges, lemons, or any similar articles, both being placed on the shelf. The drawers, fastened, should be taken out of the body and stood upon it at one end of the table, and the cone, with the shell on it, at the other end. The performer next takes the paper cone and exhibits it. He then says, standing behind the table, "This cover, which is, as you see, made simply of paper, is for the purpose of covering this solid block of wood." The paper cover is passed over the cone and shell, which are grasped firmly with one hand and slid off the table on to the other hand. The shell is then grasped a little higher up, through the paper, and the solid block jerked out of it on the floor. The paper containing the shell cone is then laid flat on the table, with the closed end towards the audience, and the solid cone picked up and placed in the drawer, which is first shown briefly round. The drawer-box is closed and placed on a side table to the left, and the performer, passing behind the table, takes up one of the two articles which are upon the shelf. This he produces in any way he pleases, taking it from the wand being the most effective method (see "Sleights for General Use"). He should then say that he requires an orange, &c., for the trick, which he will ask his wand to give him. The orange, or whatever it may be, is then placed upon the table, and covered with the paper cover, with the dummy cone inside it. The performer then explains that what he is going to do is to cause the solid cone to come out of the box and pass into the paper cover. Whilst saying this, he goes behind the table and secures the second of the two articles that were on the shelf, in the right hand. He then comes round, and proceeds: "To do this, it will be first necessary for me to remove the orange from the paper, and I accomplish the feat in this manner." (He runs the wand lightly up the side of the paper, and then produces the orange out of it, the action being somewhat similar to that used in the previous production.) "Now that the cover is empty, I can pass the block of wood into it. I take it out of the box, thus" (taps box with wand), "and, see, it is on my wand. I carry it carefully to the cover and pass it thus into it." The wand is carried very gingerly, in a horizontal position, as if the block of wood were really balanced upon it.

The paper is then taken by its very apex, and lifted carefully off the dummy shell, and the drawer-box opened, as previously explained for showing it empty. The performer, after a short pause, to allow of the free circulation of universal wonderment, says, "Ah! but perhaps I did it a little too quickly, and you did not notice how it was done. I will do it in a different way. Here we have the piece of wood, which I cover with the paper; my box, empty, I shut and place here, and the orange I take in my hand, thus" (trap it), "and rub it slowly away. I command the block of wood to pass back again into the box, and the orange to appear under the paper cover." Lift the paper and dummy together, pinching them at the base, and lay them down as before directed, and then tilt out the drawer, allowing the wood to fall upon the floor. If the cone be not very large, then the dummy may be allowed to slide out of the paper cover on to the shelf, and the paper shown empty.

There is an objection to having the dummy shell made of wood, which is that it is necessarily very light, and so easily overturned. An accidental stumble against the table will sometimes effect this untoward result. Zinc and tin are heavier, but there is an objection laid against them as well: they "talk"—that is, they make a scraping noise against the real block of wood when withdrawn from it. I leave the conjuror to decide which is the lesser of the two evils. Cones standing two or three inches in height can be successfully passed through hats, after the method employed in Houdin's die trick.

Further uses for the drawer-box will appear in the course of the description of other tricks.

Bacchus' Dovecote.—The performer advances with a bottle

and glasses on a tray, and a dove on his shoulder. From the bottle he pours some wine, and then places it upon a side table. The dove is next wrapped in some paper, from which the tail is allowed to protrude, and the performer then jumps upon it or else burns it. On the bottle being broken, the dove is found inside.

The bottle is prepared by having the bottom knocked out, which can be easily managed with a hammer, smart taps with which have to be administered, in a circle. The hand holding the bottle whilst this is being done should have a glove upon it, in case of a breakage. A dove is put into the bottle, head first, through the bottom. This is rather uncomfortable for the bird, and I cannot bring myself to think that the latter likes it; but no bad results seem to follow the treatment, which should be rendered as gentle as possible. A tin tube is passed down the neck of the bottle, secured at the mouth by means of red sealing-wax, and then filled with red wine. On the table are spread some sheets of paper, on the margin of one of which are pasted some dove's tail feathers. The exhibited dove is placed upon the centre trap, and the performer pretends to wrap it in the paper having the feathers upon it. It is, instead, passed through the trap, and the paper rolled carefully up, as though the bird were inside. The protruding feathers leave no doubt of this in the minds of the audience. The ends of the paper should be screwed up tightly, and a little hole torn in the parcel, "to give the dove air." If, when placed upon the floor or table the paper should accidentally roll slightly, the performer must attribute it to the restlessness of the bird supposed to be inside, and apostrophise it accordingly. If crushed, it should be treated lengthways, so that the feathers are not afterwards observed, or the audience might think it only reasonable that the bird found inside the bottle should be *minus* a tail if he has left it behind him in the paper. It may seem very simple on their parts, but audiences never seem to doubt that the dove apparently wrapped in paper and the one found in the bottle are one and the same bird. There is no distinguishing mark on it to identify it, and everything tends to make one think otherwise; but never a doubt is raised. This circumstance should be very consoling to the conjuror. I have even seen two doves put into a drawer-box and two other doves made to appear at the other end of the room, and no one seemed to doubt for a moment that they were the same ones that had been just before put into the box.

Doves are most docile creatures, and accommodate themselves to circumstances in a remarkable manner. When passed through a trap, they never wander about and exhibit themselves at the corners of the shelf, or otherwise expose the performer's secrets. At times, though, they will start their peculiar call, but this happens very rarely. Most regular performers, whether professional or not, usually keep a pair of doves at least. They are very hardy, and soon become accustomed to being pulled about.

The Wine-drinking Crystal Ball.—The tube in the neck of a bottle, mentioned in the preceding trick, is a very effective and much-practised deception. In the present instance, the performer selects an opaque bottle with a deep "kick" in the foot, and has a tin tube fitted into its neck. The mouth of the tube is provided with a rim turning outwards, to prevent a total disappearance of the article inside the bottle. This rim should be nicely rounded, so as to fit the mouth of the bottle neatly, as it will not do for the audience to entertain the slightest suspicion of its presence. The bottle is three-parts filled with water, and the tube with red wine. The performer is provided with two clear white glass balls, a little over an inch in diameter, and one red one, of the same dimensions. These are concealed conveniently about the person. The trick is commenced by the wine being poured into glasses and handed round. Retiring to the table, the tube is extracted and "vested," or put elsewhere out of sight, and one white ball got into the hand. By means of the wand, this ball is magically produced. The performer then remarks that he wants two balls, and manufactures another by striking the one he has in the hand with the wand; the explanation given being that the original one has been cut in two. The reader will understand that the second white ball has been got down from concealment, and exhibited at the proper moment. Two balls are not really required for the trick, but the diversion is made for the sake of increasing the attention of the audience, and for giving the trick a general completeness. If he so pleases, the performer can proceed to rub one of the balls until it becomes as small as a pea, or as large as an orange : all that is required is to be provided beforehand with balls of the necessary sizes. The ball which is supposed to be undergoing the compression or expansion can be easily palmed in the right hand, the fingers of which are engaged in shaping the latest arrival by rolling it in the palm of the left hand. To get it back to its original size from the tiny one, the small ball has only to be concealed between the roots of the third and fourth fingers (Fig. 25). To get it back from the large size, place the large ball upon the table over a trap, and, after admiring it as a splendid production on your part, pretend to take it in the hands, trapping it. After much hard squeezing and rubbing, accompanied by expressions of doubt as to the success of your exertions, all enacted close to the audience, the original ball will be produced, it having been, of course, palmed the whole time. Give it to a spectator to hold, and then fetch the bottle. Whilst retiring get down the coloured ball and introduce it into the "kick," where keep it by means of the little, or any other convenient, finger. With the bottle in the left hand, return to the audience, and, taking the white ball from the person holding it, palm it at once, retiring a few steps as you do so, holding the fingers as though they contained the ball. If the palm be kept upwards, there is no fear of the ball slipping out of it, which it possibly might do—it being an awkward thing to hold firmly—were the fingers turned downwards. Explain that you are about to throw the ball into the air and catch it in the bottle. As the ball is considerably larger than the mouth of the bottle, this announcement will naturally be received with incredulity. You, however, with the hands as widely separated as possible, toss an imaginary ball into the air with the right hand, and affect to catch it in the bottle with the left. A vigorous shake given to the bottle will cause the ball held in the foot by the left hand to rattle, and the illusion of the catch will be perfect. Now say that, having got the ball inside the bottle, you must break open the latter in order to get the ball out, and turn round, feigning to look for a hammer. This will give you an opportunity for concealing elsewhere the ball in the palm. So soon as this is done, say, " Well, perhaps I shall only make a litter with the broken glass; so I will get the ball out in a more artistic manner. Whilst I am talking, though, I fear the little gentleman inside is making very free with the wine." Ask the ball how he is getting on, and advise him not to drink too much, &c., and then proceed to get him out of the bottle by striking the palm of the right hand on the mouth of the latter with considerable force. At the third blow or so, release the ball in the " kick," and it will fall to the ground with the appearance of having been forced through the bottom of the bottle. Call attention to the fact that it is red, and consequently, as you feared, must have been drinking the wine. To test this, pour out the contents of the bottle, which, being pure water, will cause the audience to be of your opinion, ludicrous though it may appear. After this, hand round both bottle and ball for inspection. It is a great mistake to omit showing the bottle, as the audience is invariably impressed with the idea that it has an opening in the bottom.

Instead of the imaginary catch, the bottle can be stood upon a table, and the ball passed into it by any ordinary "pass." The disadvantage attending this is that the ball is not heard to fall into the bottle, as in the other method.

It is natural that a heavy ball falling into a bottle must make some noise on striking the bottom. Audiences, perhaps, are not sharp enough to remark the absence of this natural result, but there is no denying that the trick is rendered more complete with its addition. Besides, when placing the bottle upon a table, the ball in the "kick" would naturally be loose were not some method for preventing this to be adopted, and it would become a matter of great difficulty, if not an absolute impossibility, to raise the bottle again without revealing the real state of affairs. A little black wax in the apex of the "kick" serves to sustain the ball in a very satisfactory manner; but, in adopting this auxiliary, one has to dispense with what I consider to be a most necessary feature in the trick, viz., giving the bottle round for examination afterwards. The wax will tell an undeniable tale.

It is possible to vary this trick in many ways, quite according to the fancy of the performer. It is well, however, to be certain of palming and vanishing your ball quickly and neatly before attempting the trick at all, as everything depends upon this. If the white ball is observed to be still in your palm, no amount of rattling in the "kick" of the bottle, however seductively executed, will convince an audience that it has passed into the bottle.

Bacchus' Maypole.—I do not mind admitting to the reader that, where my imagination will permit, I am inventing new names for my tricks. I do this in order to save those who may hereafter undertake performances a certain amount of trouble, and also to get a little out of the beaten track. Ever since this trick has been invented it has been known as "Ribbons and Bottle." Now, that is a very poor title to put upon a programme, which, as it cannot possibly give any very valuable information to the spectator, may as well be embellished with neat terms as slovenly ones. A bottle and some ribbons certainly are used in the trick; but, as the old title does not reveal whether the ribbons go into or come out of the bottle, or whether the bottle comes out of the ribbons, a more fanciful one, so long as it is near the mark, seems just as appropriate, and much more ornamental. At the same time, it is very unadvisable to fill a programme with outrageous and ridiculous titles. I went to an entertainment once, given by a gentleman afflicted with a liking for high-sounding titles. At first I thought I was going to see something totally new, and waited for the curtain to draw up with some impatience, for the first item on the programme was thus designated : "The Celestial Mystery; or, the Winged Fairies of the Emperor Foo-Chow." This was the butterfly trick. However, although greatly disappointed, I kept up my courage, for item No. 2 was "The Sorcerer's Secret; or the Sheık's Visit to the Great Mogul." The egg bag ! I collapsed, and took no further interest in the "Arabian Necromantic Divinations," "Scandinavian Second Sight; or, the Finnish Seer," &c., for they were all tricks of the most ordinary class. Let the performer, by all means, embellish his programme with well-chosen titles ; but let him, at the same time, steer clear of the other extreme. Experience teaches one that there is more in a programme well got up than at first meets the eye.

Although there is rather more of mechanism, and less of sleight of hand, in it than I usually adopt, still this is such a very pretty trick that it would be a pity not to mention it. The performer comes on with a bottle, from which he pours a quantity of wine, beer, or other liquid, and then, either still holding it in his hand, or placing it upon a table or chair, he draws from it a ribbon of any colour that may be asked for by the audience. More liquid is poured out, and more ribbons produced.

The secret lies in the manufacture of the bottle. In most cases, an imitation one of blackened tin is used, but, as the difference between a metal bottle and a glass one is easily discernible, this is a bad principle. The best method is to procure a tapering bottle, quart size, and opaque, and get the bottom neatly cut out by a lapidary. If the glass be semi-transparent it is easily rendered opaque by being painted with Brunswick black on the inside. Into the bottom fit a block of wood nearly an inch thick, the upper half of which has been turned away half an inch, so as to form a step. To this step have fitted a long tin funnel of such a length that, when the block of wood is fitted into the bottle, the small end will be within the third of an inch of the mouth. This funnel is much smaller than the interior of the bottle, so that when it is in position there is space for a considerable quantity of liquid between it and the glass sides. The small end is closed up with a piece of metal, which is provided with a number of slits, each large enough to admit of a ribbon passing through it.

On the block of wood arrange as many tiny reels as it will take. It will be necessary to do this in tiers. There is no reason why they should be like the ordinary reel, for the smaller they are the better. Each of these reels carries a differently coloured ribbon, which has been previously passed through one of the slits at the closed end of the funnel. It will be discovered that it is not possible to wind them up quite tightly, but an inch or two hanging loose will not signify if care be taken not to cross the ribbons in any way. That end of the ribbon which appears outside the slit must have a piece of wire sewn in it, to prevent its going quite through. With the block thus prepared, and the funnel fitted firmly upon it, put the whole into the bottle, and then pour the liquid carefully down the sides of the funnel, taking care not to let any get in through the slits.

Having poured out a little of the liquid, for the benefit of the company, say that you are now going to ask the bottle to give you a colour, and request the audience to say which particular one it shall be. Of course, some half-dozen, at least, will be given by as many persons, which is all in your favour, as you may then choose which you please, or, more properly speaking, not notice any extraordinary one with which you may not be provided. Some clever person is sure to rack his brains for some impossible colour, but, as you will take no notice whatever of him, it will not matter much. Each time a colour is asked for, turn to some object of that particular hue, and pretend to convey some of it on the end of the wand to the mouth of the bottle. There is nothing in this, perhaps, but it gives an air of finish to the trick. Snatch up the bottle every now and then, and pour out some liquid fron it, and also call attention in an indirect manner to the fact that the ribbons are perfectly dry. Also tap the bottle once or twice with the wand, for the unexpresed purpose of showing that it is glass, and handle it generally in a careless manner, swinging it about by the neck, taking care, however, not to expose the bottom. This makes a very effective stage trick.

A second method, which the reader is not at all likely to have seen performed, seeing that I invented it myself, enables the conjuror to employ an ordinary glass bottle, having no preparation whatever about it. It should be a dark bottle, so as to be quite opaque at a distance. The bottle is shown for examination, and placed upon a low table or chair, and the performer extracts coloured ribbons, just as they are called for. As the bottle has been examined, no necessity exists for occasionally pouring out liquid from it, which is a dumb way of saying that the bottle is an ordinary one. Secreted beneath the vest band, the performer has his rolls of ribbon arranged. They may be either upon bent pins, stuck in the vest itself, or the performer may have a band, fitted with wire hooks, which may be buttoned on in a few moments. As the ends of the hooks or pins are towards the performer's body, the ribbons cannot fall off; but the ends of the fingers, curled slightly underneath, obtain them at once. The colours must be arranged in a certain order, which the performer will, of course, have to remember, and he must depend entirely upon his sense of touch. Directly the colour is named, the performer commences to seek for some article of furniture or dress containing it; and whilst the wand is extended towards the object, for the purpose of magically bearing away some of its colour, the other hand is getting down the ribbon, that side of the body upon which it is secreted being turned from the audience. Proceeding to the bottle, the wand affects to place the colour magically obtained into the bottle, and, as soon as the other hand has secured the loose end of the ribbon, it is brought to the mouth, and the ribbon allowed to unroll. A tiny piece of lead, sewn in the end, will assist this greatly; but the ribbons should always be kept flat, except when in actual use, otherwise they will assume a curl, which will betray the fact that they have been rolled up. If symptoms of curling manifest themselves, the wand should be held at the mouth of the bottle and pressed against the ribbon as it comes out, and it should be then taken in both hands and held stretched until placed upon the table.

By adopting this method, the performer is enabled to produce a very great number of colours; and it is advisable to have two or three of them twice over. However well the trick may be performed with the prepared bottle, the company instinctively feel that a certain number of ribbons are concealed somewhere or other, and that when they are once produced no more can come. By producing the same colours twice, the notion of an inexhaustible productive power is conveyed.

There is a third method, which can only be employed on a regular stage. The bottle is a specially constructed glass one, that part which is known as the "kick" extending upwards to the neck, and having a hole in the top. Thus there is still space left in the bottle for plenty of liquor, whilst there is an open passage up the middle of it. This bottle is placed over a hole in a table having a hollow leg (a small, single-legged round table is invariably used), and the ribbons are passed up on the end of a rod by an assistant below.

By this method, an endless supply can be taken from the bottle, but few of my readers will, I fancy, be able to adopt this method, although it could be done over a draped table under which a small boy was secreted for the time being. When the performer advances to the bottle he gives out the name of the colour very loudly, and places his fingers over the mouth, at the same time pressing hard, to prevent the bottle being shifted by the action of the ascending rod. The assistant below has his ribbons arranged in order, and, as soon as he hears the colour given, attaches the proper one to the pin at the end of the rod. When the performer is quite ready he strikes the bottle with the wand, upon hearing which, but not before, the assistant pushes up the rod. He must be in no hurry to withdraw it, but give the performer plenty of time to clear the ribbon. A suitable bottle may be manufactured by knocking the bottom out of an opaque glass bottle, and then fitting a tin lining to it, inside, which can be fixed and rendered watertight by means of putty, afterwards blackened, if white putty be used. The bottle is occasionally taken up, and liquor poured from it, as in the first method.

The Accommodating Bottle.—This is a bottle from which the performer pours any kind of wine or spirits that may be asked for. The secret, as in the foregoing trick, lies in the bottle, and it is only introduced here on account of its remarkable effectiveness in clever hands. The interior of the body is divided into a number of compartments, usually five. Each compartment has a tiny tube running from it half way up the neck of the bottle, and has also an aperture, just capable of admitting an ordinary pin, at the side of the bottle. Four of these apertures should be arranged an inch apart in a slightly curved line, so that one finger can be placed upon each when the bottle is grasped in the hand. The fifth aperture should be situated underneath the thumb. It is possible, but very difficult (owing to the absolute necessity for having the partitions hermetically closed, except at the tubes and the apertures), to have an ordinary quart bottle, with the bottom knocked out, fitted with a tin lining, properly prepared. When this can be done, it is decidedly advantageous; but, in the ordinary way, one has to be contented with a tin article, japanned.

By means of a specially fine funnel, each compartment is filled with a different wine, and great care must be taken in remembering which contains the port, which the sherry, and so on. So long as the fingers and thumb are kept firmly pressed upon the apertures, no liquid will escape, even when the bottle is inverted, as it will be by the performer, previous to commencing, to show that it is empty. Some bottles have an extra compartment, into which water is poured, in full view of the audience, and the bottle apparently washed out, the water being poured out again. The adoption of this addition is a matter of taste. A dozen or so of liqueur glasses upon a tray, and carried by an attendant, will be required, and, after calling attention to the fact that the bottle is quite empty, and that he has no pipes running up his sleeve, the performer asks a lady what particular wine she would like. It is as well to use the words " port, sherry, or what?" by way of suggesting something which you have in your bottle to start with. You will, of course, have champagne, claret, and hock, which, with the sherry and port, will make about as good a quintet as could be selected. On any particular wine being called for, all you have to do is to raise the finger covering the hole corresponding with the compartment containing the required beverage, and it will flow out; on replacing the finger the flow will cease. By using small glasses, one appears to supply so much more than would be the case with larger ones. Never more than half fill a glass, and always pass as rapidly as possible from one person to another. Of course, you will be frequently asked for a wine with which you are not provided. This, in nine times out of ten, you can manufacture out of your stock. For marsala, for instance, give a little sherry and hock mixed. For sparkling burgundy mix champagne and port, or champagne and claret. When you make a mistake, pretend to be in a great hurry to attend to another applicant, and accidentally (!) drop the glass on the floor. Never mind if the glass does break; your trick is not spoilt.

It is wonderful how much success is attained by management in this trick. In one person's hands, it falls so flat as to be almost a failure; whilst, in another's, it will probably be the success of the evening. It is especially successful in the hands of a brisk and lively performer, before, or rather amongst, a large audience of a free and easy nature. It is not a good trick to introduce before a select and stiff company. Should any particularly fastidious person be met with, he can generally be settled by the administration of a mixture of the whole five wines. If he is still dissatisfied, ask him, if the beverage is not the one for which he asked, to say what it is. It will puzzle him to answer, and you will then be able to retaliate upon him by supposing that he does not know the taste of the wine for which he was so anxious.

Some first-rate continental conjurors, who, as a rule, take infinite trouble with their tricks, perform this trick with an ordinary bottle, which, after being examined, is filled with sweetened water (ostensibly plain water), and then any liqueur is given from it. The secret in this case lies in the glasses, which are coloured, and contain each an extract of a certain liqueur. The sweetened water answers for all. By this means, it is possible to be provided with an immense number of flavours, but the trouble in preparation is such as only a professed conjuror could undertake.

The Mesmeric Suspension Wand.—The Fakir of Oolu (he is known in private circles by a far less sounding and much more cockneyfied name than that) was the first to introduce this trick to the British public.

The performer is provided with an ordinary conjuring wand, blackened all over. He passes it through one hand, to show that it is not attached to any suspending medium, and then performs a series of feats with it, which apparently entirely upset the laws of gravitation. For instance, when placed horizontally against the under side of the outstretched hand, it does not, as one would expect, fall at once to the ground, but remains in the unnatural position. When placed perpendicularly against a finger or thumb, the result is the same; and it can be just as easily suspended from the tip of the finger by its extreme end. There are three methods in general use for producing these phenomena. One is to have the rod provided with several black pins, which stand out a little from the wand, and are then bent at right angles. The heads are taken off, and the exposed ends left rough. If two of these pins be placed about five inches apart, with the points of each turned towards the other, a hand placed flatly between them will be enabled to sustain the rod in any position by merely opening out the fingers, thereby causing a pressure on the two pins. This is the whole secret of the first method. The conjuror can arrange his pins according to fancy. I find five ample viz., two about two and a half inches apart at each end, and one small one at the actual tip. There is no necessity for more; and the space of two and a half inches admits of the introduction of two fingers, which possess quite sufficient power to sustain the rod. The advantage of using two fingers only is that, by employing the middle ones, those on the outside are left free to be moved about, as they should be, to assist in abolishing the idea of any connection existing. When the wand is drawn through one hand, the action must be quickly executed, and no notice given of the intention to perform it, otherwise the attention of the audience will be sufficiently attracted to the wand to cause it to be noticed that the hand does not actually touch it, although it appears to do so. A serious pantomime of mesmerising the wand by means of a few passes may be indulged in with advantage, according to the ability of the performer in this direction;

but he must treat it seriously. If it is at all well done, one half of the audience will remain almost convinced that some influence has been exercised over the rod. The wand should then be taken in one hand, and struck smartly on the palm of the other, to show that it is solid, or it can be done previous to the mesmerism. This is very necessary, as a universal idea exists, amongst those who do not know the trick, that the wand is made of pith, and that the performer has some "sticky stuff" on his fingers. It should next be held horizontally at the end by one hand, and the other passed slowly along it once or twice, the motion becoming slower and slower until it ceases altogether. The fingers will then be between two pins, and, on the rod being released by the other hand, it will apparently cling to the under surface of the one above it. To cause it to attach itself to a finger or thumb perpendicularly, it is only necessary to hang it by one pin on the outstretched member, and the prodigy is accomplished. The pin at the tip is for the purpose of suspending the rod from the end of a finger. This is accomplished by pushing the pin under the nail. No trick could be simpler; therefore the performer must do all he can to make the audience believe in its extreme difficulty. Once or twice, at least, the mesmeric power should fail, and fresh passes resorted to in order to restore it. An effective action to introduce is that of placing both hands above the wand whilst it is in a horizontal position, and then appearing to move them backwards and forwards along it. This is accomplished by fixing the fingers of one hand only in the pins. The hands are then parted, and joined twice with considerably rapidity. The disengaged hand must not alone be moved, but the other as well, otherwise it will be seen that the wand is affixed to one hand, and the other merely moved along it. The care taken by the conjuror will make this trick the more or less successful.

The second method is to have a ring upon the finger provided with a clamp, which receives the wand in its embrace.

The only thing to be said in favour of this device is that it enables the wand to be shown round. In all else it is vastly inferior to the bent pin arrangement. The number of positions in which it is possible to suspend the rod are exceedingly limited, and the probability of the ring being accidentally exposed is by no means remote.

As it is decidedly advantageous to give the rod round for examination, it is always well for the performer to devise a method for handing round one rod, free from any preparation whatever, and then exchanging it for a prepared one. This is, perhaps, best managed by concealing the prepared one up the coat sleeve. The one that is shown round is dropped into the tail pocket, which can be specially arranged for such a use without much difficulty. The change behind the table is weak, and a large majority of the audience invariably see through it, in which case all the performer's subsequent actions with the article are looked upon as farcical. When a dummy article is to be exchanged for a prepared one, the change must be perfect, or left alone altogether. If the performer have any doubt about it, let him rather dispense with the examination and consequent exchange, for then the audience can only suspect; but, if any covert action is detected, then the suspicion resolves itself into a tolerable certainty.

The wand for this trick is very easily made, any ordinary wood being suitable, and a packet of black pins, a pair of pliers, and a file will do the rest. It is best as a stage trick, private audiences in small rooms being somewhat too close for safety.

There is, however, a third method, which I think the reader will, after giving it a trial, find commend itself highly, as it enables him to use his ordinary wand, and so avoid the suspicion naturally engendered by the employment of a fresh article expressly for a special trick. Our old friend, the silken thread, is once more the means employed, and it may be either passed round the performer's neck, in the form of a large loop, or be affixed to a waistcoat button. Experiment will at once determine the proper length, which will naturally vary with the physical proportions of each performer. The wand is, of course, given round for examination, and may be passed through the loop whilst the performer is facing the audience, although it is, perhaps, the safer way to do this whilst retreating to the stage. It will be found that when the thread is stretched outwards from the body by means of the wand, acted upon by the hands, it supports the wand by drawing it hard against the fingers. At first the wand is taken in the two hands, one near each end, and held out very gingerly. When the thread is felt to be tightly stretched, the fingers are opened, and it is as well to at once give a swinging motion to the hands. The hands should then be drawn together and parted again two or three times, both slowly and fast, a slight swinging being still kept up, and then two or three, or single fingers can be employed, as may the sides and backs of the hands. These movements will necessitate some little practice, in order to ensure facility of execution. When enough has been done by two hands, one hand should be placed in the centre of the wand, the thread passing between the fingers, when the wand will be just as securely supported. The hands should be changed, the one hand taking the wand from the other, from beneath. The *finale* to this method of doing the trick is the most startling of all, the wand being suspended by one end from the tip of a finger, and from thence given to the company. To bring this about neatly, grasp one end of the wand with the right hand and place the tip of a finger of the left hand against the other end. Let the wand assume a perpendicular position, the right hand undermost, and, at the same time, cause the thread to slide along until within a bare inch of the finger at the other end. If the wand be fitted with ferrules, as directed, the thread is certain to rest at their terminations. The pressure of the finger against the resistance of

the thread, delicately dispensed, will cause the wand to be
supported, and with it in this position the performer
advances to the company, and, with the right hand, places
it in their hands, a very slight under sweep, quite compatible
with a graceful presentation of the article, sufficing to free
it of the slight tenure the thread holds over it. As the
Fakir's wand has been on sale for very many years, there
will probably be amongst the spectators some who know its
secret. With these the method now described will be most

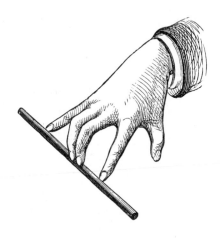

FIG. 53.

successful in creating astonishment, for it will be quite
beyond them.

A little additional sleight may be practised, which gives
finish to the trick. This is to cause the wand to apparently
attach itself to the tips of the outstretched fingers of one
hand. To the spectators, it appears as if the fingers were
merely outstretched, and the wand placed against them, when
it adheres. It is quite true that only the tips of the fingers
touch the wand, but they must be so disposed that the first
and fourth are on the inside, and the second and third on
the outside. The theory of the grip is the same as though

the wand were held between the four fingers, an inch or more down them. What the conjuror has to study is to bring sufficient pressure to bear by means of the tips only, the nails of the first and third fingers resting against the wand. The hold is really of the most fragile description, only one longitudinal half (the inside one) of the wand being operated upon. A strong and rather fleshy finger will succeed best, but, in any case, the first and fourth fingers must be stretched out as wide as they can be made to do, and the whole operation will be very materially assisted by using a wand that is neither heavy, thick, nor slippery. An unvarnished wand would be the best, and it should be as much less than half an inch in thickness as can be made convenient. Weight will then be comparatively immaterial. The performer will find the effect of his trick wonderfully enhanced if, in handing the wand from one member of the company to another, he does so by means of the apparently magnetic tips of his fingers. The sleight is illustrated at Fig. 53.

The Magi's Brazen Rod.—This is a solid brazen rod, one quarter of an inch in thickness. At each end is a brass ball, free (whether solid or not) from any preparation whatever. One ball is firmly fixed, and the other screws off and on. Some ladies' rings are borrowed, and a solid wooden ball, which is subjected to examination, is then passed on the brazen rod, and the movable brass ball screwed on. The ball ends are then held firmly by two of the audience, and a handkerchief spread over the wooden ball. The performer introduces his hands, containing the rings, beneath the handkerchief, and, in a moment, the ball drops from the wand, upon which, on the withdrawal of the handkerchief, the rings are seen.

There are many variations in the details of the trick; but the one great secret in connection with it is that, besides the solid wooden ball which is shown round, the performer has one behind the scenes that is hollow, and is divided into two equal parts, which fit firmly together, like a box and lid. In the box portion is fitted a piece of cork, in which are three slits. Ostensibly to fetch the solid ball, the performer retires behind, and there rapidly places the three borrowed rings, for the possession of which at this stage I shall presently account, lightly into the slits, closes the ball up, and palms it. Returning to the stage, with the solid ball openly in the hand, he gives it to be examined. On receiving it back, he has to exchange it for the prepared one (a feat neither too difficult nor too easy), which is passed on the rod instead, the solid ball being vested. The sequel follows as a matter of course. The solid ball is re-palmed, and secretly introduced under the handkerchief at the same time as the rings (i.e., their substitutes); the hollow ball is opened, thus leaving the rings alone on the wand, re-closed and palmed, the solid ball at the same moment being dropped on the floor. The performer must be careful not to have the wooden balls larger than is absolutely necessary, or he will find some difficulty in exchanging and concealing them neatly when occasion requires. They must be turned with circular grooves, in one of which the opening of the prepared ball is made, so as to escape detection from casual glances. The method of obtaining the rings varies considerably. Some performers put them into boxes with secret openings, and thus obtain possession of them. The simplest plan, if one has a stage assistant, is that described under the heading "Sleights for General Use." The assistant remains on the stage, holding the wand until the rings are required again. The performer then puts them in a piece of paper, ostensibly to "take better care of them," but really to make it easier for him to get rid of them, and they are palmed, along with the dummy ball, when that is taken off the wand. I have seen it attempted to place the dummy rings inside the ball before re-closing it, but the operation took too long by far in execution. If too much paper be not used, and the rings are small and tightly folded together, it is possible to pop the little parcel inside the lid of the ball. The rings could be of such a size as to allow of this. The method for managing the exchange of the rings depends much upon circumstances. The one I have given will be found generally applicable, especially as the trick is essentially a stage one. The handkerchief that is thrown over the rod should be drawn off smartly, so as to cause the rings to spin round, by the hand containing the ball just removed from the rod, which it will assist to conceal. On the completion of the trick, hand back the borrowed rings on the rod itself, and also show round the ball again.

There is no reason why this should be an expensive trick. A brazier could make the rod and knob ends for a very few shillings, and the two wooden balls should cost about 1s. 6d.

The Shower of Plumes.—This is a trick requiring a great display of dexterity, combined with considerable boldness. The performer produces, from a large handkerchief, enough plumes, each nearly 2ft. in length, to cover the floor of an ordinary room. The plumes are rather expensive articles to purchase, but, when once obtained, form an excellent stock-in-trade. The method for producing them is to take off the coat, and then, grasping a large quantity by the lower ends in each hand, replace the coat. The compressible nature of the feathers enables a dozen or more plumes to be concealed up each sleeve. Care should be taken that they lie along the back of the arm. The performer, thus padded, comes on with a large silk handkerchief in his hands, but contents himself with remaining well at the back of the stage, and also refrains from turning his back to the audience. He waves the handkerchief to and fro, to show that it is empty, and then says that he will try and find something in it. To do this, he spreads it over one hand, and, with the other, seizes the end of one plume through it. At the same moment, with a sharp swift movement, the handkerchief and plume are withdrawn, the underneath hand falling to the side, assisting thereby in the withdrawal of the plume, and also keeping the ends of the remaining ones out of sight. The hand holding the handkerchief is inverted, and the plume will be revealed. Under pretence of removing this plume, the disengaged hand seizes another plume through the handkerchief, and withdraws it with the same movement which casts the one exhibited on the floor. The second one is then shown, and the process of drawing out another repeated from each arm alternately, the production of the plumes being made as rapid as possible, the motive being to bewilder the audience, who, if the performer does not make any blunder, will never imagine that they are concealed up the sleeves. It is as well to draw out a couple at one time once or twice, for the sake of extra effect, and, with the same object in view, have the plumes of several colours. Some should be all white, some all red, and others all blue, whilst another variety can be of two or even three colours. Never attempt to produce a plume until the handkerchief has fallen well over the arm from which it is to be drawn, and let the whole trick be executed with great dash. Sometimes larger plumes are placed round the body and drawn out from the vest, the handkerchief being spread over the chest for the purpose. The attendant who picks up the plumes should make the best show he can with them. Some performers place the plumes in fan-shaped vases or other receptacles, but the operation hampers the performance of the trick too much, and also leads to too many undesirable movements to be recommended. An excellent ruse is to conceal one plume beneath the carpet, with the end just through a hole or slit in the seam. The handkerchief is spread on the floor, and the plume produced. It is undoubtedly a very difficult trick to perform well, but it produces a great effect.

The trick may be performed, in a small way, by means of ostrich feathers laid inside the shirt sleeve, the coat sleeve being turned back.

The Fairy Flower.—From a large cut-glass vase, having a

cover, cut out a large portion — say, a piece 3in. wide, and extending from the top almost to the bottom, or foot. Along the back edge of the top of the table affix a spiral spring of several close coils, the free end of which should be of sufficient length, and of such shape as to enable it to extend well over the top of the table. To the extreme end of it affix a cut rose, camellia, or other showy flower, and then bend it down until it is out of sight behind the table. A sliding pin, working in a couple of staples, and having a loop at one end, must be brought on at the side of the spiral spring, and when the end with the flower on it is bent back, this pin is pushed across it, and so prevents it returning to an upright position. A thread attached to the loop, and passed out at the side, will enable the assistant to release the spring when desired. The vase is brought on, and the best side shown to the audience, besides being rung with the fingers or wand to show that it is sound, and it is then placed in position exactly against the spot where the spring is affixed, and the cover put on. The performer then says that he will cause the fairies to place a flower inside the vase, and commands them to do so. He can either spread a handkerchief momentarily over the vase, or dispense with the operation altogether. The attendant pulls the thread, the pin is drawn aside, and the spring with the flower on it flies into the vase. The cover is then removed, and the flower taken out from the top, a strong nip of the nails being necessary to remove it. The assistant, in removing the vase, bends back the wire and pushes the pin over it. This trick is usually performed with the aid of a box-shaped pedestal, on which the vase is stood. Within this pedestal the spring and wire arrangement, with flower attached, is concealed, the working being practically the same as that just described; but the reader will, doubtless, agree with me, that the introduction of a large box is likely to bring suspicion along with it.

The Perambulating Bottle and Tumbler.—This is a trick in which absolute sleight of hand does not appear; but it calls for a certain amount of finish in execution, and, like *A Bottle of Ginger Beer*, makes an agreeable change in a programme, both to company and performer. The performer has a bottle of beer, a tumbler, and two cardboard covers, which are, in fact, mere cardboard tubes, open at each end. Beer is poured from the bottle into the tumbler, and both articles are then placed upon the side tables, and covered with a cover. After the performance of the usual magical passes, the covers are removed, when the glass and bottle are found to have changed places. The following is the ingenious method by which the impossibility is apparently brought about: Have a tin bottle made, exactly in imitation of a beer bottle, between nine and ten inches high, and japanned so as to look like glass at a distance. The bottom of this bottle is open, but four inches from the lower edge is a tin partition, dividing the bottle laterally into two compartments. The upper compartment is for the purpose of containing the beer. Passing through its very centre, and reaching to within half an inch of the top of the neck, is a tube about a third of an inch in diameter, or, at any rate, large enough to take a small funnel. Thus communication is established with the lower open compartment, by means of the tube. Then have a second bottle made, also of tin, and japanned to match, just large enough to pass over the first one. This bottle has no interior whatever, and is, in fact, a mere shell. In height it need be only the merest trifle taller than the other, and the tinman should be enjoined to keep it as narrow as possible, compatible with an easy fit over the smaller bottle. Each bottle should be decorated with a flaring beer label, taken from genuine bottles. Needless to say, they must be precisely similar, and if each has a piece accidentally (!) torn out of it, sufficiently large to be noticed by the spectator, so much the better. In the middle of the body of each bottle is cut a circular hole, nearly an inch in diameter, and fully two inches removed from the nearest edge of the label. Further will be required the two pasteboard covers, which may be of any length between twelve and fifteen inches. These must be made to fit very closely over the bottles, without actually clinging to them, consequently one will be larger than the other. Finally, two tumblers, precisely similar, will be wanted. They must not exceed four inches in height, or they will not go under the small bottle, on account of the partition there. Behind the scenes the small bottle has its compartment filled with beer, and is then placed over one of the tumblers, the large shell bottle being finally placed over both. Placing the middle finger through the holes in the bottles pressure is brought to bear upon the tumbler, which in this way may be lifted with the bottles. The whole, looking to the audience merely like a single bottle, is thus brought on, and placed upon the centre table. The two covers are shown, the performer explaining that they are merely made to cover the bottle. Suiting the action to the word, he places the large cover over the bottle, and at once withdraws it, nipping it near the bottom, so as to bring away the outer shell inside. With the other hand, the smaller cover is then placed over the smaller bottle, and at once withdrawn. The company, knowing of only one bottle, will fancy they have seen both covers placed over it. The large cover, having the shell within it, must not be laid upon its side, but stood up alongside the empty one. The performer now takes the smaller bottle in one hand—holding the tumbler beneath it as well, by means of a finger through the hole—and the visible tumbler in the other. Beer is poured out until the tumbler is filled. The performer now says that he does not want his glass too full, and, replacing bottle on table, places a small funnel into its mouth, care being taken to insert it in the tube. Half the beer—neither more nor less —must now be poured into the funnel, and it of course finds its way into the tumbler beneath. The conjuror will have to experiment beforehand, so as to discover how much liquid he must leave in the visible tumbler, and how much he must pour away, slight marks being made, with a diamond or file, for his guidance whilst exhibiting. It is highly essential that each glass contains precisely the same quantity. The visible tumbler is now placed upon one side table and covered with the large cover, containing the shell. The small bottle is placed upon the other side table, with the tumbler still concealed under it, and covered with the small cover. By means of his wand, an imaginary exchange of the articles is now made, and the covers are lifted—that containing the shell lightly, so as to leave the shell behind; whilst that containing the bottle is gripped nearer the bottom, so as to lift that article with it, exposing the second tumbler. The general method adopted in lifting the covers is to take them by the extreme top when the article contained is to be exhibited, and at the very bottom when it is to be carried away. These are certainly very safe methods; but they are unnecessarily so, and afford far too much clue to the spectators. The variation between the positions of the hand need never exceed a couple of inches. The height of the upper edge of the body of the bottles the performer may have indicated upon the outside of the cover. Half an inch below that line he has only to exert pressure to ensure the carrying away of the bottle or shell. A little above it he is clear of them, and need not fear carrying them away by mistake. A variation of two or three inches is a natural one, and unnoticeable. Poor conjurors, too, always treat a cover containing anything in a far too gingerly manner. An empty cover they flourish about with extreme recklessness, exhibiting the interior freely; but, a few moments later, they carry the same cover about as gingerly as one would a very lofty and quivering tipsy cake or jelly. Spectators cannot but notice this sudden change from extreme freedom to plainly-depicted trepidation, and generally draw very correct conclusions. The conjuror should practise to be as free and as *nonchalant* as possible with articles that are really mysterious, and study carefully how far he may go without exposing any secrets. In the present instance, the cover containing the shell should be flourished about a good deal, and finally placed over the tumbler in a careless manner.

The change made, the performer will of course offer to do it again, "in order to give everyone a chance of noticing how it is done." He may pretend to give his spectators some assistance by telling them, in confidence, that the tumbler and bottle really came out at the tops of the covers, his original statement, that the openings were there to prevent suspicion, being untrue, their real purpose being to afford easy exits and entrances for the articles. The articles then make a return to their original positions, after the covers have been replaced, the shell being carried away, and the bottle allowed to remain. The feature of the trick, which completely mystifies the company, is the transposition of the beer-containing tumbler. The fact that the bottle has been nearly inverted, in the act of pouring out the beer in the first instance, precludes the idea that it could ever have been concealed in that. Although beer is here mentioned, claret or claret and water may be used, or any other showy liquid at hand.

The Magic Omelette.—This is a very favourite trick. The performer borrows two or three rings, which are cast into an omelette pan. Eggs are broken into the pan, and spirit added, and lighted. A cover is momentarily placed over it, and, when removed, all traces of the omelette have vanished, two doves taking its place. This would, perhaps, not be so very extraordinary were it not for the fact that around the birds' necks are pieces of ribbon, having upon them the borrowed rings. Such a trick may well be admired. It is thus performed: The pan, about 10in. in diameter, and between 2in. and 3in. deep, is made of plain brass, copper, or nickel, and has a slight turnover edge, turning outwards. The cover, which is a shallow one, has a 2in. flange. This flange is for the reception of a secret lining to the pan, containing the doves, and left behind when the cover is raised, after being placed over the pan. It fits outside the cover flange, loosely, but very tightly into the pan, for there must be no danger of its being carried away when the cover is lifted. It also has a turnover edge, precisely as has the pan, and by means of this edge it is temporarily attached to the cover. The cover, on the under side, at the extreme border, has two flat hooks, an inch or so in length. These are placed on opposite sides. In the turnover edge of the lining are two slits, admitting the flat hooks. To attach the lining to the cover is therefore simple, the hooks being placed in the slits and a twist given to the cover, which has only to be twisted the reverse way to withdraw the hooks from the lining again.

Firstly, the performer sends his assistant forward to borrow the rings, which the lenders place upon the little wand he carries. In returning he changes them for dummies, as described at page 176, and at once retires behind the scenes, where he has the cover and lining already prepared with the birds inside, but not with the hooks in position. The ribbons around the necks of the birds are left outside, the insertion of a stick in the loops preventing their being pulled inside by the movements of their wearers. This pre-arrangement is necessary, as rapidity of action is essential. A ring is rapidly attached by the ribbon loop being first passed through it, and then opened out over it. When attached, the rings are popped inside, the cover hooked to the lining, and a pre-arranged signal given the performer that all is in readiness. The performer, in the meanwhile, has been making his omelette, which he must not light until his assistant signals that he is ready. Then he applies fire, and, rushing forward, shows the spectators the rings frizzling in the midst of the eggs. This is done rapidly; and it is certainly advisable to avoid, if possible, the actual owners of the rings, or the absence of a lent one may be noticed. The assistant seizes this opportunity for bringing on the cover, which he does in a careless manner; and it is as well to bring on the wand at the same time, as though both articles had been carelessly forgotten. The majority of the spectators, if not all, will, however, be engaged with the movements of the performer, who rushes back to his table, claps on the cover, his assistant firing a pistol to stir up the company to increased excitement, and takes it off again, giving, at the moment, the disengaging twist, the lining being thus left inside the pan, with the doves. The latter are brought down to the company, with the rings on their necks, and the pan shown empty, the contents being concealed between the bottom of the lining and the bottom of the pan.

To Pass a Borrowed Ring Inside an Egg.—A ring is borrowed, and placed in a handkerchief, or elsewhere, and an ordinary full egg, which may be examined, is placed in an egg-cup. The ring is "passed" into the egg, which is broken by the spectators, who also find the ring inside the egg by means of a little hook, with which they fish for it. The secret of the trick lies in the egg-cup. This may be of wood or metal—the latter for preference, wooden egg-cups being open to suspicion, whereas plated ones are not. Inside the cup, at the bottom, is cut a moderately deep slot; and when the performer has obtained possession of the ring by one of the methods described in this book, he secretly places it in the slot. The egg is now placed in the egg-cup, but, before doing so, the performer accidentally (!) breaks the shell at the small end, either by tapping the egg on the table or striking it with his wand, whilst in the act of explaining that the ring is to be found inside when the egg is placed into the cup, with the cracked end downwards. A little pressure will cause the ring to be forced into it. A small hook is now presented to a spectator, who is desired to break the top of the egg, and fish for the ring with the hook. Sooner or later, the ring will be brought to light. Particulars to be observed in connection with this trick are that the borrowed ring must not be too broad, or it may jam in the slot, nor must it be of a nature likely to be injured by the contents of the egg. The cup, with egg in it, should be brought forward on a plate or small waiter, in case of an overflow, a napkin being also necessary, for the same reason, and for the additional purpose of wiping the ring. The performer should present several eggs to the company, who select the one with which the trick is to be performed; but he should previously ascertain that each of them fits well into the cup, and does not jam at the sides. The safest plan is to have a special egg-cup made sufficiently large to take any ordinary hen's egg, as occasions may arise when the eggs will be provided by the house, as would be the case in the country. An additional feature is sometimes introduced of having a second egg-cup, without any slot in it, this one being given for examination, and the prepared one afterwards exchanged for it. The prepared one can very well be kept under the vest, and exchanged in the act of turning round.

The Flying Cage.—The performer comes forward with a square cage in his hand, containing a live bird. Standing close in front of the audience, he suddenly makes a movement as of throwing the cage upwards, when that article disappears, bird and all. The secret lies in the fact that, whilst the framework of the cage is actually of wood or metal, and the wires of real wire, the whole is jointed together at the corners with elastic, and the wires looped or hinged where affixed to the framework, so that the whole may be shut up, cornerwise, longitudinally, and made to disappear up the coat sleeve. The sleeve must be pretty large for this purpose, and the shirt cuff must offer no obstruction ; in fact, a cuffless shirt should be worn. At one corner of the cage is affixed a strong black cord, which passes up the sleeve, round the back, and down the other sleeve, where it is tied to the wrist. The length must be such that the performer is just able to hold the cage, and have the cord tight. The bird is inserted through the wires. When the performer desires to cause the cage to disappear, he shuts up the cage obliquely, and, by simultaneously stretching out his arms, it is made to fly up his sleeve. So instantaneously is this accomplished, that even those acquainted with the means by which the disappearance is arrived at cannot actually see the cage go, although the performer faces the company during the entire execution of the trick. It is advisable to purchase a cage ready made, in preference to constructing it oneself. A black frame is preferable to a brightly-burnished brass one.

The Great Dictionary Trick.—Few tricks have caused more general wonderment than this one. It is presented in various ways; but the original form, to which the reader may make what variations circumstances and ingenuity may suggest, is as follows: The performer advances with several pieces of paper, all blank. These are folded and thrown into a hat. One is selected by a spectator, and left in custody of the company. Several dictionaries are now produced, and handed round for subsequent reference. A paper-knife is placed in the hands of a spectator, who is desired to thrust it at will into the dictionary which the performer presents to him. The book is opened at the place thus indicated, the performer announcing the pages, to which the holders of the other dictionaries at once turn. The audience select which page and which of the two columns upon it shall be employed; and then, in order to ascertain which word shall be selected, a bag containing numbered counters, shown to be all different, is presented to another spectator, who draws one, and is asked to announce it. The word corresponding to that number, counting from the top of the page, is then read out, and on the paper previously chosen being opened, the word is found written upon it.

The working of this trick is as follows: The dictionary which is presented by the performer to the holder of the paper-knife is composed of two pages only, repeated over and over again, throughout the book. Thus, it makes no difference where the knife may be thrust. Say that the thirteenth word on the right-hand column of the left-hand page of the book is the one selected by the performer. He would first ask someone which page he should take. If the right hand were said, the performer immediately ejaculates, "*Your* right hand; thank you!" and immediately proceeds to have the right-hand column selected by someone else, in the same one-sided manner. The selection of the proper word is thus managed. The bag is a double one, and in one side are numbers running in proper arithmetical progression. These are shown and replaced. In the other side are a quantity of counters, but each is numbered "thirteen," so the drawer is bound to draw that number, the performer taking care to open that side for the insertion of his hand. The corresponding word has been previously written upon the paper. This may be forced upon the selector by being placed upon the crown of a hat in a circle with other pieces, the hat being adroitly turned at the proper moment, so that the desired piece of paper comes to the hand of the chooser. This force must not be insisted upon if the chooser be at all unwilling, and the performer must resort to the alternate ruse (which many prefer entirely to the force) of a change. For this, the prepared paper is held in the left hand, and a plain paper apparently put into it by the right, it being, of course, retained there, and the one in the left hand exhibited. When performed many times before the same company, different arrangements of pages will have to be adopted, or the recurrence of the same page may easily lead to detection of the fraud.

Magical Wine.—The performer comes forward with a glass of port wine in his hand. He then explains the convenience of being a conjuror, since one can always accommodate one's friends. For instance, here is a glass of port wine. The friend to whom it is proffered does not happen to care for port. In the ordinary way the wine would be wasted; but not so with the conjuror. All he has to do is to borrow the friend's handkerchief (here a handkerchief is borrowed), and, waving it thus over the glass, see, the wine has changed to sherry! But the friend does not like sherry either. What does he like, then? A little spirit? Yes! Gin, perhaps? If you please. The handkerchief is once more waved over the glass, and the sherry turns to gin, which the company are welcome to prove by the ordeal of taste.

The secret of this trick lies in two pieces of coloured glass, shaped thus : so as to fit perpendicularly into a wine-glass. One piece of glass is yellow, to represent sherry, and the other red. The performer advances with the glass full of gin, and the two glasses placed in it. The red and the yellow commingling produce the tawny port colour. It need hardly be said that the edges of the glasses must never be towards the company. The first time the handkerchief is placed over the glass the red glass is abstracted, leaving the yellow, which is removed on the second occasion. The glasses are most easily palmed. Provided with his glasses, the performer will find this a handy trick to perform extempore at the houses of friends, where water might be used if gin were not handy, or else very pale whisky. It is not of sufficient importance for the stage.

The Sack Trick.—This trick is variously performed, but I shall only give one method, as being the one best within reach of the amateur. It requires the aid of an assistant, who comes forward undisguisedly as such. A large sack is handed round to the company, along with a piece of cord, for examination. As a matter of fact, there is nothing to be discovered in connection with these articles. Into the sack the performer or his assistant steps, and it is tied securely over his head, the cord being finally sealed by one of the company. A screen is placed in front of the individual in the sack, and, in a very short space of time, he comes from behind it with the sack in his hand, and minus a boot. The sack is given to the company for examination, when the mouth is found to be firmly tied and the seal unbroken, whilst the missing boot is clearly inside, it being thereby conclusively demonstrated that it was actually the sack which contained the owner of that piece of wearing apparel. The seal has to be broken before the boot can be recovered.

The explanation is that there are two sacks, the second one being concealed up the back of the person who is tied up. So soon as he is put into the first sack he gets down the concealed one, and pops his boot into it. He then folds the mouth of it neatly, and, as his *confrère* forms up that of the visible sack for tying, he thrusts it up into his hand. The tyer, holding his hand so as to conceal the fact of there being two mouths, ties up the inside one very securely—a few folds of the cords just nipping the outside sack also, so that the hand holding them may be presently removed without any exposure resulting. The greatest care must, of course, be taken that the sealing is done upon the inside sack only, the tyer superintending this operation very closely. Everything depends upon the neatness with which he performs his part. If it is a clumsy job, the sealing must be dispensed with, or the sealer will notice the presence of two sack mouths. The material of which the sacks are made should, therefore, not be very thick, or the cord will not be able to conceal the outside sack mouth. When the screen is placed in front, the man inside carefully pulls away the outside mouth from under the cord, and he is free. The first sack he merely hangs up behind the screen—which is afterwards folded up and carried away with the sack inside it—and comes forward with sack number two, which he has never been inside, in his hand. It is a good stage trick.

The Dancing Sailor.—This is a trick which may always be relied upon not to fall flat, and should be introduced whenever the audience has had a good dose of serious tricks administered. The feat consists in taking the rude effigy of a sailor, cut out of a simple piece of cardboard, which may be freely and minutely examined by the company, and, standing it on the floor, to cause it to remain there, and to dance according to the directions of the performer, without any visible means of support becoming evident. The sailor can

be very easily manufactured in an hour or so, out of a piece
of fairly thick card. The trunk and head should be cut out
of one piece, with the arm, from the shoulder to the elbow,
protruding at a considerable angle. The forearm is jointed
on, as are also the legs, which must be in two pieces. The
joints may consist of thread, and should be very loose. The
design may be varied according to the fancy of the maker,
but he will be safe in giving to the cheeks and nose an extra-
vagantly rubicund hue, and the mouth a humorous turn.
The hat should be on one side, the trousers broad at the
bottom, and the feet large, and turned outwards, and slightly
upwards. When the jointing has been done, it is as well to
cover the whole figure with thick paper, on both sides, in
order to obtain a smoothness of exterior. In pasting on this
paper, care must, of course, be taken that the joints are not
touched by the adhesive matter employed, or they will not
work properly. The whole figure, to look sufficiently impos-
ing, should stand quite 15in. high; but if it be intended to
dance it upon the table, then 12in. is sufficient. Effect is
everything in conjuring, and a great deal may be lost by
having things just a size too small.

In performing the trick, the conjuror brings forward the
sailor, whose appearance, if properly designed, should at once
create amusement. He is given for examination, and the
performer then retires to the stage, bending, as he does so,
the arms of the figure at the armpits slightly backward
from the body. He then proceeds to show the company that
no threads or wires are anywhere about. This he does by
slashing about in every direction, high, low, and on either
side, with his wand. As a matter of fact, no threads or
wires are within his reach, so he cannot do wrong; but a
thread does exist in connection with the trick all the same.
It should be a fine silk thread. Invariably use silk for everything, as it is both stronger, finer, and more durable and
pleasant than cotton. If two assistants are available, there
should be one on each side of the stage, holding the ends.

When the performer is doing his slashing around, the thread is simply held as high as possible, the expedient of standing upon chairs being resorted to by the assistants, if necessary. It is very often the case, however, that the aid of only one assistant is possible or advisable. The thread must then be fixed on one side of the stage, at the proper height from the floor, a few inches of elastic being first tied on to counteract the effect of any unpremeditated jerk, which might easily prove disastrous to the trick. The elastic, being thick in substance, must be out of sight. If the dancing is to be done upon the floor, then the thread must be affixed about an inch higher than the armpits of the figure (to allow for the drop in the centre of the thread), and allowed to lie upon the floor, except when in actual use. If the dancing be done upon the table, the assistant must do the best he can, and the performer use judgment in the way he sweeps with his wand. When the assistant receives his "cue" from the performer, which may be done in a thousand different ways, he lowers the thread, and holds it taut. The performer then places the figure directly over it, allowing the thread to pass under the armpits. As these have been pressed back, the thread will pass across the front of them, and across the back of the figure. The assistant must watch the figure narrowly, so that no motion whatever is given to it. A rehearsal or two is all that is necessary to make it appear that the figure stands of its own accord, and without aid, upon the floor. Any swaying motion will tend to destroy this illusion. The rest of the trick follows as a matter of course. If music be at hand, the performer has a lively air, such as a hornpipe, played, or, in the absence of any instrument, the performer must needs whistle. In any case, he keeps time with his wand, and looks approvingly at the figure, talking to it occasionally. The assistant need jerk but very slightly at the thread to cause the figure to dance, and he can easily vary his motions to fast or slow. The legs of themselves assume various steps, which many of the company will think to have been brought about by design. Once or twice the performer passes his wand over and before and behind the figure whilst it is dancing, to show that there really is no connection. If it be dancing upon the table, a borrowed hat may be held in front of it, and the figure made to advance upon it and dance upon the crown. This, besides being additionally diverting, indirectly does away with any suspicion, which might excusably exist, as to the presence of mechanism within the table. When the assistant and performer are well together, all sorts of tricks may be indulged in. The figure may be made to dance *inside* a hat; and I have even seen a skilful performer twirl an umbrella between it and the floor, the sailor continuing his hornpipe merrily and unconcernedly all the while.

If the performer chooses to add to the humour of the situation, he may, if the figure be dancing upon the table, take it by the head (it should never be touched elsewhere) and lay it down, saying that there has been dancing enough. He then turns to the company, and commences to say something, as if about to explain a new trick, when the figure suddenly starts up and commences dancing with great vigour. The company laugh, and the performer goes to the figure to lay it down, this time with the wand placed across it to keep it quiet. So soon as he begins to speak to the company, however, up starts the figure a second time, the wand rolling off on to the floor, the dance being renewed with fresh energy.

When the trick is to be brought to a close, the assistant holds the thread firmly, and the performer, seizing the sailor by the head, lifts him off. Now, if I had not directed both sides of the figure to be covered with paper, a very great risk would be run of the projections at the joints catching in the thread. Properly covered on both sides, everything is smooth, and so there is nothing to catch. The figure should be instantly brought forward to the company for re-examination.

In a small way, *i.e.*, before children, the figure may be made to dance between the legs, the thread being attached to the legs. (See *To Cause a Stick or Poker to Stand on End.*) The slightest movement of the legs in an outward direction will give motion to the figure, the feet beating time with the air, whether played, hummed, or whistled, so as to cover the action. The country public-house conjuror affects this phase of the trick.

The Anti-Gravitation Ball.—The performer produces a solid wooden ball, having a thick cord passing through it, and this he allows the company to examine. It is seen that the cord passes freely through the hole. Placing one end of the cord under his foot, he holds the other end at arm's length, so that the cord is perpendicular. With the disengaged hand, the ball is raised up to the other, and, on being released, of course falls to the ground; when, however, the performer gives the word for it to remain at the top of the cord, instead of descending, it obeys. He then points with the wand to a part of the cord a foot or so down, and the ball at once descends so far, and then stops dead. To any place on the cord that is indicated by the performer or any of the company the ball will stop and remain.

The secret of this is, that the hole is not drilled straight through the ball, but has an angle, or bend, in it. The result is, that when the cord is pulled tight the ball is held, but when it is slackened the ball falls, a sudden tightening being sufficient to arrest it in its career.

A very good form of ball is that now generally sold. It has a very large hole indeed, quite a dozen times larger than the cord passing through it. This hole is slightly tapered, and the cord is passed through a small plug fitting into the hole. This plug is concealed in the performer's hand as he holds the cord, at one end of which is a big knot, or tassel. The plug has a crooked hole drilled through it, and when the ball is run down the cord, so as to get the plug inside it, the two become one, and the ball behaves precisely as it would were it itself prepared. As the spectators, however, fancy the ball to be strung on a cord that is many times smaller than the opening, the force which causes the object to remain wherever it is ordered, in defiance of the laws of gravitation, is quite inexplicable. I once saw a Chinaman with a doll which went both up and down a cord. This was very ingenious and diverting, but was too obviously mechanical.

A neat way of performing this trick, and one which I recommend for drawing-room use, is to take a ball of worsted and thread it with cotton or thread, the threading not being done straight through the ball, but crookedly. This ball will then be found quite amenable to discipline, and, of course, not the least suspicion can attach to it, the worsted being borrowed from the hostess's work-basket, and the threading done before the company's eyes. In any form, this trick is not sufficiently important for the stage, there being no variety or change in it.

To Cause a Stick or Poker to Stand on End.—For this feat the performer must be provided with 2ft. or so of fine black cotton or silk, with a black pin at each end, securely tied on. The pins may be either bent or straight, and must be fixed in the trousers at the calf, one in each leg, which will enable the operator to walk about without any fear of the thread getting him into trouble. The performer first takes a stick or poker (if a poker, it should be a light one), and, after having had it examined, proceeds to mesmerise it, as he will call it. This mesmerism should be conducted with the greatest seriousness imaginable. When the magnetic influence has been properly aroused by rubbing, &c., the performer should sit down and open his legs, so causing the cotton or silk to become stretched. He then takes the stick or poker, and stands it upon the floor in front of him. On being left to itself, it, of course, falls to the ground, but' after three or four failures, the performer brings it against the thread, and then, making several mesmeric passes with the hands, relinquishes all hold. The stick or poker will, of course, be supported by the thread, but during the whole time it is so sustained the hands must be waved over and around it, as though exercising some influence over it. Do not prolong this trick more than can possibly be avoided, but get out of sight and remove the pins and thread with all despatch. (See also *The Dancing Sailor*.)

CHAPTER XVI.

THE CORNUCOPIAN HAT.

ONE of the most taking of all the tricks performed by the
many public exhibitors is that in which a hat is borrowed
from the audience, and at once from its interior are produced a quantity of heterogeneous articles, the nature and
number of which cause, not only the greatest merriment,
but also the most unbounded astonishment that they should
ever have found lodgment in so unsuitable a receptacle as
an ordinary " chimney-pot " hat. The reader will hardly
require to be told that every article which is produced from
the hat has first to be introduced into it by the performer,
and on the skill with which this is done will the success
of the trick depend. It must be understood that there is no
middle degree of perfection allowed in performing this trick.
No one must be able to say, " Yes; he got them in pretty
well that time—I hardly noticed him." The motion which accompanies the introduction of any article or articles into a

hat must be absolutely unobserved by anyone of the audience. No extraordinary degree of speed is required, for success will depend more upon the completeness of the arrangements made by the performer for the accomplishment of his designs than upon mere rapidity of movement, which, as I have often explained, is by itself of no use whatever, it being impossible for the human hand to make any movement openly so rapidly that it cannot be followed by the human eye. The object of the performer being to introduce certain articles into a hat without detection, anything falling below this accomplishment is imperfect; but, at the same time, anything which goes beyond this in a striving to obtain an ideal perfection is useless, and results in a mere waste of energy.

The essence of the trick being that it is (apparently, at least) performed for the most part whilst surrounded by the audience, the articles to be produced must be chiefly such as can be concealed about the performer's person. Of such a nature, the reader will doubtless be astonished to find, are, when properly constructed, bird-cages containing live birds, quantities of ladies' reticules, lighted Chinese lanterns, and many other articles entirely at variance with any possibly preconceived notions of what might ordinarily be contained in a hat. The beginner, however, will have to commence with less startling productions than bird-cages, &c., and graduate in the art, as it were.

The Cannon-ball.—One of the commonest articles which it is still the fashion to produce from a hat is a cannon-ball, or, rather, the wooden semblance of one. This is introduced from the shelf, which is provided with little hollows for the reception of such unstable articles. It has a deep hole, just large enough to admit the middle finger, and is so disposed that a hand placing a hat momentarily, brim downwards, on the back edge of the table would be able to introduce the finger without difficulty. The finger firmly inserted, the hat is drawn off, and, naturally falling backwards, covers the ball, which is furthermore curled into the hat by means of the finger. If the ball were solid and made of any heavier material than wood, this would not be possible of accomplishment. The usual method is to have two cannon-balls, one a hollow one of zinc, blackened, with a hole about two inches across made in it. This hole is covered by means of a sliding lid, which lid has a smaller hole in it for the introduction of the middle finger. The ball is filled with articles, almost invariably purchases made at a baby linen warehouse, which are produced, with all possible effect, one by one, before the ball itself. Sometimes the ball is packed as tightly as possible with feathers, in which case a very large quantity can be produced, a small pinch from the ball sufficing to apparently fill the hat, which should be exhibited, ostensibly full, to the audience every now and then. If feathers are used, a large cloth should be spread upon the floor, or there will be a sad litter.

The introduction of the cannon-ball must not, however, form the commencement of the trick, but follow on something else in which a hat has been required. It would never do to borrow a hat and straightway march with it to the table, there to execute divers entirely unnecessary movements. Under such circumstances, the audience would be surprised if something were not produced from the hat. There are many tricks mentioned in which a hat is used. Whilst the result of one of such tricks is being exhibited with one hand, the other can easily introduce the cannon-ball, without fear of detection, if the performer's manner leads the attention elsewhere. The ball safely in the hat, the performer steps briskly forward to return the borrowed article, and, just as he is about to put it into the owner's hand, he makes a slight start, saying, "I did not notice it before, sir, but there is a little something just at the bottom of your hat. What is it? Something belonging to your little girl, I presume—a pair of socks," &c. The articles are then deposited on a chair or side table, and a motion made of returning the hat when "a little something else" is noticed. The ball being by this time worked round in the hat so that the opening is concealed from view, the hat can be exhibited with the ball sticking inside. After remarking that it is a very extraordinary thing to carry in a hat, and surmising therefrom that the infant to whom the clothes just discovered belong must be a "Woolwich infant," great, but unvailing, efforts are made to extract the ball. In order to make it appear to stick in the hat (which sticking makes its presence there at all seem all the more inexplicable), invert the hat, and introduce a forefinger from each hand beneath the ball. The whole can be then well jerked two or three times. It is at length got out by the assistance of your attendant, who is directed to give it to the gentleman to put in his waistcoat pocket. For the sake of effect he staggers towards the audience, but the performer recalls him, saying that he will send on the articles by parcels delivery. Whilst this is being done, the wooden ball is got inside the hat, which is once more carried down towards the owner. The discovery of more contents is made, as before, and the performer remarks that had he known that the owner of the hat carried a complete arsenal about with him he would have borrowed someone else's hat. The hat is jerked as before, and at the third or fourth attempt the ball is allowed to drop on the stage. This will confirm the idea in the audience that the first ball was solid, should there, by chance, be any wavering on the point.

The only objection to this really very effective phase of the trick is, that it has been done so often; the consequence is that so many, anticipating correctly that which is about to come, are better able to divine the means by which it is accomplished. The best way to guard against this is to introduce the features at unusual moments, taking advantage of any favourable circumstance or opportunity that may casually transpire.

A cabbage or cauliflower is often introduced into a hat in place of the solid ball, and is very effective. A hole for the finger can be made in the stalk, but it is advisable to push a tin tube into the hole, or bind the outside of it with cord, as the stalk will sometimes give way, and a disaster, in the shape of a vegetable falling down heavily from behind the table, occur. In using a cabbage or cauliflower, be careful to clean and dry it well on the outside, or a hat lining may be spoiled.

The Distribution.—The gratuitous distribution of bonbons, flowers, &c., from a hat is, owing to the expense entailed, hardly such a favourite variation of this trick with professionals as with amateurs—that is, with those very few amateurs who are able to execute it with any degree of success. It requires an unusual amount of *sang froid* and boldness, combined with a perfect dexterity. When I can obtain nothing else, I use bonbons, but they are not the best article to employ, on account of their bulk. The sweets known as "kisses"—pieces of toffee wrapped in gold and silver paper —and gelatine bags of sweets are far more showy, as so many more can be introduced at a "load." The performer must have either some black silk bags or else some pieces of black silk, in which the articles are packed and tied with the thinnest cotton or silk, which need only be just strong enough to keep all together. Three or four little parcels should be made up and stowed away inside the vest and in the breast pockets of the coat, where they can be reached without difficulty. The performer then advances, with an orange or similar article concealed in the hand, and borrows a hat. The hat is quickly taken in the hand containing the orange, and shaken, with the remark, "Why, you have left something inside, sir." The shaking is to prevent the article falling on the crown of the hat with a thud, which would too plainly reveal the moment of its introduction into the hat, which is then inverted, thereby causing whatever may be inside to fall out upon the floor. All eyes, including more particularly your own, will be turned towards it, and you seize the opportunity to introduce one of your packages into the hat. The action of stooping to see what it is that has fallen will naturally cause the hat in the hand to come against the breast. The other hand is then introduced beneath it, and the bundle slipped noiselessly in. The instant this is done, obtain possession of the orange, and be as funny as you can about it with the owner of the hat. You then discover other things in the hat, and just before one bundle is exhausted introduce another. The most extraordinary expedients will at times have to be resorted to for accomplishing this, varying according to the position in which the performer is placed. One movement that should always be tried is a rapid three-quarter turn on the heel, during which a bag is whipped in. Another ruse is to allow the wand or some of the contents of the hat to fall, and so obtain a momentary diversion whilst stooping for them. Any approach to hesitation will be fatal. When a fresh supply has been obtained, turn the hat upside down, supporting the contents with the fingers, and, shake it, thus appearing to show it empty. A splendid ruse to adopt at such a moment, in order to intimate that the hat is still empty, is to apparently read out the name of the maker (which you have previously noted), and say that you will go to him in future for your hats. Should there be no name, say you are sorry, as you wanted to know where such curious hats are to be bought.

The introduction of flowers from the performer's person is not advisable, it being impossible to keep them from being crushed. They are best introduced from the shelf, and for this purpose the following little arrangement will be found useful: Procure a tin or zinc cylinder, about two inches in diameter, and two inches long. Around the outside of this have affixed a number of small cylinders, each capable of admitting the stalk of a flower. Such an article will hold some thirty flowers at least, or even tiny " button holes " can be employed. Round the cylinder pass some wire, a portion of which form into a loop. The whole arrangement can then be suspended at the back edge of the table, or behind a suitable chair. By having some packs of cards introduced into the hat in the first instance, an excuse for going to the table or chair is obtained. Packs of cards make a great show when the hat is tossed vigorously about, so that some of the contents fly in the air and out on the floor. The last few can be taken out by the hand and thrown in the air in such a manner as to flutter as much as possible between the audience and the hat, which is, at the same time, brought into the position favourable for getting the flowers into it. The wire loop is easily found by the fingers, and, on the hat being brought backwards, when the table is used (forwards, with the chair), the bouquet is easily introduced. The cylinder arrangement is often made much larger than two inches each way, but no very increased effect is thereby obtained—certainly not sufficient to compensate for the augmented difficulty in getting rid of the article after it is done with. When made of the size I have given, it is simply concealed in the hand, as are the bags or pieces of silk in which the cards, &c., have been wrapped.

The Shower of Cups.—Amongst other things, a favourite production from hats is an enormous quantity of tin cups, very similar to those used in the cup and ball trick described in "Drawing-room Magic," but much larger. These cups, being all of the same taper, fit well one into the other, and, being also very thin, a large number can be well put together without forming a very formidable pile. Fifty is a very common number to introduce into a hat at one "load." The upper rim is turned over outwards, to give the cup a look of great solidity, and the bottoms are fairly thick, for strength. They should be wrapped in silk, and the inside cup filled tightly with ribbons or cut paper, or anything else that will make a great show when distributed. The performer then walks about the stage tossing the cups out of the hat with great rapidity on to the floor, occasionally placing a few on the table upside down. A dozen or so on a table make a good show, and they are also useful for concealing the bags and silk used previously for containing other articles. Spread out a few in the hat now and again and show it thus filled. Very few will suffice to fill a hat to the brim. These cups are, perhaps, best purchased at conjuring apparatus houses, their manufacture not being universally understood.

Multiplying Balls.—These, which are by some persons considered even more effective than the cups, can be made, for the most part, at home, with a little expenditure of ingenuity and trouble. They consist of an ordinary cloth ball covering, with an extraordinary interior, consisting, as it does, of a tapering spiral spring. Although I have succeeded in producing springs of the required shape by twisting wire round a peg top, I cannot conscientiously recommend anyone else to adopt a similar method of proceeding. A professed wireworker would do the thing much more satisfactorily in every way. The covering is a very easy matter, and any one of the weaker sex may be confidently entrusted with it. Six of these balls, when pressed tightly together and tied with cotton, take up only a very little more than the space that would be occupied by a single ordinary ball. Eighteen, or more, in batches of six, can be introduced at one time if tied up in silk. The cotton of one batch being broken, the hat will be entirely filled, and the process can be repeated, the hat being each time shown to the audience in a replete condition. A tray should be at hand on which to place the balls, great care being neccessary to prevent any of them falling to the floor, which would at once reveal their unreal nature. When the balls are used, as is not unusual, in conjunction with the cups—that is to say, either immediately preceding or following them—it is advisable to have an ordinary stuffed cloth ball, exactly resembling the multipliers, inside the inner cup. This ball is allowed to fall and roll towards the audience (accidentally, of course!), who will require no admonition to examine it. The balls can also be made to multiply in the hands. For this purpose, take one bundle and spin it high in the air (be sure to spin it well), and, catching it as it descends, give it a sharp twist, to break the cotton. As the balls will all suddenly expand, the hands must be held very hollow and kept close to the breast, against which they should be sustained. Another method is to break the cotton, but prevent their bursting out, and, holding up the hand containing them, with the back towards the audience, roll the balls into view, one by one, by means of the other hand. These effects are both good, but must be done with dash.

Both the cups and balls are best got into the hat from the shelf. The safest way to get them is, in the first instance, to introduce the cards into the hat, which, after shaking about, empty on the table with a bang. A favourable opportuuity for introducing anything is thus made. Some conjurors have an arm protruding at the back of the table, on which bundles of cups, balls, &c., are suspended, and got into the hat by means of a sweep of that article. This is an excellent method, when the performer does not make a bad shot, and sweep the whole on the floor instead of into the hat. Bringing the hat round the end of the table, and, tipping things into it from the corner of the shelf, is a method in use, but it is a bad one.

Bundle of Firewood.—Immediately after the taking out of a dozen or two of balls or tin cups, the performer may, if his previous arrangements tend thereto, proceed to extract from the hat a common bundle of firewood, which, the company may see, entirely fills the interior of the hat by itself. As, subsequent to the extraction of the balls, the performer has not even retreated to the stage, the company cannot but be at an utter loss to account for the presence of so ponderous a body. The bundle of wood is, however, far from being what it seems. That portion of it, the exterior, which is visible to the company, is genuine enough, being firewood, but this is only an outer layer glued upon a cylindrical shape of thick pasteboard, bound round, so as to look real, with a piece of string taken from a genuine bundle of wood. The bundle has only one end, made, of course, of pasteboard also, and covered with half-inch lengths of wood, which will present a perfectly real appearance. Into the open end are crammed the cups, balls, or other articles, which, being produced, enable the performer to subsequently extract the supposed bundle of wood without having refilled the hat. Some bundles are made with both ends covered, one end having a trap opening in it. This is to prevent the possibility of the unreal nature of the article becoming known; but I really do not see why both ends should ever be exposed; and, with the end perfectly open, the extraction of articles is very much facilitated. The bundle must, of course, be introduced into the hat from the shelf, it being too decidedly bulky to carry about the person.

Reticules.—A quantity of these articles are sometimes produced from a hat. They are, as may be imagined, far from being the substantial objects they represent. The ends fall inwards and lie flat on the bottom, to which they are hinged by means of calico, and the tops, sides, and bottom are hinged together also by means of calico, and so double up. A piece of cord, tape, or thin leather strap runs through two holes, about an inch apart, in the top, the ends being affixed to the ends of the reticule, inside. A pull at the centre of this cord, &c., raises the ends, which force the other portions into position. The outside is covered with cloth, and otherwise decorated to represent a small reticule. I have seen them made of playing cards without any outer covering whatever. The result was, that the audience saw through the whole thing at once, as was but natural. A dozen or more of these reticules can be introduced at once, and they make a good show. They can be easily made from playing cards, and afterwards covered.

Dolls.—Calico dolls, with spiral springs inside, can also be effectively employed. A tolerably large one, introduced into the cannon ball with the baby's clothes, is effective when produced last of all. In any case they should not be less than 6in. in height. The face and greater portion of the dress must be painted on, a few little bows, artfully disposed, serving to make the doll look as substantial as possible.

Bird-cages.—This is a trick which ranks almost as high in public estimation—the only gauge, by-the-bye, by which conjuring tricks can be measured—as the gold-fish trick. The same principal feature—the production of a substantial article, containing living things, from such unsuspected regions as the interior of a hat, or the folds of a handkerchief—is in both, and the audience is, in each instance, in the same dilemma in endeavouring to explain where the article comes. from, and how the living creatures get into it. It may sound like exaggeration to assert that two substantial cages, 6in. high, each containing two live canaries or other birds, can be produced from a hat from one "load," but such can be done, nevertheless. The cages are of wire at the top and on the sides, the bottom being solid and heavy. The sides are hinged to the top, under which they fold, when the bottom, which slides up and down the sides, is pushed up. The top being domed, the birds are safe therein, not as comfortable, perhaps, as they might be, but still unhurt. The bottom pushed up and the sides doubled under, the whole is scarcely 2in. in depth; and two cages, placed bottom to bottom, and kept together by means of an elastic band or by a thread, can be got into the hat from the coat breast-pocket in the prescribed manner. To produce them, it is only necessary to raise the upper portion, by means of the ring there affixed, and the bottom will run down into its place, causing the sides to go into their positions. These cages are also produced from handkerchiefs, in which case it is usual to have them of very large dimensions. Herrmann produced one at times which had to be concealed up his back, so large was it. This was produced, without detection, in the very centre of the audience.

Chinese Lanterns.—The production of six or more of these articles, all ablaze, from a borrowed hat, causes an effect not far from astonishing. The well-known collapsible nature of the articles would render the production of a number of them from a hat a matter of no great marvel were they unprovided with a light. What cannot be readily explained is the feature of so many lanterns being alight in the hat at one time without burning either the hat or one another, or, indeed, how they can all be alight at one time at all. The secret lies in the construction of the bottoms of these lanterns, and the positions of the candle or wick holders. The bottoms are made of tin, and on one only of each series of lanterns is the candle holder placed in the centre. This lantern I will call No. 1 (see Fig. 54). No. 2 has the holder a little on one side, and a hole through its centre to admit of

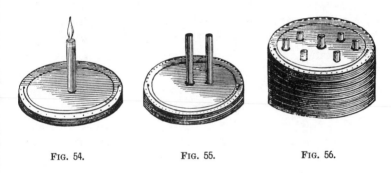

FIG. 54.　　　　FIG. 55.　　　　FIG. 56.

the candle or wick of No. 1 passing through it (see Fig. 55). No. 3 has two holes, corresponding exactly with the candle holders of Nos. 1 and 2, which pass through its bottom, and its holder is at the side of the hole through which the holder of No. 2 passes. No. 4 has three holes, No. 5 four holes, and so on all through the series, which generally consists of seven or eight, that number being about as many as can well be managed at one time (see Fig. 56). As the holder of No. 1 has to pass through the bottoms of the remaining seven lanterns, it must, of course, be very long. The holder of No. 2 will be a little shorter, and the next shorter still, that of No. 8 being of the ordinary length. By this means all the wicks will be on the same level when the lanterns are packed together. The tin bottoms do away with any danger of a flare up, and also, from their weight, cause the lamps to open easily, which is of great assistance towards the success of the trick. The upper rims are also of tin, for strength and security. A few sulphur matches, which strike noiselessly, should be affixed to the upper rims of the topmost lantern, whereon should also be some sandpaper, on which to strike the matches. The whole should be tied together with string, and concealed in the breast pocket, from whence they can be introduced into a hat in the midst of the audience. The match struck, the wicks are all lighted almost simultaneously; and, the flames burning the string, the performer is enabled to take out the lanterns in rapid succession by means of a bent piece of wire affixed to the rim of each. An attendant should be at hand with a pole or broomstick, on which to hang the lanterns. A deep round hat is better than a " chimney-pot," the extreme depth of which sometimes causes the performer to burn his fingers.

This trick is well worthy the attention of amateurs, as it is but little worked, the majority of performers being frightened at it, but without any reasonable cause. Any tinman will make the plates and rims cheaply, and the paper sides can be taken from the ordinary lanterns and transferred, so that the trick need not be an expensive one, by any means. An excellent title for it is " A Chinese Feast of Lanterns." Always remember to hold the hat as high as possible when it contains anything: premature disclosures of the contents mar the effect considerably.

Climax to the Hat of Plenty.—When the performer has a stage attendant of average ability, he can conclude this or any other trick with a hat in a very startling manner. The hat is given to the assistant to return to its owner, and, just as he is leaving the stage, he stumbles, falling heavily upon the hat, and flattening it completely. The performer is of course in despair, and after a slight scene the hat is eventually restored, it being found under the owner's chair, or elsewhere.

This exceedingly impressive and amusing trick makes a very appropriate conclusion to a performance, and is managed in two ways: Either the hat used in the preliminary trick is actually the property of a stranger in the audience, and is exchanged for the one to be destroyed, or a confederate brings it in with him, and takes his seat on a chair or sofa, beneath which his own hat has been previously concealed. In the first instance, the exchange must be adroitly managed. The excuse of going off to brush it, and returning immediately with the brush, is as good as any, although it will always be subsequently apparent to thinkers when the hat was exchanged, by whatever method the substitution is accomplished. I may say at once that this method is not so good as the second; but confederates are not always to be obtained when they are wanted. Sometimes the performer borrows two hats, and whilst he is producing something startling from one, his attendant quietly removes the other and substitutes for it a duplicate.

By whatever means arrived at, suppose the exchange effected, or, what is the same thing, the conjuror's own hat borrowed, and the assistant lying prone upon the floor. He must then rise slowly, with a rueful look upon his countenance, and, if any object, such as a tin cup, be lying upon the floor, he must abuse it as the cause of the disaster. The performer does not at first notice what has happened; when he does so, he is, of course, greatly enraged with the assistant, and assumes a very despondent look. He expresses his regrets to the owner of the hat, and asks if he would like the hat done up in a small parcel for convenience in carrying. Without waiting for a reply, he and the assistant tear the hat up to little pieces, some newspapers being produced and spread upon the table. On the shelf is a newspaper parcel containing a crinoline, a large doll, or anything else that is ludicrous in appearance. The shreds of what was recently a hat are wrapped in a piece of the newspaper, with the exception of one solitary piece, which is purposely allowed to fall upon the floor, on that side of the table opposite to where the conjuror is standing. When the parcel is made up, the performer notices this piece, and, leaning well over the table, points to it, at the same time, under cover of his body, effecting an exchange of parcels. The shred is rolled up, and a pretence made of putting it in the parcel (it is, of course, palmed), which is then given to one of the audience to hold over his head. A pistol is fired, and, if the hat be borrowed from a confederate, he is bidden to look under his chair, where, naturally, his own hat will be discovered. If, on the other hand, the borrowed hat be genuinely the property of one of the audience, it will be seen to fly across the stage and attach itself to the top of the proscenium, from whence it falls at the command of the performer, and is caught by him. This additional effect is managed by passing a black cord through a hole in the proscenium, and attaching it to the hatband by means of a very large loop. The end to which the hat is affixed must, of course, be removed from sight beforehand, the usual place being behind the proscenium. The construction of the place of performance will naturally have a good deal to do with this particular matter, and the performer must study what arrangements will be best. Wherever the hat is concealed, it must be thrown into the air when the pistol is fired, and the cord at once gathered in as rapidly as it is possible to do so. On the command for the hat to descend being given, the large loop is cut through, and the hat falls. If the cord were simply tied by a knot to the hatband, a piece of it would remain attached after being cut away, and this would give a clue to the mystery. After the hat is safely restored, open the parcel and exhibit its contents.

CHAPTER XVII.

TRICKS WITH WATCHES AND LIVE STOCK.

Tricks with Watches.—The reader has doubtless been on
the look-out for the chapter which shall initiate him in the
art of pounding up a friend's gold chronometer before his
very eyes, and immediately afterwards restoring it whole.
I have purposely introduced the subject so late in the day,
because watches are very awkward things to perform with,
and the performer should be tolerably expert before he
touches them.

On borrowing a watch, it is always as well to do, or
pretend to do, something with it that shall cause the greatest
anxiety to the owner as to its safety, and consequent amusement to the unsympathising remainder of the audience. To
expect this of a conjuror seems to be a fairly-established

custom.　One way of acquiescing with this unexpressed desire is to apparently incapacitate the watch for further use by bending it several times nearly double.　This feat is managed by holding the watch with its back to the audience between the fingers and thumbs of the two hands, the hands being on opposite sides of the watch.　If both hands and watch are worked rapidly backwards and forwards (*i.e.*, inwards and outwards) three or four times, the varying light and shade upon the shining back of the watch will cause it to appear to be really bent each time a movement is made.　The illusion is very perfect, the effect being always the same, to initiated, as well as uninitiated, eyes.　The remark, " Ah! yours is one of the new putty watches, I see, sir," will assist in carrying out this effective prelude.　Precisely the same effect may be produced with a bright florin or half-crown.

Another effective introduction is to have palmed a watch-glass that has been either well cracked previously, or cut deeply with a glazier's diamond.　Bring this glass over the one on the watch, but not touching it, and then, addressing the owner of the watch as to the strength of the glass, strike it carelessly with the wand, but not so carelessly as to break both glasses.　When the breakage takes place, of course, great consternation will be exhibited on the face of the performer, who makes profuse apologies to the owner of the watch.　The pieces of the broken watch-glass are allowed to lie on the perfect one, and the whole shown round, it being impossible to detect the presence of the perfect glass beneath the pieces.　The pieces are then put in a piece of paper, for convenience in vanishing, and the trick can proceed.

The ordinary method for destroying a borrowed watch is to have a mortar (usually of wood) into which fits an inner lining.　Over the whole fits a pasteboard cover, with a fairly large round hole in the top, in which the lining is concealed at the commencement of the trick.　The mortar is shown round and the watch put in.　The cover is then put on—for the purpose of preventing the pieces of the watch flying out, it is explained—and the false lining thus introduced. This should be done quickly, and without any show of care, which would only excite suspicion. A pestle is then introduced through the hole in the cover, and a terrific amount of pounding goes on. Some old watch works and bits of plated gold, which have been in the false lining from the commencement, are then exhibited by removing the cover only. Another description of mortar is one with the bottom revolving on a pivot. When the watch is put in, this bottom is pushed up a little on one side from underneath, and the watch falls through into the hand. The pestle used in conjunction with this is a very thick one, especially at the end, in which are concealed some watch works. The action of a piston, similar to that used in the one for *The Hatched Card*, will propel these pieces into the mortar.

A far bolder method is to be provided with a dummy toy watch, and exchange it for the borrowed one, and then actually pound it up in an ordinary metal mortar. This method will succeed best in public audiences, where an individual watch is not likely to be known by many persons in the audience. In showing round the watch, in its demolished state, in the mortar, there is no necessity for allowing a lengthened view, much less a minute examination, to oe taken by anyone; and it is as well not to allow the owner of the watch to see the wreck at all.

Instead of a mortar, a long bag, made of alpaca or any other strong stuff, and about three inches broad and two feet in length, is sometimes used. This has sewn in one end of it some solid body, fairly resembling a watch in shape and weight, and the other end is open. About four inches from the mouth a seam is stitched across. The watch, on being put into the bag, stops at the seam, whilst the performer takes up the other end, to which the watch has presumably descended, and exhibits the contour of the article or articles (a quantity of small broken pebbles is frequently used) there concealed, with one hand, the other hand holding securely the end containing the watch. The dummy end is then struck upon a table, or against the wall, several times, for the purpose of making it "go better," or of converting it into a "stop" watch. To take the watch out of the bag, hold the end containing the dummy with one hand, and invert the whole. The watch will slide into the other hand, having apparently come from the far end of the bag. An addition to this bag is to have the mouth portion divided into two pockets, each one having a flap and a button. In one are concealed some broken watch works and bits of metal. The borrowed watch is put into the empty side, and, after the process of banging about has been gone through, that containing the pieces is opened.

The manner of reproducing the watch depends greatly upon the ingenuity and resources of the performer. Every conjuror differs somewhat from his rivals. A very favourite plan is to discover the watch in a loaf or roll of bread. Another is to cause it to appear on the centre of a target, or in the midst of a bouquet of flowers. It will be readily understood that when the supposed process of destruction has been gone through, and whilst the performer is amongst the audience with the pieces and engaging their attention, the assistant unostentatiously removes the mortar or bag containing the borrowed watch, and arranges the sequel of the trick behind the scenes. If the watch is to appear in a roll, then it is put into one by the assistant through a slit, and the roll is brought on with some others. The performer takes three of these, including the one containing the watch, and puts one on each of the front corners of the table and one between them in the centre, this centre roll being the prepared one. He then asks the audience to select one of the three rolls. Of course, all three will be named, but the performer affects to perceive a majority in favour of the centre one. A great show should always be made of deferring to the wish of the audience, this being very effective, and also the best way to secure the desired end. The pieces of broken watch works can then be put into the conjuring pistol, having been previously wrapped in paper, and then fired at the roll, which, on being cut or broken open, will, of course, be found to contain the watch. Should any decided predilection be shown for one of the outside rolls, a change of tactics must be made. Remove the one selected and say, without exhibiting the slightest appearance of embarrassment, "That leaves two; which one shall I now take?" If the one containing the watch be chosen, say, "Are you quite sure, now, that you would not like the other one?" This will cause a firmer adherence to the choice, for it will appear that the other roll would be preferable to the performer. Knock the other roll off the table, and fire at the remaining one. If the watch has been neatly inserted in the roll, it can be given into the hands of a spectator to hold whilst being fired at. When a bouquet is used, the watch is merely concealed among the flowers. It should be given to a lady to hold, in which case the pistol must be directed in the air, and not at the bouquet.

The use of a target is very effective, and the target itself is not of very difficult construction. It can be either of wood or tin, and the face should be circular, about 12in. across, and affixed to a pillar rising from a square foot. The centre, or bull's eye, is pierced out and revolves on a pivot, an arrangement of watch spring or elastic causing it to keep in its place. It should be black both at the back and front, the front having a hook on which to hang the watch. The assistant, on obtaining possession of the watch, hangs it upon the hook and reverses the centre, a little bolt serving to keep it temporarily in that position. To this bolt is attached a piece of black thread, the disengaged end of which is behind, in the hands of the assistant. On the pistol being fired, this bolt is removed by the thread being pulled smartly, and the centre flies back to its normal position, exhibiting the watch to the audience. The revolution is so rapid that it cannot be detected, the watch appearing to actually attach itself to the face of the target. A good effect is produced by having the revolving centre of looking-glass, the corresponding glass on the other side, with a hook through the centre, being badly starred. It will appear as though the arrival of the watch had smashed the mirror.

Another target is one with the centre in the shape of a recess, over which a little spring blind is drawn after the watch has been hung upon a hook within it. The blind has merely to be released and will fly up, revealing the watch. This principle is carried out on a much larger scale, two or more watches and chains and a broken plate being used. The chief apparatus employed is a large picture-frame, the centre having no picture, but being made in the form of a recess. In the top is concealed a spring blind, of the same colour as the back of the recess, which should be black. The articles to be magically exhibited on the frame are hung upon convenient hooks by the assistant, who then pulls down the blind and brings the frame upon the stage. The blind has along its lower edge a piece of wire or wood, from the centre of which projects, horizontally, a small pin. In the centre of the lower portion of the frame, and inside the recess, is a small catch, working perpendicularly on a pivot. The upper portion of this catches the projecting pin of the blind, and the lower portion passes out at the bottom, where a communicating cord is attached to it. The action of pulling the cord releases the pin, and the blind flies up, leaving the articles on the back of the frame exposed to view. The means for getting the watches or other articles into the hands of the assistant are various, the most effective, in my opinion, being the following: The performer borrows two watches, with or without the chains attached, and proceeds to wrap them in a piece of paper which he holds in his hands. Underneath this piece of paper is another, in which some dummy watches have been previously folded. In wrapping up the borrowed ones, it is very easy, whilst turning the parcels round and round in the hands, to bring the dummy one to the top, and, getting away the real watches, to conceal them under the vest or elsewhere. Passing subsequently behind the table, they are left upon the shelf, from whence they are removed by the assistant. The supposed borrowed watches, still in the paper, are then put upon a plate and given to the assistant to place upon the table. Before reaching the table, the assistant stumbles, and plate and watches fly all over the floor, the plate naturally in many pieces. The usual fuss is made about the assistant's carelessness, and he is despatched to fetch the frame. The performer, in the meanwhile, gathers up the pieces of the plate (less one piece purposely allowed to remain on the floor) and the watches, and puts them into the conjuring pistol, putting in some paper to keep them in position. During this time, the frame is brought on and placed in position, the pistol is fired, and, the blind flying up, the plate is seen in the centre, and the watches on either side of it. The plate is, however, not complete, one piece being missing. The piece upon the floor is then discovered by the performer, who " passes " it towards the plate, to which it is seen to affix itself. The plate and watches are then brought to the audience, who are unable to discover any trace of joining in the plate or damage to the watches. The remarkable effect of the restoration of the missing portion of the plate is managed by having a ragged triangular piece of black cloth put upon the plate, and, attached to it, a thread. When the " pass " is made, the assistant pulls the thread, and the piece of cloth falls down inside the frame. The frame can, of course, be used for the reproduction of any class of borrowed articles. Anyone with a very light turn only for carpentering should be able to make one for himself. The pedestals or feet of both target and frame should be heavy, so as to remain firm in case the assistant pulls with unpremeditatedly extra strength.

An amusing and neat little trick with a borrowed watch is to cause it to appear on the back of a volunteer assistant from the audience. The performer is provided with a sharp-pointed hook, the blunt end of which is turned back in the shape of a smaller hook. This he has concealed about him. A watch is borrowed and immediately exchanged for one belonging to the performer, which is given to be held by one of the audience, as far removed from the owner as possible. A member of the audience is then desired to step up on the stage, where he is accommodated with a seat in the centre, and facing the audience. The performer has, meanwhile, hooked the loop of the watch on the smaller hook, and, taking the head of the assistant in the hands—the one containing the watch being behind—for the purpose of directing him as to the position in which it should be held, he affixes the larger hook to the back of his coat. He then directs the volunteer to open his mouth very wide, and pretends to pass the supposed borrowed watch into it. On finding that it has not reached its destination, the performer must surmise that he threw it a little too hard, and request the assistant to see if it be behind him. On his turning round for this purpose, the watch on his back will be revealed. An extra effect can be introduced by trying the extent of the assistant's throat capacity with the wand. The wand is taken by one end with the left hand, which is placed against the assistant's mouth. The other end is introduced secretly up the performer's right sleeve, and the right hand worked vigorously up and down the wand. The illusion is that the wand is thrust repeatedly down the assistant's throat to its full length. This should be done quickly, and only about three thrusts should be made. If the wand used for this particular effect be a special one, having an extra loose ferrule, the illusion may be rendered still more perfect if the performer keeps the loose ferrule in the hand, and slides it up and down the wand. This is a very important little addition to the trick.

A piece of apparatus that is very much used in connection with watches is what is universally known as the watch box. It is a box, the rough dimensions of which are: length, $3\frac{1}{2}$in.; readth, $2\frac{3}{4}$in.; and depth, $2\frac{1}{4}$in. The sides, ends, and top are very substantially made, and the bottom is, to all appearances, equally so; but as a matter of fact, it is made of two thin veneers, which have little blocks of wood glued between them, so as to leave an intervening space of one-sixth of an inch. The sides and ends come down flush with the bottom, and so conceal the deception. One of the ends works on pivots, the pivots being placed one-third of an inch from its upper edge; and near the lower edge on the inside is a little brass plate, with the centre keyed out. The ends, it must be understood, are fitted inside the sides. In the hollow of the bottom is concealed a catch, which protrudes just sufficiently to enter the aperture in the brass plate. No spring will be required to keep it in its place, as is usually the case, for if it be glued to the lower veneer, that will possess sufficient springiness for the purpose. The catch will of course require very neat adjustment, which is merely a matter of patience. It must be so arranged that the end is very easily closed, and opened with equal facility, by the mere pressure of a finger on the thin underside, providing the pressure is administered just under the spot where the catch is affixed. For facility in opening the box, it is usual to place two rounded pieces of watch spring on each side of the catch, adjusted so as to always bear just sufficiently against the end to cause it to fly open a quarter of an inch when the catch is released. These pieces of spring are fixed in blocks of wood glued into position for the purpose. I am not sure that the springs are not superfluous. They cause the end to fly open, certainly, and so expedite matters, but they are far from being noiseless. I have found the action of the fingers quite sufficient for opening the end. For the sake of strength, it is as well to fill in the end where there is no spring with a large block of wood. The interior should be lined with cloth or velvet, and a good lock and key added. The box is very useful for obtaining possession of any description of article that is fairly solid and that will go into the box. The following description of a trick performed with a watch will suffice to show how it can be employed:

Give the box and key into the hands of a lady, with the request to have everything examined and the lock tried. Keep very near whilst this is being done, in case of an accidental release of the catch. If there are no springs used, then this will not matter, as the end will not fly open with a "pop," as it otherwise would, which should be sufficient argument in favour of their disuse. Borrow a watch that has a light chain attached, and, winding the chain round the watch, have both placed in the box. Allow it to be locked and the key to remain in the lady's possession. Now take the box, and say, "Although there is no doubt that the box is securely locked, you may reasonably think that I have some secret means of opening the lock. To prevent the possibility of my doing this, will some gentleman kindly tie his handkerchief firmly round the box?" Hold the box in both hands whilst this is being done, by the opening end, and make a deal of fuss about the knot being tied securely. Open the end, and, tilting the box, allow the watch and chain to fall into the hands, turning round sharply to someone else at the same time. It is absolutely necessary to make a turn at this point to cover the abstraction. Give the box, at the same time closing it, into the hands of any one of the audience, with the strict injunction not to shake it—for fear of injuring the contents, you will say, but really to escape the revelation of the fact that it is empty. The watch and chain will be in the left hand by this time, covered by the wand. If there be any music available, have a little of the gentle rippling order ("The Brook" is a suitable air) played, and make passes in the air, as if clutching something, with the right hand. Finally make one vigorous clutch, and hold the hand closed for a few seconds, when open it, showing, of course, nothing. Instantly take the wand in the right hand and strike the sole or heel of the right foot, raised for the purpose, and then apply the left hand to the spot struck, the watch being allowed to drop down, a portion of the chain being held between the fingers. The several actions must follow each other with "one, two, three" briskness, when the effect will be really very fine. Naturally, it must be done far back upon the stage. Do not forget to have the knot untied by the person who tied it and the box unlocked by the lady who put the watch in. Be careful not to borrow a heavy chain. In my early days, I borrowed a huge watch with a chain only a trifle smaller than a ship's cable, and with about a pound and a half of charms attached. The result was the not unnatural one of a stoppage and visible embarrassment on the part of the performer. If there are no small chains about, rather borrow a watch without any at all. The use of the watch box does not in any way interfere with the introduction of the previously described watch-bending and glass-breaking surprises. They can come in as preludes.

It will naturally occur to the conjuror that the watch box may be used in connection with the watch target or loaf, the watch being merely placed in the box instead of pounded in a mortar. It will occasion the performer's leaving the stage on some pretext in order to get the abstracted watch or other article behind to the assistant, unless the method of placing it upon the shelf be adopted. I certainly object to the performer's absence from the stage as much as anything. If it must be done, then some suitable pretext (see *The Restored Handkerchief*) should be worked up to give it a colouring.

The watch box is a handy article to use in conjunction with *The Magi's Brazen Rod*, it being directly employed by having the rings placed in it. The rings should in this case be tied loosely together with a piece of ribbon, to ensure their simultaneous abstraction. The ribbon should be of sufficient length to enable the rings to be placed in the slits in the hollow ball side by side without the necessity of untying or cutting it. But on no account must the conjuror permit the convenient adaptability of the watch box to tempt him into using it more than once during the same performance. This is a fixed maxim which applies to all *visible* apparatus, and is one which should be always rigidly adhered to.

Tricks with Rabbits.—The gentleness and docility of the rabbit makes it, like the dove, a favourite with the conjuror, who does not hesitate to produce it from a hat, and to cause it to disappear from, and re-appear in, most unexpected places. The production of a couple of rabbits from a hat is always very startling, and requires a deal of doing. The animals are placed one in each of the large side pockets, where, if undisturbed, they will lie as peacefully as could be wished, and evidently perfectly contented with their lot. The success attending the transfer of the rabbit from the pocket to the hat will depend entirely upon the skill of the performer, and no middle course can possibly be admitted. It must be done well or not at all. The usual expedient of palming some article and introducing it into the hat directly it is taken into the hand will have to be resorted to, and the article should be of a startling nature. (A pack of cards does very well.) Whatever is put in must be emptied out on the floor, and, whilst stooping, or rather bowing slightly to see what it is, the performer brings the hat against his body and quickly introduces the rabbit into it. The animal must be helped in, as it were, by the body, and not dragged into the hat by the ears. So soon as it is in the hat, one hand should be placed under the crown, which, if not very strong, might otherwise be forced out by the weight of the rabbit. Produce the rabbit with all due affectation of surprise, and, whilst showing it about, allow it to fall. By the time it is picked up again, either by yourself or by a spectator, the second one is in the hat, and you express yourself anxious to know if the owner of the hat keeps a rabbit warren in it. So much for producing the rabbits.

A favourite and very effective method of conjuring with them further is to apparently rub one into the other. This is managed by the aid of the large centre trap. One rabbit is placed upon the table immediately in front of the trap, and the other pushed through the table behind it, a great show all the time being made of forcing one rabbit into the other. The remaining rabbit should be held up by the ears, with the rump resting on one hand, when, to the imagination of the audience, it will appear to be actually stouter than it was a few minutes before. The remaining rabbit you affect to wrap in a piece of paper, it being also passed through the trap, and the paper rolled up as though it really contained an animal, considerable agitation being communicated to it by means of the hands. The performer affects to lose patience with it because it will not remain quiet, and crushes the paper either beneath his feet or between the hands.

The reproduction of the rabbits (*i.e.*, two duplicate ones) necessitates the employment of a rather elaborate piece of apparatus, unless the performer has a friend or two in the audience with rabbits in their pockets, the production of which has a good effect, but is seriously open to suspicion. The apparatus that is generally employed is a large glass vase or goblet, some eighteen inches or two feet in height, according to pleasure (or pocket). This has a zinc lining, in two halves, fitting exactly inside it, the halves being hinged to a slightly concave top, also of zinc. The hinges are on exactly opposite sides of the top. The whole is covered with glue and then spread over with bran. There is, besides, a large bell-shaped cover, usually of thin brass, large enough to conceal the body of the vase completely. In the centre of this, inside, is a catch, which is intended to pass through a hole made in the centre of the concave top of the zinc lining. The vase is prepared by having the zinc lining, previously loaded with two rabbits, put into it. It will then have the appearance of being full of bran, a quantity of which article is spread over the concave top. A raised rim round the hole in the centre will prevent the bran falling through. The vase is brought on by the assistant, and the performer takes some of the bran from the top and throws it off, and also thrusts a thin stick or wire through the hole to show that it goes quite to the bottom. He then shows the interior of the cover, that it may be seen to contain nothing, and places it over the vase, pressing it well down. The original rabbits are next manipulated at the table; and when that matter is settled the cover is raised, gently and slowly at first, and perpendicularly, bringing away with it the zinc lining, which opens as it ascends, and leaves the rabbits in the vase. The bran can be made to transfer itself into the drawer box, previously shown empty, if the same has not been before used during the evening. A much more effective and in every way a more preferable method is to cause it to make its appearance in a borrowed hat. This is best managed by giving the hat from which the rabbits were originally produced to the assistant to place upon the table. The performer at once engages the attention of the audience with the rabbits, saying that he will make the one eat the other, &c., and so enables the assistant to slip into the hat, whilst retiring, a bag of bran that is very loosely fastened at the top. This bag the assistant has had concealed under the coat. The hat is placed carelessly upon a side table, and the bran "passed" into it by the performer as if on an afterthought, so as to avoid any appearance of premeditated effect. The bran must be first emptied out, and the bag can be abstracted, rolled up in the hand, which is inserted for the purpose of clearing the lining of any stray flakes.

If the foregoing variations are all mingled in one trick the effect is very good; but the combination requires a deal of practice, and will prove trying at first.

A Novel Welsh "Rabbit."—Employ a tinman to make a saucepan of tin, the dimensions of which should be 7in. or 8in. in depth, and about 5½in. in diameter at the widest part, which will be the top, from whence it should taper slightly to the bottom. To this have fitted an outer casing (A, Fig. 57), also of tin, that is 2in. less in height than the saucepan itself. At the line where the upper rim of the casing comes when the

saucepan is fitted into it, have a beading (B, Fig. 57), either put
on or hammered out of the metal. This will effectually conceal
the fact that any outer casing exists, which will be regarded
as the body of the saucepan. Into the saucepan fits loosely
a secret pan, about 1½in. only in depth, and into this again
fits a lid, which is ostensibly the lid of the saucepan. The
saucepan is provided with a handle, which must, of course,
come from that part which is above the outer casing. The
saucepan is prepared by having a rabbit placed in it, and
the false pan put in, the lid lying loosely on the top. Holding
it with one hand, and sustaining the casing, in which is a

FIG. 57.

piece of cotton or cambric, by means of the pressure of one
or more fingers, it is brought on, and going with it towards the
audience, care being taken to hold it high, a hat is borrowed.
Observe, on receiving the hat, that you intend making a stove
of it, and then borrow a small handkerchief, which, you will
explain, when you have obtained possession of it, you purpose using as fuel. As if indicating the meaning of your
words, put the saucepan into the hat, and, on withdrawing it,
leave the outer casing behind. Place the hat upon the table,
with the saucepan beside it, and then, removing the lid,
break an egg or two into the secret pan—apparently into
the saucepan itself. Put in any ingredients you please, not

omitting candle drippings, and then place the lid firmly on. Place the borrowed handkerchief into the hat, between its side and the tin lining within it. Pour some spirits of wine upon the piece of linen or cambric, and then set fire to it. Of course the audience, on seeing the flames, will suppose that the borrowed handkerchief is being burnt inside the hat, and mingled amusement and consternation will be exhibited. Do not allow the burning to last long, or the tin casing will become undesirably heated; but put the saucepan quickly into the hat, after affecting to cook the contents, and perform the double operation of putting out the flames and bringing away the casing. If the casing be too hot, the action of the heat upon the fingers will speedily make the fact known, so any further directions upon this point will be unnecessary. Remove the lid, which, if it fits as tightly as it should into the false pan, will bring that away as well, and then take out the rabbit. Return the hat, previously taking out the hand-kerchief, and point out that neither are injured; and also show that the interior of the saucepan is quite guiltless of any contents. If such a combination of apparent impossi-bilities as are presented in this trick do not astonish, then nothing ever will. It is a great trick for large mixed audiences. Doves or guinea pigs can be used as successfully as rabbits. I have even seen a kitten employed, but the difficulty was to get it into the saucepan.

The Bird and Card.—A very pretty stage trick this. The performer must procure what is known as a bird box, which is a pretty polished box, having a secret metal flap inside, the latter, when turned down, forming a retreat for a small bird, such as a canary. It is held down by a small catch, released by pressing the key into the lock from the outside, the double action being performed of setting free the bird and concealing the card. It is useless having such a box constructed, as it can be much more satisfactorily procured of the proper vendors. Two small cages are also necessary. They may be round or square, but, in either case, should be all wire, like a rat trap. This is merely to give them an innocent appearance. One of these cages is concealed on the shelf, behind the table. The performer borrows a hat, either for this or a preceding trick (preferably the latter), and gets the empty cage into it. This is best done by placing the hat upon the table, the opening towards the rear, and leaving it there for a time. Then. when carelessly shifting its position, the article required to be got into it may be inserted with less suspicion. In the second cage is a bird, precisely similar to the one concealed in the bird box. Place this cage upon the table, and cover with a double cloth, having inside a card-board shape. A card is forced on one of the company, and placed in the bird box, in a little slit which will be found there, just over the hinge of the secret flap. The inside of the box may be carefully exhibited at a slight distance, the blackened interior preventing anyone from noticing the presence of the turned down flap. Whilst affecting to lock it, the key is pressed hard in and the flap released. In flying back this covers the card. The performer commences by extracting the card. This he can do by having a duplicate concealed in a card-box (see page 127), and causing it to appear in that; but it will look more artistic to have one palmed and affect to extract it from the box. This done, the cloth is raised by the shape, the cage being left upon the shelf. The cloth is then shaken out and laid flat upon the floor. The box is then opened and the bird allowed to fly out, if tame, or taken out in the hand, previously shown empty, if wild. The performer will derive a great advantage from having a tame canary, which returns to his shoulder. Finally, the hat is brought forward and found to contain the missing cage.

CHAPTER XVIII.

SHAM MESMERISM, CLAIRVOYANCE, ETC.

BLINDFOLD FEATS—IMITATION SECOND SIGHT—ON SPIRIT-UALISM—THE MESMERISED POKER—THE PERAMBULATING WALKING STICK—THE ASCENT—THE TALKING GLASS: TWO METHODS — THE SPIRIT BOUQUET — THE SLATE TRICK—FIERY HANDS, WRITINGS, &C.—THE ELECTRIC TOUCH—THE ANIMATED SKULL.

Clairvoyance.—This is one of the most mysterious agencies with which the scientific world has ever had to deal. Doubted by the majority, because of its seeming impro-bability, and because of the difficulty of comprehending it, the faculty of clairvoyance or second sight has, neverthe-less, been possessed, and is possessed, by not a few. Some marvellous manifestations of seeing without the eyes have been shown, and in a manner sufficient to convince even the most sceptical of its reality. This faculty has often been imitated by conjurors, some of whom have fairly admitted that they were only imitators, whilst others have assumed possession of the actual power itself. At that now defunct institution, the Polytechnic, and other places of amusement, cleverly arranged telegraphic communication has been the means adopted for bringing a person on the stage *en rapport* with another amongst the audience. I would not recommend the amateur to take any serious trouble in the matter, but to merely make himself master of a few tricks relating to it. A very simple one is performed with the aid of a pack of cards. An assistant is blindfolded on the stage, and placed with his back to the audience. Before proceeding any farther, the performer explains that, beyond a certain point, he will neither speak nor make any sound or movement, lest it should be said that he conveyed information to the assistant. He then proceeds to "force" three or more cards in an order previously agreed upon, and the holders thereupon ask of the assistant, as the performer has previously instructed them to do, what the names of the cards are. The performer must mentally reserve to himself the right of pointing with his wand to the person who is to speak next, so as to ensure the cards being asked for in the proper order.

Instead of using cards, the performer can distribute slips of paper amongst the audience, for the purpose of having short sentences written upon them. He has a piece of paper of his own previously prepared, with a sentence upon it that is known to the blindfolded assistant. The papers written upon by the audience are folded up and placed upon a tray, or the crown of a hat, each some distance from the other. Whilst doing this, the performer contrives to effect an exchange between his own paper and any one of the others, it does not signify which. He then asks one of the audience to select one of the papers, and, manipulating the hat or tray adroitly, "forces" his own. Before it is opened, the assistant is requested to say what is written upon it.

This trick is farther elaborated as follows: The performer hands round a fair quantity of paper slips, and asks the audience to write what they please upon them very plainly. As it is advisable that whatever is written should be brief, it is best to ask to have the names of celebrated deceased persons only written. The performer has a piece of his own, previously written upon and folded, concealed in his hand. Supposing this to be in the left hand, the right takes a folded slip from one of the audience, and, under pretence of putting it into the left, for the purpose of handing it to another person, an exchange is effected, and the performer's own piece given instead. The learner will know the proper "pass" for effecting this by this time. The performer then says that he will go upon the stage and from a distance read what is upon the paper. He does so, and seizes the opportunity for rapidly opening the paper of which he has just become possessed, and of reading the name upon it. If much were written upon the paper, it would be impossible to read its contents in the limited space of time at the performer's disposal. When he turns round there is of course no trace visible of what he has been about, and he then proceeds to read the name on the paper held by one of the audience. This he does not do readily, but first names the sex of the person, and then the capital letter of the name, as if it were only developing itself by degrees and through some very mysterious medium. The first paper duly read, a second one is taken, exchanged as before, and borne off to the stage, to be read in transit. This process can be repeated any number of times, although four will be found quite sufficient, as it is a harassing trick to perform. An excellent finish is to "force" a previously prepared paper, and then have it burnt, after it has been read aloud by one of the audience. The ashes are collected and rubbed upon the conjuror's bare arm, upon which the name then appears in black. This is contrived by having the name written upon the arm in glycerine. This will be invisible, but if the ashes be rubbed lightly upon it they will adhere, and so show the name. There are chemical preparations used for the same purpose, but the method described here is by far the most simple and practicable. With this trick "Dr." Lynn created a great sensation for several months, some years ago.

Anti-Spiritualistic Tricks. — In the introduction to these papers I had occasion, the reader may remember, to refer to the impositions practised by the ancient priests and others on the minds of an unenlightened people by means of what were merely conjuring tricks, but which were made to appear before the ignorant in the guise of supernatural manifestations. Few will require to be reminded of the excitement that has of late years existed concerning spiritualism. One would have thought that, in these days, people would have been above believing that the spirits of the departed would be permitted to return to the earth for the sole purpose of answering questions and indulging in tomfoolery; but such is the simplicity of mankind, that those who have had the boldness to declare themselves capable of raising the dead, and to dress up themselves or others in muslin or newspaper, have not lacked faithful followers. The malpractices have been going on for years, and many shameless impositions have come under my notice. The victims, it will not cause astonishment to hear, were mostly weak-minded ladies, and the spirits have had the remarkable discernment to visit only those who were well provided with worldly comforts, backed by an amount of confiding simplicity wonderful to contemplate. The exertions of several amateur, and some professional, conjurors have succeeded in proving to all minds open to the workings of common sense that all those professing spiritualism as a means of gaining a livelihood are neither more nor less than scoundrels. But of course there are still thousands who would be as much imposed upon as ever by any white figure seen after dark, and, in a private way, the spiritualists are still reaping a rich harvest. Towards clearing away this darkness, conjurors, both amateur and professional, can do a great deal, and there is a definite and worthy task before them, which they can best perform by exhibiting such phenomena as are produced by spiritualists at their exhibitions by avowedly natural means. By this means ridicule, which nothing can survive long, will be thrown upon the black art, which is merely conjuring put to base uses. A performance consisting entirely of sham spiritualistic manifestations I have found take exceedingly well, especially with audiences who have seen something of conjuring, and who are not averse to a change in the programme. I do not agree with pretending to call spirits to one's aid, for it smacks of irreverence: the performer should merely explain that what he is about to do or has just done by simple dexterity is brought about by the spiritualists with the asserted aid of familiar spirits. A simple trick which seems well to commence with is—

The Mesmerised Poker.—The performer seats himself with his legs apart, and, taking a poker, stands it up on one end before him. On removing the hand the poker falls, but, after two or three fruitless attempts, it remains standing without the aid of any visible support. This is very easily managed by having a fine piece of black cotton attached to the calf of the trousers by means of a bent pin at each end. It need not be so long as to drag on the floor, and the performer can walk about with comfort and without fear of detection. The action of opening the legs draws the thread out straight and tight, so that the poker can rest against it when it is required to cause it to stand upright.

The Perambulating Walking-Stick.—This is a very amusing trick, in which a walking-stick is made to walk across the stage by itself. The invisible agency is again a fine black thread. On a stage provided with "flies," it is managed from above, in which case the only direction required is to affix one end of a thread round the head of a walking-stick, and convey the other end above to an assistant. By means of this thread the walking-stick is made to progress across the stage by means of little jumps. But on the drawing-room stage the matter is not quite so easy. Two threads will be required, and they must lie across the floor when the curtain is drawn. If possible, an assistant at each wing should hold the ends, but when one assistant only can be obtained, he must do the best he can from one side, the ends of the thread on the other being tied to the back of a chair, about the height of a walking-stick from the ground.

The walking-stick should be provided with a substantial head, and the performer must hand it round for minute examination. He then takes it back to the stage, and flourishes it vigorously to show there are no threads or wires anywhere about. The instant the flourishing portion of the business is over, the assistants must raise the threads to the proper level, and one of them, by crossing his hands, causes the threads to cross each other at about the middle of the room. The performer then places the stick, with apparent carelessness, upright on the floor, but, as he takes care to place it between the threads just where they are crossed, it does not fall on the one hand being removed from it. The assistant who has crossed his hands now uncrosses them, which action has the effect of holding the stick tolerably firmly between the threads. On receiving commands from the performer the stick is made to dance, fall down and jump up again, and walk either to the right or to the left. If it is to go to the right, the assistant on that side lowers his hands slightly, and the one on the left administers a succession of jerks to the threads, which will cause the stick to progress by means of a series of jumps. These jumps can be made alternately long and short. As a final exhibition of skill, it can be made to turn a complete somersault, by both the assistants swinging their hands round in complete circles. For this it will be necessary to have a good head to the stick. When the performance is finished hand the stick round again for examination. In my opinion the trick shows best in a room, where the audience know there is no means of concealing anyone above.

The Ascent can be performed by means of the same threads. Books, pieces of music, &c., are laid upon the floor, and rise slowly or quickly, and remain suspended in the air, where they can be made to rock about. Of course, they are simply laid upon the threads, the ends of which are then raised evenly and simultaneously. The best ascent is a sudden one, as being the most startling.

The Talking Glass.—Provide yourself with a tall, thin, and well-sounding glass vase. At a pinch a thin soda water tumbler will do. Across the room and above the table have a piece of thread or fine wire. Show the tumbler or vase round, and then place it upon the table, or on the top of an inverted tumbler, which will serve for the purpose of showing that there is no deception beneath, and will also act as a sounding medium. An assistant at the side draws the thread close against the side of the glass, and it is stretched as tight as is consistent with safety. The glass is now made to talk by means of sharply emitted sounds in answer to questions, a small code of signals being established. One sound means "yes," two "no," and so on. These sounds are caused by the assistant catching at the thread sharply with the nail, which will cause a distinct ring to come from the glass. The principle is very simple, but I have never known anyone but myself adopt it. The performer must endeavour to make his questions amusing, and, as the powers of speech possessed by the glass are but limited, they must not be too severely taxed.

If a tumbler be suspended from the wand by means of a thread tied loosely round the wand and tightly round the glass, a sound will be emitted on twisting the wand ever so slightly. With practice this movement can be made almost imperceptible. If the onlookers begin to look at the hand and wand too much the display must cease at once.

The Spirit Bouquet.—One of the most usual, and at the same time most shallow, of deceptions practised by the "spiritualist," is that of the production of flowers. The gas is (of course) lowered, a few irreverencies gone through, and, on the room being re-illuminated, lo and behold, the table and floor have flowers lying upon them! As, of course, the manifestors of these wonders could not by any possible means have the flowers in their pockets on entering the room—even if they thought of practising such a deception!—the spectators are struck with wonder. However, I shall teach the reader how to perform an even greater marvel, by causing a bouquet to glide through the air into his hand without the assistance of total or partial darkness. The bouquet can be either real or artificial—a real one, certainly, for choice. Take a piece of the finest iron wire procurable (jewellers' " binding " wire is the proper article), about 6in. in length, and tie it firmly round the stalks of the flowers, just below the buds. The other end tie round the centre flower, which is always a little higher than the others, and you will thus have a loop about 4in. in length. If the centre flower be not higher than the rest, then re-arrange the bouquet, and make it so. It is essential to have one end of the wire tied on considerably higher than the other, in order that the bouquet may hang properly. If both ends were tied round the main body of the stalks, the bouquet would hang upside down, whereas it should, when suspended by the loop, be almost upright, or, at least, only slightly on one side. From the most convenient position behind the scenes, which will depend entirely upon circumstances connected with the arrangement of the stage, have another piece of fine wire hanging, with a loop made in it at one end long enough to reach the centre of the stage. The spot usually the best for attaching this wire is at the side, as near the audience as possible. On a regular stage the "flies" are most suitable, but in the drawing-room, where there are usually folding doors and curtains (without them this trick cannot well be managed), the side must be chosen. When the trick is about to be performed, the bouquet must be put on the wire by means of the loop, and an assistant in concealment mounts a pair of steps with it and holds it in readiness. The end of the wire is so disposed that the performer can without difficulty insert his little finger in the loop thereon, under pretence, say, of shifting a chair. He then retires towards the centre of the room until he feels that the wire is drawn perfectly tight, and then proceeds to speak of the wonderful productions by humbugs, done in the dark, and finally finishes up by saying that he has only to extend his hand in the air to find something in it. With the hand that is *not* holding the wire he makes a grasp in the air, and at the same moment opens the other hand, taking care to pull the wire quite tight. The attention of the audience is naturally momentarily attracted towards the hand making the greatest movement, and at this very instant the assistant starts the bouquet down the wire. The performer, when the bouquet has reached his hand, which it will do with remarkable swiftness, exclaims, "Ah! no; here it is, see, in this hand;" and, ridding his finger of the wire, brings the bouquet forward, of course keeping the loop upon it from view. When the performer's actions have been well contrived and carried out, the bouquet is not seen until it is almost in the performer's hands; but, under less fortuitous circumstances, which are all I bargain for myself, the trick is wonderfully successful. The fact of a small portion of the aerial journey of the bouquet being observed is not by any means undesirable, the only thing to be kept from the view of the spectator being the commencement of it. The communicating wire must be fixed some distance behind, so that the bouquet is descending at full speed by the time it comes into possible view. The reader will see that the principle is so simple, as to be almost commonplace, but he must not deride it on this account. The most natural actions possible must be brought into play, and plenty of rehearsals will be required. The reason for having the loop of the wire upon the little finger is that the safe arrival of the bouquet is better ensured thereby. The little finger must be kept undermost, the hand being at an angle of forty-five degrees, with the wire lying across the palm. A great deal lies in the neatness with which the bouquet reaches the hand. There must be no bungling. Therefore I say, Rehearse.

The Slate Trick.—Everyone will naturally wish to know how this is done. "Dr." Slade, as Mr. Maskelyne correctly showed in open court, produced his "spirit writings" on the

slate by means of a thimble-shaped instrument, to which
were attached a piece of pencil and a length of elastic.
The elastic was fastened to the brace, or elsewhere, and
caused the disappearance of the thimble and pencil up the
performer's sleeve when they were no longer required. Under
the table was a little ledge which supported the slate whilst
the hand, which was supposed to be performing that action, was
busily engaged in scribbling upon the bottom of the slate,
the thimble arrangement enabling one of the fingers to
execute certain letters in a very poor and scarcely legible fashion.
The bad writing was supposed to look more mysterious;
but Slade would have written more legibly had circumstances permitted it. Anyone may try this method, but as
a conjuring trick it is poor. The trick as now sold is a
slate with an extra or false interior. The answer that is to be
given is written upon the genuine slate, and the false side
then put on. The slate is shown casually round without
leaving the performer's hands, and a question is then
written upon one side of the slate, which is waved about,
and an opportunity seized for allowing the false side to
drop out behind the table, or at any other convenient place,
and the answer is then exhibited. If the inside of the false
slate have blotting paper pasted upon it, and a blotting
pad be upon the table used whilst the trick is being performed, it may be allowed to drop out upon the table
without any attempt at concealment.

Fiery Hands, Writings, &c.—With the aid of phosphorus
a very innocent dark séance can be given. The principal
thing is to have the gas under control. This lowered, or
turned completely out, for preference, the rest is easy
enough. Bunches of cotton wool, or tow steeped in phosphorescent spirits, obtainable at any chemist's, placed upon
the ends of fishing rods, create a good effect when protruded
over the heads of the audience, and there waved about in
circles. A washleather glove, stuffed with cotton wool, tied to
the end of a rod, and wetted, is diverting, not to say alarming,

when dabbed suddenly in the face of one of the audience. Imagination will fancy it the clammy hand of death. Care must be taken to withdraw it very suddenly. The best way is to have it swinging from the end of the rod, when it retires out of reach of a possible "grab" by virtue of its own impetus. The glove must not be phosphorescent. Japanese fishing rods, with the joints sliding one within the other, will be found very useful. A good effect is produced by the performer allowing himself to be tied to a chair, to which his arms are firmly bound, and the knots sealed by the audience. His assistants, having first removed their boots, can come on and manage everything, and, as a final effect, one of them has some words or characters written upon his arms and hands, or simply has them smeared with the phosphorescent preparation in use. He then kneels behind the performer's chair, which he must approach either backwards or with his coat on, and then extends his arms from the performer's shoulders. The form of the hands and arms will be seen, and it will appear as if the performer had loosened his arms and was exhibiting them in a fiery condition. So soon as the assistant is again out of sight the gas should be turned up, leaving the audience in a state of bewilderment. The most childishly simple things can be perpetrated in the dark, when the mind is by nature more easily imposed upon than it is at any other time. The simple expedient of someone coming on the stage in his stockings, after the room has been darkened, and, by turning back the sleeve, exhibit some words written upon the arm, is a very good illustration: it is impossible for an ordinary mind to divine how the sudden appearance of the writing in mid-air is managed. The arm must be extended horizontally before the sleeve is drawn back, and it must be kept so extended until the writing is again obscured. This is essential. The slightest expenditure of ingenuity and thought will produce other effects, which will vary according to circumstances and situations;

whilst careful preparation will meet with its usual and deserved reward.

The Electric Touch.—The performer may, if he pleases, either commence or conclude those portions of his entertainments which have to do with mesmerism with a bogus explanation of the forces latent within him, the result of a natural gift. He must purposely make his elucidation a little far-fetched, in order to raise a smile, or even a remark, of incredulity. This gives him the desired opportunity for offering to practically prove the truth of what he states. Advancing to the company, he asks one of the spectators to extend his hands in front of him, palms downward. Standing immediately opposite this gentleman, the performer rubs the back of one of his own hands with the fingers of the other, and reverses the operation. This he continues for a quarter of a minute or so, and then suddenly extends his hands over the backs of those held out before him, an inch or two removed. The spectator feels no shock, so the performer continues his rubbing, and, at the third or fourth trial, the spectator jerks one of his hands away, a slight electric shock having been communicated to him. The experiment may be repeated as often as the performer pleases. A little pin is the cause of this marvellous manifestation. This the performer has about him (stuck under the vest is the best place), and often, in gesticulating, indirectly showing the hands to be empty, it is got down, with the head between the first joints of the first and second fingers, where it can be held firmly, of course pointing downwards. The rubbing of the fingers of each hand alternately upon the back of the other indirectly points to the absence of anything of the protruding nature of a pin being held in them, so the assumed excitation of electricity by friction is not the only reason for the action.

It adds to the effect when the production of the shock on the first experimenter comes only at the third or fourth attempt. With others, it may safely come at the first or second, if the performer be careful to explain that, the electric power once worked up, very little is necessary to keep it going. The rubbing is kept up throughout. The shock is, of course, produced by bringing the hand holding the pin nearer and nearer to the one beneath it, until the pin's point touches it. The touch must be as delicate as possible, as then an after feeling is experienced which necessitates rubbing. If the point enters the skin, the presence of the pin is at once detected. It being so absolutely necessary to the success of the trick that the touch should be very delicate, the use of fine entomological pins is recommended, but they must not be too long. The performer will do well to fail to produce shocks on some of those experimented upon at first, a return to them being necessary when the electric power has accumulated. Any particularly healthy and rubicund person may as well prove quite impervious, the performer explaining that the strength of mind present is too great. The company will judge by the person's healthy exterior, forgetting that, notwithstanding, the mind within may be nothing very great. As the performer is standing and the company sitting, he must slant his hands downwards, or the pin will be seen. The hands experimented upon must, for the same reason, be kept low. Should anyone suggest a pin, that article must be at once dropped, the performer being, of course, provided with reserve ones. This part of the trick is very seriously carried out, the performer congratulating himself and the company upon a state of atmosphere which enables him to exhibit such satisfactory results.

The Animated Skull.—The performer places two ordinary chairs, which may be examined, back to back, and a yard or so apart. Across the backs he lays a piece of plate glass, previously examined, a perfectly transparent table being thus formed, and one, as the performer will explain, impervious to electricity. Upon this table the performer places either a real human skull or else a pasteboard imitation of one. The imitation is recommended, the performer explaining that the reason for its use is that the feelings of some might be shocked, which really might be the case. The skull is examined previous to being placed upon the table, the company being safely depended upon for not noticing anything suspicious in the fact that the underside is very much rounded. The skull now answers questions, giving one nod for "Yes" and two nods for "No." What questions are asked must depend upon the wit of the performer, and the nature of the company assembled. Arithmetical problems should be solved, as the skull can give any number by means of nods. As a finale, the skull is asked if it would like to continue the performance, to which a couple of slow shakes are given.

Our old friend, the black silk thread, is at work again here. A piece is stretched across the stage, tied up out of harm's way when not in use. As soon as the skull is placed upon the glass the thread is brought down to the level of the mouth, and made to enter there. The imitation article has a deep indentation at this place. In other cases the thread is brought under the projecting nasal bone. A slight movement of the hand causes the skull to nod, so long as the thread is in position, and the performer may pick it off the glass at any moment, to show that no connection exists. The slow shake is done by manipulating the thread sideways. It cannot be prolonged, as it tends to work the skull off the glass. The rounded underside is to render the rocking movement easy. In some cases a tiny bead of wax is fastened upon the thread, and this affixed to the skull, at the back.

CHAPTER XIX.

FINAL INSTRUCTIONS.

HAVING at length brought the beginner to that point where he will first have to shift for himself in real earnest, I wish to leave him in a position to do credit to my tuition, and, with this object, impart a few hints for his guidance.

On the subject of practice, I would not say any more if I could. By this time, it must have become so evident to everyone that nothing can be brought to any degree at all approaching perfection without assiduous attention to detail, that any repetition of my often-expressed injunctions to practice would become nauseating. But I ought to say something regarding the best method for learning new tricks or sleights from the foregoing text. It is a bad plan to read the description through, and then immediately try to produce the result right away. The whole trick should certainly be read carefully through first, so that the mind fully grasps what is required to be done; but, after that, the hands should be made to follow, step by step, the instructions given, and no progression made until it is certain that all is correct up to each point. It will be readily understood that my instructions have not been written without a large amount of care, or without making a due allowance for the great difference between teaching by word of mouth and by book. In many instances, a single word explains a great deal; so, if the reader scans the page carelessly, it is very possible that he may miss the point altogether, and perhaps conclude, in his own mind, that I am a charlatan and an impostor. With cards, this careful following of the text with the hands is especially essential, and attention to it wi'l save much time, trouble, and annoyance at the outset, when everything new will naturally appear difficult, if not absurd. Thus much for the beginner. When he arrives at the dignity of an actual performer, let him be careful to prepare, and learn by heart, a little set speech to commence with, and also the accompanying talk for each trick. When he has exhibited for a year or two, he will perhaps be able to dispense with such preparation; but, at the commencement, few, if any, can do without it. The first appearance before an audience is in itself sufficiently unnerving, without any additional embarrassment in the shape of a consciousness that you do not know what you are going to say. Notwithstanding the most careful preparation, something is sure to go wrong at first, and unexpected difficulties will crop up on all sides, and to meet these successfully will require all the energies of the performer. It does not signify how superior the individual's natural aptitude or oratory may be—the task is too great for anyone at starting.

For the first few "shows," it is as well to perform such tricks as do not require the assistance of an attendant, for the performer must be entirely master of the situation, and dictate to his assistant at pleasure. This he could not do with freedom if he were uncertain about his own powers. Let it also be borne in mind that assistants are like money, which, when good, is a valuable acquisition, but, when bad, only gets one into trouble. Have no assistant at all rather than a bungler, or, what is, if possible, worse, one who endeavours to attach to himself some degree of consequence in the minds of the audience. Except when it is to assist the trick, he should never open his mouth, and all his work should be done as silently and unobtrusively as possible, without absolutely scurrying away. His presence on the stage should be as brief as possible, and his appearance must always be excused by the performance of some very insignificant and subordinate task. The best assistant to have is one who looks so stupid that the combined efforts of fifty conjurors could not drum into him the method for making the "pass." The worst is the one who conveys by his appearance and actions that he "knows all about it." The spectators at once attribute the greater portion of the results to his agency — not incorrectly, perhaps; but it is unnecessary that they should have any cause to do so. On no account should the attendant attempt to perform any impromptu act, however clever he may be, for he is sure to confuse the performer by so doing, and so lead to awkward results.

On many occasions, it is inconvenient, or, at any rate, highly inadvisable, to take the conjuring table. At the houses of friends it is exceedingly difficult to keep everything secret without being absolutely rude. The host (possibly followed by a friend or two—"men who understand things of this sort, you know, so you needn't be afraid") is nearly certain to take the fullest advantage of his position, and to penetrate into the performer's sanctum with all possible alacrity, and there worm from him valuable secrets. Of course, he wouldn't dream of telling anyone, not he; yet, somehow, if the tricks are exhibited on another occasion, the juveniles display an inexplicable and annoying knowledge of the why and the wherefore of them. It is of no use to say, "Oh! but no one would take the liberty," and such like; my experience teaches me (and I do not think that I, in particular, have fallen among thieves) that they do, so there is an end of it. Such articles as multiplying balls, cups, reticules, &c., are easily put out of sight; but an unwieldy table is quite another thing. Of course, immediately the trap in it is discovered, away goes your reputation for miraculous sleight of hand; and, when you really do exhibit a genuine specimen of it, you will not get credit for it. No, no risks must be run on this head—that is, if the performer cares anything for his reputation.

As an excellent substitute for the table, I have an oblong box, the rough dimensions of which are 18in. × 8in. × 6in. It has a removable sliding lid, and is covered with a dark cloth. In this I carry such of my belongings as will go into it; so, when it is seen during the performance, it is only regarded in the light of an ordinary deal box. One of the 8in. sides, however, has a trap cut in it, with a little bag inside the box for catching articles passed through. The box, *minus* the lid, and *plus* such articles as would be ordinarily placed upon the shelf, is brought boldly on, along with some of the articles which the performer will first require, as a "blind." It is placed carelessly, down within three or four inches of the back of the table, with the open side, naturally, at the back, and the trap uppermost. The table itself plays the part of the shelf, and articles are now and then placed upon the box, as they would be, in the usual way, upon a table.

Another way, much more deceptive, is to have a trap made in the top of an ordinary high hat. The crown lining should form the bottom of a collapsible bag, so that the inside of the hat can be first shown, but, so soon as it is placed upon the table brim downwards, the bag falls down. The brim should be tolerably flat, as the hat should not rock about. The crown itself will require some strengthening material, such as very thick pasteboard, glued to it before the trap is cut out, or the latter will curl up in an unseemly way. This trap hat serves for vanishing articles only. Its presence is very opportune at times. The presence of the shelf is by no means indispensable; indeed, I may safely say that I do not require it myself, except in important performances. If it be inconvenient to take the table, a programme can easily be arranged so as to dispense with the shelf entirely, but, if it can be used, then, by all means, make the most of it. Young conjurors must avoid the error of adapting their tricks to the shelf, instead of the shelf to the tricks. Experience will show what an astonishing quantity of things can be concealed in the large breast and tail pockets for hat "loading" purposes. The tail pockets will carry a bundle of fifty cups with ease, and without fear of detection; and when these can be introduced, and produced without once leaving the audience, I need hardly say that the effect is considerably enhanced. When you are using a table, be careful never to go behind it without some good reason, and let your stay there be as brief as possible. Stand at the sides as often and as long as you like.

The arrangement of the stage and the seating of the audience are matters of vital importance, and due regard must be paid to angles of vision. One of the greatest bugbears a performer meets with in private audiences is he (no lady ever sins in this way) who, under pretence of being at hand in case of need, or by means of some even more transparent excuse, plants himself, in close proximity to the stage, between it and the body of the audience. It is all very well for the reader to say, "Oh, but I would never allow that under any circumstances!" If he be young, he will find that people *will* patronise him, do what he may, or be as clever as he will; and it is in the interest of the young beginner that I am making these remarks. There will generally be somebody who thinks himself a privileged person, and who will put himself just where he is not wanted. We know what mean things people will do for money: to find out the secret of a conjuring trick they will descend almost as low. I am not romancing, but stating plain truths, such as have forced themselves upon me time after time. Under these circumstances, the table should be placed as far back as is possible or convenient, and, if little tables are used, they should be well on one side and not too far forward. But more important than this even is the placing of some large object such as a vase with flowers on a pedestal, a statue, or such like at each corner, as it is from thence that the best view of the conjuror's secrets can be obtained. A person stationed at a corner can see half of what the performer does in the vesting line, and he has an unfair advantage, which must not be permitted, when avoidable. If a pianoforte be in use, by all means put it close to one of the corners. Curtains are not of much use, as they are easily pulled aside. If he have the opportunity, let the performer arrange the seats himself, and also take the bearings of his table from the corners. Be careful that no looking-glasses are in a position to reflect back to the audience those things which are not meant for them to see, and have the light as evenly distributed as possible; but do not have any candles or lamp on the table. I object even to an upright candelabrum being placed at each front corner. They are in the way.

Programmes are a decided addition, and they should be made as interesting as possible without foreshadowing what is about to follow. The cheapest way is to have a quantity printed, with the performer's complete catalogue upon them, numbered, and then the numbers of the tricks to be performed can be announced in any convenient way. This will only do for private audiences. In performing in public the case is entirely altered.

By all means call in the assistance of a pianoforte; but see that the player of the instrument is one who will not be likely to egotistically launch out into any brilliant fantasia. Waltzes, and such pieces as can be stopped suddenly, should be chosen. The performer must be as quick as he can between tricks; but to a waiting audience one minute seems ten, so it is quite necessary to have a little music when it is obtainable. The player should finish off directly the performer comes on the stage, without waiting for any word or sign. In such a trick as the *Rising Cards* a little "magic music"—of the gentle trickling order—will be found very effective. The cards would ascend to the music.

The performer should always provide himself with a private programme, to be hung or pasted up behind his screen, or wherever his retiring place may be. On this programme should be detailed every property of each trick, down to the veriest trifle, for on trifles, be it remembered, often depends the whole success of a trick. It is also well to have written down beforehand what articles should be upon the shelf at the commencement of each part, and any preconceived pieces of appropriate wit should be put against the particular trick to which they belong. These precautions will save the performer—the beginner more especially—a world of trouble and anxiety. As a trick once written out is done for ever, it is as well to have each one on a separate card. In this case the writing out of an elaborate programme before each performance would be avoided, besides which the cards are more portable. Have the properties of each trick complete. If a knife be required in three tricks, have three knives, and not one, and let this principle be observed throughout. It is as easy to take three knives as one, and there is, besides, the comforting assurance that one will be at hand when wanted.

Do not perform longer than forty-five or fifty minutes at a stretch. Both performer and audience are the better for a short rest at the end of that period, and an interval of ten minutes or so should be allowed. This will enable the performer to re-arrange his shelf, which should always be kept as clear as possible, and to remove articles from the trap bags, &c.

Above all things, keep the hands warm, and for this purpose be provided with a pair of woollen gloves, which wear indoors as well as out, previous to a performance. No one can palm with a hand like ice.

I do not know that I can say anything more without repeating what has already appeared in connection with such tricks as seemed to me to afford the most appropriate opportunities; so my work is done.

To use the words of Byron, "I have nothing further to add, save a general note of thanksgiving to readers, purchasers, and publishers," and to wish the learner all success—but only according to his deserts—with as much true enjoyment as has been experienced by me in the pursuit of SLEIGHT OF HAND.

INDEX

A CATALOG OF SELECTED
DOVER BOOKS
IN ALL FIELDS OF INTEREST

A CATALOG OF SELECTED DOVER
BOOKS IN ALL FIELDS OF INTEREST

CONCERNING THE SPIRITUAL IN ART, Wassily Kandinsky. Pioneering work by father of abstract art. Thoughts on color theory, nature of art. Analysis of earlier masters. 12 illustrations. 80pp. of text. 5⅜ x 8½. 23411-8

ANIMALS: 1,419 Copyright-Free Illustrations of Mammals, Birds, Fish, Insects, etc., Jim Harter (ed.). Clear wood engravings present, in extremely lifelike poses, over 1,000 species of animals. One of the most extensive pictorial sourcebooks of its kind. Captions. Index. 284pp. 9 x 12. 23766-4

CELTIC ART: The Methods of Construction, George Bain. Simple geometric techniques for making Celtic interlacements, spirals, Kells-type initials, animals, humans, etc. Over 500 illustrations. 160pp. 9 x 12. (Available in U.S. only.) 22923-8

AN ATLAS OF ANATOMY FOR ARTISTS, Fritz Schider. Most thorough reference work on art anatomy in the world. Hundreds of illustrations, including selections from works by Vesalius, Leonardo, Goya, Ingres, Michelangelo, others. 593 illustrations. 192pp. 7⅛ x 10¼. 20241-0

CELTIC HAND STROKE-BY-STROKE (Irish Half-Uncial from "The Book of Kells"): An Arthur Baker Calligraphy Manual, Arthur Baker. Complete guide to creating each letter of the alphabet in distinctive Celtic manner. Covers hand position, strokes, pens, inks, paper, more. Illustrated. 48pp. 8¼ x 11. 24336-2

EASY ORIGAMI, John Montroll. Charming collection of 32 projects (hat, cup, pelican, piano, swan, many more) specially designed for the novice origami hobbyist. Clearly illustrated easy-to-follow instructions insure that even beginning papercrafters will achieve successful results. 48pp. 8¼ x 11. 27298-2

THE COMPLETE BOOK OF BIRDHOUSE CONSTRUCTION FOR WOODWORKERS, Scott D. Campbell. Detailed instructions, illustrations, tables. Also data on bird habitat and instinct patterns. Bibliography. 3 tables. 63 illustrations in 15 figures. 48pp. 5¼ x 8½. 24407-5

BLOOMINGDALE'S ILLUSTRATED 1886 CATALOG: Fashions, Dry Goods and Housewares, Bloomingdale Brothers. Famed merchants' extremely rare catalog depicting about 1,700 products: clothing, housewares, firearms, dry goods, jewelry, more. Invaluable for dating, identifying vintage items. Also, copyright-free graphics for artists, designers. Co-published with Henry Ford Museum & Greenfield Village. 160pp. 8¼ x 11. 25780-0

HISTORIC COSTUME IN PICTURES, Braun & Schneider. Over 1,450 costumed figures in clearly detailed engravings–from dawn of civilization to end of 19th century. Captions. Many folk costumes. 256pp. 8⅜ x 11¾. 23150-X

STICKLEY CRAFTSMAN FURNITURE CATALOGS, Gustav Stickley and L. & J. G. Stickley. Beautiful, functional furniture in two authentic catalogs from 1910. 594 illustrations, including 277 photos, show settles, rockers, armchairs, reclining chairs, bookcases, desks, tables. 183pp. 6½ x 9¼. 23838-5

AMERICAN LOCOMOTIVES IN HISTORIC PHOTOGRAPHS: 1858 to 1949, Ron Ziel (ed.). A rare collection of 126 meticulously detailed official photographs, called "builder portraits," of American locomotives that majestically chronicle the rise of steam locomotive power in America. Introduction. Detailed captions. xi+129pp. 9 x 12. 27393-8

AMERICA'S LIGHTHOUSES: An Illustrated History, Francis Ross Holland, Jr. Delightfully written, profusely illustrated fact-filled survey of over 200 American lighthouses since 1716. History, anecdotes, technological advances, more. 240pp. 8 x 10¾. 25576-X

TOWARDS A NEW ARCHITECTURE, Le Corbusier. Pioneering manifesto by founder of "International School." Technical and aesthetic theories, views of industry, economics, relation of form to function, "mass-production split" and much more. Profusely illustrated. 320pp. 6⅛ x 9¼. (Available in U.S. only.) 25023-7

HOW THE OTHER HALF LIVES, Jacob Riis. Famous journalistic record, exposing poverty and degradation of New York slums around 1900, by major social reformer. 100 striking and influential photographs. 233pp. 10 x 7⅞. 22012-5

FRUIT KEY AND TWIG KEY TO TREES AND SHRUBS, William M. Harlow. One of the handiest and most widely used identification aids. Fruit key covers 120 deciduous and evergreen species; twig key 160 deciduous species. Easily used. Over 300 photographs. 126pp. 5⅜ x 8½. 20511-8

COMMON BIRD SONGS, Dr. Donald J. Borror. Songs of 60 most common U.S. birds: robins, sparrows, cardinals, bluejays, finches, more—arranged in order of increasing complexity. Up to 9 variations of songs of each species.

Cassette and manual 99911-4

ORCHIDS AS HOUSE PLANTS, Rebecca Tyson Northen. Grow cattleyas and many other kinds of orchids—in a window, in a case, or under artificial light. 63 illustrations. 148pp. 5⅜ x 8½. 23261-1

MONSTER MAZES, Dave Phillips. Masterful mazes at four levels of difficulty. Avoid deadly perils and evil creatures to find magical treasures. Solutions for all 32 exciting illustrated puzzles. 48pp. 8¼ x 11. 26005-4

MOZART'S DON GIOVANNI (DOVER OPERA LIBRETTO SERIES), Wolfgang Amadeus Mozart. Introduced and translated by Ellen H. Bleiler. Standard Italian libretto, with complete English translation. Convenient and thoroughly portable—an ideal companion for reading along with a recording or the performance itself. Introduction. List of characters. Plot summary. 121pp. 5¼ x 8½. 24944-1

TECHNICAL MANUAL AND DICTIONARY OF CLASSICAL BALLET, Gail Grant. Defines, explains, comments on steps, movements, poses and concepts. 15-page pictorial section. Basic book for student, viewer. 127pp. 5⅜ x 8½. 21843-0

THE CLARINET AND CLARINET PLAYING, David Pino. Lively, comprehensive work features suggestions about technique, musicianship, and musical interpretation, as well as guidelines for teaching, making your own reeds, and preparing for public performance. Includes an intriguing look at clarinet history. "A godsend," *The Clarinet,* Journal of the International Clarinet Society. Appendixes. 7 illus. 320pp. 5⅜ x 8½. 40270-3

HOLLYWOOD GLAMOR PORTRAITS, John Kobal (ed.). 145 photos from 1926-49. Harlow, Gable, Bogart, Bacall; 94 stars in all. Full background on photographers, technical aspects. 160pp. 8⅜ x 11¼. 23352-9

THE ANNOTATED CASEY AT THE BAT: A Collection of Ballads about the Mighty Casey/Third, Revised Edition, Martin Gardner (ed.). Amusing sequels and parodies of one of America's best-loved poems: Casey's Revenge, Why Casey Whiffed, Casey's Sister at the Bat, others. 256pp. 5⅜ x 8½. 28598-7

THE RAVEN AND OTHER FAVORITE POEMS, Edgar Allan Poe. Over 40 of the author's most memorable poems: "The Bells," "Ulalume," "Israfel," "To Helen," "The Conqueror Worm," "Eldorado," "Annabel Lee," many more. Alphabetic lists of titles and first lines. 64pp. 5$\frac{3}{16}$ x 8¼. 26685-0

PERSONAL MEMOIRS OF U. S. GRANT, Ulysses Simpson Grant. Intelligent, deeply moving firsthand account of Civil War campaigns, considered by many the finest military memoirs ever written. Includes letters, historic photographs, maps and more. 528pp. 6⅛ x 9¼. 28587-1

ANCIENT EGYPTIAN MATERIALS AND INDUSTRIES, A. Lucas and J. Harris. Fascinating, comprehensive, thoroughly documented text describes this ancient civilization's vast resources and the processes that incorporated them in daily life, including the use of animal products, building materials, cosmetics, perfumes and incense, fibers, glazed ware, glass and its manufacture, materials used in the mummification process, and much more. 544pp. 6⅛ x 9¼. (Available in U.S. only.) 40446-3

RUSSIAN STORIES/RUSSKIE RASSKAZY: A Dual-Language Book, edited by Gleb Struve. Twelve tales by such masters as Chekhov, Tolstoy, Dostoevsky, Pushkin, others. Excellent word-for-word English translations on facing pages, plus teaching and study aids, Russian/English vocabulary, biographical/critical introductions, more. 416pp. 5⅜ x 8½. 26244-8

PHILADELPHIA THEN AND NOW: 60 Sites Photographed in the Past and Present, Kenneth Finkel and Susan Oyama. Rare photographs of City Hall, Logan Square, Independence Hall, Betsy Ross House, other landmarks juxtaposed with contemporary views. Captures changing face of historic city. Introduction. Captions. 128pp. 8¼ x 11. 25790-8

AIA ARCHITECTURAL GUIDE TO NASSAU AND SUFFOLK COUNTIES, LONG ISLAND, The American Institute of Architects, Long Island Chapter, and the Society for the Preservation of Long Island Antiquities. Comprehensive, well-researched and generously illustrated volume brings to life over three centuries of Long Island's great architectural heritage. More than 240 photographs with authoritative, extensively detailed captions. 176pp. 8¼ x 11. 26946-9

NORTH AMERICAN INDIAN LIFE: Customs and Traditions of 23 Tribes, Elsie Clews Parsons (ed.). 27 fictionalized essays by noted anthropologists examine religion, customs, government, additional facets of life among the Winnebago, Crow, Zuni, Eskimo, other tribes. 480pp. 6⅛ x 9¼. 27377-6

FRANK LLOYD WRIGHT'S DANA HOUSE, Donald Hoffmann. Pictorial essay of residential masterpiece with over 160 interior and exterior photos, plans, elevations, sketches and studies. 128pp. 9¼ x 10¾. 29120-0

THE MALE AND FEMALE FIGURE IN MOTION: 60 Classic Photographic Sequences, Eadweard Muybridge. 60 true-action photographs of men and women walking, running, climbing, bending, turning, etc., reproduced from rare 19th-century masterpiece. vi + 121pp. 9 x 12. 24745-7

1001 QUESTIONS ANSWERED ABOUT THE SEASHORE, N. J. Berrill and Jacquelyn Berrill. Queries answered about dolphins, sea snails, sponges, starfish, fishes, shore birds, many others. Covers appearance, breeding, growth, feeding, much more. 305pp. 5¼ x 8¼. 23366-9

ATTRACTING BIRDS TO YOUR YARD, William J. Weber. Easy-to-follow guide offers advice on how to attract the greatest diversity of birds: birdhouses, feeders, water and waterers, much more. 96pp. 5³⁄₁₆ x 8¼. 28927-3

MEDICINAL AND OTHER USES OF NORTH AMERICAN PLANTS: A Historical Survey with Special Reference to the Eastern Indian Tribes, Charlotte Erichsen-Brown. Chronological historical citations document 500 years of usage of plants, trees, shrubs native to eastern Canada, northeastern U.S. Also complete identifying information. 343 illustrations. 544pp. 6½ x 9¼. 25951-X

STORYBOOK MAZES, Dave Phillips. 23 stories and mazes on two-page spreads: Wizard of Oz, Treasure Island, Robin Hood, etc. Solutions. 64pp. 8¼ x 11. 23628-5

AMERICAN NEGRO SONGS: 230 Folk Songs and Spirituals, Religious and Secular, John W. Work. This authoritative study traces the African influences of songs sung and played by black Americans at work, in church, and as entertainment. The author discusses the lyric significance of such songs as "Swing Low, Sweet Chariot," "John Henry," and others and offers the words and music for 230 songs. Bibliography. Index of Song Titles. 272pp. 6½ x 9¼. 40271-1

MOVIE-STAR PORTRAITS OF THE FORTIES, John Kobal (ed.). 163 glamor, studio photos of 106 stars of the 1940s: Rita Hayworth, Ava Gardner, Marlon Brando, Clark Gable, many more. 176pp. 8⅜ x 11¼. 23546-7

BENCHLEY LOST AND FOUND, Robert Benchley. Finest humor from early 30s, about pet peeves, child psychologists, post office and others. Mostly unavailable elsewhere. 73 illustrations by Peter Arno and others. 183pp. 5⅜ x 8½. 22410-4

YEKL and THE IMPORTED BRIDEGROOM AND OTHER STORIES OF YIDDISH NEW YORK, Abraham Cahan. Film Hester Street based on *Yekl* (1896). Novel, other stories among first about Jewish immigrants on N.Y.'s East Side. 240pp. 5⅜ x 8½. 22427-9

SELECTED POEMS, Walt Whitman. Generous sampling from *Leaves of Grass*. Twenty-four poems include "I Hear America Singing," "Song of the Open Road," "I Sing the Body Electric," "When Lilacs Last in the Dooryard Bloom'd," "O Captain! My Captain!"–all reprinted from an authoritative edition. Lists of titles and first lines. 128pp. 5³⁄₁₆ x 8¼. 26878-0

THE BEST TALES OF HOFFMANN, E. T. A. Hoffmann. 10 of Hoffmann's most important stories: "Nutcracker and the King of Mice," "The Golden Flowerpot," etc. 458pp. 5⅜ x 8½. 21793-0

FROM FETISH TO GOD IN ANCIENT EGYPT, E. A. Wallis Budge. Rich detailed survey of Egyptian conception of "God" and gods, magic, cult of animals, Osiris, more. Also, superb English translations of hymns and legends. 240 illustrations. 545pp. 5⅜ x 8½. 25803-3

FRENCH STORIES/CONTES FRANÇAIS: A Dual-Language Book, Wallace Fowlie. Ten stories by French masters, Voltaire to Camus: "Micromegas" by Voltaire; "The Atheist's Mass" by Balzac; "Minuet" by de Maupassant; "The Guest" by Camus, six more. Excellent English translations on facing pages. Also French-English vocabulary list, exercises, more. 352pp. 5⅜ x 8½. 26443-2

CHICAGO AT THE TURN OF THE CENTURY IN PHOTOGRAPHS: 122 Historic Views from the Collections of the Chicago Historical Society, Larry A. Viskochil. Rare large-format prints offer detailed views of City Hall, State Street, the Loop, Hull House, Union Station, many other landmarks, circa 1904-1913. Introduction. Captions. Maps. 144pp. 9⅜ x 12¼. 24656-6

OLD BROOKLYN IN EARLY PHOTOGRAPHS, 1865-1929, William Lee Younger. Luna Park, Gravesend race track, construction of Grand Army Plaza, moving of Hotel Brighton, etc. 157 previously unpublished photographs. 165pp. 8⅞ x 11¾. 23587-4

THE MYTHS OF THE NORTH AMERICAN INDIANS, Lewis Spence. Rich anthology of the myths and legends of the Algonquins, Iroquois, Pawnees and Sioux, prefaced by an extensive historical and ethnological commentary. 36 illustrations. 480pp. 5⅜ x 8½. 25967-6

AN ENCYCLOPEDIA OF BATTLES: Accounts of Over 1,560 Battles from 1479 B.C. to the Present, David Eggenberger. Essential details of every major battle in recorded history from the first battle of Megiddo in 1479 B.C. to Grenada in 1984. List of Battle Maps. New Appendix covering the years 1967-1984. Index. 99 illustrations. 544pp. 6½ x 9¼. 24913-1

SAILING ALONE AROUND THE WORLD, Captain Joshua Slocum. First man to sail around the world, alone, in small boat. One of great feats of seamanship told in delightful manner. 67 illustrations. 294pp. 5⅜ x 8½. 20326-3

ANARCHISM AND OTHER ESSAYS, Emma Goldman. Powerful, penetrating, prophetic essays on direct action, role of minorities, prison reform, puritan hypocrisy, violence, etc. 271pp. 5⅜ x 8½. 22484-8

MYTHS OF THE HINDUS AND BUDDHISTS, Ananda K. Coomaraswamy and Sister Nivedita. Great stories of the epics; deeds of Krishna, Shiva, taken from puranas, Vedas, folk tales; etc. 32 illustrations. 400pp. 5⅜ x 8½. 21759-0

THE TRAUMA OF BIRTH, Otto Rank. Rank's controversial thesis that anxiety neurosis is caused by profound psychological trauma which occurs at birth. 256pp. 5⅜ x 8½. 27974-X

A THEOLOGICO-POLITICAL TREATISE, Benedict Spinoza. Also contains unfinished Political Treatise. Great classic on religious liberty, theory of government on common consent. R. Elwes translation. Total of 421pp. 5⅜ x 8½. 20249-6

MY BONDAGE AND MY FREEDOM, Frederick Douglass. Born a slave, Douglass became outspoken force in antislavery movement. The best of Douglass' autobiographies. Graphic description of slave life. 464pp. 5⅜ x 8½. 22457-0

FOLLOWING THE EQUATOR: A Journey Around the World, Mark Twain. Fascinating humorous account of 1897 voyage to Hawaii, Australia, India, New Zealand, etc. Ironic, bemused reports on peoples, customs, climate, flora and fauna, politics, much more. 197 illustrations. 720pp. 5⅜ x 8½. 26113-1

THE PEOPLE CALLED SHAKERS, Edward D. Andrews. Definitive study of Shakers: origins, beliefs, practices, dances, social organization, furniture and crafts, etc. 33 illustrations. 351pp. 5⅜ x 8½. 21081-2

THE MYTHS OF GREECE AND ROME, H. A. Guerber. A classic of mythology, generously illustrated, long prized for its simple, graphic, accurate retelling of the principal myths of Greece and Rome, and for its commentary on their origins and significance. With 64 illustrations by Michelangelo, Raphael, Titian, Rubens, Canova, Bernini and others. 480pp. 5⅜ x 8½. 27584-1

PSYCHOLOGY OF MUSIC, Carl E. Seashore. Classic work discusses music as a medium from psychological viewpoint. Clear treatment of physical acoustics, auditory apparatus, sound perception, development of musical skills, nature of musical feeling, host of other topics. 88 figures. 408pp. 5⅜ x 8½. 21851-1

THE PHILOSOPHY OF HISTORY, Georg W. Hegel. Great classic of Western thought develops concept that history is not chance but rational process, the evolution of freedom. 457pp. 5⅜ x 8½. 20112-0

THE BOOK OF TEA, Kakuzo Okakura. Minor classic of the Orient: entertaining, charming explanation, interpretation of traditional Japanese culture in terms of tea ceremony. 94pp. 5⅜ x 8½. 20070-1

LIFE IN ANCIENT EGYPT, Adolf Erman. Fullest, most thorough, detailed older account with much not in more recent books, domestic life, religion, magic, medicine, commerce, much more. Many illustrations reproduce tomb paintings, carvings, hieroglyphs, etc. 597pp. 5⅜ x 8½. 22632-8

SUNDIALS, Their Theory and Construction, Albert Waugh. Far and away the best, most thorough coverage of ideas, mathematics concerned, types, construction, adjusting anywhere. Simple, nontechnical treatment allows even children to build several of these dials. Over 100 illustrations. 230pp. 5⅜ x 8½. 22947-5

THEORETICAL HYDRODYNAMICS, L. M. Milne-Thomson. Classic exposition of the mathematical theory of fluid motion, applicable to both hydrodynamics and aerodynamics. Over 600 exercises. 768pp. 6⅛ x 9¼. 68970-0

SONGS OF EXPERIENCE: Facsimile Reproduction with 26 Plates in Full Color, William Blake. 26 full-color plates from a rare 1826 edition. Includes "The Tyger," "London," "Holy Thursday," and other poems. Printed text of poems. 48pp. 5¼ x 7. 24636-1

OLD-TIME VIGNETTES IN FULL COLOR, Carol Belanger Grafton (ed.). Over 390 charming, often sentimental illustrations, selected from archives of Victorian graphics—pretty women posing, children playing, food, flowers, kittens and puppies, smiling cherubs, birds and butterflies, much more. All copyright-free. 48pp. 9¼ x 12¼. 27269-9

PERSPECTIVE FOR ARTISTS, Rex Vicat Cole. Depth, perspective of sky and sea, shadows, much more, not usually covered. 391 diagrams, 81 reproductions of drawings and paintings. 279pp. 5⅜ x 8½. 22487-2

DRAWING THE LIVING FIGURE, Joseph Sheppard. Innovative approach to artistic anatomy focuses on specifics of surface anatomy, rather than muscles and bones. Over 170 drawings of live models in front, back and side views, and in widely varying poses. Accompanying diagrams. 177 illustrations. Introduction. Index. 144pp. 8⅜ x11¼. 26723-7

GOTHIC AND OLD ENGLISH ALPHABETS: 100 Complete Fonts, Dan X. Solo. Add power, elegance to posters, signs, other graphics with 100 stunning copyright-free alphabets: Blackstone, Dolbey, Germania, 97 more–including many lower-case, numerals, punctuation marks. 104pp. 8⅛ x 11. 24695-7

HOW TO DO BEADWORK, Mary White. Fundamental book on craft from simple projects to five-bead chains and woven works. 106 illustrations. 142pp. 5⅜ x 8. 20697-1

THE BOOK OF WOOD CARVING, Charles Marshall Sayers. Finest book for beginners discusses fundamentals and offers 34 designs. "Absolutely first rate . . . well thought out and well executed."–E. J. Tangerman. 118pp. 7¾ x 10⅝. 23654-4

ILLUSTRATED CATALOG OF CIVIL WAR MILITARY GOODS: Union Army Weapons, Insignia, Uniform Accessories, and Other Equipment, Schuyler, Hartley, and Graham. Rare, profusely illustrated 1846 catalog includes Union Army uniform and dress regulations, arms and ammunition, coats, insignia, flags, swords, rifles, etc. 226 illustrations. 160pp. 9 x 12. 24939-5

WOMEN'S FASHIONS OF THE EARLY 1900s: An Unabridged Republication of "New York Fashions, 1909," National Cloak & Suit Co. Rare catalog of mail-order fashions documents women's and children's clothing styles shortly after the turn of the century. Captions offer full descriptions, prices. Invaluable resource for fashion, costume historians. Approximately 725 illustrations. 128pp. 8⅜ x 11¼. 27276-1

THE 1912 AND 1915 GUSTAV STICKLEY FURNITURE CATALOGS, Gustav Stickley. With over 200 detailed illustrations and descriptions, these two catalogs are essential reading and reference materials and identification guides for Stickley furniture. Captions cite materials, dimensions and prices. 112pp. 6½ x 9¼. 26676-1

EARLY AMERICAN LOCOMOTIVES, John H. White, Jr. Finest locomotive engravings from early 19th century: historical (1804–74), main-line (after 1870), special, foreign, etc. 147 plates. 142pp. 11⅜ x 8¼. 22772-3

THE TALL SHIPS OF TODAY IN PHOTOGRAPHS, Frank O. Braynard. Lavishly illustrated tribute to nearly 100 majestic contemporary sailing vessels: Amerigo Vespucci, Clearwater, Constitution, Eagle, Mayflower, Sea Cloud, Victory, many more. Authoritative captions provide statistics, background on each ship. 190 black-and-white photographs and illustrations. Introduction. 128pp. 8⅞ x 11¾. 27163-3

LITTLE BOOK OF EARLY AMERICAN CRAFTS AND TRADES, Peter Stockham (ed.). 1807 children's book explains crafts and trades: baker, hatter, cooper, potter, and many others. 23 copperplate illustrations. 140pp. 4⅝ x 6.   23336-7

VICTORIAN FASHIONS AND COSTUMES FROM HARPER'S BAZAR, 1867–1898, Stella Blum (ed.). Day costumes, evening wear, sports clothes, shoes, hats, other accessories in over 1,000 detailed engravings. 320pp. 9⅜ x 12¼. 22990-4

GUSTAV STICKLEY, THE CRAFTSMAN, Mary Ann Smith. Superb study surveys broad scope of Stickley's achievement, especially in architecture. Design philosophy, rise and fall of the Craftsman empire, descriptions and floor plans for many Craftsman houses, more. 86 black-and-white halftones. 31 line illustrations. Introduction 208pp. 6½ x 9¼.   27210-9

THE LONG ISLAND RAIL ROAD IN EARLY PHOTOGRAPHS, Ron Ziel. Over 220 rare photos, informative text document origin (1844) and development of rail service on Long Island. Vintage views of early trains, locomotives, stations, passengers, crews, much more. Captions. 8⅞ x 11¾.   26301-0

VOYAGE OF THE LIBERDADE, Joshua Slocum. Great 19th-century mariner's thrilling, first-hand account of the wreck of his ship off South America, the 35-foot boat he built from the wreckage, and its remarkable voyage home. 128pp. 5⅜ x 8½.
40022-0

TEN BOOKS ON ARCHITECTURE, Vitruvius. The most important book ever written on architecture. Early Roman aesthetics, technology, classical orders, site selection, all other aspects. Morgan translation. 331pp. 5⅜ x 8½.   20645-9

THE HUMAN FIGURE IN MOTION, Eadweard Muybridge. More than 4,500 stopped-action photos, in action series, showing undraped men, women, children jumping, lying down, throwing, sitting, wrestling, carrying, etc. 390pp. 7⅞ x 10⅝.
20204-6 Clothbd.

TREES OF THE EASTERN AND CENTRAL UNITED STATES AND CANADA, William M. Harlow. Best one-volume guide to 140 trees. Full descriptions, woodlore, range, etc. Over 600 illustrations. Handy size. 288pp. 4½ x 6⅜.   20395-6

SONGS OF WESTERN BIRDS, Dr. Donald J. Borror. Complete song and call repertoire of 60 western species, including flycatchers, juncoes, cactus wrens, many more–includes fully illustrated booklet.   Cassette and manual 99913-0

GROWING AND USING HERBS AND SPICES, Milo Miloradovich. Versatile handbook provides all the information needed for cultivation and use of all the herbs and spices available in North America. 4 illustrations. Index. Glossary. 236pp. 5⅜ x 8½.
25058-X

BIG BOOK OF MAZES AND LABYRINTHS, Walter Shepherd. 50 mazes and labyrinths in all–classical, solid, ripple, and more–in one great volume. Perfect inexpensive puzzler for clever youngsters. Full solutions. 112pp. 8⅛ x 11.   22951-3

PIANO TUNING, J. Cree Fischer. Clearest, best book for beginner, amateur. Simple repairs, raising dropped notes, tuning by easy method of flattened fifths. No previous skills needed. 4 illustrations. 201pp. 5⅜ x 8½. 23267-0

HINTS TO SINGERS, Lillian Nordica. Selecting the right teacher, developing confidence, overcoming stage fright, and many other important skills receive thoughtful discussion in this indispensible guide, written by a world-famous diva of four decades' experience. 96pp. 5⅜ x 8½. 40094-8

THE COMPLETE NONSENSE OF EDWARD LEAR, Edward Lear. All nonsense limericks, zany alphabets, Owl and Pussycat, songs, nonsense botany, etc., illustrated by Lear. Total of 320pp. 5⅜ x 8½. (Available in U.S. only.) 20167-8

VICTORIAN PARLOUR POETRY: An Annotated Anthology, Michael R. Turner. 117 gems by Longfellow, Tennyson, Browning, many lesser-known poets. "The Village Blacksmith," "Curfew Must Not Ring Tonight," "Only a Baby Small," dozens more, often difficult to find elsewhere. Index of poets, titles, first lines. xxiii + 325pp. 5⅜ x 8¼. 27044-0

DUBLINERS, James Joyce. Fifteen stories offer vivid, tightly focused observations of the lives of Dublin's poorer classes. At least one, "The Dead," is considered a masterpiece. Reprinted complete and unabridged from standard edition. 160pp. 5³⁄₁₆ x 8¼. 26870-5

GREAT WEIRD TALES: 14 Stories by Lovecraft, Blackwood, Machen and Others, S. T. Joshi (ed.). 14 spellbinding tales, including "The Sin Eater," by Fiona McLeod, "The Eye Above the Mantel," by Frank Belknap Long, as well as renowned works by R. H. Barlow, Lord Dunsany, Arthur Machen, W. C. Morrow and eight other masters of the genre. 256pp. 5⅜ x 8½. (Available in U.S. only.) 40436-6

THE BOOK OF THE SACRED MAGIC OF ABRAMELIN THE MAGE, translated by S. MacGregor Mathers. Medieval manuscript of ceremonial magic. Basic document in Aleister Crowley, Golden Dawn groups. 268pp. 5⅜ x 8½. 23211-5

NEW RUSSIAN-ENGLISH AND ENGLISH-RUSSIAN DICTIONARY, M. A. O'Brien. This is a remarkably handy Russian dictionary, containing a surprising amount of information, including over 70,000 entries. 366pp. 4½ x 6⅛. 20208-9

HISTORIC HOMES OF THE AMERICAN PRESIDENTS, Second, Revised Edition, Irvin Haas. A traveler's guide to American Presidential homes, most open to the public, depicting and describing homes occupied by every American President from George Washington to George Bush. With visiting hours, admission charges, travel routes. 175 photographs. Index. 160pp. 8¼ x 11. 26751-2

NEW YORK IN THE FORTIES, Andreas Feininger. 162 brilliant photographs by the well-known photographer, formerly with *Life* magazine. Commuters, shoppers, Times Square at night, much else from city at its peak. Captions by John von Hartz. 181pp. 9¼ x 10¾. 23585-8

INDIAN SIGN LANGUAGE, William Tomkins. Over 525 signs developed by Sioux and other tribes. Written instructions and diagrams. Also 290 pictographs. 111pp. 6⅛ x 9¼. 22029-X

ANATOMY: A Complete Guide for Artists, Joseph Sheppard. A master of figure drawing shows artists how to render human anatomy convincingly. Over 460 illustrations. 224pp. 8⅜ x 11¼. 27279-6

MEDIEVAL CALLIGRAPHY: Its History and Technique, Marc Drogin. Spirited history, comprehensive instruction manual covers 13 styles (ca. 4th century through 15th). Excellent photographs; directions for duplicating medieval techniques with modern tools. 224pp. 8⅜ x 11¼. 26142-5

DRIED FLOWERS: How to Prepare Them, Sarah Whitlock and Martha Rankin. Complete instructions on how to use silica gel, meal and borax, perlite aggregate, sand and borax, glycerine and water to create attractive permanent flower arrangements. 12 illustrations. 32pp. 5⅜ x 8½. 21802-3

EASY-TO-MAKE BIRD FEEDERS FOR WOODWORKERS, Scott D. Campbell. Detailed, simple-to-use guide for designing, constructing, caring for and using feeders. Text, illustrations for 12 classic and contemporary designs. 96pp. 5⅜ x 8½.
25847-5

SCOTTISH WONDER TALES FROM MYTH AND LEGEND, Donald A. Mackenzie. 16 lively tales tell of giants rumbling down mountainsides, of a magic wand that turns stone pillars into warriors, of gods and goddesses, evil hags, powerful forces and more. 240pp. 5⅜ x 8½. 29677-6

THE HISTORY OF UNDERCLOTHES, C. Willett Cunnington and Phyllis Cunnington. Fascinating, well-documented survey covering six centuries of English undergarments, enhanced with over 100 illustrations: 12th-century laced-up bodice, footed long drawers (1795), 19th-century bustles, l9th-century corsets for men, Victorian "bust improvers," much more. 272pp. 5⅜ x 8¼. 27124-2

ARTS AND CRAFTS FURNITURE: The Complete Brooks Catalog of 1912, Brooks Manufacturing Co. Photos and detailed descriptions of more than 150 now very collectible furniture designs from the Arts and Crafts movement depict davenports, settees, buffets, desks, tables, chairs, bedsteads, dressers and more, all built of solid, quarter-sawed oak. Invaluable for students and enthusiasts of antiques, Americana and the decorative arts. 80pp. 6½ x 9¼. 27471-3

WILBUR AND ORVILLE: A Biography of the Wright Brothers, Fred Howard. Definitive, crisply written study tells the full story of the brothers' lives and work. A vividly written biography, unparalleled in scope and color, that also captures the spirit of an extraordinary era. 560pp. 6⅛ x 9¼. 40297-5

THE ARTS OF THE SAILOR: Knotting, Splicing and Ropework, Hervey Garrett Smith. Indispensable shipboard reference covers tools, basic knots and useful hitches; handsewing and canvas work, more. Over 100 illustrations. Delightful reading for sea lovers. 256pp. 5⅜ x 8½. 26440-8

FRANK LLOYD WRIGHT'S FALLINGWATER: The House and Its History, Second, Revised Edition, Donald Hoffmann. A total revision–both in text and illustrations–of the standard document on Fallingwater, the boldest, most personal architectural statement of Wright's mature years, updated with valuable new material from the recently opened Frank Lloyd Wright Archives. "Fascinating"–*The New York Times*. 116 illustrations. 128pp. 9¼ x 10¾. 27430-6

PHOTOGRAPHIC SKETCHBOOK OF THE CIVIL WAR, Alexander Gardner. 100 photos taken on field during the Civil War. Famous shots of Manassas Harper's Ferry, Lincoln, Richmond, slave pens, etc. 244pp. 10⅝ x 8¼. 22731-6

FIVE ACRES AND INDEPENDENCE, Maurice G. Kains. Great back-to-the-land classic explains basics of self-sufficient farming. The one book to get. 95 illustrations. 397pp. 5⅜ x 8½. 20974-1

SONGS OF EASTERN BIRDS, Dr. Donald J. Borror. Songs and calls of 60 species most common to eastern U.S.: warblers, woodpeckers, flycatchers, thrushes, larks, many more in high-quality recording. Cassette and manual 99912-2

A MODERN HERBAL, Margaret Grieve. Much the fullest, most exact, most useful compilation of herbal material. Gigantic alphabetical encyclopedia, from aconite to zedoary, gives botanical information, medical properties, folklore, economic uses, much else. Indispensable to serious reader. 161 illustrations. 888pp. 6½ x 9¼. 2-vol. set. (Available in U.S. only.) Vol. I: 22798-7
Vol. II: 22799-5

HIDDEN TREASURE MAZE BOOK, Dave Phillips. Solve 34 challenging mazes accompanied by heroic tales of adventure. Evil dragons, people-eating plants, blood-thirsty giants, many more dangerous adversaries lurk at every twist and turn. 34 mazes, stories, solutions. 48pp. 8¼ x 11. 24566-7

LETTERS OF W. A. MOZART, Wolfgang A. Mozart. Remarkable letters show bawdy wit, humor, imagination, musical insights, contemporary musical world; includes some letters from Leopold Mozart. 276pp. 5⅜ x 8½. 22859-2

BASIC PRINCIPLES OF CLASSICAL BALLET, Agrippina Vaganova. Great Russian theoretician, teacher explains methods for teaching classical ballet. 118 illus-trations. 175pp. 5⅜ x 8½. 22036-2

THE JUMPING FROG, Mark Twain. Revenge edition. The original story of The Celebrated Jumping Frog of Calaveras County, a hapless French translation, and Twain's hilarious "retranslation" from the French. 12 illustrations. 66pp. 5⅜ x 8½. 22686-7

BEST REMEMBERED POEMS, Martin Gardner (ed.). The 126 poems in this superb collection of 19th- and 20th-century British and American verse range from Shelley's "To a Skylark" to the impassioned "Renascence" of Edna St. Vincent Millay and to Edward Lear's whimsical "The Owl and the Pussycat." 224pp. 5⅜ x 8½. 27165-X

COMPLETE SONNETS, William Shakespeare. Over 150 exquisite poems deal with love, friendship, the tyranny of time, beauty's evanescence, death and other themes in language of remarkable power, precision and beauty. Glossary of archaic terms. 80pp. 5³⁄₁₆ x 8¼. 26686-9

THE BATTLES THAT CHANGED HISTORY, Fletcher Pratt. Eminent historian profiles 16 crucial conflicts, ancient to modern, that changed the course of civiliza-tion. 352pp. 5⅜ x 8½. 41129-X

THE WIT AND HUMOR OF OSCAR WILDE, Alvin Redman (ed.). More than 1,000 ripostes, paradoxes, wisecracks: Work is the curse of the drinking classes; I can resist everything except temptation; etc. 258pp. 5⅜ x 8½. 20602-5

SHAKESPEARE LEXICON AND QUOTATION DICTIONARY, Alexander Schmidt. Full definitions, locations, shades of meaning in every word in plays and poems. More than 50,000 exact quotations. 1,485pp. 6½ x 9¼. 2-vol. set.
Vol. 1: 22726-X
Vol. 2: 22727-8

SELECTED POEMS, Emily Dickinson. Over 100 best-known, best-loved poems by one of America's foremost poets, reprinted from authoritative early editions. No comparable edition at this price. Index of first lines. 64pp. 5³⁄₁₆ x 8¼. 26466-1

THE INSIDIOUS DR. FU-MANCHU, Sax Rohmer. The first of the popular mystery series introduces a pair of English detectives to their archnemesis, the diabolical Dr. Fu-Manchu. Flavorful atmosphere, fast-paced action, and colorful characters enliven this classic of the genre. 208pp. 5³⁄₁₆ x 8¼. 29898-1

THE MALLEUS MALEFICARUM OF KRAMER AND SPRENGER, translated by Montague Summers. Full text of most important witchhunter's "bible," used by both Catholics and Protestants. 278pp. 6⅛ x 10. 22802-9

SPANISH STORIES/CUENTOS ESPAÑOLES: A Dual-Language Book, Angel Flores (ed.). Unique format offers 13 great stories in Spanish by Cervantes, Borges, others. Faithful English translations on facing pages. 352pp. 5⅜ x 8½. 25399-6

GARDEN CITY, LONG ISLAND, IN EARLY PHOTOGRAPHS, 1869–1919, Mildred H. Smith. Handsome treasury of 118 vintage pictures, accompanied by carefully researched captions, document the Garden City Hotel fire (1899), the Vanderbilt Cup Race (1908), the first airmail flight departing from the Nassau Boulevard Aerodrome (1911), and much more. 96pp. 8⅞ x 11¾. 40669-5

OLD QUEENS, N.Y., IN EARLY PHOTOGRAPHS, Vincent F. Seyfried and William Asadorian. Over 160 rare photographs of Maspeth, Jamaica, Jackson Heights, and other areas. Vintage views of DeWitt Clinton mansion, 1939 World's Fair and more. Captions. 192pp. 8⅞ x 11. 26358-4

CAPTURED BY THE INDIANS: 15 Firsthand Accounts, 1750-1870, Frederick Drimmer. Astounding true historical accounts of grisly torture, bloody conflicts, relentless pursuits, miraculous escapes and more, by people who lived to tell the tale. 384pp. 5⅜ x 8½. 24901-8

THE WORLD'S GREAT SPEECHES (Fourth Enlarged Edition), Lewis Copeland, Lawrence W. Lamm, and Stephen J. McKenna. Nearly 300 speeches provide public speakers with a wealth of updated quotes and inspiration–from Pericles' funeral oration and William Jennings Bryan's "Cross of Gold Speech" to Malcolm X's powerful words on the Black Revolution and Earl of Spenser's tribute to his sister, Diana, Princess of Wales. 944pp. 5⅜ x 8⅜. 40903-1

THE BOOK OF THE SWORD, Sir Richard F. Burton. Great Victorian scholar/adventurer's eloquent, erudite history of the "queen of weapons"–from prehistory to early Roman Empire. Evolution and development of early swords, variations (sabre, broadsword, cutlass, scimitar, etc.), much more. 336pp. 6⅛ x 9¼. 25434-8

AUTOBIOGRAPHY: The Story of My Experiments with Truth, Mohandas K. Gandhi. Boyhood, legal studies, purification, the growth of the Satyagraha (nonviolent protest) movement. Critical, inspiring work of the man responsible for the freedom of India. 480pp. 5⅜ x 8½. (Available in U.S. only.) 24593-4

CELTIC MYTHS AND LEGENDS, T. W. Rolleston. Masterful retelling of Irish and Welsh stories and tales. Cuchulain, King Arthur, Deirdre, the Grail, many more. First paperback edition. 58 full-page illustrations. 512pp. 5⅜ x 8½. 26507-2

THE PRINCIPLES OF PSYCHOLOGY, William James. Famous long course complete, unabridged. Stream of thought, time perception, memory, experimental methods; great work decades ahead of its time. 94 figures. 1,391pp. 5⅜ x 8½. 2-vol. set.
Vol. I: 20381-6 Vol. II: 20382-4

THE WORLD AS WILL AND REPRESENTATION, Arthur Schopenhauer. Definitive English translation of Schopenhauer's life work, correcting more than 1,000 errors, omissions in earlier translations. Translated by E. F. J. Payne. Total of 1,269pp. 5⅜ x 8½. 2-vol. set. Vol. 1: 21761-2 Vol. 2: 21762-0

MAGIC AND MYSTERY IN TIBET, Madame Alexandra David-Neel. Experiences among lamas, magicians, sages, sorcerers, Bonpa wizards. A true psychic discovery. 32 illustrations. 321pp. 5⅜ x 8½. (Available in U.S. only.) 22682-4

THE EGYPTIAN BOOK OF THE DEAD, E. A. Wallis Budge. Complete reproduction of Ani's papyrus, finest ever found. Full hieroglyphic text, interlinear transliteration, word-for-word translation, smooth translation. 533pp. 6½ x 9¼. 21866-X

MATHEMATICS FOR THE NONMATHEMATICIAN, Morris Kline. Detailed, college-level treatment of mathematics in cultural and historical context, with numerous exercises. Recommended Reading Lists. Tables. Numerous figures. 641pp. 5⅜ x 8½.
24823-2

PROBABILISTIC METHODS IN THE THEORY OF STRUCTURES, Isaac Elishakoff. Well-written introduction covers the elements of the theory of probability from two or more random variables, the reliability of such multivariable structures, the theory of random function, Monte Carlo methods of treating problems incapable of exact solution, and more. Examples. 502pp. 5⅜ x 8½. 40691-1

THE RIME OF THE ANCIENT MARINER, Gustave Doré, S. T. Coleridge. Doré's finest work; 34 plates capture moods, subtleties of poem. Flawless full-size reproductions printed on facing pages with authoritative text of poem. "Beautiful. Simply beautiful."–*Publisher's Weekly*. 77pp. 9¼ x 12. 22305-1

NORTH AMERICAN INDIAN DESIGNS FOR ARTISTS AND CRAFTSPEOPLE, Eva Wilson. Over 360 authentic copyright-free designs adapted from Navajo blankets, Hopi pottery, Sioux buffalo hides, more. Geometrics, symbolic figures, plant and animal motifs, etc. 128pp. 8⅜ x 11. (Not for sale in the United Kingdom.) 25341-4

SCULPTURE: Principles and Practice, Louis Slobodkin. Step-by-step approach to clay, plaster, metals, stone; classical and modern. 253 drawings, photos. 255pp. 8⅛ x 11.
22960-2

THE INFLUENCE OF SEA POWER UPON HISTORY, 1660–1783, A. T. Mahan. Influential classic of naval history and tactics still used as text in war colleges. First paperback edition. 4 maps. 24 battle plans. 640pp. 5⅜ x 8½. 25509-3

CATALOG OF DOVER BOOKS

THE STORY OF THE TITANIC AS TOLD BY ITS SURVIVORS, Jack Winocour (ed.). What it was really like. Panic, despair, shocking inefficiency, and a little heroism. More thrilling than any fictional account. 26 illustrations. 320pp. 5⅜ x 8½.
20610-6

FAIRY AND FOLK TALES OF THE IRISH PEASANTRY, William Butler Yeats (ed.). Treasury of 64 tales from the twilight world of Celtic myth and legend: "The Soul Cages," "The Kildare Pooka," "King O'Toole and his Goose," many more. Introduction and Notes by W. B. Yeats. 352pp. 5⅜ x 8½.
26941-8

BUDDHIST MAHAYANA TEXTS, E. B. Cowell and others (eds.). Superb, accurate translations of basic documents in Mahayana Buddhism, highly important in history of religions. The Buddha-karita of Asvaghosha, Larger Sukhavativyuha, more. 448pp. 5⅜ x 8½.
25552-2

ONE TWO THREE . . . INFINITY: Facts and Speculations of Science, George Gamow. Great physicist's fascinating, readable overview of contemporary science: number theory, relativity, fourth dimension, entropy, genes, atomic structure, much more. 128 illustrations. Index. 352pp. 5⅜ x 8½.
25664-2

EXPERIMENTATION AND MEASUREMENT, W. J. Youden. Introductory manual explains laws of measurement in simple terms and offers tips for achieving accuracy and minimizing errors. Mathematics of measurement, use of instruments, experimenting with machines. 1994 edition. Foreword. Preface. Introduction. Epilogue. Selected Readings. Glossary. Index. Tables and figures. 128pp. 5⅜ x 8½.   40451-X

DALÍ ON MODERN ART: The Cuckolds of Antiquated Modern Art, Salvador Dalí. Influential painter skewers modern art and its practitioners. Outrageous evaluations of Picasso, Cézanne, Turner, more. 15 renderings of paintings discussed. 44 calligraphic decorations by Dalí. 96pp. 5⅜ x 8½. (Available in U.S. only.)   29220-7

ANTIQUE PLAYING CARDS: A Pictorial History, Henry René D'Allemagne. Over 900 elaborate, decorative images from rare playing cards (14th–20th centuries): Bacchus, death, dancing dogs, hunting scenes, royal coats of arms, players cheating, much more. 96pp. 9¼ x 12¼.
29265-7

MAKING FURNITURE MASTERPIECES: 30 Projects with Measured Drawings, Franklin H. Gottshall. Step-by-step instructions, illustrations for constructing handsome, useful pieces, among them a Sheraton desk, Chippendale chair, Spanish desk, Queen Anne table and a William and Mary dressing mirror. 224pp. 8⅛ x 11¼.
29338-6

THE FOSSIL BOOK: A Record of Prehistoric Life, Patricia V. Rich et al. Profusely illustrated definitive guide covers everything from single-celled organisms and dinosaurs to birds and mammals and the interplay between climate and man. Over 1,500 illustrations. 760pp. 7½ x 10⅛.
29371-8